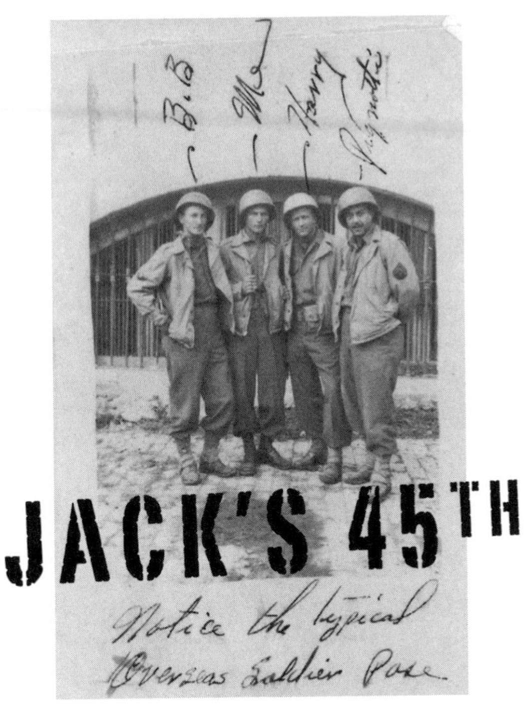

JACK'S 45TH

BY
DREW NEVILLE

Oklahoma Horizons Series

GINI MOORE CAMPBELL, SERIES EDITOR

ISBN 978-1-885596-67-3
Library of Congress Number
2008926237

Designed by Skip McKinstry
Printed by Jostens Inc. & Baker Group, LLC - 405.503.3207

OKLAHOMA HERITAGE ASSOCIATION
1400 Classen Drive
Oklahoma City, OK 73106
888.501.2059

For
Richard and Diana
Bob and Judy
John and Ted
Robert and "Jilly"
&
All the Nevilles

For
Susan
Without whose inspiration
I would not have finished

And for
Glenda
Who fought many a battle
with me for all these years

JACK'S 45TH

TABLE OF CONTENTS

ACKNOWLEDGMENTS

It was my dream that this story be told in Oklahoma and published by Oklahomans. Toward this end I approached Clayton I. Bennett, then Chairman of the Oklahoma Heritage Association with a copy of the manuscript. He encouraged me to take *Jack's 45th* to the Association's editor-in-chief, Gini Campbell. Of course fearful of rejection, it was thrilling to learn from Gini and Clay that the Association wanted to go forward with publication. Gini Campbell is a jewel in the crown of Oklahoma history. Her professionalism and charming way took me through the maze of my own faulted grammar, broken sentences, and bad syntax. Without the support and encouragement of Clay, Gini, and the Oklahoma Heritage Association, Oklahoma's "gate-keeper" of history, this publication would have never gone to print.

B.J. Rothbaum was a noted legal scholar and appellate advocate of national prominence, and reputation. He had a love of law and history like no one else I've ever known. For thirty years, B.J. was my partner and together we traveled the land trying and arguing cases in every major city in the United States until his passing in November, 2005. My eternal gratitude to the Rothbaum family, B.J., Judy, Ann and Rebecca for their generous contribution to the publication of *Jack's 45th*. In addition to the Rothbaum family my thanks extend again to Clay Bennett, Jeff Records, and the Noble Foundation for their support of this effort to preserve a piece of family and Oklahoma history.

Mike Gonzalez, curator of the 45th Infantry Division Museum, provided invaluable sources for information for *Jack's 45th*. Mike's knowledge of World War II history and role of the Thunderbirds is amazing. Mike guided me through the Division's archives where over a two year period of time he retrieved Division Artillery operations reports, recorded histories and biographies of the Thunderbirds who fought the fight for me to review and research. After discovering grid coordinate "868-293" in operation reports, it was Mike who retrieved map after map in the Division's archives to locate my father's foxhole position north of "The Overpass" at Anzio on the climactic last day of the German counterattack. Sometimes I think he was as excited as I was at this discovery. Oklahomans need to know what an incredible piece of history is preserved at the 45th Infantry Division Museum on 36th Street in Oklahoma City, Oklahoma. It is truly a marvel that everyone should enjoy and visit. The museum is fortunate to have a man like Mike Gonzalez as its curator, and my sincere appreciation and thanks go to him for his assistance, and tolerance of me in researching the Division's history and operations.

Three of Oklahoma's finest joined together to provide the Forewords for *Jack's 45th*. I am honored and thankful they would take on this task. The Honorable Ralph G. Thompson is a Judge and former Chief Judge of the United States District Court for the Western District of Oklahoma and an author of Oklahoma history himself, *Bryce Harlow: Mr. Integrity.* Judge Thompson, also a noted legal scholar, raised the standard for trial practice in our State. I am not only privileged to have tried cases in his Court for over thirty years, but to also count him as a friend. Judge Thompson brought a special connection to *Jack's 45th* as his father Lee B. Thompson was adjutant to General William S. Key, former Commanding General of the Division. As a young man, Judge Thompson spent many a hot summer day at Camp Barkeley and a few cold nights at Fort Devens. I am grateful for his review of the manuscript and honored that he lent his name to this effort.

Mike and Betty Jane Cawley have been the closest and dearest of friends for forty years. "Doc", as he is affectionately known, was one of my college roommates, and we slugged our way through law school together. Mike practiced law in Ardmore, Oklahoma for twenty years before becoming President of the Noble Foundation, Oklahoma's largest philanthropic organization dedicated to the assistance of the Oklahoma's farming and ranching industry, higher education and preservation of Oklahoma history. Adding to an already lengthy list of accomplishments, Mike was recently appointed to the Federal Reserve Board. Betty Jane was a Phi Beta Kappa at the University of Oklahoma where she and Mike met. She has kept Mike and I in line for four decades. Betty Jane sets a standard for faith and family values of which I have always aspired, but have never quite measured up. There is no one I love and respect more. Both Mike and Betty Jane knew my parents quite well and were therefore in a unique position to provide perspective to this endeavor. Betty Jane read every word of one of the earlier drafts with her typical honest and constructive criticism always clear and gratefully received. The good Lord has truly graced my life with the love and friendship of this marvelous couple. Words cannot describe the appreciation I have for their efforts toward *Jack's 45th*.

My dear friend and former college roomate, well known Oklahoma City banker and rancher Bill Johnstone was one of the first to volunteer to read the original draft of *Jack's 45th*. His usual candor and unique observations made my effort easier, and *Jack's 45th* better. My great thanks to Bill.

For more than fifteen years Legal Graphics of Oklahoma City has provided their considerable skill and talent to preparing demonstrative trial exhibits and graphics for use in our jury and non-jury trials. When I approached Sam Anderson for assistance in preparing the difficult map illustrations in *Jack's 45th*, she enthusiastically donated her company's time preparing the maps reflecting the movement and positions of the Thunderbirds during key operations. My appreciation also goes to Janice Fowler for her guidance and to Danny MacDonald who cheerfully and enthusiastically sketched and re-sketched these illustrations over the course of several weeks. Every meeting was a joy. Many thanks go to Sam, Janice and Danny.

I would be remiss in not acknowledging Flint Whitlock's fine work, *The Rock of Anzio*. My research revealed that Whitlock's book was the first published history of the Division and its operations in over fifty years. His outstanding efforts enabled me to more readily access and research the archives of the 45th Infantry Division Museum and at the same time understand from a broader perspective the roles of the various elements, and units of the Division during major operations. From the military operations standpoint, Whitlock captured every significant historical moment in the life of the Division for us all to study and enjoy.

During the war years, Oklahoma City had two newspapers which closely followed the Thunderbirds — *The Daily Oklahoman*, which of course is still published, and the *Oklahoma City Times*, which is no more. "Imbedded" within the Division was the paper's war correspondent, Don Murray, along with renowned cartoonist and humorist, Bill Mauldin, both whom regularly sent back reports of Division activities. Both papers were a major source of facts and information not only for the Division's operations, but for life on the home front. Thanks must go to *The Daily Oklahoman* for preserving these articles which kept all Oklahomans as informed as they could be during desperate times. My uncle, Gene Neville, killed in action flying the British Spitfire, worked for *The Oklahoman* as a "copy boy". After his death, Gene was eulogized on the editorial page. My friend Christy Gaylord Everest is now the President of OPBUCO. Research indicates that it was her father who wrote the moving tribute to my uncle. What a small world it is. Even today it remains one of the most eloquent and poetic pieces I have ever read. Thanks must go to Ed Kelley, Editor of *The Daily Oklahoman.* He was kind enough to read the manuscript and provide his insight and encouragement to continue my efforts.

Glenda Brown has been my assistant, secretary, confidant and counselor for 24 years. We fought many a battle together over the years in courtrooms far away. Her efforts and loyalty have regrettably gone largely under-appreciated. Glenda typed every word of the manuscript from my handwritten, often illegible, "yellow sheets". It was a huge task and one that I truly appreciate. Glenda also knew my parents very well, and her comments and perspectives on both of them enhanced the story immeasurably. Thank you Glenda.

Somewhat late in life I was lucky to find Susan, the love of my life and best friend. She gave me the encouragement and inspiration to complete this work. Without her, *Jack's 45th* would have never gotten to the finish line. Many of the final paragraphs were penned in her "Mahjone room" with an endless stream of popcorn and diet cokes to keep me going. Susan fought a courageous battle of her own with breast cancer that mirrored the spirit and love of life that were both of my parents. It is only fitting that part of the proceeds from *Jack's 45th* go to the Komen Breast Cancer Foundation as a tribute to her. I love you honey.

Last, but of course not least, Mom and Dad, and all the great men and women of their times. They fought the good fight, they persevered through hard and difficult times. They saved a world from tyranny and preserved for us all a lasting legacy of moral good, faith, and freedom. They were the Greatest Generation and will always be.

President John F. Kennedy once said that a nation truly reveals itself not only by the men it produces, but also by the men it honors, the men it remembers.

May we always remember. So Richard, Diane, Bob, Judy, John, Ted, Jilly, Robert and all the Nevilles – this is for you and for you to remember.

FOREWORD BY RALPH G. THOMPSON

I have known Drew Neville as a good friend and exceptionally gifted lawyer. I have not previously known him as a writer except in his legal briefs in my court. Now I know him as the author of this intriguing and meticulously researched account of his father's World War II experiences, spiced by a most imaginative and novel weaving-in of other events that give *Jack's 45th* such poignant character and distinction.

The gallantry of Oklahoma's legendary 45th Infantry Division has been chronicled and honored through the years but not in this form. This is an intensely personal account. As one whose father had been aide-de-camp to the Division's commanding general, William S. Key, and whose family moved with the Division to Camp Barkley, Texas and Ft. Devens, Massachusetts, as the 45th trained for WWII, the Thunderbirds have been a part of my own life, too. As another son of "The Greatest Generation" Drew Neville was inspired to write of the wartime experiences of his dad, Jack, and of the many other Thunderbirds because of their extraordinary valor and combat skills in the Division's eight major campaigns and three amphibious landings. The manner in which these battles were fought is discussed in fascinating detail, both from the broad view of the strategic importance and as experienced by the riflemen in the fox holes of the battlefield. Of particular significance is the innovative, heroic and possibly unprecedented use of artillery by the 45th in the fighting that saved the day at Salerno and Anzio. It is a part of our country's military history that deserves retelling and here it is retold very well.

Uniquely, Neville injects home-front and family recollections from the Depression era to the Viet Nam era, all of which add interesting, entertaining and touching perspectives. Also included is the fascinating but tragic story of Jack's brother, Gene, an RAF Eagle Squadron Spitfire pilot who was shot down and killed in France while returning from a combat mission.

Jack's 45th is a very worthy accomplishment. In recalling the horrors of war and the heroism and sacrifices of the men of the 45th, we are better for having read it. From it, too, we are reminded again of the enormous debt that we owe them.

Ralph G. Thompson

FOREWORD BY
MIKE CAWLEY

I have known Drew Neville since August of 1965. We were Beta Theta Pi pledge brothers at the University of Oklahoma; we were law school classmates at the University of Oklahoma College of Law; we have been seated next to each other at OU football games for 40 years; and my wife, Betty Jane, and I were guests in the home of Drew's parents, Jack and Leota Neville, on a number of occasions. Drew is one of my longest and dearest friends.

This is a challenging foreword to write because Drew was clear in his request that it come from both Betty Jane and me. Drew has a special place in Betty Jane's heart, and it is not just because he is my close friend – he is her close friend too. I think Drew often considers Betty Jane to be a special "of counsel" advisor on particular issues. Betty Jane was one of the first people to have read the original manuscript for *Jack's 45th*. So please envision these foreword comments as emanating from both of us.

Drew's dad, Jack, was a really interesting guy. In many respects, he reminded me of my dad. He was bright, charming, personable and also fully capable of a steely-eyed glare and subtle snarl that let you know right quick that he did not suffer fools lightly and expected full and strict compliance with Jack Neville's rules. He made it clear to Betty Jane and me that we were also subject to the same rules, in his house, that his kids were. But even though he growled at us, we always knew that he loved us.

I will always remember a Saturday morning in Tulsa in January of 1972. Betty Jane and I were spending the weekend in Tulsa with the Nevilles. It was semester break at law school. Jack Neville rousted Drew and me up early that Saturday morning because he wanted us to go "make the Saturday morning rounds" with him at the Tulsa manufacturing company he headed. During the "rounds," he asked if we had a pen or pencil. We did not. He proceeded to give us both one of the all-time great chewing outs – how could any prospective lawyer/businessman even think about being anywhere without a pen of pencil to take down important notes, thoughts and things to do. To this day, I remember vividly that Jack Neville remonstration when I put my pen and note card in my pocket each morning.

Jack Neville was not an outwardly affectionate man – he wasn't a hugger and I doubt that he was prone to saying "I love you" to his children. His love language was more apt to be strong words of instruction and encouragement. And I would imagine that Jack was a hard guy with whom to share words of affection and appreciation.

For me, *Jack's 45th* is much more than a chronicle of the courage and patriotism of Jack Neville and the others of the 45th Infantry Division. I see it as a wonderful letter from Jack's oldest son, Drew, telling of a son's love, respect and appreciation for his father. For Betty Jane, it was a beautiful testimony about the value of the lessons we need to learn from the previous generation.

Mike Cawley

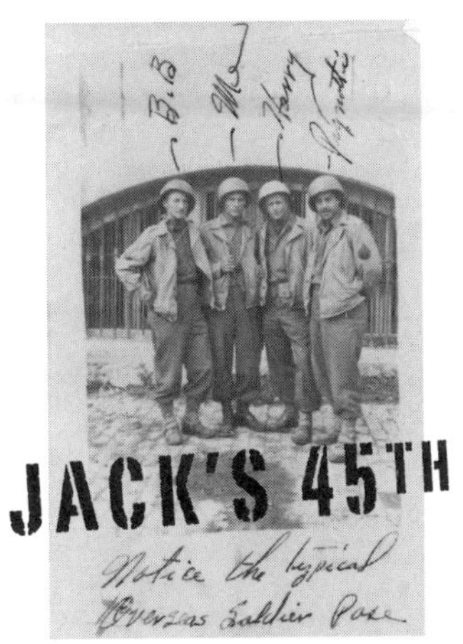

JACK'S 45TH

The 45th Infantry Division mirrored the character and courage of those men who formed and fought within the Division. For the most part, they shared a common history of hardship. They brought to the fight the ability to weather hard times, to get up from the hard-knocks of life, to adapt and modify. The history, and character of the 45th Infantry Division itself were shaped by the character of the men who were the 45th. The Division was one of the toughest, most aggressive and determined Infantry Divisions in World War II because those were the characteristics of the men who were the 45th Infantry Division. It certainly was Jack Neville.

INTRODUCTION

It always puzzled me why the 4th of July was Jack Neville's favorite holiday. All holidays at our house were special, but there seemed to be something extra about Independence Day for my Dad. Thanksgiving, Christmas, even Valentines Day and birthdays always were spent with great ceremony–but not like the pomp and circumstance of Independence Day.

Most of my memories of the 4th are still in Tulsa, Oklahoma, at 2931 East 57th Street just off Harvard. It always was a circus. The house sat slightly up an incline on the north side of 57th and on the 4th a huge American flag marked its location as if we needed to know where it was. That flag flew most every day–rain, sleet, snow, or 40 mile wind–and always on the 4th.

Dad insisted that you be there by 10:00 a.m. His insistence was not a request, it was an order. As you approached the house, smoke usually billowed from the back yard. On Independence Day Jack arose at 4:00 a.m. or earlier, fired up at least two large Hasty-Bake outdoor grills and a couple of smokers that were built at his company, Leland Equipment Co. This was done in preparation of the arrival of the entire Neville clan, ranging in ages from about 6 months to 80 years. Jack felt compelled to cook for the whole tribe. Smoked ribs, hamburgers, chicken, sausages, flank steak, you name it, it was on the

At the Neville house, the flag flew everyday.

grill or in the smoker. As with everything he did, he had to get an early start. As you drove around to the back of the house, you angled for a key parking spot, knowing that at least 10 other late arriving cars would most likely prevent an early exit should you have the guts to try and leave early. Even in 100° weather the backyard looked like something out of a Norman Rockwell painting. To the west of the cooking operation–every blade of green grass had been perfectly cut. The entire backyard was bordered in small American flags. All kinds of red, white, and yellow flowers were carefully placed in pots around the swimming pool and patio. There were enough lawn chairs to accommodate the masses. Red, white, and blue table cloths and streamers decorated four large tables underneath an awning that covered half of the patio. Vast quantities of food would be consumed underneath that awning over the course of the day, capped off with ice cream and strawberries.

Jack and Leota, my Mom, spent considerable effort arranging outdoor speakers around the patio. By 10:00 a.m. Jack had the place lit up with George M. Cohen's "Yankee Doodle Dandy," "God Bless America," "Over-There," and "It Was a Long Way to Tipporary." It was so loud that the neighbors usually complained. When they complained, he refused to turn it down and instead would usually turn it up.

There was enough beer in the four ice chests to float the entire city of Tulsa. By 10:00 a.m., Jack had consumed a substantial amount. Dawned in an apron of red, white, and blue, a "Budweiser" in the left hand, and a barbecue fork in the other, the old Sergeant of the 45th Infantry Division Artillery was the master at work.

While immediate family was invited at 10:00 a.m., the rest of the bunch usually did not show up until 11:00. By noon the party was in full swing. Usually last to arrive was my cousin Helen, her husband Bobby, and their three children, Jill, Patty, and Lee–none of whom were much older than five at the

Master Sergeant Jack Neville was also master on the grill in this picture taken July 4, 1973.

With beverage in hand, Jack's brother Nat has a good time on July 4. Roselle and Pete MacKellar stand behind Nat with the author, Jack, and Mike Neville, Nat's son in the background.

time. Jack administered the usual punishment of their tardiness by terrorizing the three girls to tears, throwing them into the pool, and then jumping in to save them, thus re-establishing heroic status. Each child under 10 had to suffer the peril of a "Jack attack," the old pool dunking. In the process, all parents consumed vast quantities of adult refreshment to both celebrate and to anesthesize themselves from Jack's antics.

Sometimes Dad's oldest brother, Baird, came from Texas. They usually ended up in a shouting match over what one had done to the other as a kid. Neither could hear the other, near deafness being a particular trait of the Nevilles. In my early days there were five brothers and three sisters, all of whom had children. All toll, when everyone showed up for the 4th, the party peaked at 50. The conversation decibel was often so loud that Cohen's "Yankee Doodle Dandy" was drowned out. As the day moved along, an almost routine like cycle developed. Into the pool, do not dry off, go to the Hasty-Bake, get ribs or chicken, then to the ice chest for a beer, sit down, visit with the multitudes, and start the process all over again. At days end, you were exhausted, but not hungry, and thoroughly tired of hearing "God Bless America" and Cohen's songs. Dad would never allow the music to be turned off and watching television was barred. On this holiday, you were required to participate with the family. Mom never attempted to police the action on the 4th, as Dad was not policable. Mom's easy way and engaging smile at least provided some degree of tranquility to an otherwise sea of chaotic revelry. It seemed that the conversation, beer, food, and songs all merged and crescendoed in volumes disruptive to a two-block radius. The Tulsa police probably were afraid to show up.

Parents and grandparents visit on July 4 while Bob Neville and cousin Jimmie Smith ready the backyard for a croquet tournament.

Scott Smith, Leota Neville's sister's grandson prepares to go off the board with Creighton Neville watching in the background.

Left to right Emily Smith, Patty Sullivan, Scott Smith, and Lee Sullivan are temporarily safe from the "Jack attack."

Jack goes off the board to bombard those floating in the pool.

Jack terrorizes Lee Sullivan on July 4 with Emily Smith waiting to be the next victim.

The 4th of July also required a bit of the Texas two-step as the evening drew to a close.

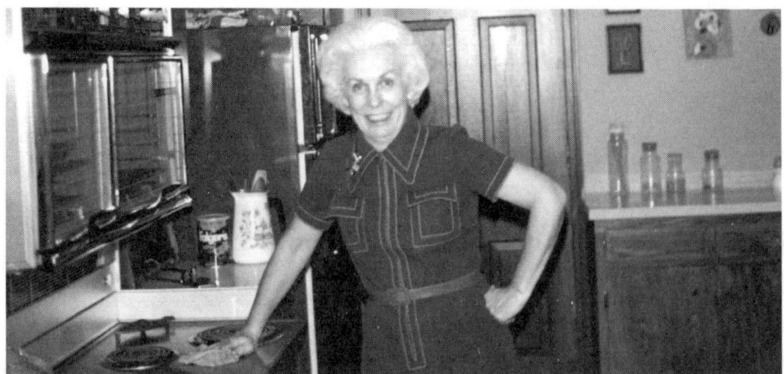

Leota Neville takes command inside on July 4.

Jack Neville and Baird Neville flank the "Queen of Mayes County," Helen on the 4th of July.

It was a grand event. Around four o'clock, the multitudes started to thin out, making their way back to Oklahoma City, Ponca City, Okmulgee, Muskogee, and sometimes Texas and Colorado.

Apart from tears intentionally inflicted on the younger set by tossing them into the pool, there never was a frown or even a stern face in this group. The joy of the occasion was infectious and real.

As the occasion ground slowly to a halt, Jack would usually find a chair in which to recline, where he would quietly proclaim what a great day it had been. And it had. Mom just looked at him and shook her head. After about an hour she would suggest that he go on to bed, which he always did without much resistance or comment.

After considerable time researching Mom and Dad's war years, the answer to the question became far less puzzling, even simple.

Why was the 4th Dad's favorite holiday? Because at Bloody Ridge in Sicily, at the Calore River at Salerno, in the freezing rain and sleet in the mountains of Venafor, on the beach at Anzio, through southern France, Nuremberg and into the death camps at Dachau, he fought for it. This is his story.

Drew Neville 2007

The entire Neville family on the 4th of July, circa 1980.

My favorite picture of Jack and Leota taken at Bob Neville and Judy Jones wedding, May 21, 1988.

PREFACE
REFLECTIONS & DISCOVERIES

As a kid, and even as hair became gray, the World War II years of Leota and Jack Neville were the "missing years." Neither talked much about them and, even when they did, the conversations always were brief, as if the words were a sound bite taken from a film clip. Jack's tales were of Spavinaw Creek in northeastern Oklahoma, near Adair, where he was born and grew up. Mom often regaled us with stories about her father who migrated from Tama, Iowa, where she was born, in search of the great oil riches of Oklahoma. Sylvester Stauffer, Leota's father, was one of Oklahoma City's most publicized wildcatters who found it and lost it several times over. Both Mom and Dad grew up in the Great Depression of the 1930s and many of the stories they told us were of that era. Never about the war. What "baby-boomer" has not heard their father preach about walking a mile to school in the snow. This message always was delivered at a time when we either felt sorry for ourselves or because some grave injustice was done to us, or when we felt the world had victimized us in some horrible fashion. Mom's touch, of course, always was more compassionate. If you were lucky, she would make one of those butter and sugar sandwiches with Wonder Bread. This cholesterol-calorie laden appetizer was her favorite as a kid in the 1930s.

At seven years old, working on my second butter and sugar sandwich, one did not reflect on what it was like for them between 1940 and 1945. And regrettably at 40, we did not give it much thought either. We never heard them complain and we never heard them make excuses about their own reversals or difficulties in life.

The undiscussed, in fact the unmentionable, were the war years–a time when life and freedom were truly at stake. Only now one wonders what it would have been like living in those years with John Lennon or The Doors as the principal song makers, rather than Glen Miller's swing or Andy Kirk and his "Clouds of Joy." It would not have been different, I suggest. History has proven that it was a time that mattered, a time when our nation was at risk and America's commitment to sacrifice the flower of its youth for a just and noble cause was firm and moral. In the war years, the dreaded telegram that Jack's mother received from the War Department was not a movie, but a real life tragedy. The fear of death in a far away land dominated everyday existence. For those at home, with a war being fought half a world away, it was often all one could do but to make it through the day, the hour, or even the minute. When America's dream and way of life were under attack, brave men left their homes and families to fight because it was their duty and the right thing to do. In the mid-1960s, at Tulsa Edison High School, we never thought about it.

None of Jack's stories of World War II came easily, if at all. He never spoke of battle, and when he did speak of the war, it was always with a "deflection," a purposeful rejection of the question and evasion of the true answer. Questions about the war were always spun into "episodes" that were theater-like adventures laced with comedy; the raid on a "Lalique" factory somewhere in France, the fruits of which are still family treasures; the beer smuggled off the landing craft at Anzio; or the return trip back across the Atlantic on the way home and how seasick most of the guys became. He never spoke of the real war, of the death or horror of being under fire, and of men being killed or maimed. It was not until after Jack's passing in 1998, that we learned he had won the Bronze Star for action in Sicily and Anzio; that at the time he sailed into the fight in the invasion of Sicily his brother, Gene, a British Spitfire pilot, had been shot down and killed in action over France; or the fact that his best war-time friend was near death from wounds suffered in Venafro, Italy.

We never had a gun in our house. I only have one recollection of Dad ever shooting a gun. Memories reflect an instance of Jack and my Uncle Dwight Williams out on an Oklahoma County dirt road sometime in the early 1950s. Dwight had a single-shot, 410-gauge shotgun and for some unfathomable reason he wanted to shoot. While everyone took their turn at a tin can resting on a fence post, Jack passed every opportunity before succumbing to peer pressure. Reluctantly, almost sadly, he raised the old 410 and squeezed off a round. Subdued that he had hit the rusty can, he silently returned the weapon to his waist and without comment handed it back to Dwight. I was 7 or 8 years old. It was the only time I ever saw him shoot a gun. He never spoke of guns, it was a subject as taboo as the war itself.

Being a child of the 1960s, the Viet Nam War dominated television news, but in Tulsa, Oklahoma, not my life. Jack listened intently to the Huntley-Brinkley evening news report of the day's events in Southeast Asia most often without comment. Despite conservative Republican views on most every social and foreign policy issue, he was against the war. While he opposed the war, he was for the kids who fought it because he was a kid who fought in his war. His view was remarkably dovish, and in today's world this veteran would be considered a liberal, at least on this issue. His opinion was straightforward–America's future should not be sent to die without America's commitment. World War

II had America's commitment, Viet Nam did not; America's youth should stay home and build their lives and future. In his eyes, it was that simple.

Jack and Leota were married in December, 1942. Shortly before they were married the 45th Infantry Division was shipped to Watertown, New York, in preparation for embarkation to North Africa. They stayed in a walk-up apartment, then it was on to Camp Pickett, Virginia, until the wives and loved ones were sent home in May of 1943. Mom returned to Oklahoma City and Dad set sail for, what he himself described in a journal, as a "great adventure." For 511 days, he saw every day of combat with the 45th Infantry Division, all the way from Sicily to Dauchau, Germany and back to the eastern seaboard. Yet, he never spoke of it.

As America's baby boomers have come to learn through the great histories written by Steven Ambrose in *D-Day*, *Citizen Soldiers* and Tom Brokaw's *The Greatest Generation*, Jack and Leota's story of the war years was an uncommon life experience shared by most of their generation. Its virtue is now realized, even though those who lived it and experienced it chose not to speak of it. Their thoughts were of the future, grateful for what they had, and filled with the dream of what could be. There was "no excuse." Jack and Leota's vision was forward, always forward. As he often said, "Don't drown in shallow water. Look for the new day for tomorrow's sun brings a new beginning." Less poetic but equally expressive was his more common rhetoric "The sun does not shine on the same dog's ass all the time." It was a quite dramatic prose for a man raised in the little town of Adair, Oklahoma. These young men and women of World War II, then in their late teens and early 1920s, as Tom Brokaw wrote "were of the Greatest Generation." And, one of the great lessons for future generations of Jack and Leota's is that these were ordinary men and women, doing extraordinary things, in a time when uncommon valor was a common virtue.

Jack Neville died January 4, 1998, three days before his 79th birthday. Leota's health deteriorated rapidly thereafter and she passed away March 24, 2000. As happens with the passing of parents, one begins to sift through the sands of time in search of the memories and the thoughts of what it was like to be "them." Somehow you search for the times you cannot clearly recollect or remember. Other times you revel in the memories forever etched in your mind. The three brothers, to one degree or the other, had great curiosity for the war years and to some extent each of us studied World War II with appreciation, but ignorant of the exactitude of Jack and Leota's war-time.

This effort produced a collage of mixed feelings and emotions, tears of joy in a real sense that provided a genuine family renewal. To our great amazement, tucked away in a dusty closet in a rarely used bedroom, were two scrapbooks that Leota had kept while Jack fought with the 45th Infantry Division. Almost perfectly chronolicled was a pictorial display of Jack's training at Fort

Sill, Oklahoma, and Camp Barkeley, Abilene, Texas. Numerous pictures detailed the good times of their life in Watertown, New York, only two weeks after they were married. They were each only 22 years old. Another scrapbook told the story through newspaper clippings more than 50 years old carefully clipped from *The Daily Oklahoman*. One headline sung out "45th SWINGS KNOCK-OUT IN SICILY." Another headline in May of 1945 shouted "WAR ENDS." The edges of the articles were brown and yellow, stained by the passage of time. There before our very eyes was the story that was never told, words never spoken–Mom working at Tinker Air Force Base for McDonald Douglas and the exploits of the Fighting 45th at Anzio, Salerno, Southern France, through the infamous Seigfried Line, and into Germany.

One of the great cartoonists of the war was Bill Mauldin. He rode with the 45th most of the war. His cartoons of "Willie" and "Joe," two dog-faces of the 45th, are still legend. There, in the scrapbook are pictures of Jack and Bill Mauldin sitting in a window sill in Marseille, France, in 1944 after the invasion of the 45th. These pictures told the story. It was all there, only we did not find it until almost six decades after the fact, and sadly only after they had both passed.

As we baby boomers hit our fifties, we become more in touch with our mortality and the need to know our own history. At this age, a true reflection sets in. Mom knew this would be the case, I believe, when she kept the scrapbooks. She knew someday we would want to know, and thought these scrapbooks would tell the story better than they could have. Mom was wrong. We would have loved to have heard about it from them. We were too late, but the scrapbooks were not. As we dusted off the old cardboard front covers, we discovered that in Mom's way she had in fact told the story. In a real sense the past was now linked to the present. So now the gap of those missing years must be recorded herein for future generations of families, of our family, to learn and appreciate.

This history is not perfect. Considerable study and some military experience teaches that it was impossible to record the war-times of the 1940s with absolute accuracy. The men of Division Artillery did not have e-mail and they did not carry laptop computers onto the beach at Salerno. Jack's own military record, upon close inspection, is somewhat vague and even Division Artillery operations reports are at times unclear, even conflicting.

After boarding ship in Virginia to embark on the trans-Atlantic trip, Jack made an attempt to keep a journal of his thoughts and travels. The six-page journal was found in an envelope tucked between two pages in one of the scrapbooks. It is handwritten and abruptly ends in mid-sentence. The evidence suggests the pages were most likely lost. Regardless, the substance of the journal provides the most direct evidence of Jack's thoughts and travels as he separated from Mom and sailed into battle in Sicily. Jack's war record indicates that upon enlistment, he was assigned to headquarters, 70th Field Artillery Brigade. This unit was later reconfigured and carried the tag Headquarters Battery, 45th Division Artillery. In those rare conversations with Jack about the war I have very distinct recollection of Jack saying he was with "Hal Muldrow's Unit." Research tells us that Hal Muldrow was Lieutenant Colonel Hal Muldrow who commanded the 189th Field Artillery, 45th Infantry Division. Muldrow was from Norman, Oklahoma.

This apparent discrepancy was resolved by Mike Gonzalez, Curator of the 45th Infantry Division Museum in Oklahoma City. Gonzalez reasoned that Jack probably was with both units at different points in time, as it was not unusual that staff would rotate between the units depending on needs. Jack's journal references an extensive review of maps and plans on his ship anchored off the coast of Oran, Algiers, before the Sicily landing. In fact, he was not allowed off the ship in Oran so that he could give his full attention to this effort. Presumably higher command was concerned that he would "spill the beans." His journal strongly suggests some degree of secrecy in planning for the assault on the Sicily beachhead. This, along with his rank and various tables of organization, suggests that he had a staff position in plans and operations probably initially with Division Artillery headquarters under General Ray McClain and, at times, with Muldrow's staff and the 189th Field Artillery. The movement of both units throughout the major engagements will be referenced herein.

One piece of evidence is clear, Jack was in a unique position to view the war not only from perspective of planning operations, but also from the perspective of participation. Infantry Regiments were the basic assault forces of the Infantry Division in World War II and those units were both supported and defended by the Artillery who were generally behind or beside the infantry position. With the exception of catastrophic situations, the war was generally in front of the artillery and Jack would have been in a situation of not only being shot at, but watching the engagement unfold before his eyes.

This history cannot pretend to precisely place Jack's movement and position during battle. Operations reports and division histories are often convoluted at best. However, having identified with a degree of certainty the units to which he was assigned, together with his rank, indications of job responsibilities, and those wonderful scrapbooks, it is possible to state with reasonable probability what he saw, heard, and felt during his 511 days of combat with the 45th Infantry Division.

How does this history serve us? It cements one's existence and sense of being. Perhaps it does something more. The courage, bravery, sacrifice, and honor of each soldier sends a message of strength to all that most of life's problems can be dealt with for the good and in a way that advances man's humanity toward one another. Jack never saw a problem that could not be handled. And man, he could handle some problems.

CHAPTER 1: THUNDERBIRDS

There are several admirable histories of the 45th Infantry Division which are commended to the readers study. Most recently in 1998, Flint Whitlock of Denver, Colorado, wrote perhaps the most exhaustive history of the Division in *The Rock of Anzio*. The other noted publication, *The Fighting Forty-Fifth* chronicles and defines the battle history of this incredible group of men and women. Any effort to simply replicate these fine works would be an injustice to the outstanding histories these two publications provide us all. However, the greatest monument to the history of this division, and those who were part of it, is the 45th Infantry Division Museum located in Oklahoma City, Oklahoma, where the moments and events discussed herein come alive through pictures and artifacts that tell the story far better than these words can ever do. Nonetheless, to place Jack and Leota's war into some historical perspective, and to better see the war through the eyes of Jack, it is instructive to set forth at least in some abbreviated fashion the history of this most celebrated group of citizen soldiers who sacrificed their youth to defeat the menace of the Nazi war machine whose objective was to conquer and control the entire world.

In World War II, the United States had 91 combat divisions. Fifty-two of those divisions served in the European Theatre of operations and the Mediterranean. Eighteen of those 91 divisions were called National Guard Divisions. They truly were, as Steven Ambrose wrote, the "Citizen Soldiers." They were the young men of the 1930s who initially saw military service as an economic opportunity. After all, you could make $50 a month if you were on active duty. If you were older than 25, you were an old man.

General George S. Patton described the 45th Infantry Division as "one of the finest, if not the finest infantry division in the history of modern warfare." This was for good reason. The division made a remarkable four amphibious landings, and fought in eight major campaigns that climaxed with the liberation of one of the Nazi's most infamous death camps, Dachau, near Munich, Germany. The first allied troops into the camp were from the 45th Infantry

Division. It was a horrible and gruesome experience. After the 45th's invasion in Southern France, they chased a retreating German army across half a continent until pounding the Nazis into submission in Nuremberg, Germany.

Incredibly, the division had eight men who were awarded the highest honor one could receive in wartime, the Medal of Honor. From July 10, 1943 to May 7, 1945, the division sustained one of the highest casualty rates of any allied division in World War II, approximately 62,500 enlisted men and officers.

The 189th Field Artillery Battalion earned its share of decorations for gallantry. Battalion members received 10 Silver Stars, 105 Bronze Stars, 173 Purple Hearts, and for its action at Salerno, was awarded the Distinguished Unit Citation. Never known or ever discussed was the fact that Jack was awarded the Bronze Star for action in Italy. The scrapbooks suggest that while he told Leota of the award, it never made its way home.

Mention must be made of the historical significance of the division insignia. Ironically, the 45th shoulder patch for many years was a Swastika. When Hitler took the Swastika as the emblem of his Nationalist Socialist Party, the division quickly adopted a symbol reflective of the heritage of the men who would form the 45th Infantry Division–the Thunderbird. The Thunderbird was adopted because of its regional identity, a symbol of Indian country. The Thunderbird was regarded as the great bird who was the giver of rain, so essential to the Southwest. It also was a symbol of good luck and fortune. Most ironically, however, was the legend and lore that the Thunderbird was the creator of thunder and lightning.

Upon reflection, I wonder whether the division symbol was adopted to reflect Jack's personality. He was thunder and lightning personified. There were many times when the brothers heard the thunder of his voice which could penetrate any wall, or the lightning of his anger that would flash quickly at one of our many transgressions.

As the war progressed, the German war machine came to fear the thunder and lightning of the 45th Infantry Division. However, in the early stages of the division's engagements, the German generals regarded all National Guard units as the weakest link. They were not professionals and not professionally trained, so the German propaganda went. The Nazi's message to their own troops even adopted a racist spin. The 45th was described as a group of disadvantaged Indians and some non-whites conscripted to a cause they were in fact against and despised. The German leaders described their opposition as lesser beings, unequal to the quality of the Arian race; therefore easily defeated when the chips were down. After the invasion of Sicily and Salerno, and especially after the epic struggle at Anzio, the German view of the citizen soldiers of the 45th Infantry radically changed. The Thunderbird symbol came to strike fear into the heart of the German soldier. The Nazis learned that not only would the men of the 45th fight, but they would kill Germans. At Bloody Ridge in northern Sicily, the fighting was hand to hand and several instances were reported of men fighting the Germans with their helmets and canteens in close quarters combat. The boys of the 45th never quit.

In perhaps the greatest artillery battle in the history of modern warfare, the fight became one of "dueling howitzers," a fight waged in a geographical postage stamp. At Anzio, the 45th Infantry Division, their backs literally to the beach-head and the success of the invasion in the balance, fought off a seven-division German counterattack. Shear guts did it. At the junction of the Calore-Sele river inward of the Gulf of Salerno, the 189th Field Artillery and the Division Artillery plugged a critical gap in allied lines that threatened the success of the invasion. Dad's unit refused to back off from a German effort to split the Allied lines. The Artillery killed them all. In some of the more controversial accounts of the war, the 45th became regarded as a take-no-prisoners unit. If Germans were in the way, they were shot, and at times this included those attempting to surrender. These accounts are defended on the basis that one of the favorite German tactics was the "fake surrender." They would show the white flag, lull the Americans into a sense of security, and then open fire. The 45th, learning of this treachery from General Patton just before the Sicily invasion, countered such trickery with a simple strategy–shoot the prisoners or so the story goes. Whichever account one tends to accept, the historical fact is clear. The boys from Indian country would get in your face. When one looks at two major battles, Salerno and Anzio, the common denominator of the German counterattack seems to be that it was aimed directly at a National Guard unit, the citizen soldiers of the 45th Infantry Division. In both engagements, the 45th Infantry Division delivered the knock-out blow that saved the day, the beach-head, and the invasions of both Salerno and Anzio. When Germans counterattacked into the lines of the boys from Oklahoma, they were clobbered by guys from Chandler, Oklahoma City, and Bristow, among others.

The great historians of World War II, John Keegan, Carlos D'Este, and even Winston Churchill have asked the question "Why?" and "How could this be so?" The Germans were a trained, professional army, many were zealots to the cause of the Nationalist Socialist Party, the Nazis. They were true believers in the Arian race and its alleged supremacy over all mankind. The Americans, on the other hand, especially the men of the 45th Infantry Division, were men of the depression, many looking for a way. Made up of minority backgrounds–Indians, Irish, Catholics–they were a melting pot of American heritage forged from hard times. It is suggested that Steven Ambrose, the author of *D'Day*, *The Victors*, and many other great works, provides the best insight, the best answer to this question.

These men of the 45th Infantry Division were free men. As free men living in a democracy, their thoughts, ambitions, and future were not chained by a government propaganda that preached suppression and destruction of any man. The men of the 45th Infantry Division dreamed of a future, of good things born by hard work. This was all they knew and all they lived. Most of them were from places like Adair, Stillwater, and Ponca City, small rural towns by any standard. They had no money and by no measure ever would be considered of wealth or prominence. But they were men, never poor of spirit, who could adapt to the hard times because they had to. And in the hard times of war, their freedom of thought that relieved them from the hardships of the 1930s spawned the ingenuity and the energy to overcome the German Army war machine.

Most of these men did not want to go to war, they wanted to be home. But once there, they faced the reality that they had a job to do. It was the same thought their fathers and family had demanded of them in every town they grew up in–get the job done. Once on the beaches of Sicily and Salerno, awash with the red blood of their brothers, they realized that going home meant go to the east, take the objective, and capture or kill the enemy. They quickly realized what they had to do if they wanted to see Spavinaw Creek, and that's exactly what the 45th Infantry Division did.

The history of the 45th Infantry Division mirrors the character and courage of those men who formed and fought with it. For the most part, they shared a common history of hardship. They brought to the fight the ability to weather hard times, to get up from the hard-knocks of life, to adapt, and to modify. The Division was one of the toughest, most determined Infantry Divisions in World War II because those were the characteristics of the men who were the 45th Infantry Division. It certainly was Jack Neville.

THE GUARD IS BORN

In 1907, Oklahoma was one of the last states admitted to the Union. Prior to 1907 a portion of what would become Oklahoma was known as Indian Territory. Before statehood, Indian Territory was governed by a territorial government with no effective structure for law enforcement. As late as the 1890s the territory was threatened by groups of renegade Indians and lawless white men, mostly robbers and thieves. It was a tough place to live and raise a family. To protect the law-abiding citizens and families, the territorial government in 1895 authorized the formation of a citizen militia. It was called the Oklahoma National Guard. The Oklahoma National Guard in those early days was a small band of volunteers that formed their own militia unit, mostly from towns in the same geographical area. These volunteers were self taught. There was little to no government support for anything. The guard was formed out of necessity for their own protection.

The guard's activity remained largely territorial until 1914. A self-described liberator, Francisco Pancho Villa, commenced a series of raids across the Mexico-New Mexico border to steal supplies and provisions to take on the government of Mexico. The United States government called upon the Oklahoma National Guard to get into the fight to protect the borders. Between 1914 and 1916, the guard was assigned to the command of General John "Blackjack" Pershing and ordered to patrol the New Mexico borders with Mexico. It was an impressive performance. The Oklahomans would fight in World War II just like they fought in Indian Territory. Ironically, at the side of General Pershing was a young West Point officer, know later as Four-Star General George S. Patton. Almost 27 years later, Patton would command the Seventh Army in the invasion of Sicily and would select the 45th Infantry Division as one of the lead units to assault the Sicilian beachhead.

Shortly after the New Mexico border action, world events changed the Oklahoma National Guard forever. On April 16, 1917, the United States declared war on Germany. It was World War I. In mobilizing America's belated entry into the war, the organization of the guard was reconfigured into two regiments, the 179th Infantry Regiment and the 180th Infantry Regiment. Twenty-eight years later, these two regiments would spearhead many great battles as two of the most celebrated infantry regiments in World War II history. However, in World War I, the 179th and the 180th became part of the 40th Division, the "Sunshine" Division. The 40th went to France, but never fought as a unit. The division was fragmented, and parceled out as replacement troops for the front-line.

The United States government learned from World War I that its military system must be reorganized and modernized. In March of 1918, plans were put in place for a detailed military system. In 1923, the 179th and the 180th were reorganized into the newly–created 45th Infantry Division. The division was headquartered in Oklahoma City, Oklahoma, and first commanded by Major General Baird Markham of Oklahoma City.

Throughout the depression years of the 1930s, the configuration of the 45th remained the same. With Adolph Hitler's rise to power in Germany, the configuration would later change. In the mid-1930s, as Hitler's Germany became real, Japanese aggression threatened eastern Asia and the Pacific rim. Still, American isolationists held that the United States industrial might back from building a formable military world force as the Atlantic Ocean separated us from Europe, and the Pacific kept us half a world away from the Japanese. As Edna Vincent Mallay, the great poet, stated most eloquently:

> "Longing to wed with Peace, what did we do? - Sketched her a fortress
> on a paper pad."

But then, in September of 1939, the winds of World War swirled into a storm of horror. Hitler's war machine invaded Poland, slaughtering and enslaving millions. Czechoslavakia, Holland, Belgium, and France quickly fell to the Nazi crush. By early 1940, the United States' most formidable ally was at serious risk. Throughout the early days of 1940, Britain's Winston Churchill begged the United States to enter the war, or at the least lend Britain the hand of its vast industrial power. Across the Pacific, the totalitarian Japanese government ordered its troops into China and Manchurian. Japanese infantry and air power quickly brought the Manchurians to their knees. The world was snarled in an armed conflict that was rapidly expanding.

Still, the isolationists held the United States back. Unlike the Viet Nam conflict of the 1960s, the "Doves" of Congress controlled a policy of absolute restraint. With the two oceans separating the war from the American continent, the United States Army was ranked a weak eighteenth in terms of its size. History records that one of the world's master mind politicians was United States President Franklin Delano Roosevelt. Keeping in close contact with Churchill, Roosevelt kept a finger on the pulse of Britain's fight for survival. Roosevelt worked his political charms on Congress, finding several ways to assist the British. Most notable was the famous "Land-Lease Program," giving British a stash of supplies and an armada of used destroyers. What Roosevelt saw in 1940, however, was that war was inevitable. It was only a matter of time before the United States was in it. Because it was next on Hitler's list, America had to prepare. Throughout 1940, Roosevelt remained legislatively stymied in efforts to lift up the American military. However, he quickly figured out he could operate by executive order.

President Franklin D. Roosevelt threw the Oklahoma National Guard unit into the modern era. On September 16, 1940, Roosevelt, recognizing that the country needed to be prepared for the worst, signed the executive order that put the 45th Infantry Division on active duty status for one year. The division was one of only four National Guard units to become part of the active duty army.

On December 7, 1941, the war came to America. The Japanese, in an unprecedented surprise attack, struck the island of Hawaii at Pearl Harbor and destroyed most of America's naval fleet. Approximately 2,500 American lives were lost.

With lives now lost, the United States was at war.

REFLECTIONS: SUMMER OF 1953

As I best recall, my first recollection of the thunder and lightning of the Thunderbird was at the age of six.

In 1953, we lived at 2118 North Shawnee in Oklahoma City. Eight years after the war, Jack and Leota bought their first house with a loan from Local Federal Savings & Loan. Mom was afraid they could not pay the loan back. Dad always said it would get done. At the time, he was an accountant for the R. Olson Oil Company. Prior to that he was employed by Kerr-McGee Corporation.

Our house was a small, two-bedroom house. Richard and I shared a bedroom. It really was not painful because Richard was neat, and quiet most of the time. Our "block" was the prototypical block of the 1950s–infested with kids, all about the same age. In those days moms stayed home, dads went to work. On our block all dads seemed to go to work at the same time. We had one car, so most mornings Mom would drive Dad to work at the old Liberty Bank Building, located at the corner of Robinson and Park avenues.

The mode of transportation for the kids was a bike or tricycle, sometimes a two-wheel scooter, and as we all moved up and down the block in mass the group was followed by a cadre of dogs. We all had dogs on Shawnee Street. Our dog was "Duke."

Cardboard playing cards were fixed to the frame of our bikes with wooden clothes pins. The playing card itself was positioned between the spokes of the wheel so that rotation of the wheel created a loud sound. Not only could the whole block hear us coming or going, but our location was easily discovered by the pile of bikes in a yard or driveway.

Jack and Leota's first house after World War II, 2118 N. Shawnee, Oklahoma City, Oklahoma.

The Shawnee Street Gang in 1953; Dickie Taylor leads the way with the author saluting on the first row, and Richard Neville fourth from the left on the first row.

The block was populated with a cast of characters reminiscent of Spanky and Alfalfa's "Our Gang." Dickie Taylor somehow thought he was Frank Sinatra. His hair was long and black, usually greased back–quite a feat for a seven-year-old kid. Dickie never went anywhere without his guitar. Ernie King lived at the north end of the block. Ernie was a small kid viewed in those days as the "crazy one" of the group. His favorite effort at gaining attention was to run out of his house totally naked yelling at the top of his lungs. Ernie, in his birthday suit, would then "pee" on the nearest tree and run back inside. This usually happened around 10:00 a.m. for those who cared to gather in front of Ernie's house and watch. Richard and Doug Perry were the smartest kids on the block. We viewed them as the "scientists," always mixing some sort of concoction for the rest of us to "test drink." The Perry boys always fancied themselves as the Flash Gordons of Shawnee Street. They never went anywhere without their tunics, or robot like wardrobe. Bazark, the local television mechanical man, and 3-D Danny also were heros of the Perry boys.

Doug Rich, Richard Roth, brother Richard, Danny Dennehy, and myself were far more versatile in our attire. We were the real trend setters of our venue, rotating various disguises of Davy Crockett, Hop-A-Long Cassidy, Superman, and various other caped crusaders of the day, including Batman and Robin. Most of the day was spent in one uniform or the other until late afternoon when one of the moms summoned us for Kool-Aid and, sometimes, those butter and sugar sandwiches. This was followed by a required nap. There were two girls on our block, Linda Sue Glidwell and Sherri Lynn Tearce. Of course, being guys, we hated the girls. Most of their time was spent making a blanket tent, under which they would sit and pretend to drink tea and discuss how ugly and mean all of the guys were. Of course, major efforts were made to disrupt their lives with the objective being to bring them to tears and force them to run inside. Often this purposeful irritation was commenced by Doug who conceived the brilliant idea of putting our smallest comrades–Richard or Danny–into an old, open-ended oil drum and push the barrel downhill, rolling over Linda and Sherri's blanket tent. Without fail, this produced the desired effect of hysteria and tears with both girls vacating the area at a high rate of speed. These transgressions were generally handled by the moms and, thankfully, not reported to the dads. Moms rarely administered corporal punishment and a good verbal tongue lashing was the aftermath of this harassment of Linda and Sherri.

On a fine summer day in 1953, about 5:00 in the afternoon, Richard Roth and myself were engaged in one of our favorite past-times–the very constructive activity of throwing rocks at cars. This effort was usually conducted with great stealth and deception at the corner of 19th Street and Roth, only a block from Shawnee Street. To disguise our identity, we dressed in one of our many costumes. On this particular day, Richard was Superman and I was Batman. I always believed Richard's selection of disguise was particularly ill-fated for this activity because Superman never wore a mask, only a cape, and thus one's true identity was readily discoverable. My own selection however for the afternoon event was far more intelligent. Batman always wore a mask, no one would ever discover who I was. We both, how-

The deputy sheriff on Shawnee Street was "Duke," the weeny dog.

Richard Neville and Drew Neville were the two-pistoled cowboys of Shawnee Street in our "Hop-a-Long" Cassidy attire.

From left to right, Richard Neville, Ernie King, and Drew Neville playing "army" in the backyard on Shawnee Street.

ever, had the cover of our capes. On this day our capes were red towels fixed at the neck with a safety pin.

On the northeast corner of 19th and Roth we had the most secret of hiding places behind the Brown's row of hedges which bordered the yard. There we stock piled our stash of rocks which had been carefully selected to fit into the small of our hands. Our plan was simple and democratic. We alternated the target selection. Richard would pick a car, I would pick the next. Having selected the appropriate target coming down 19th Street and at the appropriate distance we judged at 20 yards, we both would sprint from our hiding place, rocks in hand, our speed of foot only slowed by the capes of both Superman and Batman. We would bring ourselves to an abrupt halt and unload our pellets at the unassuming passing vehicle. Only a few of the passing motorists would quizzically look at the running dynamic duo aside the car. Having unleashed our fury, we would speed back to our hiding place, look to see if the victim stopped, and then await our next target.

The next pick was mine and I carefully selected an off-white, two-door Ford. For an instant, it reminded me of Jack's car but this was impossible. It was entirely too early for him to be coming home. Having cited our prey, and at the perfect instant, Richard and I jumped to our feet, and in full sprint, headed toward the Ford. At precisely the right moment our right arms delivered their respective payloads. It was a perfect strike, right into the side of the car. As we both wheeled into retreat we heard a most unusual and horrifying screech. It was rubber hitting the road. We looked at each other, both of us now paralyzed by fear. The driver had stopped. In shock and disbelief, absolutely frozen at the thought that someone would actually stop and come after us, we both could only stare at the car now pulled over to the curb. As we watched, the left door flew open and the driver exited in

Six of the Shawnee Street gang pile it up in the sand-box in the backyard on Shawnee Street.

a hurried fashion. The selection of the white Ford was rather unfortunate. It was Jack. He headed straight for us, ears red and nostrils flared. The Batman and Superman outfits had pitifully failed to protect our identity. We were done. He was fifteen yards away from us and coming fast. At this point we had two choices. We could take the brave and honorable course and stay put and take our medicine. Or, we could run. Regrettably, we both made yet another ill-fated decision. We ran, but not fast enough. Dragged down by our capes, we were captured.

Now in custody, the tongue-lashing began and it was loud. The most often repeated phrase of the day was "brilliant, just brilliant" which was followed by "you haven't got the sense God gave a goose." I should parenthetically note that this phraseology, on occasion, followed me all the way through high school. The decibel level was stunning and I came to fear that this verbal lashing would most likely be followed by a non-verbal one. To my great pain, I was right. Once home, I was rather unceremoniously hauled through the front door and right out the back door. Marched underneath the only tree in the backyard, I, for a moment, believed I would most likely be hung by the neck. Later, I wished I had been. As the verbal barrage continued by the man still wearing a suit, a suitable branch was selected and dismembered from the trunk. Now, the most humiliating edict was announced "drop trow and bend over." Three lashes did the trick, I was in tears, but somehow grateful the punishment phase was over. Dad's fury was undescribable. After an appropriate apology, and a few more harsh words directed toward the "non-wisdom" of my conduct, we all sat down for dinner, of pot-roast and potatoes.

Punishment was swiftly delivered and totally without due process. The message was clear. I did not throw rocks at cars anymore, and the secret hiding place was forever abandoned.

I do not know what happened to Richard Roth.

JACK NEVILLE AND ADAIR

Jack Neville was born January 7, 1920, in Adair, Oklahoma, population 290. His mother, Rosa Skinner, was born in the small town of Vinita in 1879. When Jack enlisted in the 45th Infantry Division he listed his ancestry and "national background" as "English-Indian." Dad was proud of his Cherokee Indian history. He never viewed his ancestry or the Cherokee Indian to be a minority. He always was quick to point out that the likes of Will Rogers, the world renown humorist and philosopher; Admiral Joseph Clark, the great carrier commander of World War II; Charles Curtis, vice president of the United States under Herbert Hoover; and Jack Montgomery, awarded the Medal of Honor for gallantry in action in Italy all were part of "his tribe." His brothers and sisters, however, claimed that Jack allowed his pride to overrule his common sense. Rosa had been "of record" and "enrolled" as a member of the Cherokee Tribe since the turn of the century. Most of the brothers and sisters followed suit. Jack always refused. He would not be part of a "government program," he often proclaimed, and low be the day when he would participate in a "government hand-out."

In the late 1960s, when Jack and Baird got in one of their many arguments at the Annual 4th of July gathering when Baird countered Jack's resistance to

With the exception of course of Gene, this is one of the few pictures of all the Neville brothers and sisters of Adair, taken at a family reunion in the 1960s. Front row left to right, Jim Jack, Nat, Pete MacKellar, Creighton, Baird; back row, Billy Lou, Leota, Nat's wife Ruby, Creighton's wife Juanita, Baird's wife Chola, the Queen of Mayes County, Helen, and Roselle.

Cherokee enrollment with the observation "your son could go to Dartmouth," Jack became uncharacteristically quiet. Education always was his number one priority, and a real hot spot with him. The third most often used phrase in the Neville household, with "God Damn It" and "You haven't got the sense God gave a goose" being the first two, was "you're going to get your education, get on those books." In the face of Baird's observation, Jack was forced to concede "perhaps my ass over-loaded my mouth." Still he never signed up. Jack did not want the government to help put his sons through school, he would do it himself.

On the other side of the family tree was Elzer B. Neville, born near Sedalia, Missouri to parents several generations removed from England. The "B" was not part of his given name, only Elzer, which he hated. So, he added the "B" and called himself "Bart."

The Neville clan of Adair, Oklahoma in the 1920s was monstrous. The nine included Helen, born in 1900; Jim born in 1902; Creighton born in 1904; Nat born in 1906; Baird in 1909; Roselle in 1915; Gene in 1917; Jack in 1920; and Billie Lou in 1923. The post 1909 group took the most ribbing as one would expect. They were unceremoniously referred to as the "other family" and most often by Baird as the "too-lates." There was a mad scramble for the dinner table every night.

Most of the men of the 45th Infantry Division came from small towns in Oklahoma just like Adair. Adair was a rural farming and ranching community located in the northeastern part of the state, approximately 90 miles north and east of Tulsa, Oklahoma, at the intersection of Highways 69 and 28.

Adair was initially a railroad town formed by the Missouri, Kansas and Texas Railroad, know as the KATY in 1872. The town was named after a doctor, Walter Thompson Adair, who was the regimental surgeon in General Stand Watie's Confederate Indian Army. Adair was a "flag stop" on the MK&T line, meaning if you wanted to catch the train at Adair, you had to coerce the local MK&T conductor to literally flag down the train, the signal that passengers wanted to board. A red flag usually did the trick, but in a pinch just about anything would do, including the waving of your hand in a hurried fashion. Despite the flag, the old KATY did not always stop. It was easier, to catch the train at its scheduled stop at Vinita, a few miles up the road.

Adair, even in its time, was not exactly a bustling metropolitan area. The town had one public school with six rooms for all grades. There was a lumber yard, one hardware store, the Bank of Adair, a grain elevator, a drug store, and a cluster of buildings, mostly wooden, that housed a post office, five-and-dime store, racket store, a butcher shop, the Brock Mercantile, two grocery stores, and a cream station. This square was connected by a series of wooden board walks. The wooden planks served as the sidewalks of the day. The roads leading to the business center were dirt.

Adair was not over populated with professionals. There was one dentist in town, R.V. Adler. Dr. Adler's practice was short-lived. Unfortunately, while returning from a patient's farm he was killed by an exploding steam engine. The number of doctors was reduced to one when the Dalton boys robbed the train in Adair in 1892. Dr. Goff, a by-stander to the robbery, was shot in the heal of his foot and bled to death.

For its size and station, Adair was a social hotspot. The Embroidery Club met regularly, the Masons were extremely active, and of course, one could always opt to join the Indian Territory Anti Horse Thief Association.

Although near the oil rich fields of Tulsa, the economy of the town was largely dependent on agriculture, as was the Neville family. Bart Neville owned and operated Neville and Co., one of the two grocery stores in town. Underneath the name read "Groceries and Accessories For Fine Gents." Bart received the notable acceptance of the community having been elected Adair's mayor.

Mother Rosa Neville ram-rodded the town's most prolific rumor machine, the Embroidery Club. If you wanted to know what was going on in Adair, one had to be part of this group. Legend had it that Rosa could really spin a story if she was so inclined. The one that reached into the future generations was the tale of the "Great Train Robbery" in Adair. Family history has it that at the age of 15 she saw Bob Dalton and his gang ride into town and hold up the train while stopped at the train depot. As she described it, a huge gun fight broke out, bullets flew everywhere, and half the town was either injured or killed as the Dalton boys escaped on horseback through the middle of

Jack's mother Rosa, standing to the left with her brother and sisters.

town chased by the United States Marshalls. This tale was of dubious credibility as told in the 1950s around Sunday evening supper. The *Historical Highlights of Mayes County*, enhanced grandmother Rosa's Sunday evening spin. In fact, on a warm July evening, in 1892, Bob Dalton, his brothers Grant and Emmet, and eight others hi-jacketed the MK&T payroll train when it stopped in Adair. Despite the fact that 20 marshalls guarded the train, the Daltons escaped after relieving the railroad of $27,000. They rode out of town, down the middle of main street, with guns firing. They rode off to Robbers Cave, in southeastern Oklahoma.

Oldest sister Helen followed the social suit of Rosa and was one of the most talked about among the members of the club. Helen was labeled "The Queen of Mayes County" and apparently for good cause. She was a trend setter and always part of the "in crowd." Helen, the most energetic and talkative, with the exception of Jack, was the family pied piper. All the kids gravitated toward her as a sort of surrogate mother and confidante. Helen was the queen of the family–headstrong, opinionated, and confident–an example for all.

Then there was Jack, the youngest of the brothers who was universally described in Adair as precocious, energetic, and "full of ginger." If there was trouble around Jack was usually in it. Friends came easy and Jack was the "man with the plan." However, as many recalled, it always was spirited when he was around and his enthusiasm was infectious. He always had something going. Sometimes it was good, sometimes it was bad.

At the age of seven he had become particularly adept at "flicking" lighted matches within centimeters of his chosen target. On one particular day, while the Adair Embroidery Club was busy spreading the word under the guise of embroidery, Jack focused his skills on the kitchen wood pile. He started a fire that almost burned down the south side of the house. The Embroidery Club quickly adjourned to take care of the calamity that resulted. When Bart got home, Jack was taken care of with a switch right across a bare bottom. Corporal punishment was followed by a short banishment to the hay fields of the R. E. DeLozier farm where manual labor was the final remedy for his breach of peace.

The brothers spent many a day fishing and hunting Spavinaw Creek, especially Jack and Gene. Jack could put a 22-shell through a key hole, it was said, and it was not sporting to take a rabbit unless you brought it down with a shot to the head. But his favorite sport of all was cat-fishing the Spavinaw. A little bacon on the hook always did the trick. Real sportsmen did not need a pole. A string and hook were all the tools necessary for men of skill. Jack's method of cleaning his catch became part of the folklore of Mayes County. Brother Gene would carefully hold the gills of the catfish, so as not to be speared, placing the catfish up against the trunk of a tree. Jack would retrieve a hammer and nail and drive the nail through the head of the catfish and into the tree. Once the

Nat (left) and Jack (right) square off Adair style.

catfish was rendered lifeless, Jack, with the skill of a surgeon, would remove the skin with a pair of pliers. The meat was put in a pan over a fire only a short time after this carefully executed procedure. The great Adair fisherman especially enjoyed demonstrating his craft at the almost weekly required family picnic. It was irritating to all the sisters, especially Billie Lou who usually was brought to tears at the sight of it all.

As all of the brothers reached the age of ten, they were placed into service at Neville and Co. The brothers were the labor force that staffed the store. At Bart's direction, they were involved in every phase of the store's operation. Each had their turn at stocking the shelves, sweeping the floor, taking inventory, delivering groceries, sacking groceries, and if your math skills passed Bart's muster, keeping the company books. It was Jack's first exposure to bookkeeping and accounting, skills utilized decades later to take the LeLand Equipment Co. to its zenith.

Peanut butter was one of the more popular delicacies of the 1930s. Neville and Co. sold a lot of peanut butter in those days. Each day Jack was ordered to be the man in charge of peanut butter. He hated it. In those days, peanut butter arrived at the store in large tin cans. As a customer asked for peanut butter, it was scooped out of the tin can, placed in a paper tray, and weighed. The customer paid by the ounce, that is if the customer paid. When Jack was in charge of peanut butter, every kid in town flocked to Neville and Co. Jack did his best to run out of peanut butter as fast as possible. His buddies always got good deals, usually twice what they paid for. Bart Neville always wondered what happened to his peanut butter inventory. It was said that Jack could catch catfish at Spavinaw Creek using peanut butter, but there is no real record of this phenomenon.

All the sisters flexed their vocal cords in objection to the brothers employment at Neville and Co. They wanted to be part of the business like their brothers. Bart refused. Despite constant pleas to volunteer their services, the girls were told that "business was not for women" and their place was with their mother at home. While welcomed and encouraged by Bart to visit the store, they were never allowed to work.

Bart's sexism took its toll on sister Helen. She longed to go to college and study business. She pleaded with her father to be allowed to do so. Bart refused, and further added insult to injury by explaining to Helen that he would pay for her college education if she wanted to be a teacher, but not if she wanted to study business. That was the final straw, and the result was the first Neville defection from Adair. Helen married her way out of Adair, a pharmacist fifteen years older, and in the mid-1930s moved to Okmulgee, Oklahoma where she studied business. With her marriage to the pharmacist at an end, Helen worked her way to Oklahoma City and joined the accounting firm that later became part of Arthur Anderson, one of the Big Eight in later years. Oklahoma City became her home in 1937.

Helen's strike at independence and departure from Adair had a profound effect on the rest of the kids, especially Jack. Bart preached the need for education on a daily basis and now, with Helen's departure, it became apparent that education could be earned beyond Mayes County. There was now a new horizon out there and Jack began to dream of it. A few years later Jack would follow his own dream.

The football factory at the University of Oklahoma got its start in 1897. It took a few more years for the Sooner hysteria to work its way to Adair. But it did. Early day broadcasts of Oklahoma games were via Western Union from Norman, Oklahoma. Right in the middle of the swirl of football fever in Adair, was Jack Neville. He was a one-man recruiting team for dear old Adair High.

To play high school football in the 1930s, especially in Adair, you had to be a gladiator. Most of the guys on the team had no helmets, and if you were fortunate enough to have a helmet, its thin cover of leather only awkwardly sat on your head and offered little to no protection. It was more of a nuisance than anything. Jack did not have a helmet. Three of the team members had shoulder pads. Again, Jack was not one of them. Shoulder pads were made of a heavy cardboard, or if you were really lucky, plastic that was tied to your shoulders with shoe string. Not all of the kids had football pants, but most of the team did have the same colored jersey. Jack did have football pants, minus the thigh pads, and his jersey was the color of most of the team. Only one team member had football shoes. Everyone else played barefooted or, if you could get away with it, your black shoes that you wore to Sunday School. Despite the hard times of the 1930s, Jack was vocal in his insistence that all the guys should play. While increasing the roster numbers single-handedly, he told his sister, Roselle, that he most assuredly would be the high school hero of Adair High. It was not to be. On the very first play of his very first game against Choteau, the future star of the Adair gridiron, all 5'7", 115 pounds, broke his collar-bone. His stardom was now confined to the bench. Jack's enthusiasm however remained unbroken. He was "on 'em" all the time. It was vintage Jack even at 15.

At times, despite the poor conditions of the 1930s, life in Adair took on the likeness of Norman Rockwell's rural America. It would not last much longer, however, as the Great Depression was about to end Jack's way of life.

The Black Thursday of October 27, 1929, pushed the already economic depression in Oklahoma all the way downhill. The great stock market crash signaled the start of the Great Depression. It not only shattered businesses and fortunes, it took its toll on families and towns like Adair and those living there.

In 1929 Cities Service, traded on the New York Stock Exchange, traded at a high of 68 and a low of 20. By 1932, it ranged between 6 and 1. Another barometer of economic health was the blue chip, General Electric. In 1929, the

The Adair Tigers football team circa 1935. Jack Neville is standing, second from the left.

stock floated between 403 and 168. By 1932 it posted a dismal high of 26 and a low of 8. In 1938, the Dow Jones was at an awful 100.

By 1932, 25% of the labor force in the United States was unemployed, and the nation's money market system was collapsing under the weight of bank failures. People, in acts of perceived self-defense, took their money out of the banks, hiding what they had left in tin cans and mattresses. Suicide reached record highs.

It was no different in Adair. In the early days of the depression the government left the people to suffer, there was no structure to address such an economic disaster. There was no social security, no unemployment insurance, no work, and no money.

By 1933, the dark economic cloud of depression had rolled into Oklahoma and found its way to Adair. In 1933 an incredible confluence of events occurred, never having been repeated in the history of the United States on a national scale or the State of Oklahoma. Not only were the under-pinnings of the economy collapsing from depressed prices, but the State of Oklahoma, particularly the counties in the northwest, suffered through the greatest prolonged drought in state and national history. The severe drought resulted in the Dust Bowl. An incredible natural disaster, the drought created a devastating situation. Wheat and corn commanded a smaller price per bushel than they had in the colonies three centuries earlier. People did what they had to do, they left.

By 1938, one-third of Oklahoma's population had exited the state. Most traveled and migrated in their own cars representing the entire families net worth. Many headed west in search of work and a better life as related in Steinbeck's epic, *The Grapes of Wrath*. Others migrated to the east hoping to find anything. Some looked for relief in the small rural farming communities of eastern Oklahoma. They could find food there; they just could not pay for it.

The northeastern part of Oklahoma around little Adair did not suffer the great natural disaster of the weather as those in western Oklahoma did. But they nonetheless suffocated from the tidal wave effect of depressed prices. With the huge dust storm destroying crops and lives in western Oklahoma, the rich soil of northeastern Oklahoma created huge farm surpluses. The economic problem, however, was that no one could afford the surplus, even with prices down to nothing. At the Neville house in Adair, Jack and his siblings always had food, just no money. The excess surplus of farm products and little demand due to limited money, sent prices spiraling downward. It was a vicious circle.

The economic crash in Oklahoma was further exacerbated by yet another bizarre occurrence–oil production. By the 1930s, huge oil fields had been discovered in Oklahoma City and in northeastern Oklahoma. Oklahoma's oil production was wild and uncontrolled. Like the farm surpluses, not even the discovery of black gold could get the Oklahoma economy on its feet. Huge surpluses flooded the market, dropping the price of oil to 10¢ a barrel at times.

The orders of the Oklahoma Corporation Commission to limit production so that prices might increase were routinely ignored and flaunted by those in the industry. Efforts to stop the flood on the market took some ugly turns with the governor declaring martial law, of sorts, calling for the National Guard to "barricade" the oil derricks. The objective being to at least slow up production so that prices would increase. It did not work. Oddly, the state's greatest natural asset, oil, only contributed to the economic chaos of the 1930s.

With the economic structure of the entire country collapsing, the political landscape of the nation changed forever. The economic disaster of the decade was seen as political opportunity for many, including the only three-term president of the United States, Franklin Delano Roosevelt. He entered the political arena in 1928 and was first elected president in 1933 amidst the economic and political turmoil of the times. Roosevelt's "New Deal," in a desperate effort to reverse the downward spiral of the country, created a labyrinth of federal programs, the remnants of which remain with us today. In the first 100 days in office, Roosevelt swept into play some thirteen federal programs intended to pick the country up, including the Public Works Administration and the Works Progress Administration. Roosevelt's efforts to save the economy and revive the sagging welfare of the citizen marked the birth of a philosophy of huge government spending and deficit financing to cure the problems of the day. While still controversial today, one observation was undisputable. The American people were bankrupt and spiritually broken by the hard times. The New Deal was seen by Roosevelt and the Democrats as a last attempt to save the United States from falling into the ditch of third-world country status.

Roosevelt's programs broke the fall, but by 1936, there were nine million people out of work. Many of the Roosevelt programs found their way to Oklahoma City. If one observes closely, Works Progress Administration is stamped on many buildings and bridges in the State of Oklahoma. Oklahoma City's Municipal Auditorium and the popular amphitheater at Will Rogers and Lincoln Park were built by the W.P.A. America, at least to some degree, was able to get back to work through government support and big-spending programs. Roosevelt won the support of the people. He was elected again in 1936 and 1940.

The New Deal, however, was no deal for Bart Neville and Neville and Co. The benefits of the Roosevelt program were too little too late for much of Adair and the Neville grocery store. Many of the programs brought their focus to the big cities. As a result, the City of Oklahoma City was where jobs and money were. With the destruction of the small farming communities, the migration started as a necessary way to survive. For many, Oklahoma City, the capital of the state and centrally located, was the only place to find work. By 1935, the exodus from rural Oklahoma had started.

In 1931, more than 6,000 poverty-stricken families were living in what were called "Hoovervilles" along the North Canadian River. There were more than

10,000 people unemployed in Oklahoma City alone. By 1935, a virtual network of squatter camps emerged around Oklahoma City, the worst of them being the May Avenue Camp where hundreds of families resided in extreme poverty. Despite the hard times, Bart Neville had built and owned his own store. That, along with the pride of his family, was enough. He refused to leave Adair.

Bart Neville was generous to a fault. He saw Neville and Co. as more than a business for profit, but a centerpiece of the community. Neville and Co. always served as a political platform. Bart Neville was the town's frequently–elected mayor, many times the only candidate.

In the relatively good times of the 1920s, the farmers and laborers in and around Adair could obtain their food, clothing, dry goods, and tools from Bart Neville on credit. As sagging prices came to infect the economy of small Adair, Bart nonetheless refused to turn his store into a cash-and-carry business. At Neville and Co. your credit was good for up to one year; and Jack and the brothers would even load your buggy, or in a few instances, your car. No one had the money for a tip.

The process was simple. You came into the store, placed your order with Bart or one of the boys, and told them you did not have the money to pay today but promised to later. Bart always accepted the promise to pay and entered the appropriate debit to the accounts receivable ledger of Neville and Co. Addresses and telephone numbers were not necessary, only names. As sister Roselle described the operation in the 1930s, "Bart gave away the inventory, mostly to tenant farmers who migrated out of the Dust Bowl of western Oklahoma. Neighbors and friends never went without food while Neville and Co. was open."

By 1935, Neville and Co. was suffering the beginning of the end. First to fall, however, was the Bank of Adair. The Depression claimed its first victim in 1935 when Adair's only bank collapsed and was liquidated. With prices crashing, people could not repay their loans. It was the end of a bank that had operated for 33 years. With no credit available, and most of the people of Adair with little or no money to pay Bart, Neville and Co. was on its last leg by 1937.

The economic crisis now had invaded the Neville home with devastating effect. The exodus started out of necessity and survival. Helen had left because she wanted more than what Adair could offer. Now, there was nothing for the boys to do in the store as no one came except for a hand-out. Jim left for Sedalia, Missouri, in search of work. Nat left for a job with Conoco, a new company operating in northern Oklahoma, and Creighton made his way to Muskogee and eventually found work as a clothier. Jack's Spavinaw catfishing buddy, Gene, graduated from high school determined to get his college education. He caught the train to Oklahoma City to join Helen. All efforts to keep the family together in these hard times had come to an end. Before the summer of 1936, the family was scattered. The only members remaining home were Jack, Roselle, Billie Lou, Bart, and Rosa.

The horror of the Depression continued to erode Bart Neville, his company, and his family. Before the start of Jack's senior year in high school, his father called him into the kitchen. In low tones, he explained that the family was bankrupt, the store would have to be closed. It was a grim task to explain to a seventeen-year-old that the family's survival and future required that he leave Adair to live with his brother Jim in Sedalia, Missouri. They could not make it staying together he was told, Jack had to go. Devastated, he resisted, emotionally distraught at the prospect of an unwanted separation from friends and family despite the difficulties. In the end, Jack relented. He left Adair to live with Jim.

Before the fall of 1936, Jack hitch-hiked to Sedalia with the clothes on his back and a small suitcase that carried all he owned. In Sedalia, he graduated from Smith-Cotton High School.

He did not know anyone and he had little time to develop new friends. So as not to be a financial drain on Jim, he found several odd jobs. It was not much, but at least he could contribute to the overhead and put a little change in his pocket. At Thanksgiving and Christmas, he and Jim returned to Adair for the holidays. During Christmas of 1936, he resisted returning to Sedalia and attempted to have Roselle intercede on his behalf and lobby Bart for his return despite the hard times. The Depression prevented his return to Adair. It had become a matter of economic survival; and to survive the family had to remain split.

Things remained dismal in Adair. Bart ultimately lost the store, selling out to a friend for pennies. At the close of business for Neville and Co., the accounts receivables ledger stood at $25,000, a huge sum of money in those days. Few people in Mayes County did not owe Bart Neville money. Billie Lou and Roselle, forced by the circumstances, gravitated to Oklahoma City to live with Helen and Gene. By 1938, Adair was home only to Bart and Rosa.

Devastated by the Depression, bent by the separations forced on his family Bart Neville was finally destroyed. He died of a massive stroke at home on June 22, 1938. He was 63 years old. Jack was eighteen.

The Spartan-like existence of the Depression, even in Sedalia, focused Jack's thoughts on his future. Bart Neville's message was always clear–you better get an education, go to college. That was not going to happen in Sedalia or Adair, as much as he wanted to go home. The reality of life was that Adair was dying, slowly suffocating from a horribly depressed economy.

Before his high school graduation, Jack wired Gene Neville in Oklahoma City. Gene had found his way to Oklahoma City with Helen's encouragement, secured a job as a copy boy at *The Daily Oklahoman*, and enrolled at Oklahoma City University. Gene was living on 30th Street with Helen and they could always use one more to cut down on the expenses.

In May of 1937, Jack was off to Oklahoma City. Helen and Gene met him at the MK&T depot on Reno Avenue.

Even into his 70s if you asked Jack where he was from the response was always "Adair, Oklahoma."

Through my high school days on occasion we were awakened to Jack rattling around the house as early as 5:30 a.m. By 6:00 a.m. he had the entire household up, including Leota. "We're going to Adair" was the edict. As we gathered ourselves in response to the command, he loaded his cane fishing poles into the trunk of the car. The routine was generally the same. Drive quietly through town, a quick tour of the cemetery to pay his respects, and then to Spavinaw Creek for some catfishing. Jack's unique style of cleaning the fish survived the decades. Hammer, nails, and pliers remained the necessary tools needed and careful instructions always were given. Throughout high school in Tulsa there were occasions when you were brave enough to bring your best girl home. This could be dangerous as on occasion Jack would spontaneously announce "let's go to Adair." With Jack it became almost sport to test their reaction to the site of his roots. His rational was simple. "If she can handle Adair, she might have a chance."

In the 1980s, even his grandchildren were subjected to the same routine. It was a ritual, a rite of passage of sorts. After my children, John and Ted returned from Jack and Leota's, the time honored inquiry was made "what did you guys do with granddad and grandmother?" "We went to Adair fishin'" was the usual response. They too had to clean the catfish.

The legend and lore of Adair made its way into the board room of New York City and Tulsa as Dad opened LeLand Equipment Company. Idle chat always turned to "where are you from?" The easterners, always infatuated by people from the southwest, would ask and the response was always "I live in Tulsa, but I'm from Adair, Oklahoma.'

Jack's mother, Rosa, died in Oklahoma City, in 1955 There was no uncertainty about her burial site despite the considerable distance and difficulty of a trip to Adair. A few days after her death, the funeral procession of Jack, Baird, Nat, Creighton, Helen, Billie Lou, Jim, and a tribe of families made their way up the Turner Turnpike, through Tulsa, into Adair, and to the cemetery. There, Rosa was laid to rest next to Bart. Thus ended the first generation of the Nevilles. Sister Helen bought a new organ for the Methodist Church in Adair, and to this day, Roselle sends a stipend to Geneva Eby in Adair to maintain the grave site at the Adair cemetery.

However tough and difficult the times of the 1930s were in Adair, something good came of it that lasted through the decades, and cemented a real sense of heritage, pride, and family for those that followed. Such pride in their roots was typical of the men of the 45th Infantry Division, Home and family were real to these young men. The fact was that the sense of "where they were from" and "who they were" carried them through the days on the battlefields in Europe.

REFLECTIONS—JULY 1968

In the summer of 1968, I signed on with the YMCA in Tulsa and became a camp counselor for 15 year olds at Camp Takatoka on the Fort Gibson Reservoir near Wagoner, Oklahoma. A fraternity brother and high school friend, Vic Williams, recruited me into this service at the rate of $250 per month, room and board included. We lived in huge tents and to this day Vic never has been forgiven. Every three weeks we were granted a "session break" from the stress of dealing with the campers who knew more than we did about everything. Vic and I usually rewarded ourselves during these breaks with a frolic and detour to Afton, Oklahoma and the Shangri-la Resort on Grand Lake. We would rendezvous with our buddies, drink a few "brewskies," and, of course, go on "babe-watch." We never were successful, but always hopeful. The women of the lake who cruised in daddy's new ski boat never were very impressed with a couple of camp counselors – especially from a "Y" Camp named "Takatoka."

On one Saturday morning Vic and I loaded up the old Mustang, hoping to reach Afton before noon. Our anxiety, however, over came any sense of planning or common sense on this day. As we made the turn on Highway 69, Vic asked if I had any money. "I'm sure I do" was my response as I asked Vic to hold the wheel while I reached for my wallet. I came up empty–no money. I did have a check and thought certainly that this would do.

This was brilliant. A future doctor and lawyer on the road for the weekend with no money. Nonetheless, we managed to compound the error. Rather than stop to cash a check, we would put the pedal to the metal, cruise on up to Afton, cash a check, and achieve happiness. No worry.

As I settled back into the black bucket seat of the Mustang, I instinctively glanced at the gas gauge as my foot depressed the pedal. It was not a welcome site. We were on "E." Vic quickly inquired of my groan and I broke the bad news. "Shit!" was his only response.

Of course, we ran out of gas. Embarrassingly, we coasted to a stop at the intersection of Highways 28 and 69 on a 100° Oklahoma summer day with no wind. We both sat silent in the car contemplating our fate. We concluded that our misfortune could not be remedied by simply sitting in the car.

Finally, we made the agonizing decision to get out of the car. As we exited the yellow Mustang, wearing a pair of khaki shorts, a T-shirt that said "YMCA," tennis shoes, no socks, and unshaven, there was one sign. It read "Adair, Oklahoma 2 miles."

Just great, Dad's home town. What a couple of super-stars we were. Now, I could hear Jack. "How could you ever hope to get in law school or med-

ical school, you haven't got the sense God gave a goose." The problem here, however, was that he was right and the truth was that generally when he gushed this superlative, he was right. This was not exactly a "resume" moment. To worsen the circumstances, Vic heard my audible "Great, this is Dad's home town." Vic was excited, we had been saved, out of gas in Jack's home town was a stroke of good fortune. I remained silent in further embarrassment. We locked the car and headed down the road to Adair. Vic's constant chatter, as we marched along in the heat of the day, revolved around the fact that I had to know everyone in Adair, and most assuredly everyone I knew would rescue us. Vic acted as if a marching band would greet us when we entered the city limits. I, on the other hand, was not so sure. I kept my chin down as our pace quickened toward town. I had been to Adair uncountable times, and I probably had met most of the town. But, on this day, it hit me that I had not paid enough attention during those visits to remember anyone's name. To reveal this amnesia to Vic, however, would have most assuredly resulted in a stroke in his perceived hour of greatest need. I kept quiet, but in a way I hoped we would never reach Adair. Of course we did.

For a small town in the middle of summer, Adair was quiet. Those in town seemed to be headed toward the only place open on this Saturday morning. That store became the line of march as Vic kept asking if I recognized anyone. As we neared the store, the sign out front read "Eby's Grocery Store." The name raised a faint recollection and this at least seemed to momentarily satisfy Vic's anxiety for rescue. Masquerading confidence, we entered the store. It was obvious to all that we were out-of-towners.

Joe Eby was judged to be in this fifties. He was well tanned with a set jagged jaw and large forehead. The store itself seemed small and very old. The floors were wood, and so were the shelves. Despite its size, inventory stuffed the shelves with the usual, and it was obvious that business was good. The only cash register in the place was coal black, with numbers on the buttons which were pressed to enter the amount of the purchase. It had to be old I thought. As we both approached the only check-out counter his appearance and demeanor became more and more stern. You could see it in his face–what did these two ya-hoos want? The few town's people in the store now had their attention focused on Vic and I. It was far too late to cut and run. We had to seek the moment of truth. After reaching the counter I looked at Joe Eby and reached for my wallet and the only check in it.

"Sir, we ran out of gas on the highway, and if it's okay, I'd like to cash a check so we can buy some gas." No response was the response, but we were extended a pen which was nervously utilized to fill in the blanks of the check, and then to pin my signature. I scribbled out a check for $5.00. Finally done, the check was handed over to Mr. Eby for his final verdict. As

he took the check from my hand, his giant blue eyes seemed to shoot right through me as sweat profusely dripped from my forehead. We were done. I was certain of it.

He seemed to stare at the check forever as if he were lost in deep thought. At least I had the sense to keep my mouth shut as we stood there awaiting his decision. Still no audible response. After what seemed like an eternity, he said "Need some identification."

Grateful that we were still in the ball game and that the "no" word had not yet been uttered, I grappled for the driver's license in my wallet. To this day, I think it took two hands to get my driver's license free of the wallet. Once accomplished, it was quickly surrendered to Mr. Eby. Again, no reply. He only seemed to gaze at both the check and my driver's license. It seemed as though it was certain doom.

Then his stone, rough face once again looked me up and down, but his eyes seemed distant and now watered. He asked "Son, you Jack Neville's boy?"

The question caught me totally by surprise, but at least I knew the answer. The only problem was whether or not I could get it out. "Yes sir," was my only reply.

Now Geneva Eby, Joe's wife stepped from behind a shelf. She just stood silently by watching. Joe continued to look at me. Then, with not a word said, he handed me both check and drivers license. It seemed certain rejection. As I reached for both items, Joe Eby's other hand opened a drawer on which sat the old black cash register. He took out $5.00, and extended it across the counter. "Are things all right, do you need help?" he asked.

The only response I could muster was "yes sir, but we can get our gas, and thanks a lot." It was about as inarticulate as I ever have been. The $5.00 went quickly into my wallet.

There was a pause as I now just looked at him trying to figure out what to say or do next. My mind seemed frozen as I could tell that Joe Eby was lost in thought. About what, I did not know. It seemed like forever. Finally he just said, "Son, you come from fine folks."

Now stunned, my mouth was dry. Vic's eyes were as big as quarters as he stood almost at attention in his Camp Takatoke YMCA T-shirt with his mouth gaping open. Eby's comment still rendered me speechless. "Yes sir," was my reply.

Eby's retort was quick, "Lest you not forget that son, you understand?"

That was it. I shook Joe Eby's hand and out the door we went not daring to ask for a ride back to the car. Once out the door of the store and without conversation, Vic and I proceeded to the gas station, got a gas can and filled it up at 17¢ a gallon. Then, we started walking. Grand Lake here we come.

I began to take inventory of the day's events. We left camp with no money and no gas, we both looked like crap. Jack Neville was not there, but he was right. Neither of us had the sense God gave a goose. How was I going to get in law school if I ran out of gas on Highway 69. Equally troublesome was the realization that as many times as I had been to Adair, Oklahoma, on those Saturday or Sunday spontaneous road trips, I had not paid attention to anything or anyone. All I wanted to do was catch the fish and go home. In Jack's hometown, they knew who I was, but I did not know them. Maybe I needed to start paying more attention.

Thirty-three years later I recall the events as if it were yesterday. I'm not sure why. Joe Eby's response to our predicament was of course gracious and more than necessary, but I always wondered about his silent gaze as he looked at me over that counter and said what he did. In June of 2001, I called Geneva Eby to talk about Dad and the 1930s in Adair. Much of the history of Adair comes from our discussion. Geneva Eby and her husband went to high school with Jack. They lived in Adair in the 1930s and suffered the devastation of the Depression along with the Nevilles. In that long, drawn out stare at me in his store, Joe Eby was remembering. He was a witness to those dark and ugly days that beat, and finally broke, Bart Neville. They split the family and sent Jack to Sedalia. But without saying so, he knew Jack never forgot his roots, Jack always came back and Joe Eby appreciated that. Thirty-three years later, the reason for Joe Eby's long gaze became clear. Joe Eby's $5.00 was his way of telling me that he remembered, and that Adair was home.

That was Jack Neville's home town, Adair, Oklahoma.

CHAPTER II
OKLAHOMA CITY AND THE WINDS OF WAR

To Jack, there was a relief of sorts to being in Oklahoma City. The Depression-forced exodus from Adair left a homesick feeling in the bottom of his stomach. But it was all for the best. The future for now was not in Adair. Oklahoma City was a homecoming of sorts. Helen had established herself in Oklahoma City working for an accounting firm. Gene had found two part-time jobs, had enrolled in Oklahoma City University, and even joined a fraternity, the local chapter of Lamda Chi Alpha. To Jack's surprise, Gene had found a new hobby. There was not much catfishing in Oklahoma City, so Gene had taken up flying and it had become an obsession. What little change he had left over was put into flying lessons and airplanes. By the fall of 1937, brothers Jim and Nat had gone to work for Conoco. Creighton had made his way to Muskogee to become a clothier and Baird was in Ponca City. Sisters Billie Lou and

In September of 1939, Jack, second row smiling left of "Mother" Hilburn, joined the Lamda Chi Alpha fraternity at Oklahoma City University. Gene Neville is on the front row, second from left.

Roselle opted to stay in Adair with Mom and Dad. But the reunion with his catfishing buddy and the Queen of Mayes County was uplifting to Jack. It gave him a cause for optimism generated by the energy of Helen and Gene, even though Jack had never lacked for enthusiasm himself. They all lived together at 434 Northwest 30th Street in Oklahoma City.

Both Gene and Helen immediately took their little brother under their wing. Jack enrolled in the business school at Oklahoma City University with Gene, but could not pay for it. With Helen's help he was hired by Alexander Drug Company as a clerk and stock boy. His resume item, "Neville and Co.–Groceries and Accessories for Fine Gents." The First National Bank started in a tent in Oklahoma City before the turn of the century, but by the 1930s it had grown into a 33-story building with elevators. Gene ran a shift of the elevators in the bank building and offered to split his shift with Jack. Jack quickly took Gene up on his offer. Now with two jobs, Jack could make it through school. The university social scene was not left unattended. Following Gene's footsteps, Jack joined Gene's fraternity. There were 18 members of the Lamda Chi Alpha chapter and you better be able to hold your whiskey. Neither of them missed many parties and family lore has it that Jack even found a gal from Pryor Creek to squire around campus – that is until one fine, fall day.

Sylvester Stauffer was drawn to Oklahoma from Tama, Iowa by the excitement of the discovery of black gold. He and his wife, Lottie, came to Oklahoma City in approximately 1910 with their two daughters. He immediately became a fairly well-publicized player. *The Daily Oklahoman* seemed to pick up on all the successes and failures of the Stauffer Petroleum Company. A risk taker deluxe, he pioneered the discovery of several large fields in eastern Oklahoma City, the most notable success being the Hunsaker No. 1 drilled immediately south of the Oklahoma State Capitol Building. But his appetite was never satisfied. Success bred more drilling, and with more drilling came the inevitable failures that go with wildcatting for oil, with only an occasional success. It was good enough to get by and send the girls to school.

It was Sylvester Stauffer's late Friday afternoon routine to make his weekly deposit of oil runs into the Stauffer Petroleum Company's account downtown at the First National Bank. The bank's teller stations were on the second floor in a huge expanse of space and usually a bee-hive of activity. Adorned in the art deco style of the day, the ceiling in the lobby had to be 30 feet high. On this day, Mr. Stauffer had with him his youngest daughter, Leota Pearl. In the late 1930s the quickest and most convenient way to the second floor was the elevator. Tall, leggy, well-kept, and a great smile, Leota put Jack on his heels as she followed her father onto the elevator. In the gruffest of tones, Mr. Stauffer ordered the elevator operator to the second floor. Jack's ears however had been silenced by two brown eyes and an engaging smile. It was all she wrote for Jack. Once again, this time louder, Mr. Stauffer barked the order for the second floor.

This time Jack quickly engaged. As the elevator reached the second floor and the doors opened, Mr. Stauffer exited first with Leota just a step behind. There were no options here for Jack. He could only hope and wonder if he would ever see her again. Leota's slight glance backward as she followed her father gave him the hope he needed. Of no knowledge to Jack was the fact that Leota Pearl Stauffer had just graduated from Classen High School in Oklahoma City and in the fall of 1937 she was to enroll as a first semester freshman at Oklahoma City University. So was Jack.

As a junior at Oklahoma City University, brother Gene shepherded his freshman brother into collegiate life and the ranks of the Theta Kappa Nu fraternity, which later became the local Chapter of Lamda Chi Alpha. College life and classes were the perfect elixir for Jack Neville–work, classes Monday through Friday, only a half a day of work on Saturday, then it was "party down" on Saturday night. The Oklahoma City campus on a Saturday evening was a social hot-spot, and both Jack and Gene, as they say, were participants. They never missed a big band on campus. First on the agenda for the fall semester was the Beta Alpha Phi Formal Dance on September 18, 1937. And, as the old saying goes, "there she comes, just-a-walkin' down the street, singin' do wa diddie" . . . it was the girl in the elevator. This time, however, she was unescorted and unprotected by the silver-haired Mr. Stauffer. The time was right and Jack knew now was the moment to make his move. He did.

Unfamiliar and foreign to the baby-boomer generation is the notion of a "dance card." A rather formalistic practice in the 1930s and 1940s, each girl attending a dance carried a card usually containing five lines. Custom called for her to fill in each line with the name of a lucky guy for each dance. In those days, the order of your dance partner was written down on the dance card and if you were a gentleman you had to wait your turn. Several days after Mom's passing in March of 2000 brother Richard Neville stumbled on to what appeared to be most of Leota Pearl's college dance cards tucked away between the pages of one of those old dust-covered scrapbooks. On most of Mom's dance cards, Jack's name is penned on all five lines of the card in Jack's handwriting. Probably through some slight of hand, Jack had arrested Leota's dance cards and assured that he was the only one to dance with her. Inspection of other cards revealed several "Xs" through all five lines, suggesting that those dances were reserved for no one else but Jack. Dance cards found included the Beta Alpha Phi Christmas Dinner Dance, December 18, 1937; the Alpha Omega Sorority Dance of April 20, 1938; and the Delta Psi Omega Dance of May 6, 1938. By our count, prior to December of 1940, there were some 20 dances in which Jack monopolized and dominated Leota Pearl Stauffer's dance cards.

The dance cards suggest that after the Beta Alpha Formal Dinner/Dance of September, 1937, Mom did not have a chance. She would not have wanted it any other way. They would stay together for 62 years.

The excitement of it all provided the needed escape from the dark clouds that hung over Adair, Oklahoma. Government spending had pumped new blood into the economy of Oklahoma City. The hard times of Adair were momentarily eased for Jack with two jobs and Oklahoma City University, but it was impossible to escape the sad news from Adair. The grip of the Depression had strangled Adair. Neville and Co. was gone, and in June of 1938, Rosa Neville wired the kids in Oklahoma City. Bart Neville had died.

As fast as the MK&T would travel, they all converged to Adair. Rosa would need their help. After Bart was put to rest in the Adair cemetery, sister Helen stepped up to the plate. Rosa, Roselle, and Billie Lou would come to Oklahoma City. She would entertain no debate–so it was said, and so it was done. They would live as they had in Adair, all together. Only the address changed, 523 Northwest 22nd Street.

On the heels of a new beginning in Oklahoma City came the end of the Nevilles in small Adair. Bart had done all he could do. He had fought the good fight with Rosa at his side, and it was over. Bart Neville left behind no money, no estate. He did, however, leave nine children with a better vision for the future through hard work and a lesson that perseverence through hard times was a real life virtue.

With two jobs, school, and the uplifting atmosphere provided by the Methodist-formed University, there was little time devoted to concern over world events. Nonetheless, there was a gathering storm developing in Europe that had now caught the attention of the world. Adolf Hitler's quest for world domination had begun and the Europeans were beginning to see that his power was both threatening and real. The Nazi party and Germany had become a dominant military force. In March of 1938, Hitler took his first bold step, annexing the country of Austria and making it a part of Germany. In the same month as the Delta Psi Omega Dance on the campus of the Oklahoma City University, Czechoslovakia fell to German rule. Hardly a shot was fired as Hitler's Third Reich marched into Prague and occupied the beautiful cities and towns of Bavaria. By September of 1939, Hitler's Blitzkrieg had rolled into Poland. Its tanks and planes were no match for Warsaw's horse-drawn army. It was a quick death for Poland, nothing short of a slaughter.

The Far East was likewise on the cusp of desperate turmoil. Controlled by its own dictator and military machine, the Japanese declared war on China and by 1939 their armies occupied Shanghai. Indo-China and Southeast Asia obviously were next, seen as "economically" necessary by the Japanese to satisfy the island state's thirst for oil to fuel planes and ships. Hitler and Tojo had now constructed the noose by which they would attempt to strangle freedom and dominate the world. For the most part, the free world, including the United States, stood by and watched, only voicing strong "diplomatic" objection to the tyranny. With two oceans separating the Americans from the fracas, the

United States clung to its isolationist policy. It would not last much longer.

As the decade of the 1940s arrived, the dictator Hitler's juggernaut rolled on. It was a domino-like effect as country after country fell and the threat crept closer to forcing involvement by the United States. The Germans now moved into Denmark. The United States closest ally, Britain, was feeling the pressure of invasion. Its Prime Minister, Winston Churchill reached out and pled for United States assistance. Still, the United States Congress held Britain's plea for help at bay. Neutrality and isolationists continued to fight the inevitable.

In the spring of 1940, the events in the European Theatre were gaining the attention of KOCY Radio in Oklahoma City. On Sunday afternoon, Jack had his choice between "The Chase and Sanborn Hour" on WKY, "Eddie Nicbauer's Orchestra" on KOMA, and the "London Newscast" on KOCY. The London newscast now painted a picture of death and destruction that was made more real by live reports from London. To Jack, Gene, and the boys of Lamda Chi, talk of war was mentioned seriously for the first time.

Between dances at the Kappa Tau Delta Spring Dinner Dance of May, 1940, the Battle of Britain had begun. Germany was closing in on the small island country of Great Britain and questions of its survival were openly debated. Between sets at the Phi Delta Spring Formal, Britain's death was narrowly averted by the British Army's escape of 250,000 men from German claws at Dunkirk. In June of 1940, as Jack made his way to his duties at the Alexander Drug Company, Hitler declared war on France. By June 14, 1940, the axis power had taken France and Paris was occupied by the Nazis. For the first time in its history, the tiny island state of Britain stood alone, surrounded by a war machine bent on their destruction.

Back in the United States, the eyes of the politicians were opened with Britain's fight for survival. The newscasts from London made it evident that the United States could be next, despite its separation from the European Continent by the Atlantic Ocean. On the very day Hitler took Paris, President Franklin Delano Roosevelt signed a bill that made the navy a two-ocean navy. It blew through Congress, despite screams for neutrality. The build up was real. Roosevelt was preparing for war. Churchill's pleas were being heard.

In Oklahoma, there were no oceans and no navy. While the build up was not altogether unnoticed, the last item on Jack's mind was more ships for the navy to sail the Atlantic and the Pacific. He never had seen either ocean, much less a giant war ship. His thoughts were full with two jobs, school, and his constant companion Leota.

In Oklahoma City in 1940, the summer doldrums easily were broken up with a myriad of activities and Jack was forever the planner. No one could sit around for fear of being told "we're burning daylight." The Oklahoma City Indians, the local Double A Texas League dormat occasionally spiced up with visits from Dizzy Dean, were great entertainment even for Leota. The Blossom

Heath always had a big name band and you could usually get in for 75¢. Dancing was between 9:00 p.m. and 3:00 a.m. and Leota usually made Jack stay until the very end. The most controversial forms of entertainment, roller derby and professional wrestling at the Stockyards Coliseum, were usually promptly rejected by Leota. The dating compromise was most often settled with the choice of a "moving picture" at the Criterion Theater downtown, or perhaps what was showing at the Rialto Theater, admission 10¢. Often said the greatest movie year of all times, 1939, provided some incredible choices *Gone With the Wind*, *The Wizard of Oz*, and *Casablanca*, to name a few. For the really big night, there was Spring Lake Park if you had saved your money. Leota was too afraid to ride the ferris wheel, but Jack could not get enough of it.

Gene Neville found his new hobby in the summer of 1940–flying. He loved it and Jack and all the brothers and sisters, along with Rosa, thought he was crazy. The municipal airport on 89th Street and the relatively new Will Rogers Airport southwest of town became the scenes of his free time. A copy boy for *The Daily Oklahoman*, Gene was encouraged by the paper's sponsorship of the "Oklahoma Times Air Cadet Corps" which was designed to stimulate interest in flying in Oklahoma. With his employer's encouragement, and through a pilot training program sponsored by the relatively new Civil Aeronautical Authority, predecessor to the Federal Aviation Authority, Gene learned to fly. He soloed the same summer with 8 hours of instruction.

For Jack and Leota, Sundays at the Neville's became a regular event. The whole family chipped in their change for the Sunday meals. Jack always made it a point to bring Leota to the family feast. Despite the almost mob-like atmosphere, she did not seem to mind, at least they were together. If you were lucky, you could get a good-size roast beef at the local Safeway for 15¢ a pound and, eggs were 16¢ a dozen. On Sundays it was always roast beef and potatoes–the family bill of fare.

Evening suppers were lively at 523 Northwest 22nd. Jack would find a point to debate and if brother Baird happened to be there the reparte was both loud and lively. Neither ever won over the other, but it was pure entertainment. Leota, Gene, Roselle, Helen, and Rosa could not get a word in edgewise, they were reduced to spectator status. Even in 1940, when television did not exist, you could not have dinner without the radio on.

On Sunday, September 1, 1940, the group of former Adairites, plus Leota, occupied their ususal spots in the living room, exchanging sections of *The Sunday Oklahoman* for reading while Rosa and Roselle toiled with the roast beef and potatoes in the kitchen. To this group, September in Oklahoma City had become a month of great anticipation. The oppressive summer heat would come to an end and school was about to begin. The social scene at Oklahoma City University required the girls to hop on the inter-urban trolley and make their way downtown for shopping at Brown's, Kerr's, or Rothchilds, that is if they could get the money.

Leota honed in on the Sunday entertainment section of the paper, while Gene worked the radio dial for KOCY trying to make sure that at 6:00 p.m. the London News would come through clear. This, of course, required Jack's supervision. *The Sunday Oklahoman* announced that Spring Lake Park would close its season with a Thursday night stand of "Blue Baron and the Blue Notes," admission 70¢. The consensus of the group was that this might be too expensive, but nonetheless a possibility since school was soon to start. For just 5¢ more, Leota announced that at the Blossom Heath there was Andy Kirk and his celebrated band, Clouds of Joy. You could dance until 3:00 a.m. Semi-audible groans of agony came from Jack and Gene. Perhaps they could all settle for a starlight concert at Taft Stadium, suggested Roselle. The guys remained silent. On the less expensive side of the entertainment ledger, the Oklahoma State Fair was about to open, and there was a much bally-hooed new western movie in town with a real-life hero as the star. *Stage Coach*, starring John Wayne, would open at the Rialto Theater. The admission was 10¢. Certainly Wayne would be better than that singing cowboy with a guitar, Gene Autry in *Carolina Moon*, that they saw last week. Any cowboy with a guitar had to be a sissy observed Jack. This, of course, brought a chorus of "boos" from the girls, including Rosa.

With the radio now fixed and ready for the 6:00 p.m. broadcast, Jack and Gene engaged in their ritualistic trading of pages of the sports section. The Oklahoma Sooners and Oklahoma A&M Aggies were ready for the gridiron. Oklahoma City University opened its football season with Texas Wesleyan on September 20. Everyone giggled at Jack's suggestion that he "might" play this year, recalling his greatness on the fields at Adair High. Dizzy Dean was scheduled to make his last pitching start in the Texas League at Holland Stadium, home of the Oklahoma City Indians. Sam Snead was poised again to win another P.G.A. tournament and the Cincinnati Reds led the National League. In 1940, there was no such thing as division play, and in the American League, Detroit, Cleveland, and the New York Yankees were locked in a three-way battle. Just below the National League Batting Averages in the sports section was an advertisement for a new car, the Hudson. Gene informed the group that it could be picked up for the low, low price of $695.00. The announcement was followed by laughter as not even the people who lived up on 14th Street could afford that.

The roast beef, potatoes, and carrots were finally ready and the smell of it permeated the room as the group took their places at the large round table. Gene called for quiet as the London News was about to start.

In the weeks preceding September, 1940, the news had been grim. It only got worse. London and the people of Britain were literally under siege by the German Luftwaffe. The towns and cities of small Britain were burning from the daily and nightly bombing raids of Herman Goring's German Air Force. The British Royal Air Force was locked in a life-or-death struggle for survival as its relatively small group of pilots and Spitfires, out-numbered at times by 10 to one, furiously fought off wave after wave of the German Heinkels and Dormiers in a fight to save their homeland. Edward R. Murrow's trans-atlantic broadcast reported to America's heartland a desperate story. This small group of Royal Air Force pilots, many only 19 or 20 who flew the Spitfire fighter, would write the story of the survival or death of Great Britain.

United States newscasts predicted it would be over within the next few weeks. In that time frame, Britain would either live or die depending on the success of the air war. Murrow, was detailed to London by CBS to send back live radio reports of the British struggle. Through the horror of it, Murrow's reports told of the spirit of the British to fight on against the odds. As Murrow reported:

> "I saw many flags flying from staffs . . . No one told these people to put out the flag . . . they simply feel like flying the Union Jack above their roof . . . no flag up there was white."

The 6:00 p.m. London News on KOCY brought a chill to the crowd. We needed to give them more help, griped Jack, and Gene let it out that over the last year American pilots had surreptitiously violated the 1939 Neutrality Act by going to Canada, and then on to Britain to fly Spitfires against the Germans. Lend–Lease was not enough, Jack and Gene agreed. Jack now wondered what Gene had been doing hanging out at the airports all the time. Murrow's broadcasts were a source of inspiration. The Brits would go down fighting, if they had to; they would not give up to the Hitler machine that had crushed a continent. They deserved to be saved. There was no debate about that on this Sunday evening.

After the London broadcast, Gene turned the dial to some local news. Amidst the war news in Europe also was the news of America's build-up. Despite the Neutrality Act, Roosevelt was pushing America toward a state of readiness. By September of 1940, there was open debate over a "draft" of men into military service. Both the House of Representatives and the Senate were locked in a struggle over what news reports referred to as the "conscription bill," the first peace-time draft in the history of the United States. On the campus of Oklahoma City University not only was there discussion of the game against Texas Wesleyan, but also debate over whether or not you could "be drafted."

As expected, September proved to be an exciting month, more than Jack anticipated. The next day, September 2, 1940, America's commitment to defend itself became real as *The Daily Oklahoman* Monday headlines read:

Roosevelt Calls 60,000 Guardsmen

To step up America's readiness, Roosevelt announced that four National Guard units would be mobilized for one year of active duty service on September 16, 1940. The 45th Infantry Division, the Thunderbirds of Oklahoma, would be one of those units pressed into active duty.

The war drums were now beating rapidly over Oklahoma City and the Oklahoma City University campus. The push for military readiness was no longer a news item heard on the 6:00 p.m. Sunday evening radio, but a reality and the topic on campus. The men of Lamda Chi Alpha now were paying more attention to the Capitol beat as the debate continued on the floor of both the House and Senate over the conscription bill. News came fast. On September 8, 1940, only six days after Roosevelt's announcement of the mobilization of the 45th Infantry Division, the House of Representatives reached agreement and *The Daily Oklahoman* headlines read:

House Votes to Draft Men After Election

Suddenly the opening of Stage Coach and the fact that Don McNeil had beaten Bobby Riggs in U.S. Open tennis were of lesser importance. The radio news reported the Senate version of the conscription bill was sent to a joint House-Senate conference to work out the details. The Neville brothers followed events carefully. The avenues of choice were clear. Military service was inevitable even though it was peace-time. You could sign up in the National Guard with your buddies for one year of active duty, or you could take your chances with the draft. No telling who you would do your service with or where you would go. One avenue, however, was unmistakable. College life and the good times at the Blossom Heath were going to end and Leota and Jack were going to be separated. It was only a question of how long. The brothers debated the choices without reaching any consensus.

Jim was headed for the Merchant Marines and Nat the United States Navy. Jack could not understand either choice, neither of them had ever seen, much less been on a ship or ocean. Baird and Creighton would just take their chances; whatever happened, happened. Gene's choice was easy. He wanted to fly; and fly he would with United States Army Air Corps. Jack's decision was by process of elimination. He did not like boats or planes, and besides, most of the guys were headed for the National Guard Unit, the 45th. At least he could have a chance to be with some of the guys if he joined the 45th Infantry Division. Jack carefully analyzed with Leota, it was peace-time, he could do his active duty for one year, probably at Fort Sill they thought, get back to school, and he and Leota could start their life. It was a good plan. Fifty dollars a month beat the pay at Alexander Drug Company and running the elevator at the First National Bank. Typical of the man with the plan, he looked for the best of it, not the worst. Jack made his decision. He would join up with the citizen soldiers of the 45th Infantry Division.

On September 12, 1940, Jack Neville and a few of his Lamda Chi brothers marched into the National Guard Armory on Northeast 23rd Street in

Oklahoma City, and put their name on the dotted line. Jack Neville was now a "Thunderbird."

On the day that Jack enlisted in the 45th, both the House and Senate reached agreement and the Burke-Wadsworth Bill, the first peace-time draft in the history of the United States, became law. More than 800,000 men would be called to service. The law passed unanimously in the Senate. In the House there was one dissenting vote.

In mid-September of 1940, the Battle of Britain was reaching its conclusion. By September 14, 1940, as the air-war raged over London, the outcome remained uncertain as the Brits hung on literally by the hour. Many historians write that September 15, 1940 was the critical day of the fight as the Luftwaffe bombers and fighters were turned back by the out-numbered Spitfires of the Royal Air Force in a day of furious plane-to-plane combat. Britain had won.

On September 16, 1940, the day after Churchill's pilots saved their country, President Franklin Delano Roosevelt signed the executive order that mobilized the 45th Infantry Division for one year of active duty service.

REFLECTIONS OCTOBER, 1968

In 1968, during the height of the Viet Nam war, the Beta Theta Pi fraternity house at the University of Oklahoma was a great place to live. Located at 800 Chautauqua in Norman, the house was a beautiful three-story brick structure with four pillars that semi-circled and supported a portico over the front entrance. The two front doors were made of heavy dark wood. It was an impressive entrance. The house was landscaped with two three-foot high hedges that bordered two walkways that angled from Chautauqua Street to the front portico. The outside of the house had a palatial-like appearance. Inside, the house recently had been remodeled and housed about 80 "frat rats." The furniture was new, we even had a "t.v. room," complete with the newest color model.

We lived shrouded in a cocoon like existence. Moms and dads generally paid for everything, plus you generally received some type of allowance that was most often spent on beer, girls, and gas. Norman, Oklahoma, in the late 1960s was isolated from the reality of Viet Nam. You did not hear that much about guys signing up, mainly because you did not have to. There was no draft, even though, at that time, America was a war. The only reason you signed up for ROTC was to get a few hours of easy credit and a monthly government allowance. Protests against the war were few and isolated on the campus, only a few ever attended, and no one carried a sign.

The Students for a Democratic Society (SDS), the main protestors, were considered subversive and totally uncool. They could not recruit any one to their cause. It should be noted that the largest war protest at the university was attended by about 300 students at the corner of Brooks and Asp, also known as Campus Corner. There, one warm fall day, Wendy Berlowitz became part of "Sooner" legend when she removed both blouse and bra exposing her rather unsightly pair of breasts. With this display, the SDS ensured its failure at the University of Oklahoma. The truth was we were not that concerned about the morality of United States involvement in Southeast Asia. We did not have to because we had the protection of the "Student Deferment." That's right, as long as you were in school, the United States Army could not touch you. We did not worry too much about a war half way across the world involving cities and names that we had never heard of, much less pronounce. While the NBC Evening News with Chet Huntley and David Brinkley daily reported the "body count," we were busy practicing for the upcoming intramural football game against the "Sig-Alphs." After all, the Betas were the defending champs. The more serious concern was the Oklahoma football team which had sunk into mediocrity the last four years following Bud Wilkinson's death. Maybe Steve Owens would win the Heismann.

With the insulation of the Student Deferment at an end, and with increased involvement in Viet Nam, the dreaded draft was reinstated. The government decreed that the draft would be reinstated utilizing a "lottery system." We all scurried about to figure out how it would work. The lottery system, as it was then called consisted of selection of birthdays. Dates that would be randomly drawn from a hopper. July 29 was my birthday. The later your birthday date was drawn from the hopper, the better chance you had of avoiding military service. The thought of a lottery draft stimulated more interest than Wendy's breasts displayed on Campus Corner.

Of course, most of the discussion about the lottery concerned itself with your "chances." Great effort was made to assess the odds, the hope being of course that one's birthday would be drawn late in the lottery. The mentality was on how not to serve. The engineers and math majors in the Beta house immediately went to work on attempting to quantify the "odds." The number of students who were born on certain dates were all factored into the equation of the geniuses. The conventional wisdom then emerged–if your birthday was the 50th date or less selected–you were toast. Adding to the anxiety of it all was the fact that the lottery was going to be nationally televised at 7:00 p.m. right after the weekly television series, "Batman."

Tuesday nights were an event at the Beta house. Dinner started promptly at 5:45 p.m. and ended by 6:30 p.m. With the lottery excitement running high on this particular night dinner ended even earlier. Mom Vick, our house mother, was getting up in years and her step was not quite as quick as it once was. It was tradition that she be escorted into the dinning room before dinner and from the table after dinner by the president of the house. On this particular night the "plan" was to not let Mom Vick "dilly-dally" in leaving the dining room as she was prone to do. At 6:20 p.m. the traditional dinner ending song was sung and everyone stood behind their chairs as Mom Vick was escorted from the dining room. It seemed as though she took forever, but finally she was clear. There was a mad rush for the television room to secure the most advantageous spot. While the crowd generally hooted and howled during "Batman," cheering Batman and booing the Penguin or the Joker, hardly an ear turned toward the t.v. as the weekly serial seemed to this time drone on and on toward the 7:00 o'clock hour. Finally over, the t.v. room hushed.

You could cut the tension with a knife, or at least with a quick witted one liner sporadically offered by one of the brothers usually aimed at President Lyndon Johnson. Some wondered if he had rigged the lottery as he had done in his 1956 Senate campaign. On this night not too much was funny. As the magic hour struck, the officious looking lottery officials appeared on the 36-inch box, complete with the omnibus appearing bowl that seemed to hold our fate and future. The big moment was at hand–the first number. No one in the room could remember the first eight birthdays drawn from the hopper, mainly because no one's birthday had been called. But everyone remembers the ninth birthday chosen and I certainly will never forget it, it was July 29, 1947–mine!

I was done. My days at the "Mont" faded before the next number was drawn. Friday afternoon, sipping a Coors with your feet propped up on the porch of the Beta house quickly seemed over and suddenly the body count reported by Huntley and Brinkley on the evening news took on new significance.

The rest of the lottery took on little significance. Who could really care? My number had been plucked from the caldron. Once having regained some form of composure, thoughts now turned to the alternatives–mainly, how to get out of it. Quickly dismissed were thoughts of Canada or Europe, I did not know anybody over there and besides, Jack Neville would kill me. There evolved only one available course of action; one choice lay before me.

The next morning I stood tall with a few of the brothers at the University of Oklahoma Armory, home of the United States Army ROTC. The color green would get me through law school and out of the war at least until 1972. My military career was born from the hand that drew number nine out of the hopper. My basic training started the summer of 1969 at Fort Benning, Georgia, home of the infantry.

CHAPTER III
LEAVING

Jack reported for active duty in the United States Army on September 16, 1940. The volunteer enlistees assembled to begin their processing at the Oklahoma City National Guard Armory. Five o'clock p.m. was the deadline. Jack, of course, reported early and was one of the first in line. At the Armory the new troops were met with an avalanche of paperwork and the inevitable Army way of "hurry-up and wait." But overall, given the numbers, it all went rather smoothly. However, the social shock of the day was not lost on Jack or the new Thunderbirds. Rather than enrolling at Oklahoma City University, they were enrolling in the armed services. It did not look like there would be a fall formal at the Lamda Chi House for at least a year, but the boredom of the elevator at the First National Bank at least had been broken. The first order of business was the physical. Physical examinations were performed in a perfunctory and hurried fashion. Jack never had seen so many bare-butted men standing in line waiting their turn to be poked and prodded. If you were warm, had two eyes, two legs, and could breathe and talk, at least a little bit, you passed. It was impossible to flunk the physical, and no one did. Later, the United States Army would criticize Oklahoma City for the processing of physicals as being too lax. Once at Fort Sill, a number of enlistees who supposedly had physically qualified in Oklahoma City were sent home from Fort Sill as unqualified. Then there was the endless stream of paperwork. How many times did he have to write his name, address, and next of kin to be notified in the event of death or emergency. After all, they were just going to be at Fort Sill for one year. At the end of the day all 5'7" and 145lbs of Jack Neville was in the Army; Serial Number 20830256, to be assigned to the 70th Field Artillery Brigade, Headquarters Battery, 45th Infantry Division.

At the close of the long day Jack and the rest of the assembled group received their first order from the United States Army. The Order of Movement called for the division to begin its motorized convoy to Fort Sill, Lawton, Oklahoma on September 20, 1940. Jack's unit was ordered to assemble at the armory the following day. Departure time, 5:30 a.m.

Four-thirty a.m. came early to Jack on September 21. He struggled up at the crack of the alarm and got himself together. One item of travel was noticeably absent–clothes. He did not need to take any as his wardrobe would soon take on the color green and khaki. It was a strange morning, no classes and no work, report to the United States Army. Gene and Helen had prevailed on one of their buddies for the loan of an old Model-T. At least he could ride in style to the armory. A few pair of underwear, a change of shirts and socks, and a toothbrush stuffed in a brown sack was all he needed. By the end of the day, Jack would not need that.

The morning was ugly. It was pouring down rain. The weather however provided a needed conversational diversion from the task at hand. Crossing Jack's mind was the thought that perhaps this was not such a great idea after all. Too late now, however, to turn back. There at the armory, waiting to bid farewell, was Leota Pearl. Mr. Stauffer, as Jack referred to him until the day he died, had driven his youngest daughter to the armory to say good-bye. Jack took it as a stamp of approval, but then again, he wondered if Mr. Stauffer might just as well be happy to see him go. It did not matter this morning, Leota was there. The good-bye was emotional. They had been dating three years and this was their first real separation. As Jack got set to board the 2_-ton truck for the three-hour convoy to Lawton, Leota gave him two brown sacks. It was a care package with at least a dozen peanut butter-and-jelly sandwiches, a few butter-and-sugar ones mixed in.

Jack tempered the departure with his usual optimism. Commanding General William S. Key, so the scuttle-butt went, had promised a liberal furlough and leave policy for the troops, and besides that, it was rumored that friends and family could visit on Sundays. After all, Jack explained, the general in charge of the 70th Field Artillery was from Oklahoma City himself, president of the American First Trust Company, Ray S. McClain. Surely General McClain would want the boys from Oklahoma City to see their loved ones as often as possible. It would all work out. He just knew it. Leota kept the mood up beat as was her way in such times. Louis "Sachmo" Armstrong opened at the Blossom Heath September 26, maybe they could make it. That was good for a few laughs.

Promptly at 5:30 a.m. the new enlistees of the 70th Field Artillery were ordered aboard the canvas covered 1934 trucks. Two rows of wood seats running down the sides of the beds of the truck were all the seating arrangements available. This ride would definitely be "hard on your butt" laughed everyone as they climbed aboard. Jack was the last on board and successfully negotiated the last seat looking out the open back of the truck. As the truck pulled off the armory grounds turning west on 23rd Street, Jack gave a faint wave good-bye to Leota as she disappeared in the morning dark and pouring rain. He was on his way to a place called Fort Sill, Lawton, Oklahoma. He had never been there. Neither had anyone else on the truck.

The poetic irony of the day was the opening at the Liberty Theater in Oklahoma City of *We Who Are Young* starring Lana Turner. To his relief, Jack would miss this one, but Leota would have wanted to see it.

As the fifty-truck convoy of the 70th Field Artillery departed the armory and Oklahoma City, it was a somber and quiet mood that took over the journey. The occasion and the gloomy weather did not stimulate much conversation as the seemingly endless stream of green trucks made its way down the soon-to-be Route 66 toward Lawton. The further from Oklahoma City the caravan traveled, however, the more the conversation in the back of the truck picked up. Thoughts and story-telling now started about life in the army at Fort Sill and Lawton. No one, of course, knew what they were talking about.

Rumor had it that the new troops would get to live in real army barracks–not tents. Certainly the general from Oklahoma City got the good life of the real and new wooden barracks for the "Okies," the guys from Colorado and New Mexico could take the tents. After all, the cold weather was not that far away. Most of the group in the truck had never traveled outside of the Oklahoma City environs. Norman was a big trip and on the inter-urban you could travel a good part of the way. It was quickly established that Jack was the most "traveled" man in the truck. After all, he had been to Sedalia, Missouri, and rode the MK&T all the way to Oklahoma City from eastern Oklahoma. This immediately qualified Jack as the group's expert on army convoy travel. This elevation of status quickly dissipated however when Jack summoned the courage to ask the army private driving the truck to stop so that the group could go to the bathroom. Jack's plea was summarily rejected and Jack was relegated back to "know-nothing" status. The army did not stop for bodily needs.

The convoy plugged along at 40 m.p.h. into the flat lands of western Oklahoma. The weather seemed to follow the line of march from Oklahoma City, the rain just kept coming down and down. It did not take long for the old canvas-covered truck to start leaking and when streams of water started hitting the middle of the floor-board, cold and misery soon followed. Jack's coveted spot toward the back of the truck became a place of torture that he unsuccessfully attempted to trade to another of his comrades. Water and debris continually spit up from the wheels toward the open back of the truck. The trip was turning miserable, and Jack and the others would have paid dearly to be able to stop and get out.

Half way to Fort Sill, the sun was trying to break through the horizon and finally the rain reduced from a down-pour to a tolerable steady drizzle. Both drizzle and the sun were met as welcome signs of relief. At least a little warmth of sun would break the early morning chill brought on by the rain. Jack quickly discovered that he was not the only one on board who packed a brown bag care package. Those peanut butter-and-jelly sandwiches were quickly devoured and

Jack found it easy to trade a butter-and-sugar sandwich for just about anything else the other guys had in their sacks.

Once the sun broke through and Jack and the boys were "sugared-up," life in the truck was a lot better as the caravan motored on toward the west. Jack knew the end was in sight as the convoy hit the eastern edge of the Wichita Mountain Range. The hills surrounding the Spavina Dam certainly matched these hills, but the Wichita's quickly rising mountains were in odd contrast to the surrounding western Oklahoma flat lands. It was if they had been pumped up from the ground. They were not far from Lawton and by now the group was seeing signs that Key Gate, the main entrance to Fort Sill, was only a few miles ahead. With only a mile to go there was a renewed sense of excitement and anxiety within the truck. The "to-be-privates" were soon to start Basic Training in the United States Army, and as the convoy passed through the main gate at the direction and salute of the M.P. on duty, they all knew it was the real thing. At 8:45 a.m. September 21, 1940, the army convoy of new enlistees in the 45th Infantry Division, 70th Field Artillery Brigade arrived for active duty at Fort Sill, Oklahoma.

It was a rather inglorious start. The weather remained dismal. The rain continued as Jack entered the post barber shop for the first order of business– the army haircut. "Just a little off the edges, please" was not met with any

Aerial view of Fort Sill, Oklahoma, home of the 45th in September of 1940.

laughter by the private standing behind the chair with shears and scissors. It was over with the skill of a surgeon, white side-walls all the way up. Everyone came out of the barber shop nearly bald. Next, the endless paperwork began. Jack felt like he was filling out the same forms he had completed back at the armory. "Fill out the forms son" was the only response he got. It took forever. The group once again had to take physical examinations, only this time the lines seemed even longer than at the Armory. As lights shined in your eyes, you were told to cough, tongue depressors stuck in your mouth, flashlights in your ears, bend over and grab your ankles. And then of course there were the needles and shots. Jack had no choice where the needle was stuck and the spear-thrower did not seem overly concerned about the location in his butt or arm as the men proceeded down the shot line. Line after line after line, it seemed to be a factory as the men moved from station to station at the command of the doctors.

The quarter master was not exactly like shopping at Brooks Brothers. There was not any tape-measure fitting, or even a request of your style preference. Just line up as the quarter master seargant told you. The only question for socks, shoes, pants, and shirts was "large, medium or small?" You better be quick with the answer or else you got what the quarter master threw at you.

By the time Jack passed through the quarter master area it was obvious that the 70th Field Artillery Brigade would most likely be relegated to second, third, or fourth-class status. The uniforms issued to Jack gave the first hint that the new citizen soldiers were considered part of the lower classes. The uniforms issued to Jack and the men of the 45th were from the World War I era–wool, green, and ugly. You wore what you were given, whether it fit or not. There were no alterations unless you could make them yourself.

Many of the men were from the backwoods of Oklahoma and prided themselves on their ability to hunt and shoot. Jack could shoot alright, but it had been two years since he had held the old single-shot-22. Disappointment rippled through the ranks. No rifles would be issued. The army did not have any to issue to the new trainees.

Class status slipped lower and lower as the in-processing of the troops continued. Surely those relatively new white wood-framed barracks seen coming through Key Gate would be their halls of residence. Not so.

As part of the in-processing procedure the men were issued brown or khaki colored tents and, of course, Jack and his new tentmates were required to assemble and erect their own tent in a specifically designated area outside the main post area. It was a teamwork born of necessity and survival as weather continued to plague the Fort Sill area. In all, there were 2,500 tents issued to the men of the division. The tents were supported by a wooden post that ran up the center. Only in the middle could you stand straight. Some of the guys were lucky. Wooden rectangular 2x4 frames were issued to be used as a two-to

three-foot wall around the perimeter of the tents. At least the wood frames would keep some of the rain and wind out. Those extremely fortunate received wooden planks that could be utilized to construct a floor in the interior of the tent. If you were looking for instructions, forget it. Jack was semi-fortunate. His tent-mates got the necessary semi-wall wood frames. The small group of six men who would live in the tent had to learn to deal with a dirt floor that, with the weather, became semi-mud.

In addition to packs, leggings, belts, socks, helmets, boots, blouses, hats, canteens, and underwear, each new trainee received a cot and two blankets to sleep on. No beds or mattresses were available. Along with the tent assemblage came the welcome site of stove pipes and old stove heaters. At least there was the potential for heat should the weather turn cold. The warmth of the stove was a welcome friend with the continued rain in late September. Despite the rains, perhaps the most irritating problem facing the new troops was the difficulty of obtaining water for cleaning and shaving. Sometimes access to drinking water seemed mired in the mud of the Fort. With all of the rain how could there be a problem with water; griped the troops.

With the rains came the heavy jeep and truck traffic that moved men and materials about the area. The roads in, around, and through the 45th's camp site soon became a mud quagmire. The unusually bad September weather and the pitiful living conditions created fairly serious health problems in the division. In addition to a wave of colds and coughs, 2,500 men caught the flu. Jack escaped it all. And to make matters worse, while the citizen soldiers of the 45th Infantry Division struggled in their tent city, the regular army troops weathered through it all in the comfort of real barracks. The luxury afforded the regular army troops contrasted the plight of the National Guard unit and was a constant source of irritation that created a common bond among the new soldiers. The circumstances drove the men together and many became quick friends. With six men to a tent it did not take long to get to know each other.

One of Jack Neville's new tent mates was a rather tall, lanky, unassuming fellow that was easy to be around and totally unflappable. He really wanted to fly, to be in the Army Air Corps. His name was James Pete MacKellar. The two became quick buddies.

By October 1, approximately 7,500 men were assembled at Fort Sill, Oklahoma. By June of 1943, the division numbers would swell to some 14,000.

As the ranks of the 45th Infantry Division began to assemble for basic training in Lawton, the heat of world conflict was turned up. Japan had announced

(Facing Page) Private Jack Neville on duty at Fort Sill, Oklahoma, September, 1940. The case on Jack's right shoulder probably carried survey equipment. On his left appears a clip board and books most likely to record and document his findings. Geographic survey for Division Artillery was important to the operation of the S-3 Section which was responsible for plans and operations of Division Artillery. Note the absence of any weapon.

its unholy alliance with the Germans. Now the devil was entrenched on both sides of the world. President Roosevelt in late October again cranked up America's readiness. On October 22, 1940, Roosevelt signed the executive order that prioritized defense material order to private industry. This was the first step taken by the government to control private industry and increase defense readiness. Perhaps now the men of the 45th could get new uniforms and equipment with which to adequately train. The Roosevelt Administration announced continued aide to Great Britain in its struggle against the Axis powers. Despite declarations of neutrality within Congressional ranks, on October 29, 1940 the draft became real. Secretary of War Henry Stimson, blind-folded, reached into the fish bowl and drew number 158, the first of 16, 313, 240 cards representing the young men registered.

Neutrality aside, America was preparing for a fight as Jack and the 45th began the task of learning United States Army way. Basic training was just that, basic. The trainees received instruction on such topics as hygiene, including how to brush your teeth, shave, and bathe in the field. Classes on how to salute and execute an about-face, became a welcome relief to the energy drain of physical training. "PT," as it is called, was on the agenda daily. Getting in shape was one of the main objectives of the Fort Sill training. As Jack explained, the army mode of transportation were your two feet. The new troops marched and walked everywhere, and it did not seem to matter to the commanders how far away or how long it took to get there. Each week was topped off with a ten-twelve, full-pack hike led by General Key himself. The officers of the 45th led from the front and the old man himself was no exception. The *esprit de corps* built rapidly among the men with the out front leadership style of the officer corp.

Between October of 1940 and February of 1941, much time was spent provisioning and increasing the numbers of the division. Jack's vintage World War I uniform was replaced and rifles began to appear. Soon each troop had his own weapon and intense rifle and pistol training followed. Rifle assembly and disassembly, blindfolded and in the dark, became part of the daily routine. Live fire drills became part of the schedule and most of the men of the 45th had little problem proving their exceptional skills at shooting. As the months progressed, the men got their first taste of being shot at with real fire. The obstacle course, especially at night, became a dreaded activity that required crawling with full pack and rifle a distance of 250 yards with .50 caliber machine guns firing four feet above the ground and directly over their heads. No one dared stand up.

Also on the basic training schedule was the art of hand-to-hand combat. Jack never shied away from a good skuffle as a kid, but there was something different about your opponent holding a knife and charging directly toward you. The army instructors did not hold much back and a good bruise became a badge of honor. The tendency was to pay close attention. At the conclusion of basic training Jack felt like an Olympic athlete. He could walk forever with 50 pounds on his back and carrying a 9 lb. M-1 rifle. He became used to the pup-tent even when the late November cold showed up.

General Key made good on his promise of occasional weekend furloughs for the Thunderbirds. In fact, there were Sundays when family and friends could visit Fort Sill. Jack and Leota made the best of it, and on every furlough Jack hopped on the bus or found a ride back to Oklahoma City.

James "Pete" MacKellar was no "gad-about" and the social scene was not on his list of priorities. On the other hand, Jack always was energized for the headliners at the Blossom Heath, or at least a good movie at the Criterion. Pete was going to Oklahoma City with him whether he liked it or not. It did not take long for Pete to like it. What one good turn is done for your tent mate is also done for your sister. Jack saw to it that in the late fall of 1940, Pete was introduced to his sister Roselle. They were a perfect match. They were married on December 25, 1941, and a little more than two years later, James Peter MacKellar, Jr. came along. The product of that introduction was a marriage of 57 years. On furloughs from Fort Sill, Jack made sure the foursome saw the town before catching the last hop back to Fort Sill.

The 45th marches in review in September, 1940 at Fort Sill. Note the wives, family and friends to the right of the column.

The Division Artillery's famous 155mm "Long Tom."

Of course financing the social scene while on furlough became somewhat problematic. By the time Jack paid for transportation to Oklahoma City there was not that much left of a private's pay. But the man with the plan always found a way to finance the Criterion admission, or the cover-charge at the Blossom Heath to see Andy Kirk and the Clouds of Joy. That old radio Bart had given him in Adair to take to Oklahoma City did just the trick. After arrival in Oklahoma City, Jack took the old radio to one of several downtown pawn shops, pawned the radio, and used the money to take Leota out for a night on the town before the last bus back to Fort Sill. The only problem was having the money on the next trip to reclaim the radio. He found a way to fit it into the budget, only to pawn it back the next week. Somehow Jack and Leota found a way to make it to the Phi Delta Christmas Dance on December 22, 1940.

After ten weeks, basic training came mercifully to an end, and each of the new privates reluctantly waited to see what was in store for them next. For Jack, the next phase of army life was met with indecision cured by his superiors. Most of the guys were headed to the infantry for their advanced individual training. By now the boys from Oklahoma were divided into two infantry regiments, the 179th and 180th Infantry Regiments. These regiments would go on to become two of the most famous in the European Theatre. Pete MacKellar continued to insist that he wanted to fly, he wanted to be in the Army Air Corps, and it looked like he would get his wish.

For Jack, the fact that he had obtained two years of college at Oklahoma City University was seen as an army asset. His advanced training would be spent learning how to fight a war with artillery, the big guns. With Jack's comparatively advanced education, he was immediately placed into training for a combat staff position with the Headquarters Battery of the 70th Field Artillery Brigade. Before the end of 1941, the Brigade would be reconfigured into Division Artillery of the 45th Infantry Division commanded by General Raymond S. McClain of Oklahoma City. After several weeks of intensive advanced training in the field of artillery, Jack was placed on the staff of the S-3, Headquarters Company, Division Artillery under the direct command of Lt. Col. Walter J. Arnote and Captain William Chapman. Jack's speciality was metro, survey, plans, and operations. It would win him a Bronze Star in Sicily.

The 45th Infantry Division of World War II was an organized unit of assault troops. The fundamental mission of the division was to assault a pre-determined objective, seize it, and move on to the next objective. In short, its mission was to take ground and kill or capture the enemy. It was bloody business. The tactics of accomplishing the mission were many, varied, and dependent in part on a number of factors including weather, terrain, and strength of the enemy. However, the basic design of warfare called for one, perhaps two, of the infantry regiments to assault and seize a particular position. Thereafter, the infantry regiment, or regiments, having seized the objective, would hold the position while the rearward infantry regiments would pass through the regiment to assault the next objective. In effect, the tactics called for a "leap-frogging" of infantry regiments as objective after objective was taken. The mission of the artillery, simply put, was to provide fire in support for the infantry regiments

Right to left are the 105mm howitzer, the 155mm howitzer, and an anti-tank gun, the key weapons in the 45th Division Artillery.

as they advanced against their objectives. It was risky business.

Putting fire in front of advancing infantry troops involved rather precise, and sometimes complicated, calculations involving distance and speed of travel of massive and high explosive projectiles that could wipe out a platoon of 40 men. An incorrectly calculated fire mission could put your own troops in danger. Friendly fire was just as lethal as enemy fire. The commencement of artillery fire usually was seen by the Germans as the signal of an oncoming attack. One of the many fears of artillery was that if they were in range to lob shells into enemy positions, the enemy also may be within range to lob shells back into the 45th's own artillery positions. This form of "Annie-over" could be deadly. There was no doubt about it. When the shooting started, everyone in Division Artillery, as well as the infantry, were at great risk.

The S-3 section of Division Artillery had serious responsibilities. The general duties of the section were defined as plans, operations, and training. In part, the S-3 coordinated fire in certain areas and drew up plans for missions in certain sectors of the battlefield. Maps, effective ranges of the artillery pieces, distance, and precise enemy location were critical factors that went into the mission. Hitting the enemy target meant saving American lives; miss it and the infantry's chance of success was put at serious risk, not to mention life. To perform the task, the S-3 did not have the benefit of hi-tech equipment or computers. Usually, the best they had was hopefully an accurate map with good topography and a slide-rule. With good forward observation, artillery fire could be pin-pointed on desired objectives with devastating impact. Forward observation was a touchy task. Usually the S-3 had the benefit of the information provided by the forward observers assigned to the actual firing batteries.

Taken January 29, 1941 at Fort Sill, Oklahoma is the Headquarters Battery 70th Field Artillery Brigade, also known as the Headquarters Battery, Division Artillery. Jack Neville is on the top row, fifth from the left. General Ray McClain is on the front row, sitting second from left. Pete MacKellar who married Jack's sister, Roselle, is standing, front row, fourth from the right.

Not unusual, was the need of the S-3 staffer to do their own field observing to achieve maximum results for the firing plan. Sleuthing around territory in front of your own lines carried its own high degree of risk of being shot at. Jack's primary responsibilities on the S-3 staff was the planning and coordination of fire missions. The S-3 had other duties and responsibilities besides fire coordination. Fuel, food, water, and ammunition supply all were critical to the mission of the artillery. Planning the flow of this material to the artillery fell to the S-3 and his staff.

REFLECTIONS BETA THETA PI

In the late 1960s at the University of Oklahoma, parents received their student's mid-term grades prior to the students. Regrettably, this usually happened shortly before Thanksgiving. This policy had a way of creating additional tension to student life, especially if your father was Jack Neville.

After achieving a moderate degree of academic success my freshman year, I returned to the campus in the fall of 1966, this time ready to experience the "good-life" of the fraternity house. That dreaded freshman year was over. We all had matured as young men and were now ready to enjoy the fruits of our labor. This imperative usually took the form of reversed priorities. Now experienced in the ways of college life, one really did not have to go to class, after all the professors did not even take roll; and as we learned from watching the upper-classmen, the weekend started on Thursday, not Friday night. Reveling in the new world of reversed priorities, the first six weeks of my sophomore year were a delight until one Thursday night.

Two of my closest friends were Michael Alan Cawley of Hooker and Jon Clayton Axton of Bartlesville. This history should now record that 36 years in the future Michael, "Doc" as we called him after obtaining his law degree in 1972 from the University of Oklahoma Law School, built a prestigious law practice in Ardmore and later became president of The Samuel Roberts Noble Foundation, a philanthropic and research institute with close to $1

billion in assets and the state's largest supporter of higher education. Axton, "Ax," as we called him, became a doctor. Receiving his medical degree from the University of Oklahoma School of Medicine in 1973. He is respected as one of the Oklahoma's top urologists.

However, in 1966, we were students and our weekend began on Thursday night, usually at the Mont, the local brew spot. This particular Thursday night was especially exotic. Vast amounts of beer were consumed, along with huge quantities of pepperoni pizza. Doc and Ax usually took leftovers back to the Beta House. Cold pizza was great for breakfast and Ax thought it was a superlative remedy for a hangover, after all, he was pre-med.

Our evening at the Mont came to an end at about 10:00 p.m. We had occupied the Mont since 5:30 in the afternoon and finally had pushed ourselves past our own expectations. As we departed our favorite tavern, none of us would be deemed a fashion statement. While the mid-fall temperatures had dropped considerably, we three remained bullet proof to cold weather. Further fortified with good brew, we were basically impervious to the near freezing temperature. T-shirts were the dress of the evening along with your near-worst pair of Levi's and Cole Hahns. Doc and I wore the battle scars of the evening, our shirts appropriately stained with a significant quantity of pepperoni pizza topped off with the smell of Coors. We were a proud threesome as we left Norman's hot spot that evening.

1968 Mothers Day at Beta Theta Pi, Oklahoma University. Drew Neville is sitting front row, ninth from the right with Leota directly behind.

In those days the era of the designated driver was a thing of the future and looking back somewhat embarrassingly, we often debated who the most skilled "impaired" driver was. On this night we voted Ax to guide us back to the house. Again, he was pre-med and his shirt was relatively free of pizza remnants. Ax evaded at least half of the campus police force and with great shouts of victory and triumph we found a parking spot in the Beta parking lot. Declaring the evening a total victory, we made our way to the north, down the sidewalk parallel to Chautaqua Street. Just a few feet up the old front steps of the Beta house and we could all find sanctuary in the rack.

As we opened the huge old wooden front doors of the Beta house, one of the biggest shocks and surprises ever came over us. There, standing in the house foyer, in a three-piece, blue pin-stripped suit was Jack Neville. In his right hand were my less than steller mid-term grades from the business school. His face and both ears were beet red. There was no doubt about it. He was not happy and I was about to find out why.

Not remembering the words, but distinctly forever recalling the noise that echoed through the entire fraternity, the shellacking of a lifetime took place and ended within about five minutes. No response was solicited, and none given as the major college "reaming" was administered by the master. As the story goes, Jack had returned home from a fairly hard day at the office, only to be met by Leota with the oldest son's less-than–impressive grades. He was furious. Not even delaying to get the old traditional end-of-the-day Scotch, he grabbed the grades out of Mom's hand, hopped in his navy blue Lincoln Continental, and drove 150 miles to Norman to express his view. And that he did.

There was a point in life when the three brothers believed we all had the same first name–God Damn It. These three words were generally followed by "you haven't got the sense God gave a goose." At this point in the evening, these phrases punctuated an uncomfortable scene. In conclusion, he dictated, "If you are going to go out and raise hell and drink beer, at least have enough pride in yourself to first do what you came down here to do–get an education. If this situation does not improve, by Christmas, you will not like where you're sleeping next semester. If you are going to be a drunk, at least be an educated one."

That was about it, as he did a quick about face to leave the fraternity house. As he approached the door, he turned to a stunned threesome with mouths open. Looking at Ax and Doc, he barked "And what in the hell are you two going to do with your lives?" With that, he disappeared into the darkness of the Norman night and drove back to Tulsa. It was a 10-minute visit. My grades improved by Christmas.

CHAPTER IV
CAMP BARKELEY, AND THE LOUISIANA MANEUVERS

In early 1941, General Key summoned his core commanders together for an early morning meeting. To the shock and surprise of General McClain and the others, they were ordered to make ready for a move to Abilene, Texas. The entire division would leave Fort Sill sometime in February of 1941. McClain did not have to call the Artillery commanders together to give the word as the news leaked quickly and word of the giant move spread like wildfire throughout the camp. For Jack and Pete the news was met with great disappointment. Abilene, Texas was 226 miles away from Fort Sill, and some 350 miles from Oklahoma City. The logistics of seeing Leota and the family would become far more difficult.

On February 22, 1941 the 45th saluted Lawton, Oklahoma in a farewell parade before heading off to Camp Barkeley in Abilene, Texas.

Perhaps living conditions at Fort Sill were difficult, but they had at least become tolerable, eased by the time and distance to Oklahoma City. There was no other choice for Jack or the Thunderbirds. All of his belongings were packed into his largest green duffle bag for the move. For the men from New Mexico the news was met with joy. They would be closer to home. For the guys from Oklahoma, this leaving only took them farther from home, making it more difficult to see family and friends. The distance to Abilene was shortened by the thought that in eight more months, active duty would be over. They could go home and remain on reserve status for another year. Then, it would be back to school and the Lamda Chi guys. Jack waited for the order of movement.

On February 22, 1941, much of the division left Fort Sill just as they had come the previous September. In a pounding rain storm, the division paraded through the streets of Lawton with all the pomp and circumstance the weather would allow. The Lawton citizens had adopted these Thunderbirds as their own. The town was sad to see them go.

While the biggest part of the Division caravanned to Abilene, Jack's departure from Fort Sill was delayed. He and the rest of Division Artillery stayed behind to make ready the movement of the artillery. This proved to be a considerable task. The plans for movement called for a two-column motor march to Abilene. The biggest problem was that the 1933 and 1934 trucks assigned to artillery were not operational. Most would not start. Almost five months into training, the division still was plagued by obsolete and non-functional equipment; but the men would have to do what they had done since September–adapt and modify. They did.

The S-3 planners came up with the only functional plan. The trucks that could be driven would be hooked up with chains to the one's that could not. A good part of the division would then be pulled to Camp Barkeley. On March 3, 1941, the Division Artillery of the 45th Infantry Division moved out in a two-column, 600-truck motor march, or pull, to Camp Barkeley.

The 45th Infantry Division's move from Fort Sill to Camp Barkeley was shrouded in debate, even controversy. The people of Lawton, and many Oklahomans, believed that state politicians had been "out smarted" by the more savvy Texans. Military bases were considered a gem to the economy in a time of economic despair. During leave, soldiers spending money could provide a boost to any town's fiscal base. Of course the Oklahoma political powers denied being out-foxed by the 45th's move. *The Daily Oklahoman* reported that the real reason for the move, vociferously denied by the people of Lawton, was that Fort Sill suffered from lack of water. The water supply was inadequate to the needs of the division, hence the move to Abilene. It also was widely reported in February of 1941, that the Army Air Corps had asked Oklahoma City to bid for a major supply depot to be built in the southeast of town. On April 29, 1941, the people of Oklahoma City approved a $982,000 bond issue for a new air depot and the government thereafter awarded Oklahoma City the new base. In 1942, after its construction, the depot would be named the Tinker Air Depot after Clarence Tinker, a pilot shot down during the Battle of Midway. Had the division been traded to Texas for the new air depot and the resulting boom to Oklahoma City? Or had Lawton run out of water? It did not matter to Jack. He was in the backend of a 1934 2-ton truck being pulled from Lawton in the rain.

On March 1, 1941, the people of Abilene greeted the 45th. Abilene embraced the boys of the division as if they were their very own. For the better part of 18 months they would be. Under the head line "Heros Cheers Given 45th In Texas Howdy," *The Daily Oklahoman* described the arrival of the Thunderbirds.

> "You would have thought infantry men of the 45th Division were conquering heroes as crowds lined the streets of town through which they passed and thousands jammed the business district here to welcome the men to their new home at Camp Barkeley."

To top it off, the 36th Infantry Regimental Band played "The Eyes of Texas."

The Division Artillery and Jack's unit missed the gala affair. On March 3, 1941, two days after the Texas howdy, the artillery group limped into town after the 226-mile journey. Jack prayed for a hot shower. He would even take a cot. Still cursed with bad luck, Jack discovered there would be no shower for him this night. Abilene had built inadequate water storage tanks for the division.

By March 12, 1941, the entire 45th Infantry Division was encamped at Camp Barkeley. General Key granted liberal weekend passes and the city saw to it that the men could get to town on buses that ran directly to and from camp. Bus fare was reduced to 15¢. There were several enlisted men's clubs to entertain the non-officer ranks. Jack and Pete made good use of them. The division still did not have real barracks; but at least all of the tents were equipped with gas stoves. Even though they were farther south, the stoves were a welcome amenity for the cold nights. The water issues in Abilene were quickly solved, but the division had no camp laundry. The people of Abilene saw to it that the division had access to the local laundry to wash and dry their skives. All in all, the Texans opened their arms and embraced the Thunderbirds. The leadership of Division Artillery became concerned that perhaps there was a little too much hospitality extended in Abilene. It seemed that beer consumption within city limits was breaking records.

Commanding General Key summoned the troops together with the intent to correct the behavior. The message was short and to the point. ". . . Officers or men who sow wild oats may have to eat them."

The general's effort to curb the revelry had only a short lived-effect. By April of 1941 large increases in the syphilis rates were reported by city officials. City policemen and the military police cracked down on these transgressions with the arrest of some 58 prostitutes at various hotels in Abilene.

The distance between Abilene and Oklahoma City kept Jack and Leota apart. While weekend passes and furloughs were relatively easy to obtain, the 200-mile-plus journey was time consuming and difficult. By the time Jack reached Oklahoma City on a weekend pass, there was not much time left. He did it anyway, even if it meant no sleep. Telephones were near impossible so the United States Postal Service had to do, and on those special occasions there was always the Western Union Telegraph. Jack did not miss Valentine's Day or Leota's birthday. Western Union carried the message.

The division's training at Camp Barkeley now took on a more serious tone. With Jack and the men fairly well-equipped and provisioned, the instruction centered on how to fight. For the first time Division Artillery learned how to coordinate its awesome firepower with the tactics of the infantry regiments in the attack. The concept of laying artillery shells in advance of the infantry troops put the fear of the almighty into Jack. It was one thing to survey and calculate the firing missions knowing that no actual projectile would be fired; it was quite something else to rapidly plan the artillery mission knowing that live rounds from a 155mm Howitzer would be put as closely as a few hundred yards of the moving 179th Infantry regiments. If you did not pay attention, some one could get hurt, even killed.

There was not much beer consumed the night before live fire missions. Jack wanted his mind fresh and nimble for the exercises. The level of physical conditioning, PT, also was escalated. Marches and hikes became more than once-a-week exercises, and Jack got to know almost every yard of the Jim Ned Mountains surrounding Abilene. The division spent almost the entire month of April in intense training. And, for the first time, the division was thrown into war games with other Army divisions and regiments acting as the opposition army. To Jack, the war games and maneuvers over the vast expanse of western Texas was a welcome relief to the routine of training. While the men could not play competitive baseball or football, they now had a common mission for the first time. How the mission of the infantry and artillery fit together became more clear and the men started to recognize the need for teamwork in a coordinated attack on an enemy position. The war games became extremely competitive; winning became important.

In mid-April of 1941, the division got its first crack at the war game. On or about April 10, Jack and the 45th joined 4,000 regular army troops of the 2nd Infantry Division in San Antonio for exercises in the west Texas plains. The citizen soldiers of the division originally were intended to be "fodder" for the allegedly tough regular army troops. The plan basically called for the 2nd Division to be the victors, with the store clerks and farm boys putting up only token resistence. It did not work out that way. The key objective in the exercise was a pass in the Jim Ned mountains. The race was on for who could get there first. The 45th Infantry Division arrived first and hailed themselves winners. The 2nd Infantry Division claimed the 45th had cheated and declared themselves winners of the race. The army umpires however settled the matter declaring the maneuvers a draw. Nonetheless, the division distinguished itself and sent the signal that they were not there to play. They would not lay down for anybody, and they never did.

The maneuvers were not entirely basked in the glory of victory, especially for Jack and the staff of Division Artillery. In the second phase of the exercise Division Artillery was required to practice a forced retreat. The S-3 planners got right on it, but the security for the exercise broke down rather quickly. General Ray McClain, Jack's boss, was hit by a sniper and declared out of action by the umpires. Moreover, the entire staff opened themselves up to a gas attack. There was some real butt-kicking that brought home the grim reality that perhaps this was not such a game after all.

All in all, the maneuvers went well. The boys had lived up to their own expectations and even the regular army generals were happy with the readiness of the 45th. There still was a lot of work left. In August the division would motor to Louisiana for the big-time war games. With success declared, Division Artillery "passed in review" on April 27, 1941 in Abilene as part of the festivities of the Division Bar-B-Que. Friends and relatives were invited and Jack was elated. Leota made the trip to Abilene with four other girls in a borrowed Hudson on two-lane roads. It was not an easy trip. Jack and Leota spent two days together and then it was back to work for the division and back to Oklahoma City for Leota and her buddies.

As Jack collected himself in the aftermath of the April maneuvers, he and the rest of his tent mates began to question the reasons for the intensified training. After all, by the end of August, his one year of active duty would be over and he would be back to civilian life. The thought of September made the April maneuvers in the rain and mud more tolerable, at the least the end was in sight. But it was now clear that division leadership was really cracking the whip. Rumors now were flying that the mother of all war games would take place in Louisiana in August and that the April games were only preparatory. Jack resigned himself to the inevitable, it was out of his control. If the scuttlebutt was for real, it looks like he would end his active duty life in the swamp lands of Louisiana playing war. It was a happy, but ironic, thought.

A quick look at the world scene provides the insight as to why the training in Abilene was so intense in the April, 1941, time frame. On April 6, Hitler's troops extended their dominance in the European Theatre. German armies rolled into Greece and soon thereafter Yugoslavia fell. Neither country could muster serious resistance and it was evident that the small countries of southern Europe were little match for German tanks and planes. In Egypt, Tobruk fell. In the Pacific, Japan's imperialists positioned themselves for their own plans for

In August of 1941, the Thunderbirds moved out from Camp Barkeley to participate in the Louisiana maneuvers. While Jack rode as part of the Division Artillery, many of the infantry walked.

conquest. Ever fearful of the massive expanse of Russia, the Japanese, on April 14, signed a Pact of Neutrality and Friendship with Russia.

As world events continued to spin out of control, threats to United States security became more of a concern. Rooselvent continued to press for an armed status of readiness. As a result, the men of the 45th continued to train. Leota did her best to send care packages to Jack and would include copies of *The Daily Oklahoman*. Jack usually skipped the front page going directly for the sports and entertainment section for what he called the real news. Baseball season was getting ready to start and at 20 that was more important than the Japanese-Russian Neutrality Act.

On April 29, 1941, Jack went directly to the entertainment section of the *The Daily Oklahoman*. The Spring Lake Amusement Park season was about to open. It looked like he would miss the big roller coaster this year.

Through the spring and summer of 1941, Jack continued the routine of training, training, and training. He felt he could do it in his sleep and symptoms of boredom began to plague Camp Barkeley. The August maneuvers seemed so far away and the thought of leaving yet again was depressing. It would only take him further away from Oklahoma City and Leota. There was no way that she would be able to visit in Louisiana, and besides that the rumor mill said that the division would be in the field for two full months. With every rumor, Jack was taken further from Oklahoma City and home. Rapidly developing world events, now becoming more publicized, continued to fuel the camp rumor mill and the reason for the exodus to Louisiana. In July of 1941, the Japanese, ostensibly holding the Russians in check with their "Friendship" pact, moved their army into French Indo-China. The United States reacted quickly, freezing all Japanese assets in the United States and cutting Japan off from all access to the Nation's rubber, oil, and iron. Not unnoticed to the men of the 45th was Germany's invasion of Russia in a massive Bliztkrieg across Russia's western borders. With every move and counter-move, world tensions

The bivouac was fairly spartan.

escalated. As tensions rose, so did the training regime at Camp Barkeley.

While Jack usually did his best to read only the sports and entertainment section, Leota did her best to keep Jack up to speed on the homefront news. Gene's efforts to get his wings were on the rise. Over the past year Gene had accumulated more than 160 hours solo, but he had not passed the Army Air Corps physical. Pete, however had, and was hopeful that he would be on his way to pilot training. In June, the Army Air Corps had taken over Will Rogers World Airport as a base for a light bombardment group. Gene was not spending as much time at Will Rogers as the army would allow. He remained determined to fly. Jack could only shake his head, why would anyone want to be a fighter pilot. Then again, why did Jack enlist? As August crept closer and closer, Jack searched for the positive in what everyone knew would be the near intolerable heat of the Louisiana summer. While he would be away for two months, he told Leota to keep the thought that in September his year of active duty would be over and he would be home.

In late July, Lt. Col. Arnote summoned the S-3 staff together. Their mission was to plan a route of march for the Division Artillery to Mansfield, Louisiana. The April rehearsals had proved the division ready for action. Now the generals would see what the division could do in the really big show. There was great excitement among the staff. Not only was Jack relieved of the monotonous routine of daily training, but the drone of active duty was one step closer to being over. Jack could not wait to get started.

In August, the United States Army conducted the largest peacetime maneuver in the history of the United States. For two months the war games would play out over 3,400 square miles in rural Louisiana. More than 470,000 troops would participate in the campaign for readiness. Rumor quickly spread among the 45th that all of the "big dogs" would be there. Major General George S. Patton, then Colonel Dwight D. Eisenhower, and Lt. Col. Mark Clark would all oversee the action.

On August 2, all 14,000 troops of the division departed Camp Barkeley for the brutal summer heat and humidity of Louisiana. It would take 920 trucks to move the division. Jack was lucky. For most of the way he would get to ride, as would most of Division Artillery. But for the men in the Infantry Regiments, they would slug it out over the highways on foot for at least two days. As the caravan of trucks pulling the huge Howitzers convoyed down the Texas highways towards Louisiana, and past those on foot, Jack and the rest of the S-3 staff were greeted with several middle-finger salutes followed by numerous expletives. All Jack did was smile and wave back as they passed the poor guys carrying rifle and pack.

In many respects the trek to Louisiana resembled a party march rather than a military convoy. The people of Texas were alive with excitement as the division moved through town after town. On August 6, even the infantry had been relieved of their pedestrian status as the 45th rolled into Forney, Texas. The town opened its public swimming pools and Jack did not miss a chance to wash off the Texas dust. Two days later, it was back in the truck. By August 8, the division was encamped in Marshall, Texas where they would bivouac for three days before heading towards their final destination now only 70 miles away. The Texas howdy continued. The streets of Marshall were roped off for Texas-style street dancing. By the size of the party, Jack thought he was going off to the real war. The people of Marshall even provided dance partners as the town encouraged the daughters of Marshall to extend their civic pride to the men of the 45th. No dance cards were necessary. As great as the hospitality was, the music lacked. The 189th Field Artillery Band provided the awful tunes. The Field Artillery Band would never make it at the Blossom Heath.

On August 9, the division left the friendly folk of Marshall, Texas and arrived at their Louisiana maneuver site outside of Mansfield. The party was over. For the next two months Jack would live in the mosquito-infested, insect-laden, 100° heat of the deep South. The only accommodations available were pup tents, a bed-roll, and a blanket, which you could not use because of the heat, but were afraid not to because of the insects. Life in Louisiana was miserable. At least the Division Artillery had access to what was considered the greatest amenity of all in the Louisiana misery–a shower. At times, Jack wondered if it was worth it to clean up, only to have the mosquitos gnaw at you in the night. Maybe the routine of training at Camp Barkeley was not that bad after all.

The next few days were spent getting ready for the war games. Jack spent his time planning fire missions in coordination with the infantry movement. Telephone lines were strung and command posts were set up. Jack and his group plotted and surveyed the rural town and villages in the maneuver area for the preparation of maps and grid coordinates to be used by forward observers and the firing field batteries. Supply and logistics were the subject of continued concern to the S-3 staff. The training at Barkeley was being put to good use. Jack thought they might as well work at night because you certainly could not sleep in the heat.

As the division readied for the war games, the enlisted men of the S-3 staff kept their ears to the ground so they could feed the ever active rumor mill. Once again, as had been the case in the smaller April maneuvers, the citizen soldiers of the 45th were to be the meat for the so-called more well trained regular army troops. As word spread that they were to be the "dummies" for the regular troops to scrimmage against, the competitive fires of the Oklahomans grew. General Key sent the word down to the S-3 planners. The division was not going to "lay-down" for anybody.

The United States Army Chief of Staff General George C. Marshall wanted the Louisiana maneuvers to replicate real war conditions as closely as possible. To this end, while "judges" would be appointed to grade victory or defeat, the higher-ups declared that there would be no rules. After all, if America had to go to war there would be no rules, so why have any in Louisiana. Units would be given designated objectives and targets with the general order being to "take it." While the 45th Infantry Division may have been short on state-of-the-art equipment and weapons, they did not lack imagination and determination.

Unrestricted by any rules of engagement, all division staff were put to work on a plan that would later catch the eyes of both Patton and Eisenhower. It was vintage Jack Neville. The assigned opponent for the 45th was the regular army's most talked about 1st Calvary Division. Hidden by the night and in the rain, the 45th Infantry Division received the order to move out at 2:00 a.m. on August 18. Jack giggled all the way as he and the rest of the S-3 staff hovered over the maps in the enclosed tent, lit only with a single lantern as they planned the fire missions of Division Artillery. A night movement! Why not, they could not sleep anyway so they might as well "attack" the 1st Calvary while they slept.

In the next nine hours the division moved an unheard of 80 miles. Two days later, the entire division had moved some 150 miles and "captured" some 200 trucks and numerous "prisoners." After the night movement with no sleep, the division had completely encircled the 1st Calvary Division. The entire exercise was called to a halt early when the judges were forced to declare that the 45th Infantry Division Artillery was in range of their opponent's headquarters. The judges flagged it over, the artillery would have blown the 1st Calvary apart had it been the real thing.

Of course, as the 45th declared victory, the so-called enemy screamed foul. Claims of "cheating" were leveled at the division, they had moved at night and in the rain by passing many of maneuver's "check points." The decision stood however. The 45th had won. Jack and the division gave their own "middle-finger salute" to the regular army troops of 1st Calvary.

For better, or perhaps worse, the division's exceptional performance in the 1941 Louisiana maneuvers caught the eyes of Patton and Eisenhower. Patton had not been around the men from the southwest since chasing Pancho Villa in 1915 along the New Mexico border.

The 1941 maneuvers may have been the defining moment for the 45th Infantry Division before Pearl Harbor. Throughout the eight major campaigns fought in World War II, the division became known for its aggressive and creative initiatives. The German generals were later questioned whether the division ever slept, as they just kept moving forward with unmatched speed and determination. In July of 1943, General Patton would command United States troops in the invasion of Sicily. He would have to select the troops to lead his forces on to the beaches near Scoglitti and Biscari. Patton would call on the store clerks, farmers, cowboys, and Cherokees of the 45th Infantry Division to lead the American forces onto the beach.

For Jack, the euphoria of the victory over the 1st Calvary Division was short-lived. During the month of August, 1941, Churchill and Roosevelt met at sea, off the coast of Newfoundland, to discuss the increasing threat of the Axis power to world peace. At the same time, Congress engaged in spirited debate over extending the active duty status of those troops whose enlistment was coming to an end. During the course of the August maneuvers, Jack kept his nose to the grindstone, and several days passed before he learned a piece of news that would add another chapter to his life. On August 8, 1941, after considerable debate in the Senate and the House, Congress voted to extend the active duty status of those presently enlisted for another year and a half. The measure passed by one vote. The joy of returning to Oklahoma City, nights out with Rosie and Pete, and more time with Leota quickly turned into the darkness of an uncertain future. The threat to world peace and the fact that America might be thrown into real conflict cast a shadow over the August maneuvers. Even a twenty-one-year old could see that Washington was not requiring extended service of enlistees for the practice of it all. Jack was preparing for the real thing.

With the Louisiana maneuvers over in late September, Jack climbed aboard the convoy trucks for the long ride back to Camp Barkeley. Would he really be finished in 18 months? Would he ever get back to Leota? What about school and a job? By 1941, Jack and Leota had been together for almost three years and on the trip back to Abilene, thoughts crept into his head that he was not getting any younger. But who would ever want to marry an army private who had nothing to his name, $50 a month, and a now undefinable future. Then perhaps the most profound question of all–would America really be at war? Those were the grim questions of life as Jack bounced 430 miles back to Abilene, Texas. Only a few months later, world events would provide the answers.

Years after the war, and during the height of the Viet Nam protests of the 1960s, Leota would often rib Jack about his own decision to enlist. In the 1960s the alternatives were remarkably similar to the 1940s, enlist or be drafted. Only in the 1960s the baby boomers devised another alternative unthinkable to most in the 1940s–evasion. In the 1940s enlistment in the so-called "Guard" was seen as an honorable choice of service. In the 1960s many viewed service in the guard as a "duck and dodge." The only real difference was that those who enlisted in the guard in the 1940s were activated and saw serious combat. By enlisting in the 1940s, one theoretically shortened active duty life to only a few months followed by a year or so of active reserve status in civilian life. This unquestionably was Jack's strategy and plan, only to be disrupted by uncontrollable world events.

After the return to Camp Barkeley the boredom of routine training returned. Now however, with Congress having extended the Thunderbirds' active duty service for another 18 months, more attention was focused on the world events that were driving decisions. Many believe that the first shot fired at United States forces in World War II was Japan's attack on Pearl Harbor. This may not be entirely correct. On October 17, 1941, the United States Navy reported that the destroyer USS *Kearney* was torpedoed by a German submarine off the southwest coast of Iceland. Germany, of course, had not declared war on the United States and denied responsibility for the attack. Through October and November, the Nazis continued their full court press to conquer Russia. The winter weather was slowing it up. And then, an omnibus signal of what was about to come, United States negotiations with the Japanese broke down as the Rising Sun continued its build up of forces in French Indo China over strong United States objection. On Wednesday, December 3, Jack picked up the *Abilene Evening News* to read the prophetic words of United States Senator Tom Connolly (D-Texas), ". . . if Japan wants war, she will find out we have a navy in the Pacific that can shoot, and shoot straight."

That's all we needed to do, Jack thought, was goad the Japanese into a shoot-out.

In early December, Jack received the news the division was looking for. There would be liberal Christmas leaves and furloughs for most of the division, Jack already had started packing the green duffle bag. By December 3, the division rumor mill affirmed the most awaited order of the year. Starting December 20, almost the entire division would get a ten-day Christmas furlough. Jack cabled Leota. He would be home for Christmas. The Christmas social calendar was of course the prime furlough concern. Leota was not much for western music, but there was a new group in town. Bob Wills and the Texas Playboys were at the Trianon. Leota however was leaning toward seeing "Pinky" Tomlin and his orchestra, dancing from 9:00 p.m. to 3:00 a.m. Jack did not know if he could afford that. The new movies however seemed to provide the best financial compromise. *Citizen Kane* was opening at the Uptown and *Robin Hood* was at the Bison. At the Stockyards Coliseum there was Roller Derby. Even though it was free admission for the women, it was not an option for Jack. Leota would nix that. In December, after being away from home and Leota for the better part of a year, Christmas looked like heaven to Jack.

CHAPTER V

DECEMBER 7, 1941 AND ON TO FORT DEVENS, MASSACHUSETTS

The battleship USS *Oklahoma*, commissioned in 1916, was moored in berth F-5 at Pearl Harbor on December 7, 1941, outboard of the USS *Maryland*. The ship was under the command of T.D. Cullins from Ada, Oklahoma, who had retired on shore the evening of December 6, but not before giving explicit instructions for the look-outs to remain on sharp, twenty-four-hour alert. The morning of December 7, they were at the ready.

Two hundred miles plus to the north at the break of dawn, Lt. Jinchi Goto, torpedo squadron leader on the Japanese carrier the AKAGI, climbed into the cockpit of his bomber. With three other planes of his squadron readied for take-off, Goto gathered his squadron and fixed his flight southward towards Pearl Harbor. The objective and specified target of the squadron was the battleship USS *Oklahoma* at Pearl Harbor, Hawaii.

Shortly before 8:00 a.m. the morning of December 7, Goto reached the outer boundary of the harbor. He gave the order to his squadron to arm their torpedoes and dive immediately to an altitude of 20 meters above the surface of the harbor. By 7:55 a.m., Goto's squadron was flying "on the deck" straight at the USS *Oklahoma*. Incoming was the first wave of the Japanese surprise attack.

On board the USS *Oklahoma*, the top port side look-out picked up the red meat balls on the Japanese. Zero and immediately sounded the alarm for battle stations. The ship's public address system blared out in repeated fashion. "Man your battle stations, this is no shit!"

The small Sunday morning crew did what they could but it was too little too late as hell's fury broke out all over the ship and the harbor. Goto's squadron was on the Oklahoma immediately. At precisely the correct moment, Goto released his torpedo and nosed the torpedo plane almost straight up into the air. The torpedo, specifically designed for the shallow waters of the harbor, ran true and straight, blasting the Oklahoma amidship. The huge battlewagon began to list, and then the death blow. The other three members of Goto's squadron executed their maneuver perfectly. Three other torpedoes smashed into the side of the listing giant and not long thereafter the ship began to roll. The ship was going to capsize. Amidst the chaos, fire, and death, Commander J. L. Kenworthy tried to get a grip on the situation. Commander Kenworthy, with no choice, finally gave the order no commander wanted to give, "abandon ship." As Goto's flight gained altitude and headed back to the AKAGI, his mission was accomplished.

On board the battleship there were frantic efforts to survive. Men still were trapped in the now upside down ship and Kenworthy marshaled his forces together for rescue. Cutting through the hull of the ship, rescue efforts were successful for some, but not for all that Sunday morning. Four hundred and fifteen sailors and United States servicemen died that morning aboard the USS *Oklahoma*.

In all, the surprise Japanese attack on Pearl Harbor was unmitigated disaster. But for luck, the United States carrier force was at sea delivering planes and supplies to Wake Island and Guam. However, the Pacific fleet's star troopers, its battleships, had been blown apart. As the smoke cleared later that day at Pearl Harbor, the navy reported that there were two ships that were unsalvageable, the USS *Arizona*,– and the USS *Oklahoma*.

On Friday, December 5, 1941, Jack became one of the lucky ones, Heaven's skies opened. As he described it to Leota, with good looks and charm, he was able to talk Captain Chapman into a four-day Christmas furlough to return to camp on December 9. This was near perfect, a ten-day Christmas leave starting the 20th preceded by furlough 2 weeks before. There really was a Santa Clause. Catching a small army convoy of trucks making their way out of Abilene, Jack bumped all the way to Oklahoma City courtesy of the Quartermaster Corps. It was a free ride and because it was near Christmas the entire division had been paid early. He had the bucks for a good weekend.

There was a chill about the air in Oklahoma City the afternoon of December 6. The excitement of Christmas was infectious and the surprise furlough was an extra present for both Jack and Leota. On this Saturday, Jack made every effort to beg off from doing any Christmas shopping. There were other things to do. Besides, he would be home December 20. That was plenty of time to get Christmas shopping done, but Leota would have none of it. They were going Christmas shopping. Jack finally capitulated, and they caught the Inter-Urban for downtown Oklahoma City.

Downtown Oklahoma City was a beehive of activity on Christmas holidays. Oklahoma City rarely had a white Christmas and often it was warm on December 25. This did not stop the optimists from forecasting that this was the year, there really would be a white Christmas. Brown's department store was the first stop. "Jingle Bells" did not seem to improve Jack's mood as Leota literally dragged him through a packed house. Perhaps not so subtle of a hint was delivered with Leota's stop on the second floor where the China was on display. It was a Christmas special. A service set for eight was available at the low, low

Christmas price of $14.95, 50¢ down, and 50¢ a week. Now Jack could afford that on a private's pay. However Leota's perusal of the jewelry section was not so subtle. Standing two deep at the counter, Leota suggested that they move on to Zales. After all, Zales had their own Christmas sale– a $6.95 special for ring mountings. Even Jack was quick enough to catch on to this one as his face broke a smile for the first time during the ordeal. Despite Jack's grumbling, Leota was quick about her business and after three hours Jack was relieved of duty. He would do his shopping at the last minute, it was more fun that way.

With the afternoon gone, negotiations now began for the evening activity with Leota insisting on Andy Kirk and his Clouds of Joy at the Blossom Heath and Jack initially staking out his position for Roller Derby, free admission for women. Jack's attempted compromise of *Citizen Kane* met with continued resistance. Leota adeptly noted, that Jack's ride to Oklahoma City in the back of the army truck did not cost Jack a thing. He could afford the 75¢ admission charge and they were staying until 3:00 a.m. when the last song was sung. Leota would have no more of it and Jack submitted. It would be a great evening, as always with Leota. It really did not matter what they did, they were together.

The morning product of a night at the Blossom Heath was usually a hangover dotted with alcohol-induced fatigue. The early morning hours of December 7 would be no different. For a soldier now used to sacking out at nightfall and getting up before the sun, hitting the pillow at 4:00 a.m. was pretty rough. He would tough it out on Sunday. Besides, Mother Neville would cook up the big pot roast for Sunday's noon supper, a perfect remedy for one too many rum and cokes and loud music.

Things moved slowly for the Neville clan that Sunday morning. Perhaps that late Saturday night with the Clouds of Joy caused the quiet of the Sunday morning. Jack lay half awake staring at the ceiling with the rhythm of "GI Jive" and "Com'n In On a Wing and a Prayer" still racing through his mind between the throbs. The quiet of home was a stark contrast to the hustle of even Sunday mornings at Camp Barkeley. The stillness of the bedroom was a welcome relief from the activity created by five other tent mates scrambling for breakfast chow. Jack was finally moved to his feet by the smell of Mom's Sunday pot roast diced with onions, carrots, and potatoes. The best relief for a late night was a few helpings of some home cooking, Rosa's style. Sitting on the edge of his bed trying to collect himself, Rosa cracked the bedroom door and announced that he had 15 minutes to get to the table and that Leota and Pete were soon to arrive for Sunday dinner. Jack found a way to rally. Looking at the clock, he was surprised at the lateness of the day. It was 1:30 p.m.

By the time Jack made it out of his bedroom Leota and Pete already had arrived. Both had become welcome fixtures for Sunday dinners. Despite their headaches, the conversation was lively. Pete had been granted his transfer out of the 45th and was headed to Wichita Falls, Texas for training in the Army

Air Corps. He could not wait to get going. Even getting in a few words was Rosie. She and Pete had decided to get married and there was no better date than Christmas, December 25. The conversation spun quickly toward wedding plans and who could be there and who could not. It might be tough on Nat and Gene, but Jack was a certainty with the furlough dates for the 45th already announced. Jack tried to steer the conversation away from the wedding plans. After all, Pete had pulled the trigger after only a little more than a year while Jack and Leota continued their three-year-plus date. While Pete, Rosie, and Rosa went on about the wedding plans and the excitement of their move to Wichita Falls, Jack kept his face to the plate, catching only faint eye-contact with Leota out of the corner of his eye. He would have to fish or cut bait soon. She was not going to wait forever. Mercifully the conversation changed and the topic became brother Gene.

Jack and Pete could not help but giggle at the thought that Gene had flunked the Army Air Corps physical. This physical failure did not seem to deter Gene's enthusiasm and near obsession for flying. Through the fall months of 1941, Gene had accumulated some 160 hours of flight time. The ranks of the British fighter pilots had lessened with the constant attacks on England by the German Luftwaffe. Despite political constraints and alleged violations of American neutrality, the British Royal Air Force had actively started recruiting American pilots in the United States, funneling them through Canada and then on to England through the guise of the Canadian Air Force. Probably through the Will Rogers World Airport grapevine, Gene had stumbled into the so-called Knight Committee, one of the many organizations erected by the British to surreptitiously recruit pilots for their Spitfire fighters. Perhaps not physically fit enough for the Army Air Corps, Gene was good enough for the Royal Air Force. After training in Glendale, California, Gene was on his way to Canada as one of the newest members of the Canadian Air Force, soon to transfer to the British Royal Air Force. It did not look like Gene was going to make Pete and Rosie's wedding.

Having devoured the pot roast and all of its surroundings, all retired to the living room. Jack grabbed the first available recliner nearest the RCA and immediately lapsed into a slumber like trance. Leota and Rosie busied themselves with the kitchen clean up, having given up on Jack and Pete to aide in the cause. That was "woman's work" so said Jack and Pete. Rosa was first to reach for the radio dial. Her favorite show "Listen America" on NBC was to start at 2:30 p.m. and while the rest of the crowd may not want to keep up with the world events, she did.

Half-way through the show the small group listened as the stunning news from Hawaii echoed through the room. The Japanese had attacked Pearl Harbor, Americans had been killed, the fleet destroyed. Jack and Pete were in such disbelief that silence filled the room as everyone stared intently at the RCA box.

What had happened? How could it have happened? There were no answers as Rosa wondered where on earth was Pearl Harbor. Jack spun the dial looking for more reports. The reports were all the same. The repetitive reports over the radio gave way to Jack's fury as the reality of it sunk in. Those son-of-a-bitches, gutless in the Sunday morning sneak attack. According to Aunt Rosie some 60 years later, Jack, and even Pete, became volcanic and were ready to take up arms against the Japanese.

The women of the house however were more reflective. They knew that it meant war was imminent and would take all the brothers away. Rosa was glad Bart would not have to deal with this. The worst was yet to come and she knew it before the boys. World War I had not ended that long ago as memories of men and boys lost overseas in France regrettably surfaced. There was no real glory in war and death and Rosa knew it, but the boys would now nonetheless have to fight.

Jack and Pete's hangovers from the night before were suddenly gone. They both scrambled for news of their own units and what they were supposed to do. It was impossible to use the phone, and useless to telegram the camp. Leaving Rosie and Leota speechless, Jack and Pete headed for the armory to see if they could find out what was going on and what they were supposed to do.

Once at the armory, it did not take long to find the near future. All furloughs and weekend passes were canceled and all troops were to report back to Abilene by 12:00 p.m. Monday.

Monday morning, December 8, 1941 was another good-bye for Jack and Leota, this time plagued by the reality that now America was in the fight. As Jack once again boarded the back-end of the truck, he waved to Leota, now fearful that this could be the last time. Their future was now filled with uncertainty. It was back to Abilene where the training and war games were no longer a game.

While on the road, Franklin Delano Roosevelt declared war on Japan and asked Congress for a resolution so stating. In Abilene, General William S. Key announced that the division was ready to respond to any call and would be ready to move out in 24 hours or less. All Christmas leaves were canceled.

The next day, Jack and the S-3 staff gathered around their radios in General McClain's headquarters to listen to the President Roosevelt's speech before Congress asking for a declaration of war against Japan. After a brief speech describing the events at Pearl Harbor, the United States Senate and House voted to go to war. There was one dissenting vote.

It was now official, the war was on.

At Camp Barkeley the rumor mill was at an all-time high. The most common theme working its way through the tent city in Abilene was that the division would move out at any time.

Instead, Jack and the division sat and waited. General McClain put Division Artillery in a state of readiness, be ready to move out the instant the order was passed down. But the division would stay put for at least the immediate future. Many of the Abilene analysts reasoned that the division would ship out to fight the Japanese in places never heard of rather than the Germans, they were certain of it. Of course, in World War II, the 45th did not see any action against the Japanese, only the Germans. As the days wore on the men continued their anxious wait for what was next. Frustration set in for Jack as the order to stand at the ready was the only word from on high. Jack was in no position to do anything about it from Abilene, Texas. Jack exclaimed that the S-3 section did not even have a map of Hawaii, much less the Western Pacific, and the range of those 155mm Howitzers came up a little short of any Pacific target they knew of. From Abilene they could perhaps talk the Japanese to death, but that was all.

As the sun set in the west Texas sky and taps blew at Camp Barkeley, Jack climbed into his cot lodged in the corner of the canvas tent. It was a bit cool that evening and he was grateful for the gas stove that provided the tent with heat. He stared at the old stove with a chuckle–Fort Sill seemed so long ago. The entire world had exploded at Pearl Harbor. Who knew how long it would last, or if it would ever be over. The reality was that those huge 105 and 155mm projectiles would be hurled at human beings, not just a dirt target drawn on a map. It was no longer a drill. People had died at Pearl Harbor, more people would die elsewhere. Jack stared at the dark of the canvas ceiling. Would he be one? Would he die in this holocaust? Also going down with the USS *Oklahoma* was the dream of finishing school and finding a job. Dare he now ask Leota to get married? Why would she take someone who would soon be in harm's way? Despite the horror, destruction, and death half a world away, life had suddenly become more fragile for Jack Neville and the men of the 45th.

On December 12, the word came down that no one wanted to hear. Christmas leaves were officially canceled. There would be no going home for Christmas in 1941, it would be spent at Camp Barkeley. It was not the Grinch who stole Christmas, it was Tojo and Hitler.

"Hurry up and wait" continued to plague the days as the division continued to train, be at the ready, and wait. Sitting in the middle of the country in the West Texas plains, with the enemy to the right and left separated by two oceans, Jack and the division sat in their tents, duffle bags packed, as Christmas Day drew nearer. General Key continued to echo the now almost boring words, "We are ready to respond to any call, we are ready to move in less than 24 hours." No call came.

Christmas Day did not bring much joy to the troops of the 45th Infantry Division. Letters and telegrams from Leota provided a brief relief for the anxiety and worry of what was to happen next, but in all it was a sad day not to be home with the family and Leota. In the rush to get back to Camp Barkeley, Jack barely had time to say good-bye to Leota, and not even the right way. But much worse was that Pearl Harbor had stolen Jack's Christmas spirit before he could get back to Brown's. There was no Christmas present for Leota and this year the only gift he could muster was a letter. As Jack worked his way through the chow line as the mess sergeant slammed mashed potatoes and sliced turkey onto his plate, General Key delivered the Camp's Christmas address over the public address system. General Key did his best to remind the men that the United States was a country at war and sacrifice was inevitable. The division had to be ready to defend America, even if it meant not being home for Christmas. It was of little solace to Jack and his comrades. No one wanted to be in Abilene on this Christmas Day. For Jack it would not be the last Christmas he would miss in Oklahoma City; nor would it be the last Christmas he would spend away from Leota.

On Christmas Day, Pete and sister Rosie were married in Wichita Falls, Texas. They did it alone, as time and world events kept the family away. Jack and Leota never spoke of the Christmas of 1941.

While Jack Neville waited in Abilene with the 45th Infantry Division, events moved more swiftly for Gene Neville. By December, the British Air Force were hungry for pilots. After training in Glendale, California, Gene was on his way to Canada. Pearl Harbor had removed any pretense or concern of neutrality violations by the British for recruiting American pilots. On December 13, 1941 Gene Neville worked his way through the Canadian Air Force bureaucracy and embarked for England. One day after Rosie and Pete were married he arrived in London England. He reported for duty commissioned as Pilot Officer Gene Neville, Royal Air Force Voluntary Reserve. By January 28, 1942, Gene was in the cockpit for the Royal Air Force's Spitfire participating in advanced flight

In April of 1942, the Thunderbirds marched out of Camp Barkeley.

training. By the spring, he would be over the English Channel fighting the German Luftwaffe in a British Spitfire MK VB.

After three months of frustrating routine training, the 45th Infantry Division got its marching orders. In early April, McClain called the planning staff together with directions to make ready for a move to the eastern sea board. Their destination was Fort Devens, Massachusetts. To Jack, the direction was at least now clear. If they were going to fight the Japanese, certainly the move would have been westerly. They would fight the German somewhere in Europe, no question. The strict limitations of the order however only rekindled the always running engine of the rumor machine. Would it be to England where Gene was flying Spitfires? Talk of a build up in England and an attack across the English Channel seemed logical. Would it be Southern Europe, perhaps the weakest point in the German wall? Or would it be someplace else? One thing was for sure. The division would have to cross the Atlantic Ocean. Like most of the boys in the Division, Jack, had never seen a big ship, or even the ocean. He was not even sure where Massachusetts was. A little east of the Oklahoma border, Sedalia, Missouri, was as far as he had been.

With the outbreak of the war, the movement of units the size of a division were supposed to be shrouded in secrecy. This was near impossible in the deep south where the population of the division was almost that of the nearest town. Certainly, the 45th Infantry Division was not going to be able to move out of Abilene under a veil of secrecy. Nonetheless, letters and telegrams to loved ones telling of the division's move were not permitted.

A farewell parade in Abilene, Texas, the Thunbirds on their way to Fort Devens, Massachusetts to practice and train for amphibious assault landings.

The Division traveled by train from Camp Barkeley to Fort Devens, Massachusetts with equipment loaded on flat cars for cross-country travel. The trip took five days.

On the global theater, the war was not going well for the United States. The American stronghold in the Philippines was breaking. Bataan had fallen, and the tiny island of Corrigedor in Manila Bay was under siege. After weeks of heroic fighting, United States forces in the Philippines were forced to throw down their arms, some 65,000 men put up the white flag. It was the largest United States war-time surrender in history. As the army and marines continued to build their strength and numbers at home, General James Doolittle's small band of B-24 bombers lifted off the deck of the USS *Hornet* aircraft carrier in thunderstorm conditions in the western pacific. They bombed Tokyo. While relatively little damage was done, the boost to morale was of tidal wave proportions, even in Abilene, Texas. At least we had finally struck back. The 45th Infantry Division hurried its readiness. They too wanted in the fight. On April 4, 1942, General Key reported to *The Daily Oklahoman* "My boys are ready and anxious to get going."

Training in the summer months of 1941 at Camp Barkeley was tough. Below, a tank is put through its paces.

Abilene lines the streets to say good-bye to the Thunderbirds.

At home, the face of Oklahoma City was now beginning to change. On April 4, 1942, the first airplane landed in Air Depot Field, later named Tinker Air Force Base. The industrial strength of Oklahoma City would be part of the war effort, even to the extent that by April 9, all civilian, residential, business, and road building had been banned. The city threw its money into the defense approving a war bond issue by a wide margin on April 15. Not only was the 45th preparing for war, so was Oklahoma City.

By mid-April, the Chief of Staff of United States Forces General George C. Marshall made the armed forces military objectives clear. On April 19, General Marshall announced that the United States would attack the Nazis soon by land, sea, and air. It was now certain that Jack and the division were being staged in the eastern United States for a move to the European Theatre.

Word of the division's move leaked. The City of Abilene was not going to let their favorite sons leave without a Texas-size send off. While the troops were discouraged from discussing the movement of the division, word quickly got to Oklahoma City that the Thunderbirds were heading east, and Leota was

Two "Thunderbirds" duke it out in hand to hand training.

Private Jack Neville strolling down the company street at Fort Sill, Oklahoma in September of 1940. The 45th completed its basic training at Fort Sill before moving to Camp Barkeley in Abilene, Texas.

not going to miss it. This time, it could be the last good-bye. In the week before April 19, Leota and the wives, lovers, friends, and family of the division flocked to Abilene, Texas to see their finest. For Jack and Leota it was a frantic few days. Abilene was awash with people and the population of the town momentarily swelled for the grand, and sad, departure. There was little time or occasion to be alone, but it was better than not seeing each other at all.

Shortly after, the 45th Infantry Division Artillery left Camp Barkeley as they had come, in the pouring rain. This time, however, they marched down Abilene's main street to the cheers and music of the Abilene townspeople. Jack found no real joy in the occasion. Leota had gone back to Oklahoma City, only to wait. Would she be there when he got back? Would he come back? For Jack Neville and most of the guys it was their first time away from the great southwest, and for some it would be their last. Dressed in khaki, with the black army tie appropriately knotted and tucked into his shirt at the third button hole, and duffle bag over the right shoulder, Jack boarded the train in Abilene for the trip to Fort Devens. The trip would take five days.

As the train carrying almost 14,000 men of the 45th rocked northeastward, the troops felt as if they were traveling through a twilight zone of sorts. The hills of eastern Oklahoma and the flat desert like plains of western Oklahoma, Texas, and New Mexico were a stark contrast to the soil rich corn belt of Indiana, Illinois, and Ohio. The cramped conditions aboard the train stifled much of the conversation about the future at Fort Devens as the clacking of the tracks induced a trance-like atmosphere. After the second day on the rails, the more immediate concern was when they were going to be able to get off the train and stretch as it was difficult to stand and move up and down the aisles. Going to the bathroom on a fast-moving train that rocked left and right as it moved down the tracks was a new experience for the men. Some degree of athletic ability was necessary to accomplish one's personal needs. Not for Jack, however, as he had the worldly experience of riding the MK&T from Vinita to Oklahoma City in 1937.

The closer the division got to the New England, the talk turned into the reasons for Fort Devens. Jack wondered what the division would do in Massachusetts that it could not do in southern Texas. It was now obvious to most that the division would be sent to fight the Germans in the European Theatre, and it only seemed logical that the division would be staged somewhere on the eastern seaboard before crossing the Atlantic. It seemed simple enough; get on the boat, cross the Atlantic, and fight the Germans. The division, however, was being sent to Fort Devens for training and exactly for what Jack did not know.

As the train rumbled through New York and finally entered Massachusetts, Colonel Arnot and General McClain summoned a meeting of the S-3 staff. The answer to the question was made clear. The mission of the 45th Infantry Division at Fort Devens was to train for engagement of the enemy by way of

By November of 1942, the Division was training for amphibious assault landings at Fort Devens, Massachusetts. This picture of Jack at Fort Devens most likely was taken by Harry Balkum.

In August of 1941, the 45th participated in the largest peacetime military maneuvers in history. In searing Louisiana heat, Jack is pictured in his underwear.

amphibious assault on the beaches of Europe. The division would first attack the Nazis on the beaches and fight their way inland. They were at Fort Devens, Massachusetts to learn how.

Jack and the division were made to feel special at Fort Devens. Gone were the triangular shaped canvas tents at Abilene and Lawton that often leaked when it rained. Gone was the old Sibly stove that kept everyone up all night. Jack was allowed to bask in the comfort and glory of real barracks, actual wooden barracks, complete with inside showers and bathrooms. At least for some period he would not have to tolerate the one-holers with a door that never closed or locked, if you were fortunate enough to even have a door. For the first time since basic training in September, 1940, they actually had creature comforts and it felt like they were living in the Waldorf Astoria.

While the living conditions were comfortable, the training was not. Jack only thought he was in good physical condition at Camp Barkeley; but at Fort Devens, the physical training took on a new dimension. PT took on a new meaning as push-ups, full-pack hikes, and running seemed to dominate the daily schedule. Even the S-3 staff moved at "double-time" everywhere they went. It was though walking was not permitted. The commander of the United States V Corp, the Corp to which the division was assigned, required that every soldier, from cook to rifleman, be able to cover five miles in one hour or less.

The map was the ever-present companion of the Division Artillery S-3 staff. With almost idle curiosity Jack perused the maps provided to guide the division exercises and training. After a couple of days, Jack noted what was obvious from the map. The Division was at Fort Devens for amphibious assault training. But if you look at the map, there was no water even relatively near Fort Devens; and moreover, if there was water nearby, no one had seen even the slightest resemblance of a boat since they had traveled east. No boats and no water, only the army would have an entire division train for an amphibious assault without either. The circumstances became the objects of many a joke, but not for long.

In preparing for war the United States Army and the government struggled to get on its feet with men, material, supplies, guns, and bullets. "Training simulators" were not at the top of the list for any branch of service, except for perhaps the Army Air Corps. However, at Fort Devens, Massachusetts, creativity and ingenuity made up for the lack of a boat and water. The Army constructed a large tower facility that simulated a ship. Ropes were hung over the side that fell to the ground. With full pack and rifle, every man in the division climbed the tower to the top platform, hanging over the side clutching the large net, and scaled their way downward. Jack accepted the drill as a good exercise to start with, but after a few repetitions the only next logical question surfaced. While Jack and most of the men in the 45th had never seen the ocean, they all knew that the Atlantic Ocean was not the calm of the lakes in

The 45th's Division Artillery on display at Fort Devens, Massachusetts. Anti-tank guns are to the front and to the left and rear are the 105mm and 155mm howitzer.

eastern Oklahoma. Climbing up and down those ropes on a ship that pitched and rolled in a heavy sea could prove to be a real sporting event. The ground at Fort Devens never moved, certainly the ocean would. Their questions would soon be answered with the real deal off the coast of Cape Cod.

The Army Infantry Division would basically utilize four different ships or boats to assault the enemy beachhead. The Landing Ship Tank (LST) was approximately 327 feet long, about the length of a football field. The LST displaced about 450 tons, and could carry a number of tanks. The Landing Craft Tank (LCT) was a smaller vessel, 200 feet long with a hinged ramp door. The LCT could accommodate five tanks, 10 to 12 trucks or jeeps, and a large number of soldiers. The LCI, or Landing Craft Infantry, could carry a strong company, about 200 men. In assaulting a hostile enemy beachhead, the infantry regiments would utilize nets to climb over the sides of the LCIs and into the smaller LCAs, or Landing Craft Assault boats. Once aboard the LCAs, they would align themselves abreast of each other and head for the designated beachhead. Once at the beach, the LCAs would drop their front ramps and the infantry would charge ashore.

In the Atlantic Ocean off the shore of Cape Cod and Martha's Vineyard, the 45th found it was easier said then done. The pitch and roll of the ship made it more difficult than expected. It seemed like forever before the men were given orders to disembark the LCI and board the LCAs for the run to the beach. In the meantime, the constant rocking back and forth, forward and backward at the same time it seemed, made most of the boys from the southwest extremely seasick. They were more than excited to climb down the cargo nets of the LCIs because it was a step closer to land and nausea relief. With a 50-pound pack strapped to their back and a rifle slung over the shoulder, negotiating the cargo nets took some skill that could become impaired by throwing up all over yourself and the buddy next to you. Amidst the smell of breakfast on your fatigues and the constant motion of the boats, was the fear of falling overboard or missing a rung of the cargo net. If you went into the drink with 50 pounds on your back, you sunk. The division scaled the cargo nets with each man clutching the rung of the net with a death grip. Every soldier in the division got to experience the climb down the nets and into the LCAs. But as the summer of 1942 progressed, each unit's role in the beachhead assault became more clearly defined.

If you were part of the infantry regiments of the division, the chances of being first on the beach were very high. Not so with Jack and the Division Artillery. Prior to hitting the beach, the S-3 staff plotted their respective command posts and headquarters. Most likely, the artillery would move to the beaches in the larger LSTs or LCTs. Once on the beachhead, the artillery would have to move to their designated area, set up their pieces, fix fields of fire, and be prepared to provide supporting fire to the advancing infantry troops.

It has been written by many a military historians that the amphibious landing assault is the most dangerous form of military maneuver. The physical endurance required to successfully complete a beachhead assault was remarkable. Enduring seasickness and nausea before off-loading the LCI into the LCA was difficult enough, but moving across half a mile of a swollen sea, running off the LCA's ramp, and sprinting 100 yards across a sandy beach carrying 50 pounds and a rifle totally exposed to enemy fire, required a very high degree of physical training and guts. Any man not in shape increased his chances of death. To a man, the division reached tip-top physical shape. In the summer of 1942, Jack Neville was a rock-hard 140 pounds, with little to no body fat.

The training at Fort Devens emphasized the need for teamwork and coordination. Nothing was more apparent to Jack as the Division Artillery learned their role. The infantry regiments of the 45th would storm a hostile beach relatively lightly armed with little logistics or fire support in the early going. The beachhead assault was to be preceded by heavy bombardment by air and sea. The air corps and the United States Navy would soften up any beachhead for infantry assault. Once on the beach, the infantry units, had to seize the objectives for any invasion to succeed. The artillery could not move up to support the infantry movement if the beachhead was not first secured.

The pre-invasion bombing and shelling told the enemy the exact location of the assault giving them time to mass their forces at the point of attack. Jack's role required that the infantry first do its job and seize and secure the beachhead so that the artillery units with their big guns could get ashore to support the ground troops. The S-3 planning for logistics, supply, ammunition, and fire support all assumed a secure beachhead. The map was of critical importance. Identifying locations for command posts and firing missions was essential to the success of the push inland. Once the beachhead was secured, the infantry would continue to move against the enemy positions, but now could only successfully do so with artillery supporing fire. By the time the artillery got ashore and fixed their positions, the chances were that the infantry units would be running out of beans and bullets. If the artillery did not do its job, the infantry could be left unable to advance, and worse yet stranded and isolated. For Jack it became clear that if you did not do your job, cooperate and be a team, someone could get killed. There would be one to three infantry regiments moving onto the beachhead with any given amphibious assault. Many would die on the beach. The training evidenced that not even the artillery would be out of harm's way. The pre-invasion bombardment and the actual beach assault signaled your location. This gave the enemy the opportunity to mark positions and train their big guns on the beachhead. Once ashore, while the 45th Division Artillery could zero in on enemy locations to support the infantry, the enemy could likewise fix the positions of the 45th.

During the course of the beachhead invasion, the artillery troops and guns had to wait in the LSTs or LCTs until given the signal that the beachhead was secure. Sitting off-shore, the remaining units of the 45th literally were sitting ducks for the German Luftwaffe. If the Army Air Corps, and the United States Navy guns did not do their jobs, the LSTs and LCTs could be picked off.

Failure at the beachhead meant certain death for those who ran off the ramps of the LCAs. Rescue efforts for the infantry regiment stranded in such circumstances was near impossible and most likely would result in additional deaths. Once on the beach, the artillery supporting the infantry units had to ensure the success of the invasion with pin-point accuracy. If the invasion failed, the infantry would most likely be left alone and slaughtered, and the artillery units pounded to death by German fire, or picked off on their LSTs while sitting off-shore. The reality was that successful evacuation in catastrophic circumstances likely would result in failure.

At Fort Devens, Massachusetts, the mission and grim reality of the division's purpose became apparent to Jack. If he was to survive this war at 22 years old, he and the rest of the troops, most of whom were younger than he, were going to have to pay attention, train hard, and do their job. The men may have thought of the awful scenario of being pushed back into the sea by the Germans, but the boys of the 45th never spoke of it.

As the days moved by at Fort Devens the division numbers grew to the authorized strength of slightly more than 14,000 men. The ranks were increased with draftees from other regions of the country, including Massachusetts and New York. In Jack's artillery, guys from Tennessee were filling in the ranks and with them came a bull of a man, Harry Balkum from Jackson. He and Jack became fast friends after Balkum was assigned to the Division Artillery S-3 staff. Balkum's southern drawl fit in nicely with the Oklahoma twang and his feisty ways were a match for Jack's energy.

Jack Neville had never been to New York City. Not even the Adair Public Library in the 1920s and 1930s had many pictures of the Big Apple, but on July 3, 1942, he got his first look at the concrete island. The entire division was moved to New York City to march down the streets of Broadway in the biggest Fourth of July parade Jack had ever seen. It was a grand event and the demonstration evidenced that the homeland was behind their boys. The spectacle was thrilling and for a brief day erased the home sickness that had occasion to sink in. The division commanders kept a tight rein on their troops fearful that New York City liberty would only bring the worst. This, of course, did not keep Jack and Harry from at least trying to see what they could get into, but their efforts were stemmed in every turn. The division was in and out of the big city with relative speed. It was nonetheless a grand trip, and a needed morale boost for everyone.

In Adair, Oklahoma, the site of an Indian walking down the town's boardwalk was not unusual. This was not the case in New York City. As Jack and his buddies moved down 5th Avenue, many of the New Yorkers acted as if they were fearful of the full-scale Indian uprising. Eye contact with the New Yorkers was near impossible as they passed on the street. Others crossed the street as a strategy to avoid the direct path of the tribesmen. Many gawked at the brown-skinned brothers as if they were fearful of some sort of instant savagery in front of the Plaza Hotel or in Central Park. Jack Neville was as brown-skinned and high-cheek-boned as any full-blooded Cherokee; and with his dark hair he easily mixed with the Indian brothers. And the truth was that in those times, he was one of the brothers. Jack had grown up with the Indians of northeastern Oklahoma. He did not think it any different to be in the company of the Creek tribesmen coming into Neville and Co. to buy tobacco, as he did with the Irish Catholics who threw down many a whiskey in Adair's only saloon. To him, they were all the same and the thought of crossing the street to avoid their path was something never heard of in Adair. Jack never expected the easterners to embrace those from the reservation, but he never expected such a display of outward discrimination. After almost two years of training, the division had become a melting pot that erased color or ethnic barriers. At the Biscari Air Field, five miles inland from the south coast of Sicily, Jack Neville did not care if the soldier next to him was Chinese, Indian, or lily white. All he cared about was whether his fellow soldier could shoot straight, do his job, and take care of the other when it got tough.

Jack's reaction to the sometimes outward discrimination and dislike of the Indians by the easterners was typical. Violent demonstration was not his war way, but a sort of civil disobedience was his repertoire. Along with Harry Balkum, Bill Collins, and others, they bought, stole, confiscated, and traded for every feather, sheep-skin, and drum they could find. The boredom that at

I NEED AMERICA • AMERI

The 45th Infantry Division on parade in the Boston Commons in the Summer of 1942. The Thunderbirds participated in several of these parades to promote the sale of war bonds and arouse support for the war effort.

times plagued the soldiers was relieved in part by crafting ceremonial Indian head dresses and war drums. The next time they showed up in Boston, he and Balkum, who was part Hungarian, dawned their pressed khaki pants, green three-button down army jacket, capped off with their Indian ceremonial war bonnets, and marched on down to the Boston Commons. While at Fort Devens, the division made many an effort to alter the commander's concerns over public perception. For Jack, however, Indian pomp and circumstance was a sort of an "up-yours" demonstration of his own civil disobedience. The guys were going to fight for their right to walk down the street.

Throughout the summer of 1942, Jack saw more ocean and water than he cared to. The division continued to train for the amphibious landing, but there were only so many times you could attack Cape Cod and Martha's Vineyard. The days were long and the physical training more and more intensive. General Key was getting the men in Olympic athlete shape, but with every exercise Jack realized that it was no game. He wondered if he would ever see Leota in Oklahoma again as time and distance made it all farther away. Use of the phone never seemed to work and telegrams and cables could not carry much of a message. Try as hard as he could, it was difficult to write. Some nights it was all he could do to drag his worn out 140-pound body into the sack, get a semi-nights worth of good sleep, and get up the next morning and do it all over again.

In the late summer of 1942, General Ray McClain called the entire staff together. For months the always present rumor machine continued with the message that the 45th would soon receive its first combat assignment. For the past several months, General Marshall, even Roosevelt himself, had been mulling over plans for the first attack against the Germans in the European Theatre. The Russian and British had been pleading for a third front that only the United States could bring to the war effort. Marshall and Roosevelt had now made their decision. The initial landing of United States troops would not be in France. The target would be North Africa. In the summer of 1942, General Key and McClain advised their staff to plan for an attack on German and French troops in the area of Oran, North Africa. General George S. Patton would take his army ashore in an amphibious assault in November of 1942 as part of "Operation Torch." The general's selection for the assault division–the 45th Infantry Division Thunderbirds.

CHAPTER VI
DEATH IN NORTHERN FRANCE

While Jack and the 45th Infantry Division pounded the sand off Cape Cod in amphibious assault exercises, Gene Neville got all he bargained for in his desire to fly. Between January of 1942 and at least through the end of March, 1942, Gene flew every day. Posted to a Royal Air Force training section, the young Neville's flight skills were honed to a razor's edge with a myriad of tasks. He practiced forced landings, day and night navigations, acrobatics, aerial combat maneuvers, and instrument flying. The entire package was being crammed into his head in a short period of time. In 1942, Britain's survival depended greatly, some say entirely, on its defense of the sky. The British were hungry for pilots and Gene Neville had become one of their sons.

Posted to Unit No. 58 FTS, Gene first soloed the British Spitfire, type 9891, on March 7, 1942. Piloting a Spitfire was akin to driving a powerful Harley Davidson motorcycle with wings. Powered by a 1,250-horse-power Rolls Royce Merlin engine, the single-wing aircraft was built for speed, maneuverability, and toughness. Properly equipped, Gene's Spitfire could reach an altitude of 43,000 feet. Armed with a 20mm cannon and four machine guns, it could outrun most of the German enemy with a speed of 416 m.p.h. and out-fox the German ME109 with its ability to make tight turns. It did not, however, fly itself with sophisticated electronics or aironics. The pilot had to do it the old-fashioned way. He had to fly it with his feet and hands. It took some serious skill and serious guts.

In 1942, the aerial defense of Britain was divided into sections of the country, loosely defined by geographic boundaries. Group 10 covered Western England and Group 12 defended Northern England. The action-packed southeastern area of England was designated Group 11 with the responsibility of defending the cities of South Hampton, Dover, and London. Gene Neville's first combat operational assignment was to Unit 616, or the 616 Squadron, Group 11. It was front line duty, and it was where the action was. It was hard to conceive. Twenty-four years old and from Adair, Oklahoma, population 400; and he was over the skies of England in aerial combat. It was a long way from Spavinaw

Creek and fishing for catfish with brother Jack.

Gene's flight log entries are cryptic and at times difficult to understand. However, the record is clear that after being assigned to Squadron 616, he was in the air most every day. Despite being in the air, he did not escape the horror of war. In fact, the record suggests that his initiation to the mayhem came rather quickly after being assigned to 616. On May 25, 1942, his fellow pilot officer Jack Brown lost his right eye in combat. Gene apparently witnessed pilot officer Tess Ware die when his plane disintegrated. After a mission over Dunkerque on June 3, 1942, Gene experienced engine trouble at 26,000 feet. He limped his Spitfire back to base, but his buddy pilot officer Pete Moore did not make it back across the Channel. After landing, Gene learned that Moore was "missing."

On July 28, 1942, in a mission over Boulogne and St. Omer according to Gene Neville's Flight Log eight of his squadron's planes were swarmed by "50 plus Huns." They were able to escape back across the Channel without damage and free of injury.

On July 30, over the skies of Boulogne and LeTarquet in Northern France, the 616 squadron was "jumped," as Gene recorded it, at 18,000 feet by "80 plus FW190s and ME 190s." The ensuing dog-fight got ugly. Gene lost more of his friends and fellow pilots, as Squadron 616 was shot to pieces before Gene's very eyes. As he recorded, Gene's "No. 2," Sergeant Lee crashed in flames while landing at the Squadron base at Biggin-Hill. Gene watched Lee die and there was nothing he could do. Pilot Officer Mace was recorded as "missing" over the Channel, presumed dead. The July 30 action was not without its lighter side however. Pilot Officer Large and Sergeant Cooper were shot down on the return over the Channel. Remarkably, Large and Cooper were rescued at sea the next day, having spent the night in the frigid and dark drink of the English Channel. Poetically, they were both drunk and hungover when they were rescued. While the Spitfire was heavily armed with cannon and machine guns, there was easily enough room to store a tin flask full of brandy just in case. It probably saved their lives providing the necessary medicinal and emotional relief to stick out the night. Of the 80-plus German planes that attacked the squadron that day, Pilot Officer Large reported "1 FW 190 probable." Squadron 616 had taken a beating, but at least Pilot Officer Gene Neville had survived.

In August of 1942, the power and presence of America air power was finding its way into the war. While there was no United States Air Force as we know it today, the United States was being organized and mustered into the United States Army Air Force, the USAAF. In August of 1942, the American pilots were now being transferred from British command and into all-American units. Perhaps the most famous of the units were the celebrated Eagle Squadrons, one of which was 133 America Eagle Squadron. Still under the command of the British, Gene Neville was posted to the 133 Squadron on August 9, 1942. The squadron itself was stationed in the Group 11 sector at Biggin-Hill and was under the direct command of 27-year-old Mac McColpin with orders to assimilate or transfer the squadron into the USAAF by the end of September.

With a new infusion of man power, air power, and war power, Prime Minister Winston Churchill was ready to strike back at the Germans with an offensive action across the English Channel aimed at the northern coast of German-occupied France. British intelligence had concluded that German bombers were actually guided to their targets by beams from a German-designed device known as the "Knickerbein apparatus." To this end, the Germans had constructed "Knickerbein stations" along the northern coast of France, notably near the vicinity of Dieppe, France to guide their bombers to their British targets. If the Knickerbein stations could be destroyed, the German's bombing effort would be substantially destroyed. Churchill concluded that with new resources and armed with the will to show the Germans that the allies could in fact mount an across-the-Channel attack, the British conceived "Operation Jubilee," code name for the ill-fated Dieppe Raid. The British plan of attack and strategy called for a sea-borne, amphibious assault across the Channel by a large commando force that would first silence the German flank coastal batteries. The British would be led in the assault by a 5,000-man commando raid by the Canadian 2nd Division. Assigned to provide Commando cover was the 133 Eagle Squadron. The selection of the 133 Squadron to provide air cover for the Canadians was not an idle one. Most of the Americans felt a kinship toward the Canadians as the Yanks had filtered through Canada to join the Royal Air Force. They had become brothers of sorts. In a losing battle, the 133 Squadron would fight hard for the Canadians at Dieppe despite overwhelming odds in the air and on the ground.

Gene's flight log reflects two entries, two armed attacks for the Dieppe Raid, both on August 19, 1942. The first is labeled "Commando Escort Cover–Dieppe." The log tells us that Gene was over the Dieppe area for one hour and twenty minutes, a considerable period of time for a fighter plane on a combat mission over the Channel with fuel for approximately two hours of flying time. The second entry is labeled "Commando Cover," sustained flight appearing to be 55 minutes. On Gene's first attack over Dieppe, his Spitfire exhausted its fuel. He returned to England, refueled, and flew back into action to resume the fight with the German Messerschmidts in order to keep them off the Canadian 2nd's back as they attempted to land in France. Gene's log makes it clear that the fight in the skies over Dieppe was action packed. As Gene described it, there were "more planes in one confined area of about five or eight miles" than he had ever seen before. The aerial combat was fierce with the 133 Squadron giving it their all despite being out numbered. For Gene, the horror of aerial combat engagement reached its zenith at Dieppe. As he later recorded the events of the day, he "saw several FW 190s go into the drink and burn." For Gene's squadron, the two hour and 15 minutes of combat acrobatics yielded some satisfying and impressive results–six German planes confirmed destroyed, three probable, and 10 damaged. The most impressive result of the day was no losses to 133 Squadron. Without question, on August 19, 1942, the American Eagle Squadron rode on the wings of angels. For Gene he had beaten the odds the previous three weeks and he was safe. However, the ride would not last much longer, and the odds would catch up with him over France.

Despite the heroic efforts of the Squadron, the Dieppe Raid was a colossal failure on the ground. Crossing the Channel, the amphibious force ran into a German convoy of ships and quickly were detected. In addition, and unknown to the British intelligence, was the fact that the Germans had substantially reinforced their positions all along the Dieppe area coast in fear of the allies first cross-channel attack. When the Canadians hit the beach at Dieppe they were badly mauled. Of the 5,000 men of the Canadian 2nd Division, 900 hundred were killed and 2,000 were taken prisoner. The Germans had successfully repelled the first attempted channel invasion of World War II.

The failure of the Dieppe Raid saw Churchill engulfed in criticism. It was argued that the raid was badly timed, poorly executed, and suffered from inadequate preparation and intelligence. Churchill defended the action later claiming that valuable lessons were learned in the arena of amphibious assaults that substantially aided the allied efforts at Normandy on June 6, 1944. While the British "practiced" at Dieppe, the 45th Infantry Division, exhausted and worn out from the repetition at Fort Devens, practiced the amphibious art form off the coast of Massachusetts. On the German side of the ledger, the Dieppe Raid was a wake-up call that filled the German ranks with fear, despite their victory. The raid evidenced that Winston Churchill had the courage and resolve to send troops across the Channel and storm the French beaches. This time, it was a Canadian Division. But by September of 1942, there was a new player on the block–the United States Army. The next time, the Germans feared, it could be the American and British armies assaulting the beach, not just a division. Hitler played the chess game of move, counter move, by bringing into France his best and favorite General Irwin Rommel. Rommel immediately beefed up the defense of the Atlantic Wall with concrete bunkers, huge guns that could destroy troops on the beach, and massive anti-aircraft cover to limit allied control in the skies.

One of the areas where Rommel enhanced German anti-aircraft fire power was Brest, France. Throughout August and into September, squadron leader McColpin was busy trying to fight the army bureaucracy in assimilating his men into the United States Army Air Force (USAAF). This effort was problematic as McColpin had to juggle getting his boys into the USAAF while at the same time balance British flight operations. Technically, while the American Eagle 133 Squadron was soon to transfer to the USAAF, they were still under

British command. In late August, the Eighth Air Force was fully operational, and American B-17s were flying bombing missions over German-occupied France. Critical to the bombing efforts was fighter escort. The 133 Squadron was given orders to escort American B-17s to their targeted area near Morlaix, France. Anticipated date of the mission was September 7, 1942.

Inclement weather conditions continued to delay the Morlaix mission. With conditions worsening, the 133 Squadron sat on the ground until September 23, 1942, when it was ordered to Great Samford to ready for USAAF consolidation.

After September 23, 1942, an incredible series of events unfolded that spelled the fate of Gene Neville.

Gene Neville had been technically transferred, on paper that is, to the command of the USAAF. Through September 26, 1942, McColpin shuffled his pilots in twos or threes back and forth to London to effect their transfers, keeping the remainder of 133 at homebase in the event the Morlaix mission was called up. As the men and planes of the 133 sat on the ground in Great Samford, McColpin was ordered to London to effect his own and the last transfer of the Eagle Squadrons to the USAAF. McColpin was reluctant to leave his pilots. The Morlaix mission had not been canceled and the 133 had been ordered to stand ready. The weather conditions were worsening, making McColpin dubious about the mission. Adding to McColpin's concern was that the British chain of command, in the absence of McColpin, left command and control of the 133 to Flight Lieutenant Gordon Brettrell, who was British.

Brettrell was a rather high-strung, proper, Brit who had been brought into the 133 to clean up American disciplinary problems. There was probably good reason for this. After all two pilots had been plunked from the Channel having survived the night on brandy hidden in their flight jackets. The Eagle pilots were a hard-charging, energetic group. These pilots lived on life's edge, not knowing whether they would live or die the next day. Many missions returned to Biggin-Hill with at least one of their numbers missing or dead. They stared death in the face every single day, and as Gene did, they often watched a wounded comrade's plane burst into flames or crash dive into the English Channel. The nightly medicinal was time tested, proven to provide at least temporary relief of the agony and sadness of friends lost, at least until the unit scrambled for the air the next day and wondered if they would make it back. There was not a pub or saloon in Biggin-Hill that the 133 did not frequent, always consuming vast quantities of "medicine." The tension and adrenaline of aerial combat, and oxygen at 29,000 feet, tended to clear a heavy head rather quickly, the following day. If they survived the day, they celebrated life in the night no matter what rules Brettrell would attempt to impose. As many a proper Brit complained, the only problem with the Yanks was that they were "over-paid, over-sexed and over here." However, for the most part, the British loved the American Royal Air Forcers. They were not required to fight for

Britain, but they chose to do so. While the Yanks did not like Brettrell's rule making or at times his rather pompous attitude, they did have respect for his fighter pilot skills. As Gene noted in his log, Brettrell had downed a FW 190 over Dieppe. Perhaps questioned as a leader, Brettrell was at least a fighter.

Before leaving for London, McColpin cautioned Brettrell concerning the Morlaix mission and warned him against exposing the 133 unnecessarily to severe weather conditions. Nonetheless, with McColpin gone to London, and after breakfast the morning of September 26, 1942, Brettrell ordered the 133 to fly 200 miles west to Bolt Head on the plain of Devon to the immediate south of Plymouth. The 200-mile flight was perilous. In a torrential downpour the ceiling never reached more than 200 to 300 feet. At this low altitude, the American pilots found themselves dodging barrage balloons and church steeples. As related by Pilot Officer Bob Smith, the difficulty of the flight was elevated by the fact that most of the men were hungover from the previous night's activity, but as Smith observed the oxygen and execution of the dangerous fight "diluted the effects of the previous night." Despite the troublesome course set by Brettrell, the 133 miraculously arrived safe at Bolt Head sometime before noon.

The record, at least as related in The Eagle Squadrons is unclear as to whether Brettrell was ordered to Bolt Head the morning of the 26th or whether he took it upon himself to move the 133 despite the expressed concern of McColpin regarding the weather and Morlaix mission. The evidence seems clear

Gene Neville was buried in the American Cemetery in Brest, France. In the forefront his marker appears in a picture taken by Jim MacKellar, son of Pete MacKellar.

This is one of the few pictures of Gene Neville, sitting to the right of his American Eagle 133 Squadron Commander McColpin. Gene was shot down and killed over Guingamp, France on September 26, 1942.

that the chain of command for the 133 Squadron was a scrambled egg. On September 26, 1942, most of the Eagles were administratively in the USAAF. Gene Neville was now Lieutenant Neville, no longer Pilot Officer Neville. The unit itself, however, was still a British unit temporarily commanded by a British lieutenant.

After lunch on September 26 the briefing for the Morlaix mission began in the ready room. With the exception of Brettrell and one other section leader, the Eagle pilots did not attend the briefing. It appears evident that Gene chose not to attend the mission briefing. By this time the men of the 133 had flown more than 60 missions. They were an experienced group, they had been largely successful, and they were cocky. The mission called for a 150-mile flight to target in lousy weather. Most likely, the mission would be scrubbed. There seemed to be no need for a British briefing.

The Morlaix mission was a bombing mission aimed at Focke-Wolf aircraft maintenance plant near Morlaix, France. The secondary targets were the German submarine pens on the Northern French coast at Brest. The mission would be carried out by eighteen B-17s of the 97th Bombardment Group, USAAF. The 133 was to provide escort for the B-17, rendezvousing with them at 25,000 feet over the English Channel and then proceeding to the target. Take-off was scheduled for 4:00 p.m.

If the mission itself was not a monumental blunder in its planning, certainly the weather briefing was. The British forecast called for a 35-knot headwind at Eagle mission altitude, 28,000 feet. In fact, the Squadron would be disserved by a 100-knot tailwind. The mission forecast would prove fatal, despite the fact that the squadron did not attend the briefing. It must be concluded that Brettrell and George Sperry, who attended the briefing, advised the squadron of the forecast so that each pilot could navigate accordingly, should the squadron separate.

For the raid, the 133 was organized into three sections, Red Section, Blue Section, and Yellow Section. Each section contained four new Spitfire IXs. The Eagles would put twelve planes in the sky to meet up with the B-17s. As the mission briefing was concluded Brettrell selected his pilot line-up. After "scramble" was sounded, Dusty Miller, Gene's roommate hurried to his plane. As he double-timed to the Spitfire IX, Brettrell instructed Miller to stand down. He would be spared this trip. Substituted in at the last minute was Miller's close friend and roommate, Gene Neville. Gene climbed aboard and strapped into Miller's plane and readied for taxi. Gene would fly in the Red Section, with Brettrell taking the lead, followed by Sperry and Dick Beaty.

The freakish events of the day continued as the 133 moved toward take off. Brettrell's Spitfire blew out its right tire on taxi. Brettrell quickly exited his plane and switched planes with Beaty who was given instructions to grab another plane, take off, and put the pedal to the metal to catch up with the section over the Channel. Many of the Spitfire IXs were difficult to start without auxiliary battery and power units. On this day, the squadron only had three such units for the entire squadron. Ten of the twelve planes, newly off the factory line, choked and sputtered as the pilots cranked the huge Rolls Royce Merlin engines. Unable to get started, the helter-skelter created by pilots yelling and demanding an auxiliary boost with ground crews running amidst the swirling propellers only added to the calamity of the day. The leader of Blue Section gave orders to change radio frequency for the mission to one of the pilots; that pilot failed to advise the others. In essence, Blue Section would fly the mission on different radio channels. Unable to communicate with each other except for hand signals, the bad luck of Blue Section continued when one of the section's planes narrowly missed colliding with the tail section of another Spitfire on taxi. Many of the pilots of the squadron never believed the mission would actually come to be. The operation would call for the Spitfire IXs to operate at maximum range in horrible weather making navigation difficult.

Believing the mission would probably be scrubbed, the squadron imbided in British "cider" after lunch. As one of the 133 said–"The cider we had for lunch had more authority than we realized, and most of us went sound asleep under our airplane wings." And to top the day off, many of the pilots forgot to take their escape kits, a packet that contained money, maps, and compasses in the event they were downed in enemy territory.

In historical hindsight, it was a near miracle that the squadron got off the ground on September 26. But, at 4:00 p.m. that afternoon they did. However, the bad luck and misfortune continued to follow the ill-fated squadron as they climbed into the skies over the English Channel.

Eagle Squadron 133 was to rendezvous with the B-17 bombers 15 minutes after take off. At approximately 4:15 p.m., all three sections of the 133, including Beaty, were over the rendezvous point; however, the bombers were no where to be seen. Not known to the squadron was that the bombers were 20 minutes ahead of the Spitfire IXs and continuing their southward flight toward Morlaix. The bombers had decided to fly their mission despite the apparent absence of fighter cover.

The 133 Squadron was now at the critical decision point. The rendezvous had been missed and weather prevented visual observation of the ground except at extremely and dangerously low altitudes which would expose them to anti-aircraft fire. The Squadron knew the target was Morlaix, but they did not know where the bombing group was unable to communicate with them. Unaware of the 100-mile-per-hour tailwind and not knowing the location of the B-17s, these brave young men made the decision that the mission came first. They would continue southward toward Morlaix in an effort to provide the fighter protection the B-17s would need to return home. They would not leave the bombers and their crews stranded in the skies over enemy-held territory. And so the order was given, the Eagle Squadron would continue on.

Approximately 35 minutes later as the Squadron steered southward, Gene Neville's Spitfire IX developed engine trouble. Gene radioed Brettrell of his difficulty. Brettrell ordered Neville to turn northward and return home. Dick Beaty was dispatched from Red Section to escort Gene and his plane back to Bolt Head.

The vice of the weather forecast raised its ugly head to write the final epitaph of Gene Neville. Gene's location at the time his plane experienced engine difficulty is not known. However, approximate calculations of cruising speed coupled with the tailwind reasonably suggests that he was approximately 367 miles south of Bolt Head, most likely over the Bay of Biscay, south of France. Having turned northward, apparently believing he now had the aide of a tailwind, but still unable to establish radio contact to fix their position or see the ground below, both Gene and Beaty concluded that after a half-hour of flight time they would be over friendly shores. They were wrong. They were over German-held territory approximately 40 miles east of Morlaix near Guingamp, France.

Believing they had reached safe harbor, Gene and Beaty put the nose of their Spitfire IXs downward and descended through the dark soup of rain and clouds. As they broke the cover of clouds they began the frantic search for a spot to land as by now both planes were near fuel exhaustion. As they maneuvered their planes, looking for what they were sure was safe haven, the surprised Germans had fixed the positions of the duo gliding downward toward a flat piece of land. The Germans unleashed a deadly volley of fire with their 88s and anti-aircraft batteries. For Gene it was over quickly. Now taking fire, he pushed the throttle to the max to gain altitude to escape while at the same time trying to return fire with the Spitfire IX's machine gun. It was not enough. The Nazi guns had turned the British Spitfire into a red and black thunderball. It was over at approximately 5:20 p.m. on September 26, 1942. Second Lieutenant Gene Neville of the 133 Eagle Squadron, from Adair, Oklahoma, died in the skies over Guingamp, France.

Somewhat miraculously, Dick Beaty escaped the death of German fire. Powering his plane to the safety of the clouds, turning invisible to the German guns, Beaty flew until his fuel tanks were empty. As he prepared to bail out over the English Channel, the cliffs of England appeared. Out of fuel and his plane now on a downward glide-pattern, Beaty steered the exhausted Spitfire over the cliffs to a crash landing on its belly. Dick Beaty struggled out of the crashed Spitfire as fire engines sped toward him. Although safe and relatively free of injury, he was emotionally shaken. Someone would have to tell Dusty Miller, Gene's roommate and friend, what happened.

An equal share of fate awaited the remaining 10 planes of Eagle Squadron 133. As Gene and Beaty headed to the north, the remaining planes of the squadron continued south. As they sped southward, the 97th Bombardment Group finally concluded that they had flown past the target. It took the observation of the Pyrenees Mountains in Spain for the B-17s to realize they needed to turn around and head northward. Finally, the 97th Bombardment Group met the remaining Eagle Squadron. Brettrell turned his group around and now both bombers and Spitfires sped northward in search of the Morlaix target.

The 97th Bombardment Group fought to find their targets amidst the confusion and navigational disorientation that resulted from the day. Unable to establish radio contact with the home base and unable to visually identify land marks because of the weather, the B-17s were unable to locate their targets. Now running low on fuel, the bombers jettisoned their bombs and struggled to make it home. They made it.

After two hours of flight time at high altitude and near maximum speed, the 133 was desperately low on fuel. Yellow Section leader William Baker, now on fumes and believing they must be over home soil, signaled Brettrell to take the squadron down. Brettrell agreed and turned his Spitfire groundward. Breaking through the cloud cover, the group was sailing over the German held harbor at Brest, France infested with its beefed up anti-aircraft guns laying in wait for the gas hungry British fighters who were now almost 100 miles west of the intended target of Morlaix. The entire squadron scattered in absolute panic reaching for the safety of altitude and the darkness of the clouds. It was too late as the German guns were fixed on the Spitfires. The 133 Eagle Squadron was shot to pieces.

The final chapter of the doomed Morlaix mission was written over the sky of Brest, France. Four pilots were killed and six taken prisoner. Beaty had survived the crash landing of his Spitfire, and Gene Neville had died over Guingamp. The Morlaix mission was a failure. All planes of the squadron were lost, and eleven of the twelve pilots captured or dead. Adding misery to the already gruesome result, not a single bomb fell on the German aircraft maintenance facility at Morlaix, France.

Gene was the only Neville who died in the world's greatest and most horrific global war. Falling in the sky over France, Gene Parks Neville was 24 years old, two days shy of his 25th birthday. Gene Neville was laid to rest in the American Military Cemetery in Brest, France. Aunt Rosie says it is a beautiful place cared for by the people of Brest, still grateful for the American sacrifice made to save their country. To this day, Aunt Rosie sends her monthly stipend to Geneva Eby to care for Gene's marker in the Adair Cemetery.

The Neville brothers of the 1960s; from left to right, Jim, Baird, Nat, Creighton, and Jack. The empty chair in front of Nat and Creighton was for Gene Neville, killed in action flying his spitfire in Northern France.

CHAPTER VII
GRIEF ARRIVES AT THE NEVILLE'S

At 63 years old, Rosa Neville had resigned to her life in Oklahoma City, however almost three years past Bart's death, she still missed her home in Adair. Although not the up-town of Oklahoma City, she had her friends, her family, the Methodist church, and, of course, the Embroidery Club in Adair. The house at 523 Northwest 22nd was not quite the white frame two- story home that sat on the edge of the Adair inhabited by a husband and energy that nine active children could muster. There were days in Adair when she prayed for the relief of solitude and quiet that rarely came with a household of humanity. Now, however, she experienced times when she longed for it all to be back, a time when she felt so alive. The Adair house sat outside of town. In Oklahoma City, however, eves of the house on 22nd Street were separated from the homes on the east and west by only a few feet, and at times you had to make sure that the blinds were drawn, or else your neighbors may well receive an eyeful of your business. Barely 2,000 square feet, Rosa at times felt as if she lived in a barrel. The two bedroom, five-room brick house was only 50 feet or so from the not-so-busy street between Walker and Dewey. The avenue of approach to the house was a cracked two-foot-wide concrete walkway that split the yard in the middle. A large evergreen flanked the west side of the house, partially covering the porch and protecting the house from the hot sun.

Even before Pearl Harbor, and certainly by September of 1942, Rosa was writing a new chapter in her life. The kids had grown up, they had their own lives, and the onslaught of world conflict had robbed her of three sons. Nat was now in the United States Navy; Jim in the United States Merchant Marines; Baird still in Ponca City with Conoco as part of an "essential" industry; and Jack at Fort Devens, Massachusetts with the 45th Infantry Division, most assuredly going to Europe and the war. Only Creighton, because of his age, was not pressed into some form of service.

Helen once again found the man of her dreams and remarried. Thankfully, Helen always was a frequent visitor, and Billie Lou was still home, but would soon be off to marry Charles Storch. By now Roselle and Pete, in the United

States Army Air Force, were stationed in Wichita Falls, Texas. And, of course, there was Gene, so far away, and so difficult to communicate with, not a day went by that she did not go to sleep and wake up with a knot in her stomach over worry for his safety. For security reasons, the family never knew exactly where or what Gene was doing. But the daily reports of the war in Europe provided ample basis for concern. There was heavy fighting in the air over the English Channel and the conclusion had to be that Gene was right in the middle of it. As only mothers can be, she was of course right. Ten o'clock in the morning was the most difficult time of the day. It was this time that the mail generally arrived, and it was the time of highest anxiety and fear. If just the postman came, it was a good sign. The postman, in those days was a well-recognized member of the block and knew the families who had loved ones fighting the war overseas. With "ginger" in his step the postman acted as delighted to deliver the "good news" as Rosa was to receive it.

Thursday, October 1, 1942, was just such a day. Bounding down the sidewalk at about 10:00 a.m. was postman Robert Delaney acting as if he already had read the cable he was about to deliver–probably because he had. With a big grin on his face, he handed the cable over to Rosa, exhorting "you've got to love it! British Broadcasting Corporation, New York," and a letter from Gene. Rosa hollered for Billie Lou and ripped open the letter from Gene as Billie Lou tore into the cable. It was the good news. Gene wrote that things were good, that he was excited. Soon, he said, his unit would be officially transferred from the Royal Air Force to the United States Army Air Force. The transfer was now only a few days away, and the best part of the trade was that his pay would be three times what he made with the British. Censorship and secrecy of course precluded Gene from writing of his missions, even his location. To spur the spirit of the homeland, the United States and British had formed the American Eagle Club. A club comprised of the American pilots who flew in the Eagle Squadrons for the Royal Air Force. In conjunction with the British Broadcasting Corporation, the pilots of the American Eagle Club tape-recorded messages to their loved ones. The taped messages were then played from London, over the British Broadcasting Network, to its affiliates in New York, and then on to the homes of the Eagle pilots. The excitement of a cable from the British Broadcasting Corporation in New York was beyond their words. Together, Billie Lou and Rosa, with four hands on the envelope, struggled to open the rather official looking envelope from the British Broadcasting Corporation.

John Hooley of the British Broadcasting Corporation of New York wrote to advise that Gene had recorded a message on September 3, 1942, and that all ears should be tuned to the local mutual station on October 3. At that time, the British Broadcasting Corporation would broadcast Gene's message from London to New York to KOCY Radio in Oklahoma City. The excitement ran wild. Rosa called Helen, Billie Lou was dispatched to call, cable, and wire the other family members that Gene was going to be on KOCY on Saturday night. Seven o'clock was a little past the regular dinner hour, but given the occasion close enough for a Saturday night family get together with the old RCA right in the middle of the dining room table. At last, some relief that Gene was safe, they would get to hear his voice all the way from the fighting front in London, England. Saturday seemed too far away.

October sunrises always seem to come late. Friday, October 2, 1942, was no different. The sun did not reach the cloudless sky of bright blue until shortly before 8:00 a.m., but Rosa Neville had been up for hours. *The Daily Oklahoman* always was prompt in the war years and Rosa was able to retrieve the paper well before the crack of dawn. In the quiet of the morning she could plan the celebration of Gene's voice over the British Broadcasting Corporation with the rest of the Nevilles in Oklahoma City. Grabbing the morning paper, she rushed immediately to the grocery store ads. She would make the list and see to it that Helen carried it out. At the local I.G.A., arm roast was on sale for 27¢ per pound along with beef ribs at 17¢. But, on this Saturday night it would have to be T-Bone Steak, even though it was a little expensive at 39¢ per pound. Besides, if Gene was there, he would want steak. In a sense he would be coming home, at least his voice would be.

With the main course now planned, it was time for a quick perusal of the front page. Very few reports of the battle over skies in England found their way to the Oklahoma City paper, and when there were reports of such skirmishes, there were few indications of the units or squadrons involved. It was almost impossible to track the Eagle Squadrons in the papers, and Gene's letters home gave little hint of mission operations or location due to censorship. Rosa knew that Jack was in Massachusetts, but little else. *The Daily Oklahoman* was reluctant to print the precise whereabouts or activities of the 45th Infantry Division. It was frustrating to Rosa not knowing the whereabouts of her boys, but on Saturday night she would surely know Gene's. Although having little interest herself, Gene loved baseball. Rosa quickly checked the sports page thinking that she would tell Gene Saturday night that the St. Louis Cardinals and the New York Yankees were battling it out in the World Series. The series was tied. The front page of The Daily Oklahoman told of Roosevelt's tour of the United States manufacturing plants all across the nation. By October of 1942, they were reaching full capacity. This was of little interest to Rosa, compared to the joy and excitement of the BBC broadcast from London.

With the Saturday night gala planned, and the paper read, Rosa turned to the morning chores. Although not big, she saw to it that the house was dusted almost every day. At least it was something to do and when done in tandem with the 10:00 a.m. Mid-Morning Melodies on KOMA Radio, cleaning provided some distraction from the constant and worrisome thoughts of her boys so far from home.

As Rosa moved about the house the sun broke through the old elm tree in the front yard. The northeastern Oklahoma fall had a bright cheer about it, but the Oklahoma City fall seemed almost brown and rust in color as the sun filtered through the aging elm and into the front living room. But at least the sun was bright and shining on this windless October Oklahoma morning.

Fussing about the lamps in the front room surrounding the normal hour of the postman had come and passed. At 11:00 a.m., as Rosa looked out the front door in search of the letter carrier, a strange green colored four-door Hudson rolled to a slow stop at the edge of the sidewalk just under the elm. On the door, the lettering read "United States Army." At first partially obscured, two men wearing army khakis and black hats emerged from the sun's glare and moved toward the front porch. They did not have to get to the door before Rosa sank to her knees in tears. World War II had reached into the Neville's home and family with devastating news.

On October 3, 1942, Group Captain F. W. Trott of the Royal Air Force Delegation cabled Mrs. E. B. Neville that her son Pilot Officer Gene Parks Neville of the Royal Air Force Volunteer Reserve, while on a mission over France on September 26, was reported missing in action. No details were available. Struggling for strength, Rosa called Helen.

Gene's letter of September 30, the cables of October 1 and 2, threw the situation and family into a state of confusion. Gene's letter suggested that he had been transferred into the USAAF, that he was no longer with the Royal Air Force, so surely there was a mistake. Besides that, word had come that Gene's voice would come to Oklahoma via the BBC on Saturday night. There had to be a mistake, it just did not add up. Rosa and Helen found hope in the confusion and for a few hours they found a self-induced relief from the devastating cable. They just did not want to believe it.

Struggling through the night, Rosa waded through the house on Saturday, October 3. Surely the BBC broadcast from London between 7:00 o'clock and 7:30 p.m. would provide some answers. It did not. Turning the dial to KOCY at the appointed time, yet another signal of despair was sent. The broadcast had been canceled for unknown reasons.

Monday, October 5, 1942, brought more tears and anxiety to the Neville home. Writing once again, Captain Trott wrote Rosa to convey the few details that he had available.

> "I am afraid that the details I have at present are very incomplete. They do however include the fact that on September 26, 1942, your son was the pilot of a Spitfire flight . . . and that between five and five thirty on the afternoon of that day, together with a number of other Spitfires, he set out on an operational flight from which he failed to return. The location of the squadron at the time is not stated nor is the cause apparent."

Without assigning any deliberateness, the Trott letter of October 5, 1942 is of course misleading. Dick Beaty, Gene's flying companion, struggled back to

England and was rescued on the day of the mission, September 26, more than a week before Trott's letter. Beaty obviously knew and presumably related to the Royal Air Force that he and Gene were ambushed by anti-aircraft fire over Guingamp, and Beaty obviously knew they had separated from the rest of the squadron due to Gene's engine trouble. Further, Beaty may have seen Gene shot down as Beaty's recollection at least in part appears to be the source of this history of events related in The Eagle Squadrons. Nonetheless, the Royal Air Force was prompt in its communication with Rosa and Trott's October 5 letter can in no way be described as a government form letter advising families of their son's casualty. Trott's cable was some four paragraphs long, extremely sincere both in tone and manner. Without actually knowing, perhaps the compelling need for war-time secrecy mandated the vagueness and inaccuracy of the British letter. The day after Trott's October 2 cable, *The Daily Oklahoman*, carried the front-page headline–"City R.A.F. Pilot Is Missing."

The Royal Air Force delegation further reported to Rosa and the Nevilles on October 7, 1942 that the American Eagle Club Program Broadcast of Gene's taped message scheduled for October 3, was canceled because of "poor reception conditions" apparently in New York. Now Rosa was advised that the program was rescheduled for Saturday, October 10 from 8:00 to 8:30 p.m. This communication rekindled the Neville's hope that perhaps Trott's October 2 cable was in error, and that surely on October 10 the family would learn that Gene Neville was alive, well, and in the arms of safety. After all, certainly the message would not be sent if all was not well.

It was not to be. Like the sorrow and grief that poured out of the confusing events of the last few days, all emotions sunk to new despair when John Hooley of the British Broadcasting Company of New York wrote Rosa to advise that Gene's message had in fact been recorded on September 3, 1942, and "BBC policy necessitates deletion." Gene's tape-recorded message to the home folks of Oklahoma City would not be heard from London. There is no history that suggests that the message was in fact ever heard, or that the tape was ever recovered.

The emotional roller-coaster of the Morlaix mission continued however with further correspondence from the Royal Air Force. On October 31, 1942, Group Captain Trott again wrote Rosa.

> "The Air Military signal states that No. 133 (Eagle) Squadron reported that 12 Spitfires set out at 4 o'clock in the afternoon of September 26, 1942 to act as escorts to a number of Flying Fortresses engaged in a bombing operation over France. For a number of reasons the operation was unduly prolonged with the result that the Spitfires ran short of petrol and the majority were forced to land in enemy occupied territory. This information is contained in the report of one of the Spitfire Pilots who returned to his aerodome in the United Kingdom, and there is reason to believe that the majority of his brother officers in the

> Squadron named, landed safely and are prisoners in enemy hands.
>
> The only definite news on this subject, however, has been received from the International Red Cross Committee, which confirms that three of the pilots amongst whom your son was not included, have been reported by the Germans as being prisoners of war. Enquiries are still continuing and I shall again write to you directly any further news arrives."

Once again, observation of the inaccuracy of Trott's letter cannot go unmentioned, at least if the account of the Morlaix mission in The Eagle Squadrons is to be accepted as true. The mission was prolonged because the British had mis-forecast the weather conditions, especially the fact that the 133 Squadron had a 100-knot tail wind, not a 35-knot head wind as otherwise projected, thus causing the squadron to fly too far south. While the main body of the squadron that flew over Brest, as well as Gene's Spitfire while over Guingamp, were perilously low on fuel, the fighters descended through dense cloud cover because they all believed they were over England when in fact they were over occupied France. While probably not historically material, Trott suggested that Gene was with the entirety of the squadron, when in fact he and Beaty had split off from the squadron due to Gene's engine trouble. Perhaps most egregiously fabricated, were Trott's statements that ". . . the Spitfires ran short of petrol and the majority even forced to land in enemy occupied territory. This information is contained in the report of one of the Spitfire Pilots who returned to his aerodome in the United Kingdom."

The last sentence is an obvious reference to Dick Beaty, the only Eagle to make it back on September 26. Beaty was not with the majority of the Spitfires, he was with Gene, and therefore had no knowledge as to the fate of the rest of the squadron. Further omitted from Trott's account of the day is the fact that Beaty, Neville, and the rest of the 133 Squadron were shot to pieces by German anti-aircraft fire. It must be concluded that Trott's report that the majority of the squadron landed safely and simply were captured is at best a gross understatement of what Trott must have known by October 31. The Morlaix mission was a complete failure in both planning and execution. The colossal calamity of the events of September 26, 1942, reflected a certain ineptness by the British in the execution of war-time flight operations at a time when the Americans were initially throwing their air power into the fight.

In fairness to Trott, and the British, it must be noted that his observation and conclusion that Gene could have been captured and therefore possibly alive, missing in action, is a fair and just conclusion drawn from then-known facts. Beaty in fact may not have seen Gene shot down and if he did see Gene go down, there may have been reason for Beaty to believe that somehow Gene had survived. Trott had reported that the Red Cross had learned that a number of the 133 Eagle Squadron had been captured by the Germans.

For Rosa and the rest of the Nevilles, the factual detail of the Morlaix mission may not have been that important to them in the fall of 1942. To family, the Trott report that Gene could have been captured, and was a prisoner of the Axis, gave hope that the dark of the day could yet be replaced by the glimmer of an Oklahoma sunrise.

The truth would not be known until January of 1943.

News of Gene's reported missing in action conquered Jack's every emotion. It was more than a devastating blow, it consumed his every thought and motion. Perhaps the horror and grief of it all would have been easier to deal with if the report had been that Gene was killed in action, although there seemed a grim finality to both. At least there would be certainty in knowing one way or the other. But now, he would have to find a way to march on in the sands of overwhelming anxiety with every day giving rise to a new set of emotions. Why had Gene strained so hard to fly for the British? Why did he believe it worth such extraordinary effort? Gene never seemed to be a risk-taker, how dare he subject himself to an against-all-odds adventure with no apparent prospect for gain. At times, Jack found himself angry at Gene for pushing the envelope too far and too fast. At other times his emotion spoke of unreserved admiration for a brother who had the guts to go do it.

Gene's story was one of great adventure, of daring do, of what truly good men did in evil times. Gene's odyssey had to be pure of heart, certainly there never was, or even could be, any financial reward or material trappings for such volunteer risk-taking in the skies of Europe. There was goodness, a purity in Gene's deed, and perhaps that is what Gene Parks Neville was in search of when he left Oklahoma City for London, England in December of 1941. At least that is how Jack resolved the wave of grief.

But the fickleness of war, and death in war, now laced through Jack's every thought to such a degree that life took on a new celebration, a new living. As the old pop song goes, you better "love the one you're with." Gene Neville had been in Europe for only ten months. He had been assigned to Eagle 133 for some six weeks and in combat for only a few short months. It had apparently ended all too quickly, and not even by his own hand.

The now certainty of it all told Jack that his march to the war, to face death, was inevitable. It was only a matter of time and he would face the odds as Gene had. This reality focused many a man's thoughts on living and life.

The war and the Germans had now invaded the Nevilles. Rosa Neville, as she saw it in October of 1942, had lost one son to the world conflict, and now but a short time later, another son would stand in line to do his duty in harm's way. Nothing could wrench a mother's gut more than the fear of burying not one, but two sons. She would live with the thought until May of 1945, when the war was over. For Jack, the news of it all made life more precious; and on the other hand the reality of it all told him that the war games and training were no longer a game. Jack knew he would get his chance to see death's eye. He had better be ready.

CHAPTER VIII
TO CAMP PINE

On November 7, 1942, the then largest Army-Navy armada in the history of modern warfare set out to attack the Germans by invading the shores of North Africa in what came to be known as Operation Torch. For the previous two years, the Prime Minister of England, Winston Churchill had pleaded with President Franklin D. Roosevelt for a second front that would divide the Axis forces. Now he had it. Under the command of General Dwight D. Eisenhower, 35,000 American troops left Norfolk, Virginia bound for French Morocco; another 39,000 Americans sailed from England to Oran; and 10,000 more set out for Algiers. All toll, 107,000 British and Americans boarded more than 300 war vessels to invade North Africa. Within only a few days the British and American Troops occupied three key cities on the North African coast, Rabat, Oran, and Algiers. The Allied forces consolidated their supply lines and massed forces for the greatest desert tank battle in history. American-British forces fought and clawed their way eastward against Irwin Rommel's elite desert Panzers. For months the Allies traded brutal blows until April of 1943 when Rommel's troops were finally beaten and forced to withdraw. Operation Torch was a success and now the Allied forces had the springboard of North Africa to attack the Germans in southern Europe.

Commanding the 2nd Armored, 3rd, and 9th Division of the United States forces was the old friend of the 45th Infantry Division, General George S. Patton. He would wait for the 45th in North Africa to later invade Sicily.

The fall of 1942 brought other changes for Jack and the 45th Infantry Division. General Key, who had commanded the division since Jack's entry into the service was reassigned as the Provost Marshall General of the European Theatre of Operations. Appointed as the Commanding General of the division was Troy Houston Middleton, the comptroller and the dean of administration at Louisiana State University. Despite his title in civilian life, he was no lightweight. A veteran of World War I, Middleton had won the Silver Star and five Bronze Stars fighting heroically in the Meuse-Argonne. Remarkably, after the war in Europe erupted, Middleton volunteered for service and he was rejected.

In November of 1942, the Thunderbirds moved from Fort Devens to Camp Pine in New York. The division's arrival was reported as a "Wild West show comes to town." The weather was miserable and training efforts plagued by heavy snow as shown in this photograph.

After Pearl Harbor, at the age of 53, he was recalled. Middleton's assignment to lead the 45th spoke volumes to Jack and the other G.I.s. Middleton was a combat soldier, a fighter, and the division was now close to getting into the thick of it. Middleton was the man who could be followed across the battlefield. To Jack's relief, citizen-soldier Ray McClain would remain Jack's boss as the general in charge of Division Artillery.

With the appointment of Middleton as Commander of the 45th, the division was on the move again, this time to Camp Pine, just northeast of Watertown, New York. Beginning in early November of 1942, the entire division exited Fort Devens by train and motor convoy to establish residence at Camp Pine. Reports indicated that the citizens of Ayers, Massachusetts, the small town nearest Fort Devens, were not exactly saddened by the division's departure. The division drank more beer than the entire city could store and it was evident that the boys of the 45th were itching for a fight. Local law enforcement earned their pay in Ayers, Massachusetts, and they were glad for the opportunity to see Watertown's law enforcement receive the opportunity to keep the peace.

By reading the Watertown Daily Times, one would have believed the circus had come to town as the local paper announced the division's arrival on the front page of the Friday, November 13, 1942, edition, under the headline "45th Infantry Division Now Stationed at Camp."

The division's arrival was reported as "wild west show comes to town" with the people of Watertown being told that cowboys and Indians from the southwest made up the ranks of the 45th. Of course, they did. Jack and the boys looked upon the newspaper report as a source of pride for their heritage as the New Yorkers were told that more than 50 tribes comprised the division, mostly

Shawnees, Seminoles, Creeks, Osages, Comanches, and Apaches. Jack was disappointed that the by-lines did not go to the Cherokees. While identifying the division as cowboys, Indians, gold miners, oil field workers, and cotton growers, somewhat overlooked was the fact that Colonel Walter Arnot, a Cherokee Indian, was a Harvard graduate and that most of the commanders of the division were college educated. Described as a "colorful unit," and a "top-notch fighting machine," the 45th Infantry Division became part of Watertown legend, but not entirely for good reasons. In a rare war-time reporting moment, *The Daily Oklahoman* on November 15, 1942, in a small back page article reported the division's presence in New York under the headline "45th Is Now Stationed in New York." This was the first time that the Oklahoma City paper had reported the location of the division in more than six months.

The exact military reason for the move from Fort Devens to Camp Pine seems obscured by time and history. For whatever the reason, the historical facts suggest that the division actually did little training at Camp Pine. The

The wood paneled barracks at Camp Pine did little to shield the cold and misery from the division.

division arrived at Camp Pine without adequate winter clothing or equipment. Efforts to engage in serious military training efforts were severely hampered, most often restricted by snow and temperatures that often ranged between 35° and 50° below zero. In sum, while at Camp Pine, it was all the division could do to keep warm.

While the weather was miserable, the nightlife was not. To mitigate the stir-craziness that resulted from an entire division being cooped up in winter, the United States Army authorized the opening of a USO center in the town of Black River just outside the camp's perimeter. The army hosted a weekly series of dances at the Black River USO with all of the "eligibles" of Watertown encouraged to attend. Learning of the division's rather raucous activities in Ayers, Massachusetts, the USO's efforts were a rather obvious effort to keep the boys of the division out of the town of Watertown. It would not work for long. Despite the bitter cold of New York and its stifling effect on combat training, *The Daily Oklahoman* announced that the division was in the lap of luxury. On November 24, 1942, it was reported "Luxury of 45th Division New Camp Pleases Oklahoma Soldiers."

Jack's performance through the Fort Devens encampment was more than commendable. Impressed with his efforts was General McClain who nominated Jack for Officer's Candidate School (OCS) for the artillery. Jack viewed the nomination as a tremendous reward for his two years of service in the division. He was grateful for the honor and opportunity; he was even more grateful for the occasion as the OCS for the artillery branch was in Fort Sill, Oklahoma. It was a welcome relief from the brutal cold in the northeast and the boredom that had infected the division because of the inability to train. But more than anything else, the return to Oklahoma, only 100 miles or so from Oklahoma City and Leota, was a much needed remedy for the daily depression that seemed to constantly linger from Gene's unaccounted-for absence. Home was where the heart was and home was where Leota and family were. In November of 1942, Jack threw his worldly belongings into the now-worn-out duffle bag and caught the train west.

CHAPTER IX
MARRYING LEOTA AND WATERTOWN

Forever lost to the ages are the details and circumstances surrounding Jack's proposal of marriage to Leota. These privacies were never discussed with three boys, perhaps if Jack and Leota had borne at least one girl the circumstances may have been revealed. They never were. As we three brothers grew up through the 1950s our own activities and schedules seemed to dominate every waking hour. We played every sport imaginable and participated in all school activities at the insistence of both Jack and Leota. The family focus always was on what we three were doing and, looking back, it was never on Mom and Dad or what they were doing. Hence, their relationship and how it came about that they exchanged vows was never a topic. Besides, as a kid, you never thought about your parents being "in love." The truth is, as boys, we just did not ask. We should have.

Accordingly, for our history these intimacies will not be disturbed by speculation and we must accept that Mom and Dad simply chose to keep "this one" to themselves.

Based on childhood, there are a few observations however that can and must be made. First, without doubt Jack Neville must have approached and asked Mr. Stauffer for his daughter's hand in marriage. This had to be a challenge. He was one tough customer, a veteran of the early-day Oklahoma oil boom with rags-to-riches-to-rags experience. He was watchful of his daughters, especially the youngest one who was pursued by this high-strung student turned soldier. My own recollections of "Grandpa" are to this day clear. Very slight of build with striking gray hair that only grandfathers of the 1950s seemed to have, he was high energy. With raised cheekbones and a square rugged jaw, he was formidable in appearance and demeanor. No doubt Jack had to pay his dues. Indeed, Jack Neville always referred to Sylvester Stauffer as "Mr. Stauffer," even after his death. Mr. Stauffer was a current affairs addict and a tough questioner of one's goals and objectives in life. Even at seven he found a way to provoke your thoughts about one's future at 20. As a father, Jack Neville could cross-examine as well as any courtroom lawyer. While it came naturally, he had to have learned his technique in part from Grandpa Stauffer.

Another observation, perhaps rather obvious, leaps from the pages of time and circumstance. Jack and the 45th Infantry Division would be in combat in a few short months. Gene Neville was reported missing only a few weeks after his initial combat engagement and at the time Jack and Leota had to have been discussing marriage. The harsh reality of it all was that Leota could be a wife one day, a widow the next. If they were married there would be no time to make a home in Oklahoma City, or anywhere else. Once having completed Officers Candidate School, Jack would have to report back to the division at Camp Pine with disembarkation certain before the summer of 1943.

Other facts to be weighed included the reality that Leota did not have a job, and Jack made slightly more than $50 a month. Neither had a house, or apartment. Leota still lived with her parents at 1200 Northwest 42nd Street, and if Jack had not enlisted in September of 1940, he most likely would have continued to stay with Rosa on 22nd Street. Neither had any furniture or the other customary trappings that go with being young and married. They had no investment accounts, no savings accounts, neither had a car, or even the financial means to buy one. While Leota had a closet of clothes at home, Jack's wardrobe was all green and khaki. By today's standards they had nothing, by the measure of the day in 1942 they had very little. Some could argue with reason that the facts of the day did not spell marriage.

Leota's parents, Lottie and Sylvester Stauffer. It had to be difficult to ask Mr. Stauffer, as Jack always referred to him, for permission to marry Leota.

What they did have was each other. As one reflects on their circumstances and stations in life some 60 years later, they were in love and that was all they needed. Perhaps marriage in December of 1942 could be viewed as impulsive, as Jack was sometimes known to be. However, the events of the times evidence the contrary. Jack and Leota were certainly not rushing into a relationship. They had been together since the fall of 1937. They spent considerable time together and, probably at times to their chagrin, with each others' families.

Jack and Leota in November of 1942, about one month before they were married.

Jack and Leota were married on December 5, 1942 and left by train two days after the ceremony to rejoin the Thunderbirds at Camp Pine near Watertown, New York.

They had weathered some tough times–the good-bye for Fort Sill, the attack on Pearl Harbor, the long separation, and sparse and difficult communications from places then considered far away. And, of course, the still uncertain fate of Gene Neville, still thought to be missing in action. The times and events of young people were enough to drive relationships apart, but not for Jack and Leota. There is no evidence that through all of this that they ever saw anyone else, or that they even wanted to. By December of 1942, their relationship had stood the test of difficult times and reached a certain maturity. Their relationship lasted 61 years, their marriage 56.

There is another compelling observation that serves as a lesson for future generations. Jack and Leota never saw the glass half empty, it was always half full. They both never made plans based on the possibility of gloom, doom, or failure. They saw the future in terms of what they could accomplish and do that which was good.

They, of course, had to realize that Jack would most likely sail for Europe in only a short time. They had to know that at best the separation would be long and difficult, and the possibility Jack might never come back. Nonetheless, if Jack were to meet Gene's fate, he would meet it together with Leota and she obviously felt the same. They would make a life together for however short or long it would be.

December 5, 1942, promised more rain and snow in Oklahoma. Even at this late date, the Oklahoma Sooners were to kick it off against Williams and Mary. The Sooners would lose 14-7 and Jack Neville happily missed the game.

On this Saturday, while home on weekend leave, Leota Pearl Stauffer and Jack LeDrew Neville were married at 10:00 a.m. at the Crown Heights Methodist Church in Oklahoma City. The Reverand John R. Abernathy presided and one of Mom's good friends, Bette Gibbons, played the piano. Mom's sister Eleanor was the matron of honor. Jack's brother Baird served as the best man. Leota wore white and Jack his only suit of clothes, his Army green and khaki uniform. After the ceremony, Eleanor had a small reception at her house. With no time for a honeymoon, Jack and Leota left immediately to catch the train for the five-day ride to Watertown, New York, and Camp Pine.

Despite the joy of the occasion, there was sadness to the departure. The day after Jack and Leota left for New York, Rosa Neville's picture appeared on the front page of the Women's Section of the The Sunday Oklahoman with three other women from Oklahoma City whose sons also were missing in action.

Self-described as the "Capital of Vacationland," Watertown was a fun city for young soldiers and couples. In 1942, the main hub of the city was built around an oval, the center of which contained a large spherical monument and a flag pole that reached above the roofs of the city's buildings. A trolley system and buses from the camp made transportation relatively easy. Very few of the soldiers had cars. Live music, bars, and the USO band and the orchestra at Black River just outside of the camp provided plenty of entertainment. Living arrangements for young army marrieds were spartan. Jack had to spend most of the week at the camp doing what training the weather conditions would allow. But the weekends were better than good. Jack and Leota were not the only couple to marry in the winter of 1942. Many others followed suit. Jack's closest friend, Harry Balkum, a star highschool quarterback from Tennessee married his high school sweetheart from Jackson. In December, they too were on their way by train to Watertown from Jackson, Tennessee. Jack and Harry made arrangements for Maxine and Leota to stay together while they were busy at camp. It was not much, but it made due. A small white wood-frame duplex located in a residential area. Jack and Leota's first address as a married couple was 506 Washington Street. They shared the house with Harry and Maxine. Nobody seemed to mind at all.

For a few brief weeks in Watertown, the times of the war seemed to stand still, as if Jack, Harry, and the division had been lost or perhaps misplaced. Not a weekend, and many a week-day night, was missed as the inseparable foursome made the most of their time together. They seemed to find every party. Not a bar or tavern was over looked, and not a single dance night at the USO Center was unattended. While "adult beverages" were officially discouraged,

Leota's picture announcing her engagement to Jack in December, 1942.

the organizers of such events did not mind overlooking the large brown sacks poorly hidden and bulging underneath Jack's overcoat.

There was no such thing as casual dress. The guys wore their Army green and khaki complete with khaki tie with its square knot drawn tightly to the neck and appropriately tucked in at the third button hole. The women always donned their finest. The girls without fail put on the fashion of the day with loose, knee-length dresses, high heels highlighted with eye-catching buckled

This picture of Jack is believed taken just before leaving for Watertown, New York to rejoin the 45th after being married at the Crown Heights Methodist Church in Oklahoma City on December 5, 1941.

ankle-straps, and of course a hat, slighted cocked in one direction or the other. Maxine Balkum had a full length mink coat appropriate for the trip to New York given to her by her mother. She and Leota traded the coat back and forth in exchange for each other's accessories as they paraded the streets of Watertown's party circuit. Jack, Leota, Harry, and Maxine never left the dance floor until the last dance was played and the orchestra was packing up. Jack's favorite step was the Rumba, and Leota was considered the "queen of the Jitterbug." The basic training at Abilene barely allowed Jack and Harry to keep up with these two ladies of the evening. Among Leota's favorite tunes of the day were "Sleepy Lagoon," "Comin In on a Wing and a Prayer," and of course "G.I. Jive." For a brief few weeks it seemed as if time stood still. The Nevilles were dealt a heavy blow on January 18, 1943, at 4:26 p.m. in the afternoon.

Once again, the ugly green four-door Hudson sedan pulled to a slow stop at 523 Northwest 22nd Street in Oklahoma City. Two young men dressed in their army best delivered to Rosa the telegram she prayed daily would never come. The telegram brought the final certainty of Gene's mission over Morlaix.

> "The Secretary of War desires me to express his deep regret that the report now received your son Second Lieutenant Gene P. Neville was killed in action in defense of his country in Western Europe September 25, letter follows."

Sister Helen once again was called to the scene to tend to the family grief. The next day, January 19, 1943 at 12:58 p.m. Helen sent a Western Union telegram to Mrs. Jack L. Neville at 506 Washington Street, Watertown, New York. The words spoke with devastating finality – "Secretary of War Reports Gene killed in action September 26, letter follows, Helen.

It was left to Leota to tell Jack of his brother's death. The news shattered the last remaining innocence of their near perfect few weeks in Watertown.

The Balkums and Nevilles at Camp Pine in January of 1943.

The women who followed their husbands to Camp Pine in January of 1943 became fast friends. Left to right are Eileen Thompson, unknown, Mom, and Maxine Balkum huddling from the cold of up-state New York.

Returning from festivities at the Black River USO at Camp Pine in January of 1943 with Jack, of course, leading the charge.

Somehow Watertown had insulated Jack and Leota from the war-times and the plague of not knowing Gene's fate. Now they knew, on the eve of the division shipping out, that Jack would soon sail for Europe to fight for his country, and his family, knowing that the German's had killed his brother.

Following the telegram of January 18, 1943, was the War Department's letter to Rosa Neville. By this time the transfer of all United States pilots from the Eagle Squadrons to the USAAF had been completed so it fell upon the shoulders of Adjutant General's Office of the War Department of the United States to notify next of kin of United States servicemen killed in action. On January 19, 1943, Major General J. A. Ulic wrote Rosa expressing profound regret of the death of her son. By January of 1943, United States casualties were on the rise as American participation in the war increased. To promptly process the notification of family in cases of casualties, the War Department's letters took on a rather deathly coldness. After expressing "profound regret" in the first paragraph, three paragraphs were devoted to the business of death in war-time, "arrears in pay are payable to legal heirs," "It is not necessary to employ the services of an attorney or claim agent in order to obtain government benefits," "Army Emergency Relief is writing you under separate cover." Sadly, the phrases, as they had to be, were too often repeated during the course of World War II. Rosa probably never got to the last few paragraphs before she put the letter down.

In January of 1943, Rosa Neville, her sons, and daughters had the burden of the uncertainty of Gene's fate lifted from their shoulders only to be replaced by the mystery of exactly how he had met the end.

A POSTSCRIPT

In the fall of 1997, Susan Parker and I traveled to Westminister, Missouri, to watch her son, play football for Westminister College. Westminister College is located in the small beautifully wooded town of Fulton Missouri, east of Kansas City. There in 1952, Winston Churchill delivered one of his most famous speeches that was heard by all of America wherein a post World War II setting then known as the "Cold War," Churchill described the "Iron Curtain of Communism" that was being drawn across the continent of Europe. He warned of a third world war. In tribute to Churchill, the Winston Churchill Museum was created and remains a focal point of this town and college. In the northeast section of the museum is a tribute to those brave American pilots of the Eagle Squadrons who sacrificed their lives in the defense of freedom and country. Gene Neville's name is appropriately displayed on the Honor Roll of the Dead. It is a fitting and emotional tribute.

Gene Neville was one of the favorite "copy boys" employed by The Daily Oklahoman *and the Oklahoma City Times. Two days after Rosa and the family were told of Gene's death, the* Oklahoma City Times, *in a gracious expression and remembrance of Gene devoted its editorial page to their adopted son. No writing could capture with such remarkable eloquence the essence of Gene Parks Neville as did the tribute which appeared in the Wednesday, January 20, 1943 editorial section of the* Oklahoma City Times.

Thirty-three years after Gene's death and almost forty years after those spontaneous sunrise trips to small Adair, Oklahoma, the cemetery now takes on a new meaning with discovery of this history. Even as Jack's hair turned grey, I can recall him staring at Gene's marker on the hill at the Adair Cemetery that stood next to his father's grave and the other Nevilles. No one ever knew the thoughts that raced through Jack's mind standing on that hill in those days as the wind kicked up and the sun cracked the Oklahoma sky. And no one ever asked, not even mom. But Jack was returning home, to an admired and loved brother, to Spavinaw Creek, and to a small unknown piece of America's heartland, to pay tribute. To remember, always to remember.

Boy!

GENE NEVILLE was a very quiet though friendly youth as he worked in this office. Those who knew a little of his life despite his reticence were aware that he as a self-reliant, brave young man, carrying a heavy load, studying hard as he worked. It was a humble, prosaic job.

"Boy!" This, by an old newspaper tradition, is the stentorian cry that booms from the city desk when copy service is needed. Gene Neville, of slight frame, but eager and alert, was always ready for his call.

It seemed a bit strange when this seemingly frail youth suddenly announced that he was quitting his job to ferry monster bombers across the Atlantic. He got into the war before the United States die. He knew what was coming before most Americans.

In fragments, but not with finality, through the thick curtain of censorship, has filtered the news that Gene Neville, after transferring from R. A. F. to the American flying force in Britain, was killed in action.

Somewhere—perhaps no one knows—perhaps in gray, grim loneliness miles above the North Sea, possibly in the infernal flak of German ground batteries, he gave his life for the rest of us, as quietly as when he carried copy and tended the pneumatic tubes.

Like many copy-boys, he dreamed of being a reporter, to be sent out on great business, or perhaps an editor. But while we who stay at home are obscurely safe, he was called to do an assignment that only the greatest men know, and their wisdom is written on copy-sheets that are seen only by immortal men. "Boy!" This time the summons is infinitely tender, for the Editor at the Great Desk has given him the greatest accolade that a man can get. No knight of ancient time ever achieved a more magnificent mission. Gene Neville has been promoted far above any of us earthlings, and has been told: "Greater love hath no man than that he give his life for a friend." His friend is the United States of America.

January 20, 1943 editorial section of the *Oklahoma City Times*

CHAPTER X
CAMPS PINE, PICKETT AND PATRICK HENRY, AND GOODBYE

The story of the division at Camp Pine, New York is unique to its history, and to say the least unusual. Initially, the small town of Watertown did everything they could to welcome the soldiers of the 45th. On November 12, 1942, the division's arrival was promoted in the press as if it were a triumph of sorts. The local citizenry sponsored many a welcome dance. Top notch entertainment was brought to town. Crowd favorite Harpo Marx brought the house down one evening at the Black River USO, former members of the Xavier Cougot band provided the hottest music of the day, and the USO went to extraordinary lengths to broadcast the Army-Navy football game. And on Christmas day, soldiers were invited to the homes of the locals for Christmas dinner. In its way, the division attempted to reciprocate the town's generosity. The Thunderbird's Southwest Hill Billy Band and Forty-Fifth Indian Dancers formed the Thunderbird Frolics playing to packed houses at Carthage High School, and other schools across town. However, the love affair between town and the division's soldiers did not last long as many of the soldiers turned the quiet little Watertown into a 1940's version of Dodge City and the Gunfight at the OK Corral.

Five days after the division's encampment at Camp Pine, the local constabulary arrested 33 soldiers embroiled in a brawl on the public square in the middle of town. One soldier shot and killed another with his .45 smuggled off base and there were multiple stabbings in the skirmish. This incident was enough to cause the Military Police and the local police department to join forces. From now on, an MP would ride with two police officers in every squad car to help keep the peace. Watertown taxi cabs became particularly vulnerable. Taxi cab drivers and liquor stores were robbed, one soldier was killed when he fell out of the fourth floor window of the Hotel Woodruff and broke his neck. Another jumped off the River Street Bridge and into the Black River. Even the locals were put at risk by giving soldiers a ride from camp to town as their cars were stolen.

Only a few weeks after their arrival, approximately seven of the division's finest walked into a local favorite Washington Street restaurant and announced that they were going to "tear the place apart." Obviously an alcohol-related event, the restaurant's owner, a former professional football player, accommodated the soldiers' request and a brawl broke out. It took the town's entire police force to break it up.

The Christmas season brought no joy to law enforcement. At Gene's Tavern on December 8, 1942, police searched in vain for a soldier who had bitten the ear off another soldier; a private's wife, depressed that her man was going to war, drank a bottle of poison believing that surely he would now have to stay at home with her. She died. And, to top it off, at 2:00 a.m. Christmas morning, using a Thompson sub-machine gun, two soldiers commandeered a taxi cab for a joy ride all over the county before finally being apprehended. In all, by year-end December, 119 soldiers were arrested on charges ranging from intoxication to bank robbery to murder. During the month of December alone, the police and MPs quelled 172 disturbances, more than five per day.

With remarkable understatement, the Watertown Daily Times editorial page reported that "Several things have happened in Watertown over the last few weeks that were too serious to be dismissed as unfortunate incidents."

On December 31, 1942, the army insisted that General Middleton try to patch things up with the town. Invited to the Chamber of Commerce dinner by the Black River Dinner Club, Middleton attempted to apologize. "There has been some unfavorable publicity, but the men were trained with a fighting spirit, and incidents were expected." It did not go over well.

Shortly after January 19, 1943, the 45th Infantry Division received orders to make its second major move within a four-month period. This time, the division was moving to Camp Pickett, Virginia. Encampment to a southern city near the sea port navy base of Newport News where Operation Torch departed was an unmistakable signal. The division would be going overseas and relatively soon. For the people of Watertown, it was "good riddance" to the unruly boys of the 45th. Cooped up in the cold winter of northern New York, the division had liberated every beer keg and whiskey bottle within a two-county perimeter. As Whitlock reported in *The Rock of Anzio*, "they were not shy about settling an argument with fists, chairs or beer bottles" and "they apparently had forgotten the manners that had impressed the locals in Abilene."

Law enforcement and citizens alike would cheer the departure. At Lawton, Oklahoma and Abilene, Texas, the 45th departed with great ceremony, pomp, and circumstance. Bands played, flags flew, troops marched down the street to the citizens waving good-bye and yelling "good-luck," some with tears rolling down their cheeks. But at Camp Pine, New York, in mid-January of 1943, there was no fanfare, there was no parade, the division quietly slipped out of town.

It did not take long for Jack and Leota to pack for the three-day trip to Virginia. A couple of suit cases and duffle bags were all it took as Jack and Leota and Harry and Maxine boarded the train in Watertown for the trip to Blackstone, Virginia, near Camp Pickett. The stay at Camp Pickett was unlike

After Camp Pine, the division was staged at Camp Pickett, Virginia in May of 1943.This picture was taken of Jack and Leota in Crewe, Virginia where Leota and the other wives rented an apartment.

that of Camp Pine. At Camp Pickett there was no on-post housing. Jack and Harry were required to remain on post, at least through the week. Maxine and Leota were left to find their own housing along with the hundreds of other wives who followed their husbands for the last good-bye. The wives were left to search for cheap hotels, boarding houses, or a single-room rental. The town of Crewe, Virginia, 10 miles northwest of Camp Pickett was the closest Leota and Maxine could get. There they found a boarding house and were able to rent a room for the both of them. Sadly, they knew they would not be there long, but at least they were close to Jack and Harry.

There was no uncertainty about the training routine at Camp Pickett. It took on a brutal intensity designed to ready the division for attack against the Germans. Mountain combat training in the Blue Ridge Mountains was exhausting and little rest was given before the division once again renewed its amphibious landing exercises on the beaches of Virginia's Solomon Islands. At Camp Pickett, their was little time for the Rumba or the Jitterbug, and now Jack and Leota were grateful for those days and nights at the Black River USO in Watertown.

At Camp Pickett the rumors flew fast and furious. The division knew they were only 100 miles from the Norfolk Naval Station, and therefore departure was imminent.

Troy Middleton, like William Key, was an out-front leader. The men of the division were used to seeing Middleton mingle in their ranks. However, in April of 1942, Middleton became noticeably absent. Unknown to Jack and the division was that General Middleton and his staff had been summoned to Morocco in North Africa to meet with General George S. Patton. In Morocco, General Patton laid out the plan for the invasion of Sicily in July of 1943. It would be known as "Operation Husky."

Patton's choice to spearhead the first United States attack into the European Theatre of operations was the 45th Infantry Division Thunderbirds. Middleton gave the order to prepare for overseas shipment.

With Middleton's order, the division swung into a frantic pace, still with some lingering doubt as to the destination. The heavy bet however was on Europe and what little uncertainty existed was put to rest when General George C. Marshall, Army Chief of Staff, himself, told the 45th's officer corps at Camp Pickett:

> "You are going to make an amphibious landing in Europe. Your job and that of the few divisions who will land with you is to keep the enemy busy and occupied while we prepare a huge American Army."

It did not take long for Jack and Harry to ferret the destination out of Colonel Arnote and Captain Scott, but not even they knew exactly where the division would put its foot ashore. In early May of 1943, Jack broke the news to Leota. It was Europe, and the good-bye was close at hand.

By mid-May, the 45th's direction was made firm and clear. On May 25, 1943, the division would move approximately 100 miles to the east to Camp Patrick Henry, very close to the naval base at Norfolk, Virginia. On May 24, 1943, all civilian personnel, wives, friends, family, children, and lovers would say their final good-byes to the men of the 45th Infantry Division.

Words do little to tell of the emotional drama that must have unfolded on May 24, 1943, at Camp Pickett, Virginia. Jack and Leota had been together since September of 1937. In the last few years they had shared several tough good-byes. But this was different. There was no guarantee of when, or if, they would ever see each other, be with each other, or speak with each other again. The war would make communication difficult and uncertain. Jack would be half a world away on the continent of Europe.

Gene Neville had lasted only a few months in the fire of the combat zone.

In January of 1943, the 45th received orders to move to Camp Pickett, Virginia to ready for overseas deployment from Newport News. The accommodations were not the best as the division set up its "field mess" tents and equipment.

What made it likely that Jack would survive any longer? The tears had to flow, and the final embrace long, with eyes locked standing on the edge of Camp Pickett. In these terrible circumstances, with America's youth about to embark on the greatest crusade the free world had ever seen, Leota and Jack's thoughts had to be of only each other on this Virginia spring day. You could not say enough "I love you," "I'll think of you each day," "write as often as possible," "I'll miss you," "take care of yourself," "keep your head down," or "stay away from the European babes." The phrases had to have been repeated over and over. On the afternoon of May 24, 1942, Leota kissed Jack good-bye at Camp Pickett. The next embrace would not be for two years. Without question, Jack Neville promised Leota that he would be back, he would somehow make it through.

And, he did.

Testament to the emotion of the day is Jack's handwritten diary of an unknown date. The first paragraph spills out his feelings.

> "On May 24, 1943, my wife kissed me good-bye at Camp Pickett, Virginia with both of us knowing that it would be sometime before we saw each other again. I must say that the departure from my wife was hard to take as we had been married only 6 months and so far lived the perfect life in the way of matrimony. Even though I feel like that I still couldn't feel too sorrowful. There was lots of excitement in my blood as I know the adventures and experiences which lay before me were to be that of excitement and all that goes with war."

For Leota, she and Maxine Balkum caught the train for the long ride back home. First through Tennessee and to Maxine's family, and then on to Oklahoma City and the Union Station where Mr. Stauffer met Leota. Through the war, Leota would stay with her parents on 42nd Street. She and Maxine had become genuine friends in the cold of New York. They had the common bond of Jack and Harry. Throughout the next two years, they would regularly correspond with each other, and through the summer each would visit the other.

In November of 1942, the government had announced an operational expansion at the Tinker Air Depot and surrounding area. Almost 30,000 women were expected to join the labor force in Oklahoma City alone with upwards of 18,000 women to be hired at the Douglas Plant just outside Tinker in Midwest City. Leota took her place among the women at the Douglas Plant. She was hired as a secretary in one of the production sections of the plant that assembled the famous C-47 transport aircraft. With the new job and living with her parents, Leota began the long and agonizing vigil of the war-time fear and uncertainty of the homeland, never knowing and always wondering. At least she would be at the Douglas Plant when the postman delivered the mail.

Three days after Leota left, May 28, 1943, Jack and the 45th Infantry Division boarded trains to Camp Patrick Henry, located only a few miles from the giant Naval Base at Norfolk. Once at Camp Henry, the next few days consisted of "hurry up and wait." Final physical examinations, clothing checks, and equipment checks were the routine for the next few days as Jack and Harry watched a massive armada assemble off the Virginia coast.

The early morning of June 4, 1943 was it. The division formed for the last time on United States soil, and loaded the convoy trucks for the point of embarkation. For Jack, the precise location of his departure was the Hampton Roads Port of Embarkation, Newport News, Virginia. As the trucks pulled to the pier for off-loading, the huge Army Band was in formation and playing at such a decibel level it was difficult to hear. Jack's journal recorded the moment:

> "...As we pulled in the pier there was a band playing "Over There" and "It's A Long Way to Tipporary." At that time, I began to realize all that lay in front of me. My throat kinda got clogged up and I wasn't the only one you could see the same expressions on all faces of the soldiers."

The division was "combat loaded" over the day onto the huge troop transport ship the USS Leonard Wood. The phrase combat loaded is a term of art meaning that the men, equipment, and vehicles were arranged on board in the most effective order to disembark on a hostile shore. The Headquarters Battery of Division Artillery was split in half. Jack and Harry were assigned to the forward echelon along with infantry troops of the 179th who were part of a battalion landing team. Loaded in this manner, Jack would be one of the first off the ship once they hit the landing area. Jack was billeted below decks with mostly infantry troops as each scrambled for beds or hammocks stacked four to six high. Your nose almost touched the bottom of the bunk on top of you. To say the least, it was miserably crowded.

In the early morning of June 5, 1943, the USS Leonard Wood and Oklahoma's best of the 45th Infantry Division pushed away from the pier at Hampton Roads, Newport News, Virginia. For many, it would be the last time they saw the United States. For Jack, he would not return for two years.

At those raucous Fourth of July family parties on 57th Street, in Tulsa, every patriotic song known to man was played and played over the speakers in the all-day feast. All of George M. Cohan's songs were re-spun until you found yourself repeatedly mumbling the verses as you went for your third or fourth batch of ribs, beans, and beer. The songs most often played again and again were "Over-There" and "It's a Long Way to Tipporary," the same two songs that the United States Army Band played as Jack boarded the USS Leonard Wood on June 4, 1943. Seemingly always out of place in the house on 57th street was a beautifully framed, but a rather ordinary looking poster of troops marching and a band playing. I remember it hanging in the hallways of every house we ever lived in. The title to the poster is only now significant – "It's a Long Way to Tipporary" was scripted at the very top of the poster. Two slight and subtle hints of Jack and Leota's war years were there before our very eyes, and no one seized upon the significance of the poster or the song. We all were too busy, and Jack and Leota never spoke of it.

CHAPTER XI
THE WAR TO NORTH AFRICA

When the USS Leonard Wood pushed away from the pier at the Hampton Roads Port of Embarkation, the 45th Infantry Division was a formidable fighting force. The division was self- sufficient from beans to bullets. Every soldier was trained to do a job and their tasks were interlocked, each dependent on the other. The Infantry Regiments could fight, but not without ammunition. Someone had to make sure the boys up front had the ammunition. These young men had to eat, if they were going to fight the Germans, they would need food in their bellies. Someone had to make sure that at the end of a long day or night no one went hungry. The list of such examples is endless, but for it to work every man in the division had to pull together.

In 1943, a United States Army Infantry Division was comprised of approximately 14,253 men under the command of a major general. Division Headquarters was comprised of approximately 140 men and Headquarters Company with 110 men. These units were responsible for the planning and execution of the division's mission and operations. The Military Police Platoon with 73 men generally had the responsibility to keep the trucks, jeeps, and cargo carriers moving in the right direction. With approximately 700 trucks in the division, traffic could be a problem. And, of course, the MPs were charged with the duty of keeping the peace among the division population. The Ordinance and Light Maintenance Company was made up of 147 men to maintain possession of weapons and ammunition. The division had to have a "repair crew" to fix equipment that eventually broke down. The division's Quartermaster Company was responsible for, among other things, all supplies and uniforms. Soldiers had to have boots, leggings, canteens, shirts, blankets, trousers, and food. It took 193 men to handle these tasks.

The Signal Company, made up of 226 soldiers, had the responsibility for all communications with the division. Radios, telegrams, and walkie-talkies all were essential to engaging the enemy. Every unit in the division, down to the smallest level, had to be able to communicate with each other. The Calvary Reconnaissance Troop, mechanized was made up of 156 soldiers. Sometimes referred to as the guys in the "up-front," this unit had the dangerous responsibility of reconnoitering the areas forward of the division's movement. They would observe and report the location of the enemy, if found, and "recon" the terrain forward and around the division's line of march. The Engineering Battalion was populated with 647 men with varied tasks. The division would have to cross rivers whose bridges had been blown up or did not exist; roads would have to be carved out of the countryside; mine fields would have to be dealt with; and explosives would have to be laid. The division had its own unit of doctors, nurses, and corpsmen trained to care for the wounded or dying. The Division's Medical Battalion was made up of 465 people.

The 45th Infantry Division consisted of three separate infantry regiments whose main responsibility was to assault, capture, or kill the enemy. Assigned to the three infantry regiments were 3,118 men who were organized into battalions, companies, platoons, and squads; the numbers of which varied from time to time. The infantry regiments were assigned objectives and thereafter ordered to "take-it." In accomplishing their tasks there were many tactics and strategies utilized, but generally the regiments and units would advance by "leap-frogging" each other. The infantry regiments were to directly and aggressively engage the enemy troops. By leap-frogging, the enemy could be constantly and continually attacked with no one unit having to sustain the sole burden of continuous advance. This tactic required extensive training, coordination, and communication supported by every unit in the division.

The next most populous unit was Jack's Division Artillery made up of 2,316 men. The Division Artillery was broken into four different units, Headquarters, Headquarters Battery, three battalions of 105mm Howitzers, and one battalion of 155mm Howitzer. Division Artillery was commanded by Brigadier General Ray McClain. Jack was specifically assigned as a master sergeant in the headquarters, Headquarters Battery to the S-3 staff of Colonel Walter Arnote. The S-3 section was responsible for the plans, operations, and training of the Division Artillery. There were 10 master sergeants in Division Artillery, two of which were assigned to the Headquarters Battery. Jack was one of the two.

By necessity, Division Artillery was motorized so Jack in many instances had the questionable luxury of being able to ride. With the Luftwaffe still active through much of 1945, trucks and convoys were more of a target liability than a corporate benefit. Division Artillery was stocked with an incredible array of equipment and firepower. Thirty-six 105mm Howitzers and 12 155mm Howitzers were the major source of the artillery's firepower. These big guns were mounted on wheels and usually towed by trucks to their firing locations, thus giving maximum flexibility and mobility to the artillery's mission. They could move when they needed to move with relative speed. The two mainstays of the artillery packed a powerful punch. The approximate range of the smaller 105mm Howitzer was approximately 12,000 yards. As for the larger 155mm

Howitzer, the approximate maximum effective range was 16,000 yards. Each shell weighed 95 pounds. The 155mm required a crew of 14. If you were within 50 yards of an exploding shell fired by one of these guns you were killed or seriously wounded. It took 60 ammunition trucks to service the division's guns, and an incredible 434 trucks of various sizes to move the remaining men and material of the Division Artillery from place to place. Despite the use of some 700 trucks, the division had only one wrecker.

Division Artillery also had 10 airplanes at its disposal for forward observation purposes. These planes were broken down for transport and then reassembled once an airstrip had been built or captured. The soldiers of the artillery were not without the means to protect themselves in the field. The division had 1,682 .30-caliber M-1 rifles, 79 .50 caliber machine guns, 267 .45 automatic pistols and 166 rocket launchers. Last but not least, artillery had its own assigned medical detachment consisting of 53 personnel and two chaplains.

The primary mission of the artillery was to support the infantry regiments in their advance against the enemy, "to move, to shoot, to communicate . . . responsible for delivering fire on the target at the time and in the amount necessary." The motto of Division Artillery appropriately characterized the persona of its men as "Semper Anticus," meaning "Always In Front."

The soldiers of the Infantry Regiments were the best-equipped fighting units in the history of modern warfare. At their disposal were 5,262 rifles, nearly two for every man in the regiment, 90 .30 caliber machine guns, 235 .50 caliber machine guns, the most powerful machine gun in the world, 14 assault boats, and an incredible number of trucks and transports. The spiritual support for the 45th Infantry Division came from 37 Chaplains.

Without doubt, the "fighting" units of the division were the three Infantry Regiments and Jack's Division Artillery. In support of the 3,118 soldiers in the field who would walk, crawl, fight, sleep in inclimate conditions, and suffer the oppressive heat were almost 12,000 men. For every single soldier in the Infantry Regiments and the Division Artillery, three soldiers were there to provide the necessary support for their effort to take the fight to the Germans.

The 45th Infantry Division also had a band. Thirteen men made up the division band; they also carried rifles. At Salerno, even the drummers would be in the fight.

The task of identifying with some degree of specificity the strength, material, and firepower of the 45th Infantry Division is necessary to emphasize the degree of difficulty that had to exist in moving the division from place to place. Getting on the ship and getting off the ship was a monumental task. Organization to fight once off the ship was an almost greater feat.

It was rather an inauspicious beginning for the 45th and the USS Leonard Wood as they moved away from the pier at the Hampton Roads point of embarkation. Once under way, the big transport steered her way into the

Chesapeake Bay, idled to a stop, and dropped anchor. There was, of course, no air-conditioning below decks and the summer heat baked the division into misery. The only relief was on deck when hopefully an Atlantic breeze would provide the necessary relief to the sweat and smell of cramped quarters. The heat and boredom of sitting in the Chesapeake Bay would last three full days. Jack remembered "There we lay 'til June 8 sweating and cursing the heat for all we were worth."

As the hours and days crept by, Jack spent as much time on deck as possible. So did everybody else. On June 6 and 7 the boredom was broken with the sight of other transports, cruisers, and destroyers arriving at the rendezvous point. Jack and Harry stood on the ships rail watching as a vast armada slowly came together in the Chesapeake Bay. By June 8, an incredible array of ships massed in the Chesapeake Bay awaiting the signal to weigh anchor and steam into the Atlantic.

At 7:30 a.m. the order was given, and the convoy known as "Cent Force" made its way into the Atlantic Ocean with the men still not knowing their ultimate destination. Jack put the count of ships at 40 transports, 14 destroyers, and four cruisers. What Jack did not know as they sailed was that elements of the 1st and 3rd Infantry Divisions also were part of the Cent Force convoy.

The sight of such a convoy moving into the Atlantic Ocean all aligned in formation was excitement enough, but the anxiety rose to a different level when the USS Leonard Wood's naval personnel began instructions on what to do if the convoy was attacked by German submarines. The most depressing instructional advice was how to abandon ship "in an orderly fashion" if hit by a torpedo. The combination of heat, cramped living conditions, and fear of submarine attack kept most of the men top side a good part of the trip. Jack was no exception. By June of 1943, the United States Navy was achieving substantial success in repelling the threat of the German submarine wolf packs. However, the threat of submarine attack still was real. Cent Force was moving far to the south of the more-traveled routes. Jack grabbed the ship's rails and marveled in amazement at the site of the destroyer escorts racing past the lumbering transport ship in defense of the convoy. The destroyer escorts were not the division's only line of defense. Most of the heavy cruisers with their big guns pointed outward or forward of the convoy's path also were also mounted with aircraft. As the destroyer sped by, the cruisers would launch their anti-submarine aircraft to patrol the waters on all four sides of the giant group of ships. Once completing their patrols, the cruisers would pause to retrieve their aircraft from the Atlantic waters only to have the process repeated over and over again. It was quite a site for Jack and the boys, most of whom had never been on such a vast expanse of water where land could not be seen in any direction; however, Jack's concerns of submarine attack were not altogether put at rest. He recorded "The cruisers carried planes for anti-subs and we all felt reasonably safe."

After two days at sea, and with the novelty of the Navy's anti-submarine efforts wearing off, the ship's broadcasting system announced the destination of the convoy. At sea, Jack learned for the first time that the USS Leonard Wood was streaming as fast as possible for the northern coast of North Africa. With the announcement of the destination, and the division somewhat squared away for ocean travel, General McClain put in place required physical training aboard ship–pull-ups, sit ups, running in place, and push-ups. Some of the men would rather have experienced the unpleasantness of sea sickness than face McClain's ship board PT regimen. One thing was for sure, the 45th Division's leaders were not going to let the men get soft. The division also was constantly busy cleaning and checking their equipment and weapons. Perhaps some of this routine was intended to relieve the boredom of long days on the ocean, but ship board training also sent another signal–with each passing hour they were getting closer to the fight.

There were ship-board activities designed to provide tension relief from the trip. The chow line was not too bad and the navy attempted to provide a nightly movie. Not exactly a luxury cruise, the USS Leonard Wood rather quickly became a floating "crap game." Jack always fancied himself quite skilled at the art of shooting craps, a skill he learned aboard "the Wood." Jack claimed he never lost. Poker games and even roulette also were easy ways to lose your money while at sea. Many of the men did not seem to care if they lost what money they had. After all, where they were going, you could not spend it anyway.

At times, the entire ship took on an atmosphere of the Las Vegas strip. Absent, however, were the bright lights and dancing girls. Much of the time only a light bulb hung from the ceiling deck of the ship as someone's bunk served as the "gaming" table.

Maintaining personnel hygiene was a serious challenge. On board the USS Leonard Wood there was no such thing as privacy. When you had to "go," you generally were joined by a cast of thousands. Toilet paper quickly became a valuable commodity. A change of clothes and underwear were a luxury. The June weather allowed one to sleep in their "wear." There was no closet or clothes rack from which to pick your shirt or trousers, rather you dug down into your duffle bag when your own smell became too much to tolerate. The close quarters created sights and smells that some soldiers complained had to be worse than war itself, especially when some one got seasick below decks.

There were only so many times you could clean your weapon and it did not take long to conclude that the physical training and "equipment checks" were more designed to save the division from boredom once the convoy was at sea. But despite the efforts of command to keep the crew busy, and despite that constant chatter that drove the poker games and the craps table, there were many times when the wind on the sea blew lonely. Jack was never one to sit, and good money would bet that on the voyage to North Africa he and Harry Balkum wore out the ship's decks. There's no telling how many times Jack and

Harry paraded through the decks of the giant ship. After a full week at sea there was no land in any direction, only a constant horizon of ocean broken by the sunrise, sunsets, and the ships in the convoy. But in those quiet moments of thought that had to exist, Jack continued to inventory his life. He of course had not spoken with Leota since May 24, and circumstances made it impossible to receive or send mail. One could certainly write letters home, but there was no real chance of mailing them until they got to Africa. There was no "air-mail" that moved westward as the convoy continued to chug eastward. There was no telephone to call home. As difficult as it was at times, Jack focused his mental energies away from Gene's death. It did no good to contemplate dying, but the thought of it crept into his thoughts during those times of solitude. Equally unproductive were thoughts of the more material possessions of life. There was no house, savings accounts, checking accounts, and investment portfolios were unheard of. He had no job to go back to when, or if, he returned from war.

At times, those old Sibley stoves at Fort Sill were not so bad after all, and most of the men remembered the good times of training, like the night-time movements of the division in Louisiana maneuvers that so infuriated the so-called professional soldiers. Trickery had won the day. It may have been all misery then, but now at sea those times past were a source of pride and more often comedic relief. Even the unbearable cold of Camp Pine occasioned with the big dance band sounds of the Black River USO were events the men longed to repeat. And as Jack had to reflect, six months was too short of a time to be married before going off to war, but from his brief journal of events it is evident that those six months were the best of his young life. There were 14,000 psychologists in the Cent Force convoy, very few with any education past high school. Events were driving the men together, and if you got down someone was there to bring you back up. Extending deference to the work of a noted historian Steve Ambrose, the citizen soldiers of the 45th Infantry Division were becoming a band of brothers.

Overall, the trip across the Atlantic Ocean was uneventful, with seas and weather relatively calm. On the morning of June 21, 1943, land surfaced on the ocean horizon for the first time in 13 days in the open sea. As recorded in his journal, it was "the best sight . . . seen in many days." At approximately noon on the 21st, the Straits of Gibralter came into view and by 2:15 p.m. Cent Force was sailing into the Mediterranean Sea. Jack and the men of the division hung on the rails of the ship as the convoy passed the Great Rock. Most of them had never seen the Rock of Gibralter, and only a few had seen pictures of the mammoth wonder.

By May of 1943, the Alliers had run Rommel's vaunted "Africa Korps" out of North Africa. Cent Force would land in North Africa unopposed in friendly hands. On June 22, 1943, the USS Leonard Wood and the Cent Force convoy dropped anchor at 3:00 p.m. at Mers-el-Kebir, just off the coast of the port city of Oran, Algeria.

Excitement ran rampant through the ship as the division neared anchor. After almost two weeks at sea the men felt like caged animals ready for release. Some even thought that two feet on the ground was better than Christmas. As the USS Leonard Wood readied for disembarkation, Jack and the other Division Artillery master sergeants were summoned to a meeting with Colonel Arnote, Captain Chapman, and to Jack's surprise, General Ray McClain himself. In vague, almost ambiguous terms, McClain explained that the division was only a few days away from engaging the enemy by way of amphibious assault. He did not identify the objective. McClain related to Jack and the other sergeants of the Division Artillery that the division would shake off their sea legs for a couple of days on the beach of Oran, then resume vigorous training for approximately two weeks before once again forming up the Cent Force convoy for the attack on the Germans. Anxious to get ashore, Jack was both shocked and surprised to be told that he would not be going ashore. He, and two other master sergeants of Division Artillery would remain on board "to work on the next operation." While initially disappointed that after 13 days at sea he would remain parked on the USS Leonard Wood, Jack recorded that he "felt greatly honored by being picked to work on the plans."

Jack's writing does not identify with exact specificity the work he performed on board ship. It may be assumed that he intentionally failed to record the specifics of his efforts for security reasons. The entire division knew they would hit the Germans soon, but the particulars of it all were successfully kept shrouded

Jack and the men of Division Artillery boarded the troop ship USS Leonard Wood in May of 1943 for the trip to North Africa. Here, the "Wood" is anchored at Oran, just prior to the invasion of Sicily.

in secrecy. Keeping "the planners" on board for the next few days would ensure the secrecy of the objective for at least the near term. For the next two days Jack and others poured over a number of maps provided by Arnote. Except for towns and roads, the maps were not identified by country, and the small towns depicted on the maps were not known or even pronounceable. However, after a full day and a half, Jack was finally able to "definitely know where we were going to invade." The 45th Infantry Division would unload on the southern coast of Sicily in July. On June 25, 1943, Jack was admitted to the conference for planning the invasion of Sicily. Broad strategy decisions involving the movement of divisions and armies were not left to master sergeants. However, the fact that Jack was instructed to review maps of Sicily for almost two days coupled with the fact that he was in Col. Arnote's S-3 section of Division Artillery lead to some reasonable conclusions as to the tasks he performed in June of 1943 while on board the Leonard Wood.

Once the infantry troops were ashore and the beachhead secure, the Division Artillery pieces, principally 105mm and 155mm Howitzers, would be put ashore to support the inland advance of the foot soldiers. In order to accomplish this, division and battalion command posts would have to be established, fields of fire, and area responsibilities would have to be plotted and assigned to keep the artillery going. Logistical plans and routes would have to be charted. The S-3 section, responsible for plans and operations, would have to learn the road network inland from the beachhead, distance to objectives, and topography of land in order to plan the artillery's support of the 45th's three infantry regiments. Along with aerial photographs, the only other tool available were maps. Working knowledge of maps and photographs were the type of detail left to the master sergeants of Division Artillery.

While anxious to get ashore, it was just as well for Jack that he was ordered to remain aboard the Leonard Wood. The 45th's entry into Oran was not exactly spectacular. The division was instructed that disembarking the ships would take the form of a practice amphibious landing at night no less. Only one infantry regiment hit the correct beach, and the other two missed the mark by 12 miles due to inexperienced navy coxswains.

Happy to be on land quickly turned into vocal displeasure punctuated by four letter expletives. While Jack remained onboard, the rest of the division set up camp in an area near the city of Oran. After a few days, many of the men wished they were back onboard the Leonard Wood. It was not exactly the Oran Hilton. Setting up their two-man pup tents in the barren fields of sand and dirt was no beach vacation. Conditions worsened as an army of desert lizards, sand chiggers, and other local snakes and vermin never seen by Oklahomans seemed to invade the camp. The lesser evil of the Oran area were the constant appearance of the Arab traders seeking "to do business" with the new American faces. In many instances it was a spectacle now worthy of television sport–the

Cherokee, Choctaw and Seminole Indians negotiating with the Arabs. It had to be quite a site.

Nonetheless, while bivauced in Oran, the Thunderbirds shook off the effects of a two-week trip at sea, cleaned the sand out of their weapons and uniforms, and wrote letters home. Then there was the never ending physical training. How many more push-ups and sit-ups would they have to do before firing the first shots at the Hun? And the constantly asked question, "where and when would they attack?"

On June 27, 1943, General George S. Patton, now a three-star general, assembled the troops of the 45th in their desert camp. Patton explained that the division would soon attack the Germans and they needed to be ready. The Thunderbirds were told they needed to "lock and load" and "saddle up." This was no exercise, no drill. This was the real thing, they were going to kill the Germans and no quarter should be given. Patton's presence was inspirational, but the objectives and destination remained a secret.

The United States Army stood on the edge of "Operation Husky," the invasion of Sicily, and the 45th Infantry Division would lead the attack.

By June of 1943, the Port of Algiers, shown here, had become a massive staging area for the attack into Southern Europe.

CHAPTER XII
THE INVASION OF SICILY OPERATION HUSKY

As Jack and the men of the 45th prepared to depart Camp Pine in Watertown, New York, the major allied war leaders were meeting in North Africa. On January 14, 1943, Roosevelt, Stalin, and Churchill met at the historical Casablanca Conference in Morocco. With America only in the war for a little more than a year and having cleaned the Axis out of much of North Africa, the stage was set to launch another attack on the Germans in the "soft under belly" of Europe. No one from the 45th ever would believe that the under belly of Europe was soft. At the Casablanca Conference, Stalin and Churchill argued for the United States to continue to press the attack in the south, thus diverting and relieving the British and Russians from German pressure in the north and in the east. Convinced that a second, or third front was the best move, the more tactical question remained–where to hit the Germans next? At the conference, the three world leaders selected Sicily as the next target of opportunity.

The island of Sicily sits off the southern coast of Italy. As Whitlock points out, it was no stranger to warfare since the days of the Greeks and Romans fought their way across the volcanic island. Just off the "boot" of Italy, Sicily is the approximate size of Vermont, with its most significant landmark being the 10,000-foot Mount Etna in the northeast corner of the island. Rugged mountains cut across the center of the island and the road network was considered poor. The roadways that bordered the coastline were generally passable and provided the easiest routes of march and convoy. However, the center of the island was difficult to traverse, in many instances only donkey trails allowed access over or through parts of the mountains. The strategic value of Sicily lay in its location. Just off the southern tip of Italy, the island provided a variety of avenues of attack. In the northeast, the Strait of Messina separated Sicily from Italy by approximately 10 miles, and the northern coast of Sicily and the Tyrrhenia Sea provided avenues of attack up the entire west coast. Additionally, the taking of Sicily would allow the allies to move their aircraft, especially their fighters and bombers, into key positions that allowed more extensive use of air power. Mission time could be shortened considerably, and targets reached more quickly. Sicily was a prize worth taking.

The military historians who have studied the invasion of Sicily agree that it was the greatest seaborne assault of World War II. Launching the attack would be nine Allied Divisions consisting of 115,000 British and 66,000 American troops. The assault would stretch across a 100-mile stretch of beach. The invasion fleet itself consisted of six battleships, 15 cruisers, 128 destroyers. All toll, there were 2,760 ships involved in the attack along with 4,000 aircraft. It was a massive array of sea, land, and air power.

The fundamental plan of attack was as follows. The British 8th Army, under the command of General Bernard Montgomery, would land along the coast road near Syracuse in the south and east of the island. Montgomery's army was made up of the 5th, 78th, 50th, 51st and 1st Canadian divisions. The United States 7th Army, under the command of General George S. Patton would hit the beaches between Licata and Scoglitti to Montgomery's west. Patton's Army consisted of the 3rd Infantry Division, the 1st Infantry Division also known as the "Big Red One," and the citizen soldiers from Colorado, New Mexico,

In July of 1943, the Thunderbirds spearheaded the Allied attack into Sicily. At home, Mom got the word through *The Daily Oklahoman* headline "45th Swings Sicily Knock-Out."

Left to right, General Troy Middleton, Commanding General of the 45th Infantry Division, General Owen Bradley and General George S. Patton, Commanding General of 7th Army, in Sicily during the Summer of 1943.

Texas, and Oklahoma. Montgomery would attack and seize Syracuse and move up the coast road north and east to Messina. Patton would advance relatively parallel to Montgomery and protect the British flank. The Allied Commander of both the British 8th and United States 7th was General Dwight D. Eisenhower. It was a plan that would rather quickly fall apart with Patton racing northward for the coastline highway and Montgomery slugging his way eastward, both with huge ego's attempting to first capture the City of Messina.

As for the 45th Infantry Division, it was given the key mission of the operation to the west of Montgomery. The battle order called for the division to capture two key airfields at Biscari and Comiso approximately 12 miles inland of the beach. The airfields would provide safe haven to allied bombers and fighters who would then have the range and capability to attack most anywhere in Italy. The division would land south of the airfields near Scoglitti and advance inland to the airfields. The 1st Infantry Division would cover the 45th's advance on the left flank landing at Gela and the 3rd Infantry Division would go ashore to the left of the 1st at Licata and proceed inland. Within the 45th itself, the 157th Infantry Regiment would form the southern border of the advance, flanked to the left by the 179th Infantry Regiment, who in turn was flanked to the left by the 180th Infantry Regiment. Packed into an approximate 60-mile stretch of beach on the southern coast of Sicily were 66,000

American Troops, most of whom were not more than 20 years old. The 45th line of march would take them directly into the teeth of the veteran and battle-hardened elite German troops of the Herman Goering Panzer Division who occupied the southern one-third of the island. The young men of the 45th would lead the attack against Germany's so-called best.

In hindsight one could question the wisdom of sending a national guard unit up against the Herman Goering Division to capture two key airfields in the allies first invasion of the European continent. History however hinders such second guessing principally because "they won." Patton "knew" the 45th and he had confidence in its leadership. The division's performance in the 1941 Louisiana maneuvers evidenced that the division was aggressive, innovative, and unintimidated by regular army troops, or anyone else for that matter. In Louisiana, General Key moved the citizen soldiers in an all-night maneuver that captured the 3rd Infantry Division's headquarters. The division's rather blemished, unsavory record at Watertown, New York and Camp Pine proved they would fight anybody, anytime, anywhere. Patton knew that the banker from Oklahoma City, Ray McClain, and the dean of administration at LSU, Troy Middleton, would get it done. He was right.

A good argument could be made for the proposition that a corpse saved Jack's life in Sicily. While the British could be legitimately criticized for their questionable planning of tactical missions, they had in fact refined stealth and deception in war-time to an art form. In other words, the British were sneaky in Operation Husky. Borrowing a corpse from a London morgue, the British draped the dead body in the clothes of a British major. Stuffed within the fabric of the British major corpse were the false, fictitious invasion plans of the allied armies. The plans planted on the corpse called for an allied invasion of Greece and Sardinia, not Italy. Packed into a submarine, the corpse was transported and dispersed off the coast of Greece. Washed ashore by the June tide, the already dead British major, along with the top secret plans to invade Greece, were discovered by the Germans. The artful deception almost was unveiled when an American B-17 bombing mission on June 17, 1943 conducted near Sicily forced the surrender of some 4,600 Italian soldiers. Despite the bombing near Sicily, the Germans took the bait. Accordingly, Hitler shifted many of his troops to the east and away from Sicily, believing the invasion of southern Europe would come through Greece, then Sardinia. Perhaps more directly responsible for shifting the odds favoring successful beach invasion were the efforts of the 82nd Airborne Division. On invasion night, 3,000 United States paratroopers were flown in 266 C-47 transports and dropped near the beaches of Gela to protect the 45th's right flank. Despite the stealth of the British, heavy pre-invasion bombardment, and the night action of the 82nd and a elite force of Army Rangers, the Axis powers would defend the island of Sicily with 50,000 Herman Goering Division veterans, later to be backed up by 40,000 regular German troops, and 315,000 Italian soldiers. If one counts the numbers, the allied forces were out numbered at least one and one-half to one. In war-time, these are not good odds.

The men of the 45th would again sail as part of the Cent Force convoy aboard their old friend the USS Leonard Wood. General McClain and the men now referred to the ship simply as "the Wood." On July 5, 1943, "the Wood," now combat loaded with men and equipment, set sail eastward for their destination, Sicily. Once safely at sea, the men were officially advised of what Jack already knew, that the invasion of Sicily was on, with D-Day to be July 10. Jack recorded in his journal ". . . when troops were notified excitement ran high and men lived with anticipation of D-Day."

As they chugged eastward, Jack began the serious task of "saddling-up" for the invasion. There was a dress code for the occasion. Most noticeably gone were the light and comfortable tan khakis easy to wear on the warm trip across the Atlantic. On his bunk were a steel helmet, wool shirts, ankle-high service shoes with canvas leggings, and an ammunition belt that carried 80 rounds. The mainstay of the wardrobe was the canvas pack stuffed with rations, mess kit, wool blanket, poncho, and half of a shelter. If you wanted a roof over your head at night you would have to find a buddy to provide the other half of the shelter. Also lodged into the haversack were socks, underwear, toothbrush, shaving gear, and whatever else you could fit in. To complete Jack's invasion ensemble, he attached to his belt a 16-inch bayonet, an entrenching tool, and two canteens of water. There was no such thing as a bullet proof vest. At Jack's further disposal were his weapons of choice, a .45 pistol strapped to his hip, and a .30 caliber M-1 rifle. Also part of the invasion paraphenalia was a book that all the troops had a difficult time taking seriously. It had to be a trick or joke, but lying on Jack's bunk was the book A Soldier's Guide to Sicily.

Perhaps the most disturbing item of required wear were "dog-tags," complete with name and unit identification to assist the grave-diggers in the event the worst happened. The command also required that the dog-tags be taped together so as to prevent them from rattling. They had thought of everything right down to the smallest detail.

As Jack strapped on his gear, the reality set in. After more than two years of training and field exercises, this was no drill.

As the Cent Force voyage began the days were sunny and the nights were clear. Things quickly changed. Slipping past Malta at 6:00 pm. on July 9, 1943, the weather began to deteriorate rapidly. Soon the convoy was engulfed in a storm that was feared would stop the invasion. So severe were the seas that the very bottoms of the destroyers could be seen as the giant waves rolled the ships from one side to the other. Many of the men became extremely seasick. Jack recorded that ". . . The small ships such as destroyers PC were wallowing in the sea and at times one could see the bottom when she rolled from side to

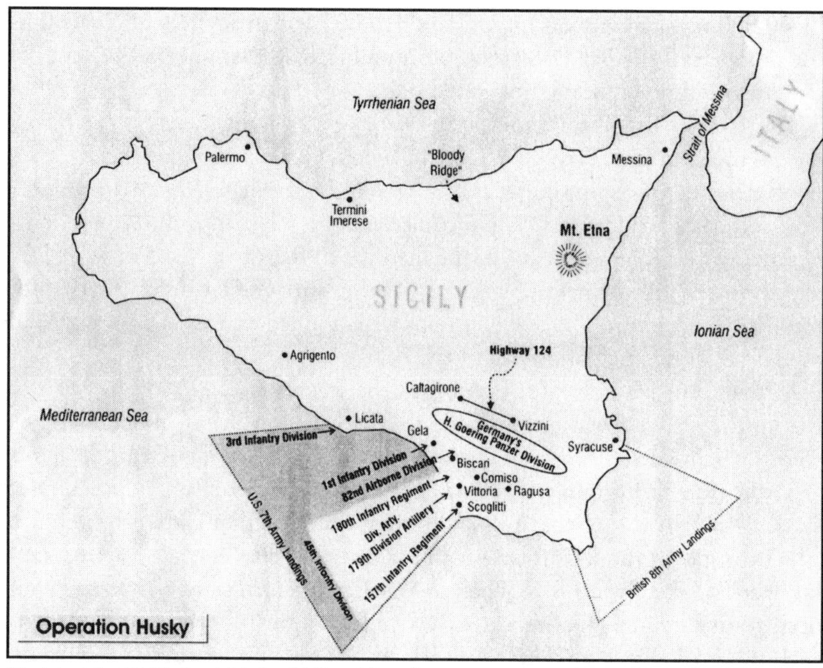

On July 10, 1943 the 45th hit "Yellow" Beach near Vittoria and Scoglitti with the objective of taking the Biscari and Comisco airfields. Jack Neville went in behind the 179th Infantry Regiment.

side." Jack was one of the few who did not get sick. He recorded in his journal "Many men were seasick, surprisingly enough I wasn't much to my relief."

The conditions aboard ship were miserable. In the bottom of the ship, where many of the men choose to seek sanctuary from the sea and storm, vomit was one inch thick. It was as if the weather had sided with the Germans to thwart the invasion. The fighting force was being eroded before they ever stepped foot on the ground. Jack wondered whose side God was on.

Jack's journal recorded the anxiety created by the incredibly difficult conditions, ". . . We all felt as if the heavy sea continued it would be called off and if it wasn't what a hell of an invasion it would turn out to be.

For four hours the Cent Force convoy crept along at the mercy of a storm that threatened Operation Husky. Still miles from Sicily the capability of the invading army had been dented through no act of their own. The weather had become the enemy, but the men and ships had no choice but to ride it out.

At 10:00 p.m on July 9 God seemed to suddenly change sides as if to ordain the allied invasion of Sicily. Jack wrote "God must have been with us for at approximately 2200 the sea began to calm down."

At midnight "the Wood" slowed to a halt and dropped anchor eight miles off the coast of Sicily. The weather had forced a delay in "H-hour" which was now set at 3:45 a.m. on July 10, 1943. The big show was getting ready to start. Everything the division had trained for since September of 1940 was now on the line. The Thunderbirds were focused and ready.

Without hesitation the navy crew and the men of the division readied to off-load the Infantry Battalions into the landing craft as they had practiced many times. The beaches had been designated Yellow, Green, and Red from right to left and covered a line of 7,000 yards in the Scoglitti area. It has been recorded that Ray McClain's Division Artillery were the most aggressive in the war. Some reports indicate that on more than one occasion he and his men were ahead of the infantry with nothing but small patrols protecting their advance. McClain did not intend to go into Sicily behind his own men and artillery. McClain would go in with the infantry, reconnoiter the beach area, locate his command posts and be on the beach to direct and lead his Division Artillery when they came ashore. McClain's plan called for him to go in behind the 179th Infantry Battalion. As for Master Sergeant Jack Neville, he would go in with McClain. Along with McClain and Arnote, Jack would follow the 179th onto Yellow Beach in the invasion of Sicily.

As the men of the 1st Battalion, 179th Infantry readied to off-load into the Higgins boats, Jack rushed to B-Deck. The sight was incredible. There were boats and ships everywhere and everything seemed to be moving at the same time. It was the biggest 4th of July fire works show that Jack had ever seen. Red tracers streamed through the sky and giant German flares slowly dropped seaward in hopes of silhouetting the ships for the German shore batteries. The landing craft circled about the dropped cargo nets, their coxswains shouting and barking instructions in preparation of receiving the men who would first

Elements of the 45th head for the beach in the landing of Sicily.

step onto the German-held Sicilian shore. At half an hour past midnight, the men of the 45th's Division's 179th Infantry Regiment began their climb down the cargo nets and into the waiting landing craft. While the sea had calmed, the swells were still large enough to pitch and roll the small personnel carriers. Off-loading onto the small landing craft took focus and attention that was made more difficult by the night darkness. The 179th already was seasick and it would be almost three more hours before they would be on land. As Jack stood on B-Deck, he wondered how these men could fight with the dizziness and vomit that goes with your stomach being turned inside out by five foot ocean swells. But the men assembled and did as they had trained and practiced many a time. Quietly and methodically, almost patiently, the men of the 179th made their way down the nets and into the waiting boats. Jack remained on deck and stared out in absolute amazement. At 3:30 a.m., the United States destroyers Tillman and Knight, and the USS Philadelphia, one of the cruisers, opened up fire as they raced in to protect the infantry assault waves as the boats lumbered toward shore.

As the landing craft moved toward shore, Jack now readied himself. McClain and his staff would go in with the 1st Artillery battery at daybreak, approximately 5:00 a.m. Jack and Harry Balkum gathered their maps and other paraphernalia making sure to waterproof their packages. Wet maps on the beachhead would serve no purpose. Each did an equipment check on the other. Their hands were so full of what was needed ashore that their M-1 rifles were returned to the quartermaster. They would go on to Sicily with only their .45 holstered on their hips. Given the mission, they would not have time to shoot at anybody anyway. With the artillery battery and McClain's jeep now

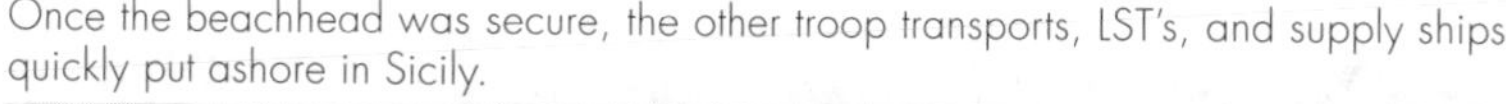

Once the beachhead was secure, the other troop transports, LST's, and supply ships quickly put ashore in Sicily.

loaded onto the landing craft, Jack descended the cargo net and timed his leap from the net perfectly to hit the rolling deck of the small craft that would ferry McClain's party to the beach. As they waited for the signal to shove off for the beach, the grand laser show continued to the background sounds of the giant navy guns blasting away at the Krauts.

At 3:45 a.m. the 179th Infantry Regiment stormed ashore at Yellow Beach on Sicily relatively unopposed. However at 4:30 a.m., as the 179th hit Yellow Beach, Jack's landing craft and the men it it were experiencing their own heightened state of anxiety. In an effort to stop the approaching armada, the Germans had launched an air assault with aircraft they had on the island. The Luftwaffe was unloading their bombs all over the landing force as the cruisers and destroyers attempted to put up defensive fire. It was sometimes close as Jack's landing craft moved toward shore, but it was "no cigar" for the Germans.

As the navy coxswain moved closer to the shore, the waves seemed to get higher, pitching and rolling the boat in an almost uncontrollable manner. Now, for the first time, Jack could see the aftermath of beach invasion. Landing craft were strewn all over the beach as if they were toys left in the sand to be played with the next day. Some of the landing craft were stuck in high sand bars as far away from the shore as 100 yards. Some of the men of the 179th had to swim more than 100 yards with 50 pounds of equipment on their backs. How could they have survived that, Jack wondered. To Jack's relief, there were no dead bodies afloat as they approached. Then Jack's boat experienced its own difficulty. One-hundred yards from the shoreline they ran aground. The coxswain slammed the boat in reverse, then forward, then in reverse again in an effort to dislodge the boat. Those on board readied their weapons as they were sitting ducks. No enemy or friendlies were seen.

After near Herculean efforts, the navy boatmen backed the craft off the sand bar. On the second try they reached the beach successfully. Jack and McClain exited the boat in record time attempting to get a fix on their location. While equipment and boats littered the beach, to Jack's amazement he observed no bodies of American soldiers. Relieved, he and the others looked for a way off the beach quickly. Maybe God was watching after all. Efforts to depart the beachhead however became complicated when McClain's jeep containing critical radio communication equipment became stuck in the sand. Again, they were again sitting ducks. As luck would have it this day, the enemy offered no fire. The men pushed the jeep off the beach and away from open view.

From the conditions, it appeared that the 179th had come ashore free of serious opposition. The line of march of the 179th was readily observable and easy to follow as the foot soldiers had crushed a pathway through a cane break just off the beachhead. If the avenue cleared by the 179th was good enough for them, it was good enough for McClain's small party; and through the cane brake they went. The roadway through the cane in short time led to a rocky

Jack along with General McClain followed the 179th Infantry onto Yellow Beach in a Higgins boat like the one shown here.

The 45th's landing at Sicily was relatively unopposed as men and supplies quickly piled up.

Once ashore on Yellow Beach, the deep and soft Sicilian beaches bogged down many a jeep making the going slow getting off the beach.

road where the maps indicated a left-hand turn northward toward Vittoria and Scoglitti was necessary. Approximately one-half mile north on the rocky road, McClain gave the order to set up the first Division Artillery command post (CP). The CP was located one mile from the beach and seven miles from Vittoria.

McClain wasted no time in ordering Jack and most of the others to remain at the designated location for the CP and make every effort to become operational. With a secure beachhead, the field batteries next would be coming ashore. As Jack remained behind to assist in the organization of the CP, McClain and two others were down the road in McClain's jeep to make contact with other units. By 12:00 p.m., July 10, 1943, Division Artillery CP was up and operational, and word was sent back to Cent Force to send in the artillery pieces. In the meantime, in preparation for the arrival of the 105s and 155s, Jack and Harry broke out the maps they so intently had studied aboard "the Wood." Maps reviewed and communication somewhat established, Jack stood ready.

Pictured, left to right, are Bill Bell, Jack, Harry Balkum, and Al Pagnati somewhere in Sicily in the Summer of 1943.

Unknown to Jack at the time, was that the 179th was like a race horse headed for the finish line. The regiments had swept north toward Vittoria largely unopposed and along the way had captured many prisoners, mostly Italian. So quickly had the 179th moved, that after only a few hours the regiment stood on the edge of Vittoria with Division Artillery not yet ready to fire in support of their movement. However, by 5:00 p.m., Division Artillery was ready, and the 179th waited for the order to advance. Even McClain was stunned at the speed and efficiency of the division's performance. In less than 12 hours, the 179th had taken the beachhead and progressed to Vittoria. In the mix, Division Artillery had readied itself to provide the fire support necessary to take Vittoria and support the other two infantry regiments in their advance on the airfields of Biscari and Comiso.

The 157th Infantry Regiment hit their beach relatively unopposed almost ten minutes after the 179th. However, the 180th, ashore to the left flank of the 179th, was desperate. The regiment was deposited several miles west of their assigned beachhead and had run into stiff resistance. The commanding officer of the 1st Battalion had been captured and the regiment was beginning to take casualties. Nightfall left the 180th in a precarious position. Having the CP operational, McClain sent word to his master sergeants. The CP would be moved before nightfall. Jack and the staff disassembled and before the sun set moved the CP almost three miles to a position two-and-one-half miles southwest of Vittoria. Division Artillery was now in a position to support the 180th to the north in its hope for advance against the Biscari airfield, and to support the 179th and 157th movement against Vittoria, Scoglitti, and the Comiso airfield to the south. It was unlikely that Jack slept the night of July 10, 1943. Jack "dug in" with his trenching tool and wrapped himself in one of the many parachutes found as they moved off the beach. The old hammock looked pretty good compared to the dirt bed dug into the Sicily soil.

The sun did not rise friendly for the men of the 180th Infantry Regiment. On July 11, 1943, the Germans mounted a serious counterattack. German tanks and infantry had blasted through regimental lines to the extent that they were running "unchecked" through even the regiment's command post. Radio and wire traffic flooded the Division Artillery CP in efforts to plot and identify fire missions to stop the Germans. With remarkable effort, the entire fire power of Division Artillery was ashore and positioned on July 10, with the exception of the 189th Field Artillery. The division's artillery was ready to ride to the rescue of the beleaguered 180th now stranded and endangered on the left flank.

History should note that after the division swung the knock-out blow of the invasion of Sicily, the bad boys of the 45th became the adopted sons and heroes of the town folk of Watertown, New York. They embraced the soldiers from the southwest with love, admiration, and thanks in an editorial that has become part of the division's colorful history. Appearing in the Watertown Daily Times in September of 1943, was the following tribute.

> "The Forty-fifth Division, as all will recall, was at Camp Pine for two months. They came just as the leaves were departing from the trees in early November last fall and remained until the middle of January. They were a rugged, rollicking group. They made the Fourth Armored, which preceded them, appear as docile as Dagwood Bumstead. It took us a few weeks to get used to them and frankly speaking the town was considerably quieter after they were shifted elsewhere. Raw November and December weather never cooled their spirits. They cut high, wide, and handsome capers on our streets. They broke up a tavern or two. They gave local police and MP's a real workout. Yet we look back with affection upon the Forty-fifth. They were fighting men. Woe to anyone who fell in their path. Now, if it is true they are in Sicily, they will find conditions exactly to their liking. If General Eisenhower wants Catania taken, let him shove the Forty-fifth in battle. They will deliver any town, mussed up perhaps, but thoroughly conquered."

Without doubt, the division tested more than the patience of the local Watertown constabulary. However, as the division marched through the war, the Watertown Daily Times reported each division victory as if their own were on the front lines and, in a sense, they were.

Men and supplies pile ashore at Yellow Beach in Sicily, on July 10,1943.

As the day of July 10, 1943 wore on the 45th secured the beachhead and quickly moved inland to capture the Comisco and Biscari airfields.

At 3:45 a.m., July 10, 1943, the division hit "Yellow Beach" on Sicily's south shore.

RECOLLECTION JUNE 15, 1977

On June 15, 1977 the sun did not rise friendly for Bob's group of best friends.

Bob Neville is the youngest brother. He came along nine years after me and seven years after Richard. Accordingly, he suffered through many indignities as a child that would now most likely be labeled as child abuse.

In 1959, Jack worked for an affiliate of the Madison Square Garden Company of New York and he was transferred to Palm Beach, Florida. Jack and Leota purchased a beautiful white stucco-walled, adobe roofed home in the small nearby town of Lake Worth, just south of Palm Beach. Richard and I were 10 and 12 respectively, Bob only three. The backyard was a kids delight highlighted by a large rectangular shaped swimming pool. Waterskiing was the year-round sport. This was easy enough to take advantage of as the house sat across the street from Lake Osborne we were only three miles inland of the Atlantic Ocean.

At only three, Bob, of course, had a communication problem. Nonetheless, to us it was irrelevant what he wanted or said as long as he did what we told him to. Richard and I, along with friends, conceived a brilliant plan to teach Bob how to waterski. Grabbing every roll of adhesive tape in a three-block area and, with little objection from Bob, we placed his feet in the rubber footings of skis. The rubber footings, of course, engulfed his feet. Thereafter, over now strong objection from Bob we taped his feet to the skis. We did have enough sense to put a life jacket on him before his first ski lesson. Weighing only a few pounds, Bob was carried to one end of the pool and held under his armpits by Richard just over the top of the water, his skis barely touching the water's surface. Bob then was instructed to hold on to the ski rope handles. He did so out of pure fear. At the other end of the rope were four twelve-year-olds who, on Richard's command of "he's ready," pulled and ran as fast as their strength and speed would allow. He only made it a few feet before we had to dive in and rescue the screaming and yelling three-year-old. This activity was good enough for a one-month grounding after a major Jack "shellacking." Leota allowed Jack to pronounce the sentence, standing and shaking her head. They both immediately sought the relief of the Scotch decanter.

Perhaps the most egregious indignity inflicted on Bob, but certainly not the most demeaning, was the continual securing to poles or staircases and hiding in closets. On our summer family trips Bob was instructed by

Richard and I, as we sped along looking out the car window, that horses were cows, that pigs were dogs, and on and on. This of course elevated Jack and Leota's blood pressure to the point that we quickly found a Holiday Inn to end the day.

It is now understood why Bob is the quietest of the brothers and many believe it remarkable that he even survived. It should be noted that Bob went on to obtain his undergraduate degree from the University of Oklahoma and is a vice president of a major Oklahoma City bank where he manages millions of dollars daily. However, it should also be said that Bob was not only the target of his brothers' pranksterism, he and his friends were often put to great unease by the "Jack attack."

In the summer of 1977, the United States Open Golf Championship returned to Tulsa and the Southern Hills Country Club. If you liked golf or a party and were a friend of Bob, Richard, or myself, you had an open invitation and a ticket at the pleasure of Jack Neville. The house on 57th Street was only three blocks away from the golf course so the ease of access made the occasion even more inviting. My group of pals were, of course, older and wiser tournament goers than Bob's buddies by virtue of our experience in the 1970 P.G.A. Championship. Translated, this means that my comrades got to the Neville house early and staked out all available beds and inside sleeping areas, leaving Bob and his army to fend for themselves. Bob turned this minus into a plus and promptly sent word to his group to bring their sleeping bags; they would all sleep outside around the swimming pool. At twenty, this was "no problemo" as all were "bullet proof" anyway. Bob's band of merry men had much more nefarious plans at play, and their submission to the sleeping arrangements was not done through acquiescence. Bob may have been the quietest, but Richard always believed Bob was the sneakiest. Their reasoned acquiescence was fairly college simple–they did not plan to spend much time at the house as they intended to party most of the night away and watch the golf tournament during at least part of the day. In addition, if they all stayed outside around the pool, Jack and Leota really could not discover when they returned from their evening entertainment or discover how many adult beverages had been consumed during the course of the evening. Twenty-four years later it must be conceded that they totally out-smarted the older guys, and totally underestimated Jack.

For such gatherings the backyard and pool area always were immaculate, much the same as the 4th of July. Grass perfectly cut and flowers planted and arranged, no one wanted everyone around the house more than Jack. To tend to the backyard, Jack had a number of tools and equipment at his disposal which included a rather large and lengthy water hose. If need be, this hose could have been used by the Tulsa Fire Department to put out multi-story building fires. With enough pressure, which could only come with nighttime usage, it was all one could do to stand up to the force of the stream that blasted out of the nozzle. It was a real piece of work.

On the Wednesday night prior to the start of the United States Open, Bob's group carried out their strategy to near perfection. Departing the house at approximately 6:00 p.m., this group of college all-Americans tripped back into the driveway and pool area at about 4:00 a.m. the next morning. There was little quiet involved in re-entry into the backyard and I was awakened by the deep tones of slurred speech and the effects of the staggered gait of this tribe. The performance of this group would have rendered any Breathalyzer device inoperable and without question each needed a blood transfusion. Still believing their activity undetected, each slipped into their sleeping bag after stripping down.

Only a few minutes later Jack was out of his and Leota's bedroom. With commando style stealth, leaving all lights in the house out, Jack sneaked his way down the hallway, through the living room, into the kitchen, out the back door, and into the garage. All of this was done without detection, except for me and Mike Cawley. Curious as to what the old man was up to at such an hour, we peered through the curtains of my bedroom, onto the moon-lit patio and pool where the once merry band could be heard for two full blocks. It did not take long to find out, and hear, what Jack was up to.

Within seconds of hearing the back door to the garage, we could hear the unmistakable sound of the outside water faucet. Next, the old sergeant was adjusting the nozzle of the hose to achieve its full force. His effort was not without great result as water erupted from the hose with the power and force of "Old Faithful," the geyser at Yellowstone National Park. So on the mark with the point of his hose was that Danny Jordan was rolled over in his sleeping bag. All were slow to awake from their slumber, Jack's tool was wholly indiscriminate in nearly drowning everyone that was pool side with gallons of water. In literally seconds, the group of ten scattered like a covey of quail punctuated with some rather majestic four-letter phrases. In less than two minutes, the grand event was over. As Jack looked and laughed at the bewildered crew, he announced that "breakfast would be served in ten minutes, the first United States Open tee-time was at 6:30 a.m." He expected everyone to be there. They were.

With this, the old sergeant cooked up several sides of bacon, dozens of eggs, sausage, and biscuits and forced a cafeteria-style serving on the now hungover and hungry group. Off they went to the United States Open.

As they all exited the house for the tournament Dad fired up his famous Hasty-Bake smoker. First on the grill were the ribs, then the brisket, then the chicken. At the end of the long day at Southern Hills, everyone returned home to a grand feast prepared at Dad's hand. Worn out, hungry, and stuffed, that ended forever all plans for drinking and late night carousing at the 1977 United States Open.

When the P.G.A. Championship revisited Tulsa a few years later, all returned.

The Comisco Airfield was a principal Thunderbird objective in the invasion of Sicily. This picture shows a nearly destroyed hangar and control tower taken on July 14, 1943.

CHAPTER XIII

YELLOW BEACH, BLOODY RIDGE, & VICTORY

With German infantry running through and around the position of the 180th, laying artillery fire down was tricky business. Coordinating with destroyers off-shore and the forward observers in the 180th area, on July 11, 1943, Division Artillery threw their shells at the Germans as if they were darts. In an effort to drive the Americans into the sea, the Germans launched a Panzer-tank counterattack. Patiently, Division Artillery pelted their position as the forward observers with the 180th called in the enemy positions. The giant 155s picked the German tanks off one by one. The German assault was stopped, but only two miles from the beachhead, and less than one mile from Jack's position. Now the 180th was regrouped and ready to move forward against Biscari and its airport. Fighting fiercely, the 180th pressed their way up a steep plateau toward the town and airport. The assault up the slope became hand-to-hand combat with one Thunderbird beating a German officer to death with a helmet. With near-perfect coordination, just as the division had practiced in the west Texas plains of Abilene, the Artillery shattered the German tanks, troops, and machine gun positions, and routed the Germans out of Biscari. By July 14, 1943, Biscari and its airfield were in Allied hands with the Germans in retreat.

With heavy activity, Division Artillery had to juggle its attention with the movement of the 157th and 179th to the east and south near Scoglitti. The 157th and the 179th had the easier time of it and the Scoglitti airfield was under the division's control on July 11, 1943, only one day after the invasion. The action had to have run high for Jack. The Division Artillery CP was only two miles off the beachhead and two miles west of Vittoria in an olive grove. The action north and west of the CP in their area at certain points was only a mile to Jack's left flank and the action at Scoglitti less than two miles away to his southeast. Jack was right in the middle of it all.

For five days the division worked with efficiency and bravery. Division Artillery had reacted to the plight of the 180th, coming to their rescue with 155mm and 105mm rounds in the right place at the right time. The Infantry

Regiments aggressively pursued their objectives with hand-to-hand fighting when necessary. The "leap-frogging" battle tactic had worked with one captured German officer quizzically asking "How do they fight all night, when do they sleep?" In five days of fighting the division had achieved its assigned objectives with great speed, capturing 5,000 prisoners, 150 aircraft at both airfields, 220,000 gallons of gasoline, 38 artillery pieces, 700 machine guns, and more than 10 million rounds of ammunition. An unknown number of Germans were dead.

With confidence that came with success, McClain called his S-3 staff together in the olive grove CP just outside Vittoria. The division, consistent with the pre-invasion plan, would move to the north toward Highway 124, the road between Vizzini and Caltagirone. As per the plan, Division Artillery would move to support the advancing Infantry Regiments. Division Artillery needed an operational plan of advance and support in short order. The Division Artillery CP then was promptly moved forward to a point five miles north of Vittoria. There, Jack and Harry set up shop very near and slightly forward of the now-advancing infantry regiments. The CP's radios were crackled as the artillery's forward observers moved closer to the Vizzini area. Expecting significant German movement west on the road due to Montgomery's landing at Syracuse, the Division Artillery headquarters was a buzz with activity. The 157th had moved northward, ready to assault Vizzini across Highway 124 with Division Artillery to provide the supporting fire. At 5:00 p.m. on July 13 the unexpected shocked McClain's headquarters. While German troops were moving westward on Highway 124, so too were the British. With the Germans in the very cross-hairs of Division Artillery, orders were given to stand down as the fields of fire planned in the assault on Vizzini would now endanger the British. Fury and frustration laced through the S-3 section. By now, the forward observers were radioing back to the S-3 section that they were actually watching German columns move along the road, without interdiction by Division Artillery. The S-3's irritation in not being able to execute their mission was recorded in the Historical Summary of the 45th Infantry Division Artillery on July 14, 1943.

> ". . . At 2100 instructions were received that the limiting line of artillery fire was 1 mile south of line yellow, on Highway 124 as the British were planning an advance on the highway. . . enemy vehicles were observed moving . . . *but we were unable to fire although the targets were well within range.*"

Jack Neville seethed as he knew that many would escape, only to shoot at the Americans later. They needed to kill them now, but could not because the British were advancing east to west as the 45th advanced from south to north.

The Highway 124 fiasco was a product of the British 8th Army's inability to promptly overcome German resistance at Syracuse. Montgomery could not move north and east up the coastal road as was the plan for Operation Husky, so Montgomery took it upon himself to move westward. The real vice of Montgomery's shift to the west however was his ego-driven refusal to communicate and coordinate his move with higher command and, in particular, his counterparts Patton and Troy Middleton, commanding general of the 45th Infantry Division. Substantial numbers of German troops actually were trapped. With communication and planning, Montgomery could have pushed the Germans into the deadly fire of the 45th Division Artillery. Instead, by running across the northern section of the 45th advance without warning in close proximity to the Germans, Montgomery had assured that German columns would escape to fight another day, as the 45th's artillery could not shoot. With certainty, Jack and the rest of the S-3 section must have railed at McClain. McClain, as the Germans passed safely by, phoned Corps for permission to shoot, telling Eisenhower that the British needed to get out of the way. Eisenhower however refused and McClain reported back to his disappointed staff that "... orders were orders."

Accordingly, as McClain put it in his diary, "we sat tight."

In a real sense, Montgomery's decision had increased the odds against Jack's survival. German troops who could have been captured or killed, would fight the 45th again in northern Italy; and now the entire division would have to pull out of their line of march, move westward, and thereafter northward over

After taking their initial objectives, the Thunderbirds pushed to the northern coast of Sicily, and Termini Imerese, and the Battle of Bloody Ridge near San Stefano.

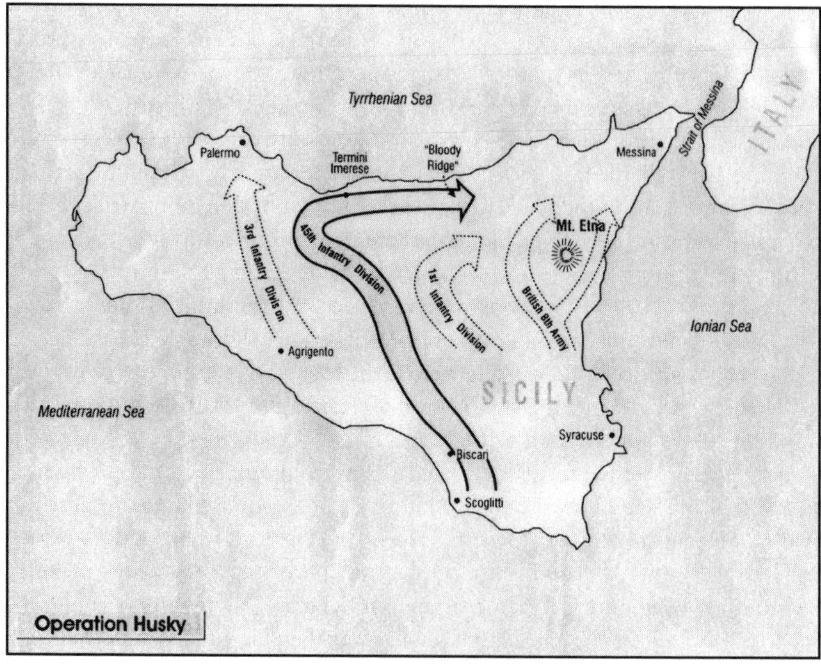

the rugged mountainous terrain of central Sicily.

However, as the division called up the trucks to convoy the 45th's pivot to the west, General Patton saw opportunity. With the 1st Infantry Division and 3rd flanking the 45th's spearhead, Patton's Seventh Army would begin a sprint for the northern coast of Sicily, then eastward. Patton was going to beat Montgomery to Messina. Luckily for Jack, he would get to "truck" it most of the way. The dough boys of the infantry regiments would have to slug it out much of the way on foot. To the northern coast from Biscari, it was more than 100 miles in the tough July heat of Sicily.

For the next three days, the division would fight all day and all night. Confined to a single, narrow northbound road, the infantry regiments leap-frogged to attack 24 hours a day. Fortunately, resistance was fairly light. For Jack, his group could not move the Division Artillery's CP quick enough. With the speed of the northward movement, an operational plan for one day could not be used the next, and at times, Jack found the division moving "off" the map. While at least the rearward infantry regiment could get some sleep and rest, not so for the S-3 staff. Through Mazzarino, then Pietraperzia, by July 18, 1943, the division was advancing on Caltanisetta in the near center of the island. In only three days, 14,000 men had moved more than 50 miles up a single-lane road in mountainous terrain.

At 4:00 p.m., the 45th Infantry Division took Caltanissetta with little resistance and, for the first time, Jack would be able to get some rest and shave. In Caltanissetta, the Division Artillery CP was established in an abandoned palace allegedly owned by a fascist leader who had fled. In the courtyard of the palace, Jack and Ray McClain had the luxury of bathing and shaving in the palace's fountain. While short-lived, it was a welcome relief to digging a slip trench to sleep in overnight and even better to get the 10-day stink off their faces.

The luxury of the fascist palace lasted less than 24 hours. The next day Jack was trucking through San Caterina when, five miles west of town the CP was set up in a granary. McClain was pushing hard, and now the Division Artillery was moving ahead of the infantry regiments. On July 21, Division Artillery raced through Vallelunga, then Caltavituro, and by July 21, 1943, McClain's troops, Jack, and the CP were an incredible three miles ahead of the infantry regiments and in full chase of the enemy. By July 23, 1943, McClain's troops had hit the coastal road near Termini Imerese and were moving rapidly eastward. Going through Campofelice, the CP was set up in the coastal town of Cefalu. By now, elements of the infantry regiments were catching up and the division was on the heels of the Germans.

The Nazis were in fact retreating, conducting a strategic withdrawal designed to allow a substantial number of their forces to escape Sicily across the Strait of Messina. The 45th would catch up with the Nazis near San Stefano in what history called the "Battle of Bloody Ridge."

While the division met little resistence in its drive northward, the move through the mountains of Sicily on a narrow winding road gave Jack his first look at the savage effects of war on the people, towns, and villages of Sicily. Somewhere along the way Jack was able to commandere a camera. Throughout his war years he was able to take a number of pictures which he either sent or brought back and were made part of the scrapbooks kept by Leota. The pictures themselves, along with the words of the many sources for this writing, tell a horrific story of despair, destruction, and poverty that Jack, at the age of 22, witnessed daily. They were the by-products of a world at war. Most of the buildings in the war-plagued towns of Sicily had been reduced to mere darkened black shells, usually walls only, many without roofs. If the Americans were met with German fire coming from a town's buildings or houses, the offending structure was quickly destroyed out of necessity to save American soldiers' lives. The Sicilians in the way were lucky they had a place to at least partially shelter themselves. Often the best they could do was build a fire next to a wall that was once a house or home. What had been quaint villages for decades now were only rubble and broken stone. The Nazis and Fascist conducted a reign of terror on the people. Whatever they needed to support the war they took from the villagers, including food, leaving the citizenry with next to nothing to survive on. Poverty was rampant and as the 45th moved through the villages. Townspeople begged the Oklahomans for any food or clothing the soldiers could spare. Every village became the same.

Most towns were inhabited by only old men, women, and children. Unable to fight, they were in the war's way only to be shoved aside. The younger women prostituted themselves for most anything, including cigarettes, panchos, utensils, and food. The most despairing site of the miserable pictures were the horrible plight of the children. Many were orphaned by the war. They were alone, no parents, no family, and homeless at the age of ten or younger. Many were caked in filth and dirt with no one to feed them or care for them. Many had only the dirt stained shirts on their backs that fell to their knees and no shoes. The skin of their feet and hands were bleeding, broken from walking through the rubble that was once their home The male population was for the most part conscripted into the cause of Mussolini's Fascist Regime, or the war machine of occupying Germany. When the Americans arrived in the small Sicilian town, they were gone with the retreating forces. There was no work, no jobs, no food, no money, and no hope–it had all been destroyed by war.

The Germans had a bad habit of leaving grenades along the sides of roads or booby-trapping the bodies of dead soldiers with explosives or grenades. Poverty ridden and scavenging for anything, children walked the streets maimed and bloody from their naive curiosity and desperate drive. Jack witnessed substantial poverty and hard times in the depression, but war took it to a different level and it was sickening. It was a site that would too often be repeated as Jack rolled through Europe with the Thunderbirds. He never spoke of this, but the pictures tell the story of a great sorrow, and the tragedy that sadly befalls the by-standers of war. This awful scene was one that was destined to repeat itself often as the division continued the pursuit of the Germans through Italy, France, and Germany. But, at Dauchau, the Nazi death camp, it would be worse.

Through July 24, 1943, Division Artillery and the division continued to press eastward along the Sicilian northern costal highway 113. Now on the very heels of the Germans, the forward elements of the 45th met stiff resistance at Pizzo Spina and pressed on toward the small town of Tusa. The Germans fought fiercely in their retreat fleeing across the Tusa River. Once across, the Germans took up heavily-fortified positions on a rocky ridge just west of San Stefano where they dug in to wait for the advance of the 45th. On this ridge the Germans massed their forces. The Germans would make their last stand in hopes that the rest of the Herman Goring Division could escape across the Strait of Messina and into the momentary safety of Italy. The forward observers of the 157th radioed back the now-entrenched position of the Germans. As the radio crackled the coordinates, Jack wrestled with his map. According to the maps, the Germans were entrenched on Hill 335. The Thunderbirds would call it "Bloody Ridge." Jack and Harry immediately commenced planning for the fire missions that certainly would soon come with the infantry's advance. The brave men of the 157th were the first to assault up the ridge. They were forced back down by German artillery and a counterattack. In so doing, the German gun positions were exposed and plotted by the 45th forward observers and Division Artillery. Mortars of the 157th pushed the Germans back up the ridge. So intense and close was the fighting that the 45th attackers were within yards of the enemy. The big guns of the Division Artillery were not called on for fear of killing their own. The give and take of attack and counterattack went on all day. In the early morning hours of July 29, the Germans mounted a massive counterattack that put the 157th in desperate straits. The regimental commander of the 157th believed the entire regiment was in danger of annihilation. He played his card of last resort. Radioing in, he called for all available artillery fire support. Jack stared at McClain and Balkum in disbelief. Once again, artillery would be laid on the 45th's own positions. All four battalions of Division Artillery responded unleashing hell's fury at Hill 335. It lasted fifteen minutes and more than 1,000 rounds of steel and horror were unloaded on Bloody Ridge. Once fire lifted, the 157th again moved up the ridge, only again to be pushed back. This time Division Artillery, along with Naval cruiser gun fire from the bay, beat back yet another German counterattack. By its own fire, the division's positions were now identified by the Germans and their counter-battery fire was now aimed at the 45th.

Jack and Harry were too busy to think, their actions were instinctive, born from their training. By now, explosions were everywhere as the CP itself was taking fire directly from the German batteries. "Incoming" was the often-used phrase signaling Jack to take cover in the slip-trench dug overnight. Mercifully, the CP itself avoided a direct hit, but ammunition trucks near the CP erupted in explosion. Jack was lucky, he escaped unscathed with everything else about him in a firestorm. Fortunately, Harry and the rest of the CP escaped the death of the flying metal.

As the hours of July 29 moved on, the resistance let up and eventually the Germans retreated off Hill 335. By July 30, Division Artillery caught the Germans attempting to filter through the village of Motta and the big guns unloaded their payload on the gray clad Nazis. It was brutal retribution for the Germans. During the night hours of July 30, 1943, the Germans walked out of Motta with almost every German soldier carrying another. The "Battle of Bloody Ridge" was over on July 31, 1943 and the 45th had won. The victory however was costly–163 Thunderbirds were killed or wounded.

On August 1, 1943, Jack's Sicilian Campaign came to an end. The 45th

The dotted line marks the general line of the Thunderbird advance through Sicily, the approximate size of the state of Massachusetts. It was at Palermo that Jack saw the first Bob Hope USO show and where General George Patton addressed the division following the invasion of Sicily.

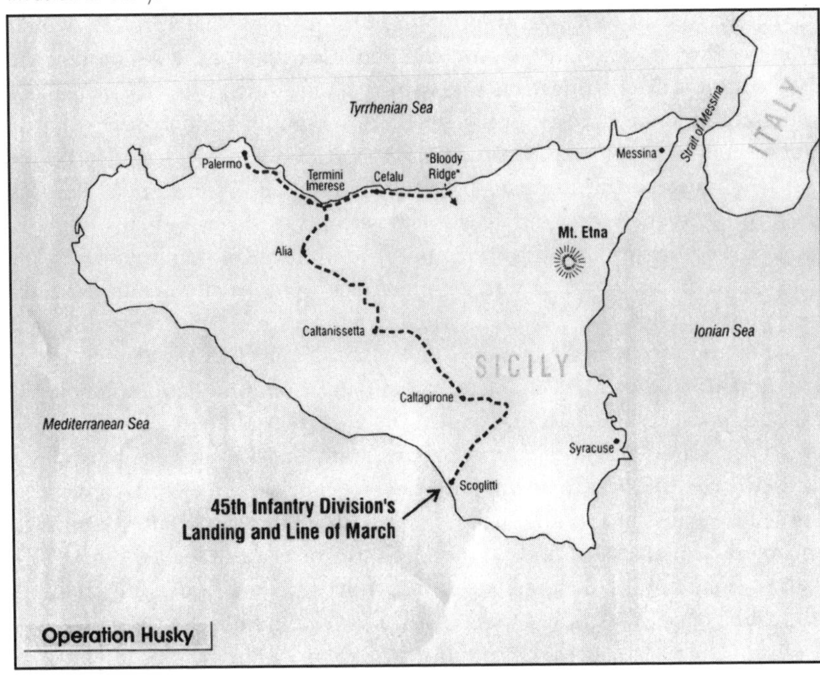

Infantry Division Artillery was relieved by 3rd Division Artillery and moved into a bivouac area on the northern coast of Sicily between Termini Imerese and Cefalu. After 22 consecutive days of combat, the Division Artillery, and most of the division, were told to stand down, clean up, and rest. In taking the Thunderbirds off the spearhead and out of the line, General Patton told the division "You were magnificent."

Patton continued his drive eastward toward Messina with the 3rd Infantry Division and two units of the 45th Infantry Division. On August 15, 1943, the 157th Infantry Regiment 2nd Battalion and the 158th Field Artillery Battalion made an amphibious end-run landing behind German lines, only 25 miles west of Messina. Two days later, Patton won his race against Montgomery to see who would get to Messina first. At 4:30 a.m., the 157th of the 45th Infantry Division entered Messina.

For the citizen soldiers of the Thunderbirds, the division proved in the Sicilian Campaign that it was the equal to any division in the United States Army. The division fought with courage and bravery the entire campaign, taking the point of the attack much of the way. The stories of heroism under fire became legend. Captain Otho Butler of the 180th led his men up Bloody Ridge with malaria in the face of a German artillery counterattack. He was killed. Again at Bloody Ridge, against a German counterattack, four machine gunners, all privates, refused to leave their machine guns while they covered the withdrawal of the 157th. They died at their guns so their comrades could get back down the ridge. They all were awarded the Distinguished Service Cross posthumously. Almost 60 years after the war, the price of Sicily remains incredible. In Sicily 302 Thunderbirds were killed, 163 of which died at Bloody Ridge. More than half of the men killed in Sicily died in a fight to take a ridge line on the northern coast. All toll, there were 3,914 men of the division killed, wounded, injured, or missing in the battle for Sicily. Just as humbling, of the slightly more than 14,000 troops in the division, almost 29% were casualties in one form or another of Operation Husky. As the war went on, it would only get worse.

For Jack, the Sicilian campaign was exhausting, physically and emotionally. Twice, in southern Sicily and at Bloody Ridge, Division Artillery placed fire down on, or near, the division's own troops. On one occasion, again at Bloody Ridge, he was lucky to escape death when the Germans shelled the artillery CP hitting an ammunition truck and not his bunker. At 22, he was eyewitness to the death and destruction war brings. Cities, towns, and villages were destroyed. There were more casualties in war than the soldiers who fought it. Forbid that it ever reached the shores of the United States, or the city limit of Oklahoma City. Jack felt lucky to be alive, but burdened by the lingering thought–would he ever make it home

Study of the Sicilian Campaign reinforces the regrettable thought that we, as family, never made serious efforts to press and learn the history of Bloody Ridge and Yellow Beach until after Dad's death. Tucked away in those old scrapbooks was a brown faded memo that awarded Jack Neville the Bronze Star for service in combat in the Sicilian Campaign and the Italian Campaign citing his "unusual initiative" in maintaining high efficiency in his combat section. It would have been exciting and meaningful to hear from him exactly what he did to earn this wonderful honor for his service. He never once spoke of it.

Back home in Oklahoma City, Leota's only means to keep up with Jack was through the newspaper and the radio. It was impossible for Jack to write letters or send telegrams that chronicled the division's movement, and in July of 1943, there was no CNN or Fox television crew to follow the Thunderbirds. As the war in Sicily moved along, Leota clung to the radio, never missed a newspaper, and bravely awaited the postman, praying "that" letter would never arrive. With boys from Oklahoma on the front lines in a big way, Leota had a general accounting of the division's whereabouts from *The Daily Oklahoman*. Although Leota was relatively certain that the Cent Force convoy was headed for North Africa, which left on May 24, the home folks did not know where or when the Thunderbirds would meet the Germans in battle. What mail that could be sent was censored to guard against any leak, but most of the division did not know the final invasion destination in any event until they were on board "the Wood" and away from Oran.

Through the entire month of June of 1943, with no word from Jack, the family was left to guess, worry, and pray that a second Neville brother would not be killed in action half a world away. Then the word came. On the very day that Jack hit Yellow Beach at Scoglitti the headlines blasted "Allies Invade Sicily." Interestingly the article did not reference any of the specific units involved in the invasion, but the "Okies" knew it was their boys. By July 17, 1943, as Jack pushed toward the northern coast, the state's largest newspaper confirmed that the 45th was in Sicily under the headlines "States Own Division at Last Sees Fighting." Even the fighting at Hill 335 was reported to the city on July 29, 1943 with "45th Drives Germans Back." Every Sunday at 2:00 p.m. Leota turned her dial to "Army Hour on WKY Radio." Once a week the Armed Forces Radio broadcast direct from the war sight of the 45th Infantry Division.

The reports were very general, sometimes vague, and obviously censored, but at least when she listened she felt linked to Jack if only in a small way.

The very first United States Army newspaper to be published was the 45th Division News. Edited by Sergeant Don Robinson, a former reporter for the Oklahoma City Times, and published in Vittorina Sicily. Jack's boss, General Ray McClain, saw to it that the small paper got back to the people of Oklahoma. Interestingly, it was this paper that first featured "Willie and Joe," two 45th Division dog-faces created by the world renown cartoonist and humorist Bill Mauldin. When Leota needed a laugh, and perhaps a real peek at what life on the front was like, she looked for Mauldin's "Willie and Joe" in the 45th Division News. By today's standards, access to information was meager, but in 1943, Leota was thankful for the news that she had. Perhaps the most satisfying headline of all carried by *The Daily Oklahoman* that summer came on August 17, 1943. The headline read "45th Swings Sicily Knockout." Operation Husky was over. It was enough to conclude that Jack had probably made it. She was right.

As the 45th achieved its remarkable success in Sicily, even the Watertown Daily Times could not resist once again embracing the soldiers once seen as undisciplined ruffians. In a second editorial praising the division and now defending their conduct while at Camp Pine, the paper wrote.

> Each day, as I read the accounts in the newspaper of the swell job the Forty-fifth Division has been doing in Sicily, I think back to last winter. . . . The Forty-fifth had just pulled into Camp Pine from Fort Devens, Massachusetts, and what a load of unfavorable publicity had accompanied it; how the boys had wrecked the town of Ayer, Massachusetts, and what a relief to the townsfolk of Ayer when the Forty-fifth pulled out. Consequently, the people around Camp Pine were a little wary of these Oklahoma boys, when they first arrived and it was tough going at first to make friends in Watertown. There were the usual fights. People just didn't like them very much because they were too wild. . . . What the smug citizens who censured these soldiers did not realize was that here, in their midst, had been one of the roughest, toughest infantry divisions in the whole United States Army. Those fellows were just itching for combat duty. They had to blow off steam some way or other, so there were a few rows in beer joints or other public places. However, when those same holier-than-thou critics read the newspaper accounts of what the Forty-fifth has been doing, I'm sure they feel a bit of guilt. Because, in order to win, this army of ours has got to be the roughest, toughest of any army in the world.

For almost two weeks after being relieved from the front on August 1, the men of the 45th Division Artillery were able to relax, enjoy themselves, and thank their lucky stars they were still alive. One certainty existed, the entire

Division Artillery smelled. Jack had only bathed once in the last 31 days and the odor was enough to topple strong buildings. The warm saltwater of the Mediterranean became one of the chief cleaning ingredients of life in the bivouac. A shower and a warm meal were heaven. Even a "one-holer, port-a-potty" was seen as Waldorf Astoria luxury. The High Command issued the expected occupation orders to the division troops shortly after they were taken off the line. The boys of the 45th were not to drink the Italian wine and they were absolutely forbidden to fraternize with Sicilian women. Violators would face court martial. These orders were paid their due respect, and of course promptly ignored. The war had ravaged the Sicilian economy and countryside, but in August of 1943, Jack and Harry saw to it that enough "vino" was consumed to revive the capital city of Palermo. And hats off to the USO who provided some pretty nifty entertainment after Operation Husky. American icon Bob Hope got his start entertaining American troops in August of 1943 on the northern coast of Sicily. Along with Hope, Jack and the boys were treated to the likes of Frances Lankford and Humphrey Bogart while they rested on the beach east of Palermo. For a time they were able to set the war aside, but home was where their hearts were.

By August 18, 1943, with the Sicilian Campaign now over, the division went back to work. Overhauling equipment and replacing the worn and broken pieces of their weapons, the division began training for their next mission. As with Operation Husky, the specific destination remained top secret. Shortly after August 18, Jack was sequestered with the rest of the "planners." Again, the names of towns and cities were mostly unfamiliar, but study and study the maps he did for hours. As Jack pondered the maps for logistics and fire operations, he knew the modus operandi would not measurably change. McClain, staff, and Jack would go in early, just behind the infantry troops. McClain would be there when his Division Artillery arrived, ready to move inland with the infantry regiments. Speed of movement would be key and Jack needed to plan for it. In 39 days in Sicily, Division Artillery had established more than 16 command posts in their near 200-mile march northward. McClain would demand the same speed of movement for the next operation. As Jack worked on the maps and studied the geography and terrain of Italy, he wondered how many of the Nazis that had escaped death and destruction at Highway 124 would fight the division again in Italy.

The hours over the maps at the CP made the next objective clear and evident. The 45th Infantry Division would again be part of an amphibious assault, this time on the west coast of Italy at a place called Salerno.

For the Allied Armies, the invasion of Sicily was a resounding success. In slightly more than one month every pre-invasion objective was seized. The Biscari and Comiso airfields in the south were seized by the 7th Army within five days of the invasion, and the valuable sea ports along the northern coast were under the control of the 45th and the United States Navy. Now the Allied Forces had both airfields and seaports from which to attack most anywhere up the Italian coast. With the fall of Sicily, men, material, equipment, and ammunition could be stockpiled on the island to provide the necessary logistical support for yet another amphibious invasion. The 45th Infantry Division alone captured 11,266 Germans. Overall, 32,000 Germans and 132,000 Italian soldiers were either killed or captured with a total of 20,000 casualties on the British and American side. The Italian forces were neutralized for the remainder of the war with the success of Operation Husky. Moreover, the Allies had proven, despite the problem at Highway 124, that they could plan and coordinate the extremely complicated maneuver of a multiple beachhead amphibious assault. As for the 45th, their metal was tested and proven with success in spades. The Thunderbirds were up to the fight. The Sicilian victory was not without its blemishes. As the United States 7th Army and the British 8th moved across Sicily and toward Messina, the Germans fought an effective strategic withdrawal of their forces. Slowing Montgomery's advance in the south, and delaying Patton's forces in the Battle of Bloody Ridge on the northern coast allowed 40,000 German troops, 9,600 vehicles, and 47 tanks to escape across the Straits of Messina and into Italy. Whitlock reports that Allied Forces entered Messina as the last German transport moved away from the port. For the Germans it was a scaled down version of the British escape at Dunkirk–they fought so they could fight another day.

Anger spread through the 45th as rumors swirled of the German escape. How many of the Germans who had escaped across the Strait had been on Highway 124 when Division Artillery was told to cease fire. Jack was afraid that they would find out in Italy.

As Jack hovered over the maps for the next operation, he felt lucky. German bombs missed their mark as his LC approached Sicilian soil and there was little enemy resistance at Yellow Beach. The shooting and bombing in southern Italy stayed a mile away from his location and at Bloody Ridge, the German artillery got very close to the CP, but no one was hurt. He was fortunate indeed. But, at the junction of the Calore and Sele Rivers at Salerno, Italy, Jack Neville, for the first time, would look death straight in the eye.

As word of the 45th's success in Sicily drifted back to Oklahoma City in fragmented stories reported to *The Daily Oklahoman*, citizens responded with extraordinary patriotism and war-time generosity. In tribute to the men of Oklahoma who lost their lives fighting in Sicily, city leaders and the Neighbors Services Corporation, chaired by J. I. Meyerson, knocked on almost every door in Oklahoma City to raise $45 million in war bonds. It was an incredible display of civic pride for the boys across the Atlantic.

CHAPTER XIV
SALERNO AND OPERATION AVALANCHE

As Jack and the Oklahomans dangled their toes in the warm sea of the Mediterranean and saw what sites were left to see in bombed out Palermo and Messina, Sir Winston Churchill on August 5, 1943, boarded the Queen Mary and sailed with his wife and daughters westward to meet his new best friend, President Franklin D. Roosevelt. At Roosevelt's suggestion, and with the victory in Sicily, a conference was called to meet this time in Quebec to discuss the future strategy of the war. Code named "Quadrant," the conference's primary agenda item was Operation Overload, now targeted for the late spring or early summer of 1944. Also high on the agenda was the continued pursuit of the Germans in southern Europe, specifically Italy. On August 24, 1943, the two world leaders decided that the Allied Forces would attack by land up the boot of Italy and by sea on the western coast of Italy. The two left it to the military commanders to decide the precise places, dates, and times for the next operation, designated "Avalanche." Noticeably absent from the conference was Joseph Stalin and the Russians who were locked in a savage struggle with the Nazis in eastern Europe.

After Quadrant, and three days after Jack and the division were put back to work, General Middleton and parts of his staff were ordered to Algiers on August 21, 1943, to plan for the invasion of Italy. The allies would again attack the Germans with a one-two punch. Again under the command of Montgomery, the British 8th Army would attack in southern Italy, directly across the Strait of Messina and move northward up the center of the country. Montgomery was to move from Sicily, across the Strait, and into Italy between August 30 and September 4, 1943, the specific date to be chosen by Montgomery. The United States Forces were to be reformed into the Fifth United States Army under the command of General Mark Clark. Clark had won acclaim for his planning of Operation Torch, the invasion of North Africa. Joining United States Fifth would be British Forces. The United States 36th Infantry Division, the British 56th and 46th Divisions, United States Rangers, and British Commandos, and the now veteran 45th Infantry Division would total 70,000 men for attack on the west coast of Italy.

It was a given that the invasion would require crossing the narrow 10-mile Straits of Messina and this task was assigned to Montgomery's British 8th Army. The invasion's objectives to the north and along the west coast of Italy were more problematic. Rome was too far north for air cover and logistical support. Naples, the next thought of objective, was too–heavily defended for direct assault, leaving Salerno and the Gulf of Salerno as the only viable military option for an amphibious landing. The beaches of the Gulf of Salerno were perfect for an amphibious assault as the landing craft could run far into the beach before the troops had to disembark. On the negative side was the fact that the open beaches provided unobstructed fields of fire from elevated positions. To the east of the beachhead was a mountain range as high as 4,000 feet at the north end of the beach to 1,500 feet the center and south. In essence, the beach was hemmed in by mountains and hills providing the Huns the advantage. While it may have been an ideal place to land, it also was an ideal place from which to defend. In essence, the Thunderbirds would be in a shooting gallery.

Flowing out of the mountains from the east to the Gulf of Salerno were two rivers, the Sele River and the Calore River. Both rivers joined together approximately 15 miles east of the beach and five miles southwest of the small town of Persano that fed into the Gulf in the approximate middle of the beachhead. Highway 18 ran north out of the town of Paestrum parallel to the beach and crossed the Sele and Calore rivers at a key bridge approximately seven miles inland. Highway 18 ran on northward to the town of Battipaglia. From Battipagila it was a straight shot on Highway 19 to Salerno, Naples, and Rome. The military value of the objective lay in the harbors and airstrips. With the seaports of Salerno and Naples in hand, the allies would have a valuable stage to launch further pursuit of the Germans.

The allied plan called for Col. William O. Darby to put his famous "Darby's Rangers" on shore at Maiori to the far north of the beachhead and seize Highway 18, west of Salerno. The British Commandos would attack almost directly at Salerno. More to the center of the beachhead, the British 46th and 56th Divisions would attack north of the mouth of the Sele River advancing toward the town of Battipaglia and its important intersection of Highways 18 and 19. The United States 36th Infantry Division, seeing its first action of the war, would unload on the southern beaches near Paestum and thereafter move to the east and north. As early as September of 1943, the allies were piling up supplies and material, including landing craft, all over the British Isles in preparation for Operation Overload, the famous D-Day invasion into Normandy. As a result, Operation Avalanche suffered from a shortage of landing craft and the 45th Infantry Division would act as a "floating reserve." The division would remain on board its troop carriers until needed on shore. The division's precise objective would be defined by the invasion circumstances. It would prove to

be a critical role. The selection of the division for the floating reserve was the subject of debate. Certain members of the Allied High command wanted the 3rd Infantry Division for this role. Dwight Eisenhower, however, personally selected the 45th Infantry Division for the key mission.

Ironically, Italy would not be defended by the Italians. By "Avalanche D-Day," the Italian Armed Forces had surrendered and the Germans still occupied the country. The Germans refused retreat, and accordingly, Italy would be defended by the Germans and by two of its finest generals. In charge of the defense of northern Italy, from Rome northward, was the arch nemesis of the United States and British in North Africa, General Irwin Rommel. The German leader in the south was Field Marshall General Albert Kesselring. It was Kesselring who had planned and managed his troops' escape across the Messina straits in Sicily. Kesselring had at his disposal an impressive array of infantry, artillery, and tanks. With Sicily lost, the Germans knew that the next invasion in southern Europe would come somewhere in Italy. Six of Kesselring's Panzer Divisions would be ready to meet the allies. While the allies saw Salerno as the most logical landing site, so did Kesselring. With constant air patrols and the luck of decent weather, the Germans detected the Allied Armada almost as it sailed. In response, Kesselring massed three of his divisions near the beaches of Salerno–the 15th Panzer Grenadier Division, the 16th Panzer Division, and the 29th Panzer Grenadier Division. Under the direct command of Heinrich

Jack left Sicily for Salerno on board LST 404. The division landed near Paestrum and moved to plug the gap in the lines at the Sele Corridor on September 10, 1943. Here is a photograph of the Thunderbirds on the Salerno beachhead.

Von Vietinghoff, 17,000 men, more than 100 tanks, and substantial German air cover would be near the beach to greet the invading forces.

In addition to the talents of Hope, Lankford, and Bogart, the division was treated to the showmanship of General George Patton in his last days on Sicily. Despite his success in Operation Husky, Patton came under severe criticism for slapping two enlisted men while visiting wounded G.I.s in hospitals. Thereafter, Patton was forced to apologize for his conduct and command of Operation Avalanche was handed over to Mark Clark. Military history forever will debate whether Eisenhower punished Patton by sending him to England after the Sicily victory, or whether it was in fact a ruse to divert the Nazi's attention. The Nazis always believed Patton to be the best Allied Commander and wherever Patton went invasion was sure to follow. In August of 1943, the entire 45th was gathered to hear Patton's farewell to the division.

"The 45th is one of the best, if not the very best division that the American Army has ever produced. . . . I love every bone in your heads, but be very careful. Do not go to sleep or someone's liable to slip up behind and hit you over the head with a sock full of shit, and that's a hell of an embarrassing way to die." The whole division roared with laughter.

RECOLLECTIONS ON PATTON

Hearing old "Blood and Guts" was the emotional lift the division needed before Operation Avalanche left the northern shore of Sicily. It must have stayed with Jack the rest of his life as Jack delivered more than one "Patton-ish" speech to the brothers through the years. Interestingly, when the Academy Award-winning movie Patton was released, Jack was rather anxious to see it, and in his later years I recall watching the video version with him on 57th street in Tulsa. Jack loved Patton's speech delivered at the beginning of the movie with the giant American Flag serving as background. As George C. Scott, playing Patton, delivered his final lines of that speech, Patton posed the question of what the G.I.s would tell their grandchildren they did in "the great World War II." Pausing dramatically, Patton answered his own question, ". . . well, you won't have to tell your grandchildren you shoveled shit in Louisiana."

Dad would laugh uncontrollably, but thereafter only sporadically watch the rest of the movie. I did not think about it then but Dad had been in both Louisiana and Sicily. Bob Hope, of course, went on to become a national treasure. We rarely missed The Bob Hope Christmas Show as he entertained United States Troops all over the world. Incredibly, never once as we watched The Bob Hope Christmas Show, did Jack ever hint that in August of 1943 he first saw Hope on the northern shore of Sicily during the great war. Also, just as remarkable, was the fact that not once did Jack ever tell his grandchildren, or his sons, that he and the division were with Patton in the 1941 Louisiana maneuvers, or that the 45th was under Patton's command in the first Allied invasion of Europe. With sons and grandchildren asking what he did in "the war," the usual response was delivered in a few short words, "I was with the 45th." Proudly stated, that was it.

Jack's silence on such matters is further testament to the ugliness and brutality he witnessed. The Salerno beach would not be a Hollywood movie. The players were real, and many would never again see Bob Hope, or sit in their living room watching the video version of Patton.

Jack's whereabouts during the invasion of Salerno are ascertainable from the division's historical record. While the 45th readied to embark at Termini-Imerese, the British 8th Army attacked across the straits of Messina at dawn on September 3, 1943. Four days later, the division commenced to combat-load on transports at the port of Termini-Imerse. Just as they had done in Virginia and again in Oran, Jack and the elements of Division Artillery boarded on the "first lift" with their old friend the 179th Infantry Regiment in the afternoon of September 7, 1943. Jack and the entire artillery staff boarded the British LST 404, along with McClain.

General Patton addresses the 45th in Palermo in August of 1943.

Outside of Palermo, the Sicilian hucksters offered postcard pictorials for a price next to nothing. On September 7, 1943, Jack Neville made a pictorial postcard of himself and mailed it to Leota just before boarding LST 404. He knew he would not be able to write again after they sailed. On September 8, 1943, at 2:00 a.m., the Division Artillery headquarters and its staff, the 179th Infantry Regiments, and the 157th Infantry Regiments, less its 2nd Battalion, pushed away at Termini-Imerese in 16 LSTs, and 23 LCIs to rendezvous with the rest of the invasion force. As Operation Avalanche was the stepchild of the build-up in England for the Normandy D-Day Invasion, the 45th's 180th Infantry Regiment was forced to remain on shore due to a shortage of ships.

North of Palermo the ships carrying the 45th met with the rest of the invasion force. The armada now consisted of more than 500 ships and a British aircraft carrier to provide air cover if necessary. In relatively smooth seas, the division sailed directly for the Gulf of Salerno when at 6:30 p.m. on September 8, 1943, the ships loud speaker blared out the voice of General Eisenhower. He announced that all Italian Forces had laid down their arms and surrendered. Huge cheers went up around LST 404. But McClain could only look at his staff with word that the Germans were still there, we had not won yet.

After 18 hours at sea LST 404 sailed into the Gulf of Salerno. The Germans had heavily mined the entire Gulf area and, as a result, the giant LST dropped anchor 12 miles off the Salerno beachhead in the southern end of the beach near Agropoli, south of Paestum. Now at rest, in the darkness, the division sat and waited. As Jack looked off the rail of the ship he felt as if they were a sitting duck in a giant still pond just waiting to be plucked. The reality of the division's position and location sparked a scary thought. If the floating reserve was called into action, it was a 12-mile run to the beach across open water. In the early morning hours of September 10, 1943, the Germans began their search for the flotilla they knew was off shore. Giant German flares woke up the night and the ships carrying the 45th were silouetted against the sky. The German Luftwaffe jumped on the British LSTs illuminated by their flares in a furious aerial attack. The guns on deck blasted away and the destroyers and cruisers fired in search of German targets. The white of the search lights intersected with the red traces and blasts coming from the muzzles, and all Jack, or anyone else of the 45th, could do was hang on the rail, watch, and pray they would not fall victim to a German shell. Many of the men wished they were with the Texas 36th, at least by now they were off the ships and into the smaller target of the LCI. The luck of the Thunderbird carried the night hours, not a ship of

At Salerno, the 45th played a key role as a floating reserve. With the beachhead in jeopardy, the division was rushed in to plug a gap in the lines ultimately saving the beachhead with a last ditch stand at the junction of the Calore-Sele rivers to the south and west of Persano.

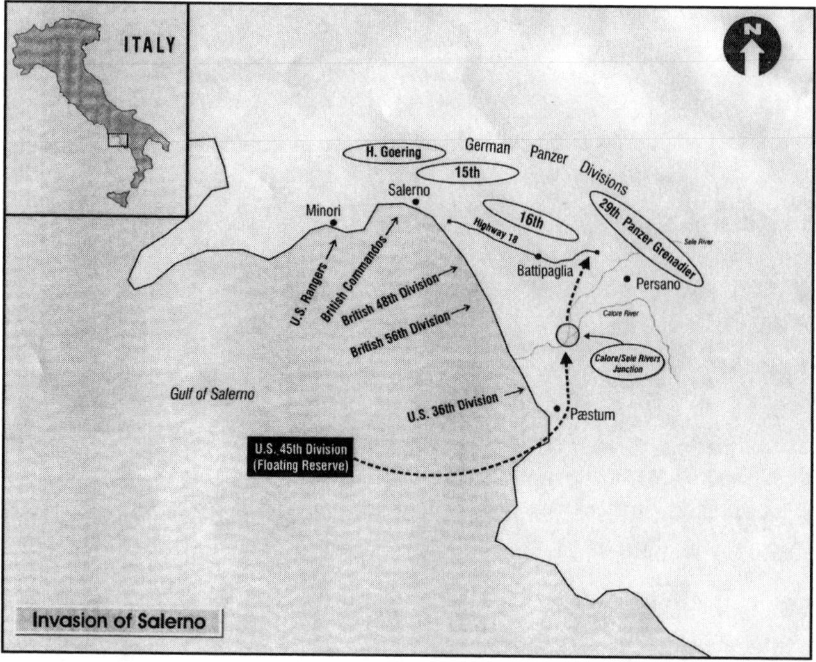

the 45th was hit. But, for Jack and Division Artillery it would be another 24 hours before they could get off the water. All they could do was wait, watch, and listen as bombs and shells fell and flew about them. As night turned into day, the carnage left by the Germans air attacks became evident as black smoke and red flame billowed from the armada. The British ships HMS Uganda and Warspite were damaged; the USS Savannah, a crusier, was burning and out of action; and the United States destroyer Rowan, destroyed.

Churchill wrote in *Closing the Ring*, that surprise, violence, and speed are the essence of amphibious landings. Violence and speed may have been with Operation Avalanche, but surprise was nowhere to be found on September 9, D-Day. Hours ahead of the 45th were the ships carrying the lead elements of the troops who would first assault the Salerno beaches. To the north of the Sele River, parts of the British 46th and 56th landed on the wrong beach due to the havoc reeked on the beachhead by German fighters. In time, they were able to regroup and move inland. To the south, near Paestum, the United States 36th Infantry Division came in at 3:35 a.m. The German 16th Panzer Division was hidden, waiting for the Texas boys. Patiently, Von Vietlinghoff let the first wave come ashore unopposed. Seven minutes later, the second wave hit the beach and all the fury of the German Division was unleashed. Whitlock described it as a "killing field" with machine guns ripping at both waves as shouts of "Medic, Medic" screamed through the air. German artillery at near point blank range disintegrated LSTs and LCIs carrying both men and equipment. The battle for the beachhead near Paestum raged most of the day, but by mid-afternoon the fortunes of the 36th turned for the better. The Americans were piling up ammunition, men, and supplies on the beach, and along with the infantry, American fighters were able to destroy two-thirds of the 16th Panzer Division. Shear guts and determination won the beach and late in the afternoon of September 10, the 36th was moving inland, seizing its objectives.

During the morning hours of September 10, 1943, General Mark Clark could see the battle for the Salerno beachhead taking shape. While struggling, the British to the north of the Sele River and the United States 36th broke through the beachhead. Later in the day, the 36th Division took Altavilla, far inland, and the British looked as if they were on their way to the Battiaglia area. However, the Allied advance uncovered a developing gap in the lines of some seven to 10 miles between the British 56th and United States' 36th. Both Kesselring and Clark discovered the gap in short order which came to be known as the "Sele Corridor." Like pawns in a chess game, Kesselring hurled what was left of the 16th Panzer Division into the gap. The objective was brutally simple. If the Germans broke through to the beachhead, they could divide, split, and destroy the invasion. Clark's counter-move called for the 45th Infantry Division, to plug the gap. If the Thunderbirds could not hold the corridor and the beachhead, Clark would have to evacuate the Allied Forces. The Thunderbirds were given orders to disembark LST 404 and head for the beach. As Whitlock eloquently and appropriately described the situation, the 45th was now on a collision course with the remaining elements of the 16th Panzer Division and the 29th Grenadier Panzers, and to the winner would go the victory of Operation Avalanche. The invasion now hung in the balance. With the 45th Infantry Division committed, the allies had no troops in reserve.

Word came aboard LST 404 that the 45th would head ashore in the late morning hours of September 10 to plug up the Sele Corridor. As the order filtered to McClain and down to the staff, plans were made for the division to hit the beach west and slightly north of Paestum to stop an anticipated run at the beach by the Germans. The division prepared to load the LCIs with the primary planning worry now being the under-strength of the division. The 180th Infantry Regiment still was steaming toward the Gulf of Salerno as was the 2nd Battalion of the 157th Infantry Regiment. The Thunderbirds would be short an entire regiment and battalion when the ramps were dropped. As Jack reviewed the situation maps, his constant thought was "they better hurry." As Jack readied for his second amphibious landing in two months, he once again caught himself staring down at the tools of war spread on his bunk. Slightly superstitious, he kept the routine the same. The M-1 carbine went back to ordinance, the .45 holstered and strapped to his waist, extra ammunition, and a stuffed pack complete with entrenching tool. He would probably have to dig his bed again. He was lucky in Sicily, would lady luck again be with him at Salerno.

The ships loud speaker called for the 179th Infantry to man their stations and prepare to disembark the LST for the LCI which would ferry the men to shore. Jack and Harry both went to the rail to watch the infantry's climb down the nets into the pitching and rolling LCI. Jack and Harry shook their heads at each other. These guys had some serious guts.

As the 179th disembarked 404 into the LCI, were stunned at the sight of the next cadre of troops readied at their stations for the second wave's ride onto the Salerno beach. Neatly dressed, but without rifles or pistols, were 40 women nurses of the Medical Corps who would go ashore at Salerno on the second wave. As they lifted themselves over the railing and climbed down the nets, not a cat-call could be heard, only loud applause and cheering. The guys were proud of them. They were warriors too and it was comforting to know that if you got hit they would be there. Jack Neville could not help but giggle "My God, the women were going in before Division Artillery, nobody at home would believe it."

The plan for Division Artillery was basically the same as it was for Sicily. McClain intended to lead the artillery from the front. Once again McClain, Jack, and the staff would go in behind the last wave of the 179th, establish the command post, direct the big guns to their planned location, and prepare to support the 179th's move inland. McClain's concern for the man power shortage of the division at Salerno found its way into his draft of Citizen Soldiers.

> The 36th Division had landed and was fighting for the beachhead. Part of the convoy was in Sicily. We had but one combat team with us, Middleton's headquarters, and mine.

Nonetheless, at 11:40 a.m. on September 10, 1943, the little LCIs carrying the 179th begun their full speed sprint for the beach and the landing south of the mouth of the Sele River. As the ramps dropped, the scene was mercifully quiet and the regiment moved quickly inland. The march off the beach was uninterrupted by enemy fire until 20 minutes after the last wave came ashore. Appearing out of the deep blue sky came the German Luftwaffe strafing and shooting at the men running off the beach for cover. They seemed to be gone almost as quickly as they came. Back on board LST 404 Jack could hear the war at the beach and he could see the German planes strafing the beach. Jack and Harry could only look at each other. The 179th moved inland unopposed by German infantry troops, established their assembly area two miles south of Paestum, and waited for further orders to move into the Sele Corridor.

With the last elements of the 179th going ashore, it was now Jack's turn to make his way over the rail and down the nets. Safely aboard the LCI, the small craft carrying McClain and his staff rumbled toward shore. All eyes were skyward searching for the German planes they had seen from the LST. The German fighters chose to stay away. Balkum was convinced the German pilots knew he would blast them from the skies with his .45 pistol. They did not dare show up. It was good for a few laughs as the craft splashed on. As the little boat made its way toward shore the sounds of war became more clear. To the south and to the north of their landing area, the boom of the 36th and British 56th's artillery could be heard blasting away together with the crackle of rifle fire and the stacato of heavy machine guns. There was fighting all around them, but fortunately none in front of them. The luck of the Thunderbirds and the angels rode on their shoulders all the way to the beach. They landed without incident. The small party wasted no time getting off the beach.

McClain moved quickly through the lines of the 179th, once again ahead of the infantry units and established the Division Artillery CP slightly north of Paestum by mid-afternoon, September 10, 1943. The 179th received orders to move out and proceed northeasterly, across the junction of the Sele and Calore rivers, along the east bank of the Sele toward the towns of Eboli and Serre.

With this movement to the northeast, and directly into the "Corridor" the luck of the Thunderbird ran its course at Salerno, and for the next four days, the life of the division would hang by a thin reed. That afternoon, as the 179th moved northward into the Sele Corridor, Jack and the Division Artillery CP moved into the junction of the Sele and Calore rivers in support of the advance. That same afternoon, the 157th Infantry Regiment, less its second battalion, landed–but at the wrong beach. On the 157th's run to the beach, the regiment was heavily bombed and strafed by the German fighters that had left Jack alone. Instead of landing north of the mouth of the Sele as planned, the regiment was forced to put ashore to the south. Now, on the wrong beach, the 157th was in a weak position to provide the flank support of the advancing 179th. With the 180th still not in the Gulf, the 157th on the wrong beach,

The Allies invaded Salerno in September of 1943. The beachhead was in jeopardy as the 45th landed on September 10 to plug a gap in the Allied lines. The Thunderbirds held the line and saved the invasion with a last ditch stand at the junction of the Calore-Sele Rivers. Here two Thunderbirds huddle behind their tank.

and most of the big guns of Division Artillery not yet on shore and not scheduled to arrive until the next day, the 179th was on its own as it marched into the gap. Division Artillery was the only unit between the 179th and the Gulf of Salerno. The Germans were not idle. The 29th Panzer Grenadier Division made its way into the area near Persano only seven miles from Jack's position and the 16th Panzer Division also was flooding into the corridor, becoming more crowded by the moment.

In keeping with the speed and aggressiveness demonstrated in Sicily the 179th, on foot most of the way, marched all night and by dawn on the morning of September 11, 1943 had crossed into the "Y" above the junction of the Sele and Calore rivers. Without the flank protection of the 157th, the line of march ran them directly into the teeth of two German divisions. The fight was on. Throughout the day, the 179th was locked in a bitter struggle with German tanks, artillery, and infantry south and west of Persano. With only Lt. Col. Jess Larson's 160th Field Artillery available for support, the American 105s were in a muzzle-to-muzzle duel with German 88s as the regiments forward observers were now reporting 200 German tanks massing north of Persano near the town of Serre. As for Jack and the Division CP, there was little they could do but sit at the river's junction with their field glasses glued to the action in the valley between the rivers and wait for the arrival of the 155s and the other artillery battalions. The view to Jack was surreal as he watched the fight between the German and American armor. The giant muzzle flashes and concussion of the big guns rumbled through the valley, shaking the ground, and drowning out the rifle and machine gun fire. If the Germans broke through the 179th now, Jack's .45 pistol would serve no purpose against German armor. As Jack was fond of saying "it's like pissin' on a forest fire."

Without flank support on the left, the German 16th Panzer Division pushed across the Sele River and into the left flank of the 179th. It became man against tank with the German tanks working their way to the rear of the 179th position. The 179th was suddenly encircled and, as Whitlock described, being "hammered from all sides." The 179th was in desperate shape, completely surrounded, and with little chance of survival.

Back at Division Artillery CP, the plight of the 179th was apparent. As the day wore on, the rest of the Division Artillery was getting ashore and the 157th was regrouping, crossing the Sele River, and moving northward. But could they get in position soon enough was the question as Jack and Harry struggled to firm up the firing maps and cement the vital lines of ammunition supply desperately needed to unleash on the Germans.

As night fell Jack dug in and prepared his slip-trench for what little sleep he could get before dawn. In the darkness he could hear the sound of rifles and the 179th trying to hang on. Hopefully with the light of day, Division Artillery would be released to fire-in rescue of the 179th. Meanwhile, the 157th marched north all night, taking a position that would hopefully allow relief of the 179th.

As for the men of the 179th, as the sun turned to moon, the Oklahomans fixed bayonets, dug-in and stared into the darkness of night waiting. As Major Pete Donaldson told his men "... Tonight, you're not fightin' for your country, your fightin' for your ass because they're behind us."

In an interview with *The Daily Oklahoman* after the battle in the Sele Corridor, Lt. Col. Jess Larson described the horror and grim plight of his men who were surrounded that September night.

> "... We lived 100 years in 36 hours ... at night the moaning of the wounded sickened us, men were killed, we buried them quickly."

With sunrise of September 12, the luck of the Thunderbird legend returned to the Sele Corridor. Miraculously, the Germans did not attack. By the 12th, the 157th had worked their way into a position north and west of the 179th to provide support and Division Artillery. Jack and Harry were energized with the thought of pounding back at the Germans. Division Artillery unleashed its firepower on the Germans, shelling Persano, and keeping the Germans "undercover," allowing the 179th to hold on through the day. As night fell, the 179th was able to strengthen its defense and realign its positions with the 157th sufficiently to beat back a German attack the night of September 12 .

The fighting was tough at Salerno. Here, a wounded Thunderbird is attended by medics

Having survived the German counterattack, the 179th was nearly out of ammunition, food, and supplies. Without support they would not make it through the day. At this most desperate hour, General McClain organized a convoy stuffed with ammunition, medical supplies, a vital cache of artillery ammunition, a few good men, and charged directly at the encircled 179th. McClain himself led the rescue party the last few yards through a mine field. The seige of the 179th was lifted. McClain later was awarded the Distinguished Service Cross for gallantry in the rescue of the 179th. With unbelievable understatement, The History of the 45th Infantry Division Artillery recorded this heroic event rather simply:

"The 179th was encircled at Persano, but rescued."

Lt. Col. Jess Larson had a more descriptive view of the rescue in his interview with *The Daily Oklahoman*, "Brigadier General Ray McClain was the first man through, he looked like Pancho Villa [coming to the rescue]."

The heroics surrounding the relief of the 179th were short-lived. To the east and between the 45th and 36th, the Germans were poised for yet another attack down the Sele Corridor, this time directly at the confluence of the Sele and Calore rivers. The only units between the Germans and the Salerno beach were the 189th Field Artillery, the 158th Field Artillery, McClain's staff, and Jack Neville. The 16th Panzer Corp was headed directly at Adair's son.

With only troops of the 45th standing between the German juggernaut and the beach, General Mark Clark gave the order to the Corps staff and the ships off shore to prepare for evacuation as the invasion was now likely to fail. Word of Clark's concern made its way to Troy Middleton, Commanding General of the 45th Infantry Division. Clark's order raised the hair on Middleton's neck and he sent out his own response, "Put food and ammunition behind the 45th. We are going to stay here."

Badly out numbered, Middleton had drawn a bold line in the sand, but he was determined to hold the position. The division would dig in on the banks of the river and wait for the Nazis. Middleton summoned McClain with the decision to stay and fight. With this, McClain gathered his staff. Jack was given orders to stop all movement toward the beach, turn any withdrawing troops around, and form a defensive perimeter with all available troops on the west bank of the Calore River near its junction with the Sele. With the situation near catastrophic, the artillerymen became riflemen; cooks, clerks, truck drivers, and members of the division took their place in the last stand at the river's edge. Jack was no exception, and neither were the nine members of the regimental band. As McClain noted in his draft of Citizen Soldier, "My headquarter's staff also took their carbines and went out to the fire fight along the river bank."

In the afternoon of September 13, 1943, Jack Neville grabbed his carbine and took his position on the defensive line along the Calore River. It all had to be similar to Crockett's last stand at the Alamo as the relatively small number of "Okies" faced a large foe with superior firepower. Jack's entrenching tool was put to good use this day. Jack dug and dug until he could stand in the foxhole and rest his arms on the ground. Having grabbed an M-1 carbine and eighty rounds of ammunition, Jack, and what there was of Division Artillery, stood ready for the test which most assuredly soon would come. As Jack surveyed down the eerily quiet valley, the big 105s and 155s lowered their giant barrels to zero elevation, as low as they could go. In these close quarters, the forward observer and map grid coordinates would be of little use in calling the shot. Breach citing, looking straight down the barrel and down the valley would be the effective method of aim. Jack put his rifle down range into the valley and peered through the open sights. Two hundred yards and he was certain he could hit the target.

At 4:00 p.m. on September 13, 1943, the German's 16th Panzer Division started their charge down the corridor. The attack force consisted of 10 to 12 tanks with supporting infantry. As the attacking force drew closer, Jack and the men dug in on the defensive line and could hear the unmistakable screech of steel meeting steel–the treads of the German Panzer creeping along. As Jack looked down the valley, the tanks were in the open, in plain view with the gray tunics of the Nazi infantry sprinting about and around the tanks. Still out of range, Jack practiced picking a gray clad target waiting for the enemy to get within range. As General McClain described it, "the boys on line kept their cool," there was no panic. McClain's artillery stayed put laying down direct fire at 200 yards.

At 200 yards, the Germans were within the effective range of Jack's M-1. Almost like puppets dancing up and down on the ground, Jack and the other riflemen carefully selected the moving gray targets who at this range still remained faceless. Jack could only believe that they were as afraid as he. With 80 rounds in his sack, he tried to make every shot count. As the Germans moved forward and closer, the sounds on the battlefield became deafening. The 189th Field Artillery under the command of Lt. Col. Hal Muldrow of Norman, Oklahoma, were firing the 105s as fast as they could stuff shells into the barrel, and the longer 155s were doing the same. It was a literal curtain of steel that rained down the valley at the German tanks and infantry. It became so loud at times that Jack could not hear his own rifle firing and if you had to talk to the soldier in the foxhole next to you, shouting barely got it done. There was no time to look around the battlefield, stay down, focus on the faceless nameless gray suit, and squeeze off a round. If it fell, search for another. As the great battle wore on, the scene down the Sele Corridor became more and more clouded with smoke and fire. Great chunks of black metal were all over the battlefield and dead gray bodies spotted the ground. With no time to think about it all, Jack just kept firing. It was impossible to count the rifle ammunition spent that day, but General McClain recorded that by sunset the two battalions of artillery had shellacked the Germans with 3,650 artillery rounds into a corridor slightly more than one-mile wide, firing at an incredible rate of 8 rounds per minute per gun. As night fell, the fighting continued with Jack having few, if any, targets to focus on. The evening hours brought on more artillery fire on enemy position silhouetted by burning fires on the battlefield in front of the 45th. By midnight the fighting subsided. The Germans fell back to regroup and reports were now filtering through the lines that the enemy had amassed more tanks, and more infantry with the purpose to finish off the 45th when the sun rose. It was at this point in the battle that Clark sent the order to the ships off shore to prepare to evacuate the division off the beach. But just as quickly as it was given, Middleton responded that the boys of the 45th would stay and fight, "send in the ammo" was the call.

There is no recorded history of what Jack's thoughts were as he crouched in that foxhole. He had to wonder if the morning would bring the end, if it was the last day he would see the sun, breathe the air. As he sat there in the dirt banks of the Calore, he and every man around him had to be scared as they gazed out into the darkness of Italy. There was no dishonor in fear. Every man this night had to feel it. No one could have slept that night as each and every sole recorded their past and wished for their future.

Supply lines to the beach still somewhat in tact, the ammo runners brought what was left of the bandoleros now containing the last few rounds of ammunition. With the limited resupply of rounds it was now obvious to those standing in foxholes that the division was low on ammunition and supplies. C-Rations were dropped off with the ammo. The beans were always a little better mixed with dirt that fell off the edges of the foxhole. Appetites, however, were a little difficult to come by. As the front lines were resupplied with what was left, the scuttle-butt for the morning was that the Germans were mounting yet another attack, this time more tanks, more artillery, more infantry. The rumors would prove true.

As dawn came, Jack could see the destruction and carnage wreaked on the countryside. It was nothing short of horrific. Bodies and body parts littered the ground. In the distance, he could hear the sounds of pain and agony, men screaming for help that did not come. Animals and birds picked over some of the German remains as if they were a last supper. The screams of the dying and wounded pierced the morning air both on the defensive line and down "the gap." How could they possibly come back through that corridor. The once beautiful trees and woods that painted the little valley between two rivers were now gone, pulverized into little more than kindling by the cannon fire. Smoke painted the blue sky gray. Farm houses that once dotted the scene were gone, still burning, and horses and cows seemed scattered amongst the now lifeless figures of the German soldiers. In this battle there were brave men on both sides, but as Jack studied the scene he found it difficult to believe they would come again. He was wrong.

For a time that morning Jack wondered if they would ever come, almost wishing it so, at least it would be over and finished after standing, kneeling, and lying for more than 14 hours in a hole. But down the valley they came. At 10:00 a.m. on September 14, 23 German Panzers with infantry were once again headed at Jack's position. This time, however, the Germans were about to see a new hell. The giant 155s, now restocked with their last supply of shells, opened fire on the German advance at 700 yards over open sights. At that extended range, Jack was helpless to shoot at anything; but the adrenalin of joy rushed through his body as the sight and sounds of the heavy guns blasted away at the German tanks with devastating effect. Muldrow's boys were on the mark, but still the Germans kept coming in one last desperate gamble to breach the 45th lines. As the Nazis continued to stumble forward, two battalions of the 105s opened fire with the heavy machine guns. The thunderous roar of the cannon continued for hours with Jack having to fire few shots. In a remarkable display of physical stamina and courage, the artillerymen kept the Germans at bay with 6,687 rounds fired that day, almost twice that of the previous day by McClain's count in Citizen Soldier. The smaller 105s of the 158th and 189th fired at an incredible rate of 19 shells per minute, the maximum rate possible previously had been estimated at only six rounds per minute. When the smoke and dark haze cleared, the entire German force had been annihilated. Twenty-three German tanks and numerous 88s destroyed. The Germans had been stopped.

As Jack crawled from his foxhole, the entire valley seemed an inferno. Filthy after more than 24 hours in a hole that probably saved his life, he gazed down the valley with rifle in hand. The most ghastly sight of all was the gray carpet of dead German soldiers that covered the floor of the battlefield. Standing by his hole, physically exhausted but relieved that this one was over, Harry Balkum stumbled by. Jack could only smile, his buddy had made it. Happy they were both alive, Jack looked at Harry with his mischievous grin and asked "Do you think Andy Kirk and his Clouds of Joy are in town tonight?" They both roared with laughter as they walked off in search of the rest of the S-3 staff.

Late in the afternoon the 180th Infantry Regiment arrived off the coast near Agropoli. The fear of course was that the Germans would return. The S-3 staff reassembled, gratefully surrendering their status as infantrymen. Even the cooks were happy to go back to cooking. The eyes of the artillery, the forward observers, were again deployed to detect any renewed effort by the Germans to come back down the corridor, and Jack and the staff continually raised their field glasses and prayed they would see nothing. They did not.

On September 15 the division continued to improve its defenses, consolidating their lines in anticipation of another Nazi move. The forward observers were now reporting tank activity in their rear positions and accordingly the 155s primed their pieces to lob their giant shells into the German's positions believing yet another German counterattack was imminent. As the artillery readied their fire, Jack grabbed his binoculars to surveil the valley down range. And then, across the radio came the order from one of the field battalions to hold their fire. Jack steadied the glasses on the corridor. To his amazement, walking into the line of fire were German soldiers. They were unarmed, without helmets, and shirt tails out. They were carrying shovels, axes, picks, and body bags. It took some time to realize that a German burial detail had been sent to retrieve the bodies. It was a gruesome reality filled with the ultimate irony of war. Only hours before the Germans were trying to kill the Americans, and vice versa. Now, with guns silent, the unarmed Germans marched into the fields to retrieve their fallen brothers. In near reverence, the United States soldiers watched the Germans retrieve their dead and bury their fallen comrades in a quiet peace, free from fire. It seemed an awkward civility extended to the enemy, but perhaps one that was due if for no other reason to pay some form of homage to humanity. Jack wondered if the Germans would do the same for those fallen men of the 45th or if they did the same for Gene Neville. It seemed hours before the Germans cleared the battlefield of their dead and wounded. Once in the clear, the forward out posts reported armored activity in the town of Persano, toward the rearward positions of the Germans. Over the 15th and 16th of September, the artillery shelled the German forces into submission and reduced the beautiful town of Persano to a casualty of war.

By September 18, 1943, the Germans had withdrawn their forces to the north, evacuating most of their troops at night. By September 19, 1943, the bloody battle for the Salerno beachhead south of Naples, Italy, was over. The 45th Infantry Division had won against all odds, and Jack Neville could only breathe a great sigh of relief that he was still alive.

Despite relatively light resistance in their move up the center of Italy, the British 8th did not get within 100 miles of Paestum at the critical stage of battle for the Salerno beachhead. Somewhere along the way Montgomery decided his men needed a two-day rest while the soldiers of the 45th slugged it out with the 16th and 29th German Panzer Divisions.

RECOLLECTIONS SEPTEMBER ,1943

September of 1943 was excruciating for Leota back in Oklahoma City. After the mid-August victory in Sicily the 45th Infantry Division "disappeared" off the map and the pages of the press. War-time security required the Thunderbird's whereabouts be shrouded in secrecy. No press and no mail, the division had become a ghost. The daily routine of trekking to the McDonnell-Douglas Aircraft Plant in Midwest City and back to 42nd only to be met by a "45th black out" put life on the edge. There was nothing she could do except write letters to "45 APO" in New York and commensurate with others whose husbands and family members were overseas. Was "knowing" worse than "not knowing." Leota's recurring and burdensome question had become unanswerable. Little news came across "Voice of the Army" on KOCY Radio through the latter part of August and new movie releases at the downtown Criterion Theatre, such as "So Proudly We Hail," did not seem to generate enthusiasm.

Most entertaining however was Sylvester Stauffer's rather vocifuous and violent reaction to the September 2, 1943 ruling by the Oklahoma Supreme Court that held it unconstitutional to require children to salute the American Flag. Sylvester always viewed himself victimized by Roosevelt's big brother government. Controlling the glut of Oklahoma crude during the Depression years was unAmerican, unconstitutional, and now the liberal communists had invaded the Supreme Court of Oklahoma during wartime forbidding children's flag saluting. "My God, we've got boys fighting and dyin' over there and those little kids ought to damn well salute that flag there-a fightin' fore," he would proclaim. Such protest was the closest Sylvester came to acknowledging the difficulty of Jack and Leota's separation, but he nonetheless saw it as an expression of enthusiastic support. And, in his way, it was.

By September of 1943, the press was becoming more skilled at covering the events of the war and the United States Government, and its Armed Forces more cognizant of the great power of the press to generate patriotism and support for the war effort. The reporters were "pooled," grouped together. Choosing one of their numbers, the "war correspondents" were assigned to various fighting units to report and bring the battle to the folks on the homefront. With press reports heavily monitored and censored, the reports of the Allied war efforts made their way to the hometown press in the towns and cities across the nation. Purposefully vague, general, and at times ambiguous, reports carried in The Daily Oklahoman *became Leota's only message home from Jack, her only view of the fighting front. The descriptive, eloquent words of Ernie Pyle and* The Daily Oklahoman's *Don*

Robinson allowed Leota to paint some picture of where Jack was and what he was going through. The speed of communication coupled with streamlined military censor reviews allowed the war to be reported almost as it occurred, and certainly within a couple of days of the events. As a result, the Oklahoma City paper, which carried two editions, morning and afternoon, became a coveted missive that Leota read closely each day and night.

The first clue in weeks of the location of the 45th came on September 3, 1943, when The Daily Oklahoman *headlines reported in giant bold print "Allies Invading Salerno." Every sentence was scoured for word of the division as the Supreme Allied Headquarters reported that the British 8th Army had attacked across the Straits of Messina. With some relief for Leota, it was reported that the Thunderbirds were being held in "reserve." With the Allies on the move once again in southern Europe, the paper took on an everyday importance. On September 9, the front page reported that "Allied Armies Land At Naples," with headlines three days later blaring "Allies Expand Hold at Naples, Seize Salerno." Of course the report was somewhat misleading because the 45th Infantry Division did not invade Naples, protected by heavy German defenses and the Sorrento Peninsula. In fact, the 45th was some 40 miles south of Naples in Paestum. The reports created mixed emotions. Jack had to be there someplace and there was at least some satisfaction in knowing the division's approximate location. On the other hand, the battle reports now clearly put the division in harm's way; however, as of September 12, the 45th had not been identified as being involved in the fighting. Just maybe, she hoped, the division was still in reserve.*

Every day in Oklahoma City was now a roller coaster as the city was locked to the news to hear reports about their boys. The emotional barometer spiked upward again on September 14, 1943, when The Daily Oklahoman *headlines read "Yanks Advance on Salerno Front Against Fierce German Defense." For the first time the Allied Supreme Headquarters was allowing reports that the soldiers on the front were sustaining heavy casualties. Leota's fears only deepened as the worst reports of the war in southern Europe clearly indicated that the fight was bloody, Oklahoma boys would be killed. Ironically, the first reports that the 45th was locked in fierce combat with the Nazis came from the Germans themselves. Broadcasting from Berlin, the Germans reported that the 45th Infantry Division was locked in a brutal struggle with German tanks at Paestum. This broadcast was picked up in London, and the British Broadcasting Company forwarded it on to the Yanks in New York. It only took a few hours for the information to find its way to the front page of* The Daily Oklahoman. *On September 15, 1943, the sickening fear of Jack's death now invaded the Neville and Stauffer homes. In a two-day period of time the news had turned awful. Heavy ca-*

sualties were reported in fierce fighting on the Salerno beachhead with Jack obviously right in the middle of it. The gloom of the reports darkened all spirits. News of the battle took on a secondary significance to the reports of casualties as the fear of deaths escalated to a real-life high. The entire situation spelled a horrible tragedy. At the McDonnell-Douglas plant working wives searched for any hint of optimism to end the depression. Perhaps the British would get to the boys in time, they had to be close, all they had to do was hang on. The fact that Ava Gardner had gotten divorced in Nevada did not even make the coffee room gossip.

Of course, what Leota did not know at home was that the British were not even close to rescuing the division, but rather the Thunderbirds had rescued themselves in the gallant stand at the river's edge. By September 15, the war at Calore-Sele rivers was over, and Jack was safe; however at home in Oklahoma City Leota felt as if she was on death watch.

As the next few days wore on, reports of the success of Operation Avalanche drifted into the news, along with the increasing lists of men killed, wounded, and missing in action. Twenty-two years later on television's Huntley-Brinkley Report it was rather clinically called the "body count," but in 1943 the name of every casualty was prominently, proudly in a way, reported to the home folks in the pages of The Daily Oklahoman *and Oklahoma City Times. Each day brought a sigh of relief as Leota went down the ugly lists, only to be replaced by the anxiety of yet another day's wait.*

Reports of the invasion of Italy bettered over the next two days. The city breathed deep relief as on September 17, it was reported "Sooners Hold Lines at Salerno, Blasting Vicious Panzer Attack," and again on the 18th with the front-page article "State Soldiers Rescued From Nazi Trap in Italy." For Leota each passing day brought promise, and then delight. "That" letter never came, and "Neville" failed to surface on any list. Jack had made it she was now convinced, and so had Leota.

In the near aftermath of the Salerno fight, waves of patriotism rolled across the city as the citizens were challenged to do what they could to support America's war machine. In an emotional editorial on September 21, 1943, entitled "Of Course They Stayed," the virtues of the 45th's last stand in the Sele Corridor was eloquently extolled on one hand while the citizens were lambasted and chastised on the other hand for not doing their part.

> *". . . We are lagging in our bond purchase campaign. . . . We wait and dilly dally and argue and procrastinate while they are breaking bones and giving their own red blood."*

Leota bought every bond she could, all she could afford was $100.00.

It was not until mid-November of 1943, that Leota learned of the serious game of daring jeopardy played on the Italian beach south of Naples.

Seriously wounded, Lt. Col. Jess Larson of the 160th Field Artillery and one of the soldiers entrapped and encircled with the 179th Infantry Regiment returned home to convalesce. Larson was from Oklahoma City, and for the first time Leota, and the city, learned of the near catastrophic events of the 179th plight south of Persano, and the division's last ditch stand at water's edge. With every word of Larson's account, Leota was reminded that the war moved on, it was all so fragile for Jack, and with every fight, she would have to live through it again thousands of miles away.

Almost 60 years after the guns have fallen silent on the Salerno beachhead, the gallantry and heroism of those days in the Sele Corridor have been misplaced, even swallowed up by the more titanic battles of World War II, if not forgotten entirely. By September of 1943, Operation Avalanche had become the stepchild of Operation Overlord. The priority of men, ships, and material were given to the preparation for the D-Day landing that occurred the following June, 1944. As a result, the Thunderbirds sailed into a tough battle woefully under-strength. The 45th fought in the Corridor with more than one-third of its infantry strength still on the ocean. At Salerno the Germans had superior numbers and firepower, but still the Oklahomans prevailed. The 179th Infantry Regiment moved inland too far, too fast, and became entrapped and encircled by an entire German Division. Low on food and ammunition, the regiment refused to give up. They bravely fought on for two days until McClain's convoy rode to the rescue. For a day frozen in time, more than two-thirds of the division's fighting strength was either trapped by the Germans or on the ocean with only the 157th and Division Artillery. Then was one of the most courageous struggles ever in the European Theatre of operations, the last stand at the conjunction of the Sele and Corridor rivers. As they say, this one was for all the "marbles." While Clark hesitated in his ship offshore, even to the point of giving orders to prepare to evacuate the beach, the Oklahomans never backed off. "Send in the ammo, the 45th stays" was the battle cry, as Jack Neville and the rest of the Thunderbirds dug in at the river against tanks, artillery, and waves of infantry. They were the only troops between the Germans and the beachhead. If the Germans took back the beach, Operation Avalanche would fold like a house of cards as the United States 36th to the south and the British to the north would be cut off from their life lines of supply and ammunition that could only come from the beach. The 45th did not break. They held.

As feared, the casualty count at Salerno was abysmal. The Americans suffered 1,084 killed in action, 3,252 wounded, and 869 missing in a nine day period of time–total of more than an entire infantry regiment. The Salerno beachhead has a rightful place of honor and remembrance in the greatest struggle to save freedom the world had ever seen.

CHAPTER XV
UP THE BOOT, VENAFRO, & THE WINTER LINE

With the break out of the Salerno beachhead successfully underway, the 45th Infantry Division moved northeast through the towns of Persano and Eboli. For Jack, he was lucky that he did not have to walk through the destruction and death that the division had reeked on the Germans. As Division Artillery motored through Persano the stink of death was everywhere. It was impossible to breathe without a handkerchief covering your face. Some of the men could not hold it and let it go, throwing up over the sides of the trucks. There was nothing Jack could do to conceal his eyes from the horrific sights all about him. The little town of Persano was no more, totally destroyed. Once the battle for the Sele Corridor began, the town's citizens left their city and home, certain to die under a hail of shrapnel if they did not. As the Artillery staff moved on, the sadness was overwhelming. An entire town was rubble, and its citizens gone. There was only one way to handle the death and destruction of Persano and that was to ride away from it and try to forget it. Jack had to have found it difficult. After uninterrupted days and nights of fighting, the division continued eastward. Battle weakened and fatigued, the men became sick with the flu, colds, and malaria. Once at Eboli, the 45th was positioned for a move northward. There, they dug in to wait for orders. They did not have to wait long.

Having lost the Salerno beachhead, the Germans engaged in another of their patented strategic retreats. They would make the allies pay for every bridgehead and river crossing between Salerno and central Italy and take up fixed defensive positions in the "Winter-Line" south of Rome in hopes of stopping the allies advance. One of the Nazi's biggest allies would become the sleet, rain, and snow of the approaching winter. With the allies move into Sicily, and then Italy, the Germans began preparing four lines of defense that ran across central Italy. To the north of Naples was the "Barbara Line" of defense, and behind this line the "Bernhard Line." Yet another line of defense was behind these two positions, the famous "Gustav Line" that stretched the entire width of Italy just south of Rome. The Gustav Line was the German's last line of real defense in Italy, an extremely heavily fortified position made up of bunkers, gun employments, and a complicated trench system. Along with these three lines of fixed positions, was one last line intended to protect the south of Rome the "Hitler Line" running from Cassino to the sea. These four lines collectively became known as the Winter Line, thought to be impregnable by the Germans. Defending the Winter Line was the German 10th Army, made up of 11 divisions inclusive of the 45th's Sicilian foe, the Herman Goering Division.

The Allied plan of attack up the boot of Italy called for a massive six-division assault the width of Italy directly north into the teeth of the Winter Line. From west to east the British 7th, 46th, 56th and the United States 3rd, 34th and 45th would move through the Apennine Mountains, through Piedmonte Di Alife, and Venafro just across the Volturo River. To position itself on the eastern flank of the 5th Army's advance, the 45th would have to move further eastward from Eboli to the town of Oliveto. To the east of the 45th would be the British 8th Army, that is, as Jack thought, if the 8th could get there given their performance south of Salerno.

As the Division Artillery moved toward Oliveto, Jack found the only thing soft about the underbelly of Europe was the mud. Heavy rain slowed all movement and the advance became more difficult, plagued by the desperation of German tactics. Every bridge between Paestum and Oliveto was booby-trapped, mined, and blown. In fact, between the two towns, the Germans brought the division to a near halt by blowing up 25 bridges. With bridges destroyed, Jack had to call for the engineers to construct their erector-set "Baily Bridges" so that the huge artillery pieces could make their way across the swollen rivers. As Jack sat in the truck waiting on the engineers, he and the rest of the men were stationary targets for the German snipers and camouflaged machine gun positions. No trick was left unturned by the Germans as they left soldiers behind in civilian clothes to observe movement and report grid coordinates to German artillery to fire on the 45th while the Baily Bridges were being built. It only took one barrage to send Jack and Harry off their truck as the engineers did their work. Stop, wait on the engineers, and take cover became the modus operandi of the day. The sniper situation became so disruptive that the men removed all insignia from their uniforms as the Germans were attempting to pick off the officers and higher ranked non-commissioned officers, like Jack. It did not take long for the preferred method of advance down the narrow roads and trails be by bull dozer. With their huge front-end blades raised slightly off the ground, machine gun fire and sniper's bullets ricocheted and provided the shield necessary to move ahead.

As the division crept toward the town of Oliveto the fighting became more bitter. The infantry units were in near foxhole-to-foxhole combat with the Germans who would just not let go. The S-3 staff was non-stop preparing firing and logistical plans to provide the fire support necessary to aide the "leap-frogging" tactics of the foot soldiers who were literally having to dig the enemy out.

The unbelievable courage and heroism at Salerno was not left on the beaches. In brutal hand-to-hand fighting near Oliveto, Lt. Ernest Childers, a Creek Indian from Broken Arrow, Oklahoma, won the Medal of Honor, as did Corporal James D. Slaton. By September 22, 1943, the Division Artillery CP was set up in fallen Oliveto and the Thunderbirds were poised to chase the Nazis further north.

For the next three weeks the division would play a cat-and-mouse game of sorts with the Germans. On September 23, 1943, the 45th took Valva, where Jack's Division Artillery set up shop, only to lose contact with the Germans the next day. On September 25, Jack's CP was established at the village of Calabritts, only the next day to move again to a position along the Sele River to support the continued pursuit of the Nazis. The weather again became the ally of the enemy. Torrential rain bogged down the advance and many of the men again became sick with flu, colds, and the stomach bug of Italy. The tension and fear of the deadly sniper fire began to take its toll, along with the harassing tactics of the withdrawing Germans. Col. Charles Ankorn, commanding the 157th Infantry Regiment, lost a leg to a mine. Sniper fire continued to haunt the division by maiming the arms and legs of the men moving slowly through the mud.

From the west came the first good news since the Salerno beach breakout. While the 45th lost contact with the enemy in the east, on October 1, General Clark and the rest of the allied forces had taken Naples. With the fall of Naples there was little doubt that the Germans were in full retreat heading for the refuge of the Winter Line defenses.

On October 2, 1943, the Thunderbirds were ordered to pivot their line of advance northwest toward the city of Benevento. It would be a 50-mile convoy march up the boot of Italy abreast of the other five divisions, with the 45th continuing to hold the right flank. This march would prove every bit as miserable as the move out of Paestum. The weather worsened. The cold rain and wind never seemed to let up. Jack, at times, thought it better to walk than ride, you could not stay dry anywhere. The trucks pulling the 105s and 155s and the men seemed to sink only deeper into Italy's mud. For a time, the trek became one of pushing and shoving spinning truck tires out of deep mud-filled ruts and rescuing the giant guns when they slid off the path. Dirt, filth, and mud caked Jack's face, hands, and fatigues in layers only to be washed away by the continued torrent of rain. There seemed no relief. For the next six days the division slogged their way northward fighting both the elements and the Germans. The snipers continued and the German's mine fields plagued the pace of the march. At times, the men were afraid to take a step in any direction for fear of an exploding mine. If the mine did not kill you, it most probably would take off a foot or a leg. Jack found himself no longer looking down the road, but at the road in terror that his boot would touch off the tentacles of a

Moving up the boot of Italy in October, 1943, the small Italian town of Benevento was the scene of intense fighting until it was laid to ruins on October 8, 1943.

deadly mine planted in his path. Jack even gave a second thought at wondering off the beaten path to "relieve" himself. Fear ripped through the ranks when Lt. Col. John Patterson of the 180th was blown to bits walking into the regiment's bivouac area. No path was safe. It was all under fire of some sort.

After what seemed an eternity, the division reached Benevento on October 8, only to regroup for the continued move north. With the soldiers absolutely spent, the 45th received the order for yet another treacherous and lengthy march, this time of 20 miles. As part of Clark's planned offensive north, the division was ordered on October 9, to move north out of Benevento, and to proceed westward along the northern bank of the Calore River toward Telese. Division Artillery prepared to support what again would be a slow advance. Along the advance, the towns of Cerreto and Guardia were taken in rather quick order, but at Telese on October 12, with the division getting closer to the Winter Line fixed positions, the Germans formed a pocket of fierce resistance and mounted a panicked counterattack against the 180th. Now experienced in the way of the German counterattack, the 180th drifted back to allow the entirety of Division Artillery to focus their sights on the Germans. At the ready, the artillery stopped the Germans cold in their tracks.

There was still no rest for the wearied Thunderbirds. They pushed on toward the Barbara Line, the first of the German Winter Lines of defense that stretched the width of Italy. Having been chased out of Telese, the Germans attempted to consolidate their position to the north in Monte Acero and the town of Faicchio. The Division Artillery established its CP north of Telese to plan and position their supporting fire on the two small towns. The 179th met stiff resistance at Monte Acero. With the inevitable German counterattack the guns of the artillery put a halt to another German attack. Now routed out of Monte Acero, the Germans 26th Panzer Division retreated further northward to Faicchio. With the Nazis bunkered down in Faicchio, the incredible rain and cold came again. There seemed no end to the miserable weather conditions, but on the heels of the Huns, the Thunderbirds would not let go. Wet, cold, and fatigued beyond description, the Division Artillery pounded Faicchio all day October 13. It was at Faicchio that the Germans introduced their multi-barrelled mortar capable of firing six rounds at a time. As devastating as it was on the infantry's advance, the "Screaming Meenie" as it came to be known, was no match for the 105s and 155s. Fortunately for Jack, the German mortar could not reach the Artillery CP. Sleepless, near physical exhaustion, the 179th Infantry Regiment mounted a night attack at Faicchio. The fighting continued for 24 hours in a down pour, but Faicchio refused to fall, and the first effort by the 45th failed. Throughout the night and on October 15, Division Artillery unleashed all of its fire power on Faicchio. The town was nearly destroyed and the German troops were forced to scatter into the surrounding

On the road up the boot of Italy in the fall of 1943, is Jimmie Smith, Jack's brother-in-law, who drove a truck he named "Sick, Lame and Lazy."

hills. By October 16, Faicchio finally fell in a bloody struggle. With ferocious determination the division continued to ferret out the Germans at every turn of the road. The only way to get home was to keep moving, and by now no one wanted to stop. They all knew it was the quickest way, just keep going. The towns of Gioia and Auduni fell to the Thunderbird advance. After the two towns fell, and eight miles out of Faicchio, the division was poised on the city limits of Piedmonte di Alife, approximately 20 miles south of the Barbara Line. Thankfully, the division did not have to destroy its fourth town in less than 10 miles. The city was spared and taken against relatively light opposition.

Worn out and worn down, eyes sunk deep into their faces, sleepless ghost-like in appearance, exhausted, nearly out of ammunition, food and supplies, the Thunderbirds were cooked. General Middleton mercifully called a halt to the division's gallant and unprecedented sweep northward. After 40 days of continuous fighting, the division was relieved from the front lines by the United States 34th Division for a well-deserved rest and placed in Corps reserve,with the Division Artillery CP and moved back to Faicchio. For the citizen soldiers from the southwest, it was the longest period of time an American division had been on the front lines in the European Theatre without relief since the war started.

Jack, left, and his pal Harry Balkum, right, taken somewhere in Italy after the Salerno invasion in September of 1943.

Once again for Jack, the luck of the Thunderbird and the angels rode his shoulders all the way up the boot of Italy. Although there was heavy artillery activity at Benevento, Telese, and Facchio in fighting back German counterattacks, Jack was relieved that he did not have to climb back into a foxhole again as he had to do on the Salerno beachhead. At Salerno he at least had the enemy in front of him. In the fight northward to Piedmonte di Alife he rarely saw the enemy but had to endure a different kind of terror in the war–snipers, mines, booby-traps, enemy artillery fire–and all it seemed aided and abetted by the miserable and constant rain and mud of the narrow Italian roads. He had for now survived and it was all he could do but look skyward and say thank you to the heavens.

For the 45th Infantry Division, the boys were setting new standards for toughness and courage under fire. In 40 days, the division had clawed and scratched its way over 200 miles. They had liberated 274 towns and villages, chasing out the Nazis and Fascists. It was not without great cost and heartbreak that the Thunderbirds lost 30% of their strength to death, illness, and other casualty.

None of it would get any better as the soldiers would next move to Venafro, and soon the titanic battle at Anzio.

The 45th proceeded up the right flank of the 5th Army's move northward up the boot of Italy and into the face of the German Barbara Line and Bernhard Line in November of 1943.

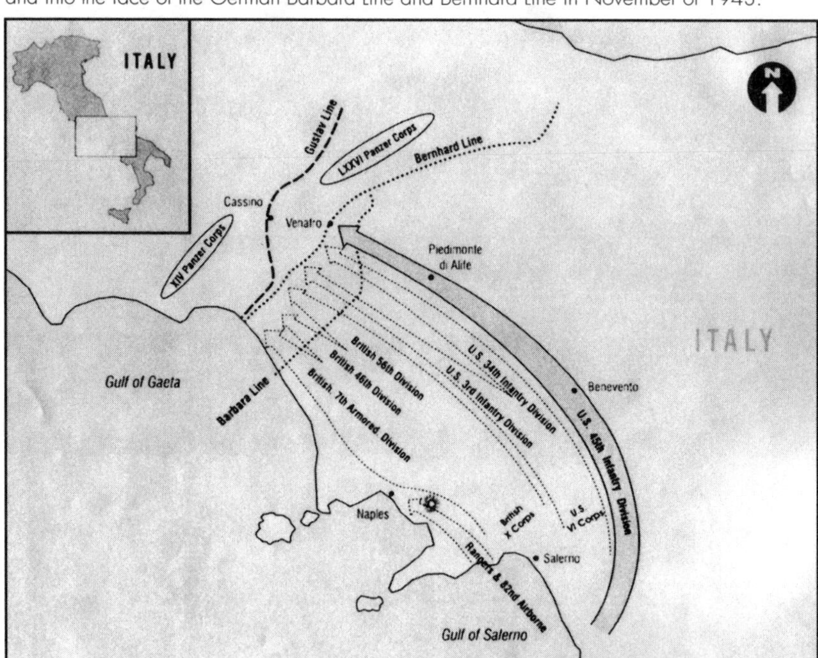

REFLECTION JUNE, 1959 LAKE WORTH, FLORIDA

The greatest place to live in the world in the 1950s was Oklahoma City, Oklahoma. For a kid growing up we thought we had it all. By the mid-1950s Jack and Leota were moving to the north side. By 1956, Bob Neville had come along and Jack found greener pastures with the R. Olson Oil Company as an accountant. With a new addition and a new job, Jack and Leota were ready for a new house. Excited at the prospect of having my own room, because I was the oldest, Mom quickly dashed my hopes for solitude when she commanded that one-year-old Bob would have his own room, not I. Bob's arrival required an extra bedroom, but Richard and I were forced to bunk up again. It was traumatic. At first we both hated it. After all Bob could not talk, and he could barely eat. He could not even change his own pants. Why did he need his own room? For some reason Richard thought he would get his own bedroom and of course sibling rivalry kicked in with loud shouts accusing the other of being a "dork," "stupid," "wimp," and so on. This was quickly ended with Jack's arrival home and one of his patented "shellackings." Mom was right, the general commanded, Bob would get his own room, that was it. Peace in the house was restored rather summarily once the sheriff got home from work. The move across town was made with ease. A lot of my pals made the same trek northward excited about the new Monroe Elementary school at 48th Street and Villa Avenue. After all, if your friends go too, nothing can be too bad about a new school at 10 years old.

By 1956, throwing rocks at cars and stealing bubble gum at Katz Drug Store was replaced by baseball, basketball, and flag football. At Monroe we had the coaches, the players, and the team, but no baseball field to play on. This was taken care of in rather short order. On a Saturday morning at 6:00 a.m. I arose to the clang, back-firing, sputtering, and smoking site and sound of a three-wheel farm tractor with a front-end grader chugging down 48th Street and into our driveway. The driver was Jack Neville; we were going up to school to build a baseball field. Two of my buddies, Jim Stacey and Jim Mosely, climbed aboard and to the disgust of the cars and traffic behind us, we slowly made our way to the school. In an all-day event, Dad and Coach Leland Mosely measured 50 feet to first, second, and third, thirty feet from home plate. While Stacey, Mosely and I played catch and did nothing at all to help, Dad and Coach Mosely graded, leveled, and carved out of the southwest corner of the school yard, a baseball field complete with a back stop. By days end, it was done and we were ready for play.

In those days the Monroe Redbirds, as we called ourselves, played in the Midget "A" YMCA league against the likes of Billy Grimes and the Madison Magpies, and the O'Toole brothers of the Mayfair Chipmunks. We loved to beat up on the rich kids north of us–the Nichols Hills Wildcats. We were the scourge of the league with speedster Jim Stacey stealing bases like they were candy and Ron Kise's fastball looking more like an aspirin than a baseball as it whizzed toward home plate. We did not have tailored uniforms, only a pair of Levis rolled up to the ankles, high-top tennis shoes, a cap with "M" on the front, and a tee-shirt with "Monroe Redbirds" stenciled on the front. There were no numbers or names on the back. What we really had however was fun, and Jack and Leota never missed a game. Richard and I played the games while brother Bob, in his stroller with grape popsicle juice all over his face, sat behind our bench. In the summer of 1958, we actually got a black and white television set and Saturday afternoons were spent with Jack watching the first televised Major League baseball games announced by Pee Wee Reese and Dizzy Dean. I thought Dizzy's excitement that Mickey Mantle "sludded" into third was good English. It was quickly corrected by Mom who expressed horror at Diz's abuse of the King's English. There were times when she insisted that the television be turned off. It took some work for Dad to overcome the objection. In the summers of the mid-1950s, the Oklahoma City Indians were a big thing. A farm club of the St. Louis Cardinals, Mom and Dad always insisted that we invite a friend when the "Cards" came to town with Stan Musial and Oklahoma's Lindy and Vaughn McDaniel.

The Oklahoma Sooners were the nation's juggernaut on the gridiron. In the 1950s Bud Wilkinson's Sooners went on a 47-game winning streak, the longest in the history of the NCAA. Grab a buddy and go, we never missed a home game in the 47-game streak. My pal Jim Stacey was the usual beneficiary of a ticket bought near the Armory for $1.00 right before kick-off. "Bud's boys" usually blew the opposition out early with margins of victory exceeding 40 points or more, but we never left early. My Saturday heroes were Tommy McDonald, Clendon Thomas, Jimmy Harris, and Jerry Tubbs. They ran with impunity up and down Owen Field and the Big Eight Conference soon became known as "Oklahoma and the Seven Dwarfs." We loved every minute of those lop-sided games; that is until November 7, 1956, when the Fighting Irish of Notre Dame came to town. In the 1950s, you did not wear jeans, tennis shoes, and tee-shirts to Oklahoma home games, coat and tie was the dress code and the women were no exception. Mom never went to a game without her high heels and a below-the-knee suit or dress. Bud Wilkinson always wore a shirt and tie, and so did all the men in the stands. You would have thought we were going to church as many believed Bud to be God himself residing in Owen Field. My buddy Jim Stacey quickly learned that if he was going to Norman, he better dress *up, even though he was nine. With the Catholics coming to Oklahoma all the way from the Golden Dome of South Bend, Indiana, as Jack explained it, Saturday called for your wardrobe's finest. We all were dressed to the nines for the big battle, but Mom refused to allow Jack to wear his red-saddled over white shoes. Our seats were on the east side of the stadium, right on the twenty yard line in the north end of Memorial Stadium about 30 rows up. While Jim and I were attentive to the game as best as nine year olds could be, we spent little time in our seats and Mom and Dad were content to let us roam the 60,000-seat stadium at will. Both teams, unbeaten and ranked one and two in the nation, moved up and down the field all day, but going into the fourth quarter it was zero-zero. Then, with only a few minutes left, came the play that changed Oklahoma football forever. Dick Lynch took a pitch out circling right end. His teammate, Nick Petrasante, delivered the last block on OU's Carl Dodd and Lynch sprinted untouched into the north end zone. The streak was over. It was the first time I saw grown ups cry. In shocked disbelief, Memorial Stadium was an ocean of tears as Jack and Leota tried to explain that Jim and I had just witnessed one of the greatest football games of our time, an event we would remember forever.*

According to Mom's scrapbook, basketball was Dad's favorite sport. Through the winter, "b-ball" was the game and the Gilt Edge Cowboys were the ten-and-under team. With my buddies Kenny Womack, Gary Kizzar, and Rod Eskridge leading the way, we were the kings of the hardwood. Two state championship trophies sat on the mantle. With my pals and sports, life in Oklahoma City was good.

Then, in June of 1959, it all came crashing down when Mom and Dad gathered Richard and I around the dining room table for the big announcement. The then New York City-based mega-corporation Grand Paige Corporation had bought the R. Olson Oil Company and Dad was being transferred to a new job in Palm Beach, Florida with a real estate company, A.E. and R.F. Raidle Co. They tried to put their best spin on the situation but to me it all sounded awful, the very end of the world itself. There would be no democratic vote of whether or not to go. No more Cowboys, Sooners, Redbirds, or my buddies at Monroe Elementary. We were gone. After three difficult days of driving, mostly in silence, we rolled into Palm Beach County at 2020 Lake Osborne Drive. At twelve years old, the worst two days of the rest of my life were the first two days of school at Lake Worth Junior High.

In the morning of that first day after a massive breakfast of bacon, eggs, and toast Mom handed me my lunch pail and gave me a big hug as I climbed into Dad's car for the lonely ride to school. Believing he was doing me a favor, he dropped me off very near the front steps of the school. This, of course, was very uncool as everyone else was afoot. To add insult to injury, no one else carried a lunch pail. Climbing out of the car in great agony, I was certain I looked like an elephant in short grass. All Dad could say was "Good Luck." I knew Mom would have extended more sympathy than just a sober, unfeeling "Good Luck." Peering up the steps to the front door, it seemed like a walk to hell itself. No pals, I did not know a soul. Everyone was cheerful and happy to be back at school. Everyone seemed to speak to everyone else as chatter bounced off the walls through the halls. Except no one spoke to me; and I spoke to no one. I was clearly the new kid in town. The lunch room was the loneliest place in the world those first two days. While all the kids had a lunch ticket and pushed their trays through the line, I had a lunch pail with Vienna sausage and mustard spread on white Wonder Bread. I sat alone in silence at the end of a long table. This was all my parents' fault. They had ruined my life. No one could feel more sorry for themselves than me, and I did a champion's job of it in those days.

By the third day, I had enough. A boycott or protest of some sort was in order. After the usual gigantic breakfast, this time of oatmeal and brown sugar, I returned to my bedroom, again shared with Richard, to retrieve my jacket and school books. Summoning every bit of courage and willpower possible, ready to take the Jack shellacking I was sure to receive, I left the books on my bed and marched into the living room. Dad asked me where my books were, said that we needed to go. I did not reply and instead sat on the edge of the sofa assuming the most defiant posture possible. Jack's jaw was set sensing the impending exchange, his hands at his waist, he bellowed "What in the hell's the matter?" Mom quickly hurried to my side and in a quiet voice asked me to tell her what the problem was. Legs crossed and locked at the ankles, arms tightened across my chest, I blurted out that I was not going to school, I knew no one and had no pals. With some relief it was all off my chest, I was now prepared for the inevitable ass kicking.

It did not come. Dad's hand dropped off his hips, his jaw relaxed, and his head dropped. It was a signal that he understood and Mom's immediate silence told me so did she. Maybe it would be okay, they would not make me go to school, and we could all go back to Oklahoma. No such luck.

On this morning I was extended full due process for my grievance. Uninterrupted, I explained that I was odd man out with this lunch pail. At lunch, I felt as if I were Robinson Crusoe marooned on an island alone. When I put my glasses on to read the blackboard, weird looks shot my way and if and when I ever spoke, the giggles of the kid with the Oklahoman twang sung out. I felt like I had gone from hero to weirdo. Worst of all, I had no friends. A silence took over the room as Richard's head peaked around the corner of the hallway and Bob wondered about with an orange juice bottle hanging out of his mouth just gurgling. Bob, of course, did not understand anything that was going on and it was slightly embarrassing that Richard probably did. Mom resumed the conversation as Dad remained silent quizzically staring at me. "Drew, you've got to go make friends, you've got to make the effort to show them that you are the good guy that you are. Sitting in the corner will only add to your misery. Life is full of changes and this move is just one of them If you don't try, you will only be and feel the worst for it, and you can do it if you'll just let yourself. If you make the effort to make a friend, I promise, so will they," these were Mom's closing remarks.

Dad would be next as I now dug my fingernails into the edge of the sofa ready for the on slought that did not come. To my relief it started and ended quietly, probably to Richard's disappointment. He always enjoyed seeing me get reamed by Dad. "I know it's a tough time, that you left a lot back in Oklahoma, but I had to make a difficult decision for what I believed was the best for the entire family. We all left friends behind, but you know what, they are still your friends and will be forever. And now you've got an opportunity to have a new group of friends and buddies. Good pals don't come easy, you've got to try to make a friend and then work hard to be a buddy, and let me tell you that school will be less difficult if you'll work at being a friend. It's much easier to weather through difficult times with a buddy than without one." To my amazement, Dad's eyes actually started to water up a bit. "I know what it's like to lose friends, in the very worst of circumstances," he continued, "but sometimes it's life's way, and you've got to move on or life's path only becomes more difficult to walk."

The words seemed to work, maybe the sun would shine again. After all, football season was approaching with sign-up near. There had to be a teammate out there someplace if I could just find him. I vowed that I would.

Of course, none of Dad's speeches ended without some type of instruction, and this one was no exception. First, I was going to school but I did not have to take the lunch pail. I was not going to get to stay home and no we were not going back to Oklahoma. The final verdict was that before day's end I was to make a friend at school, make an effort to get involved, and be prepared to render my report of the day's effort by dinner time. With that we headed off to school with Richard suggesting that I was a "whiney wimp" while running out of my near grasp. By the time Dad drove me up to the front of the steps of Lake Worth Junior High School, I had resigned myself to the task.

Lee Jackson Keie became my Florida soulmate. It came as a great and welcome surprise that he too was a new kid in town. His mother and father had just divorced with his mother moving back to Lake Worth to be near her parents. He knew no one, and we became fast friends. For the next three years we became known as the "Bobsy-Twins." We went everywhere and did everything together and it did not take long for our twosome to grow into a good circle of friends, Bobby McGill, Kim Golden, Pete Smith, and

Larry Hogsett to name but a few. Instead of the Monroe Redbirds and the Gilt Edge Cowboys, it became the Lake Worth Junior High School Warriors with Lee leading the football and basketball teams to Palm Beach County Championships. We missed the Pony League World Series by one run in the bottom of the seventh, and I could occasionally catch an Oklahoma football game on television. Life was now good and the Redbirds and Cowboys became fond, never-to-be-forgotten memories, as 12 turned to 13.

For some reason, now at the age of 60, my memory of this event is as vivid as yesterday as a life lesson difficult to learn. As a kid, the thought of your parents actually understanding the importance of pals was impossible to fathom. Mostly, you believed they did not know anything about anything. My folks however knew the importance of friends and their own life lesson in this regard was not far off from my own. Mom knew no one in Oklahoma City when she moved from Tama, Iowa; Dad knew very few when he got on the truck at the Armory in September of 1940, and they only knew a handful when they went to Camp Pine and Camp Pickett. Yet they persevered and made the most of those around them.

Dad's rather stachato, halting statement that difficult times were easier with a buddy was certainly a lesson learned in war; and regrettably for him the difficulty of losing a friend became a lesson learned when the 45th Infantry Division moved into Venafro, Italy in November of 1943.

CHAPTER XVI
VENAFRO WINTER DEATH

After 41 consecutive days of combat, ten days in Corps reserve felt like Heaven. Jack finally got to shave with warm water and the men were ecstatic over a hot shower. Little things became life's pleasure. A new pair of socks and a new pair of boots, Jack was sure his old ones had grown to his feet. Off with the old ragged uniform, and on with the new. It was Christmas in October with a change of underwear and tee-shirts. Perhaps the greatest relief, however, was the respite from the constant fear of being shelled by artillery, ambushed by mortars, picked at by the German snipers; and with the sound of war in the distance a decent night's sleep was possible in a cot, rather than in a hole dug into the ground. Corps reserve was not all vacation. All knew the rest would be brief, so time was taken to ready for the return to the front that was sure to come. Weapons were cleaned, worn parts of the big artillery pieces were replaced, vehicles and motorized equipment were repaired and made ready for what all knew would be another push north to attempt to break the German Winter Line.

In the 41 days up the boot of Italy there was little time to think or reflect. It was all more instinctive reaction rather than thought. Taking too much time to think on that narrow mountain trail could be deadly, actions at times were born out of a will to survive, rather than reasoned. But once removed from the hysteria of battle, the Thunderbirds realized that events had driven them together as family, strong bonds of friendship forged from hard and difficult times. Their continued dependence on each other, of team work, of every man doing their job no matter how seemingly small worked toward the good, and for the survival of all. The company cook was as important as the infantry rifleman. You could not fight on an empty stomach. The privates driving the ammo truck down the muddy road were a critical cog in the wheel. You could not fight without ammunition. As brave and courageous as were the infantry men of the rifle companies, they had to have the support of the artillery, and vice versa. They were inextricably intertwined. For Jack Neville, Harry Balkum, Bill Collins, Basil Thompson, Walter Arnote, Arthur Large, William Chapman, and Ray McClain, officers and enlisted men alike, they had become an extended family. The title of Steven Ambrose's great book captured the spirit, the essence of what they had become–Band of Brothers.

As the cool of November came, the 45th Infantry Division "locked and loaded" once again to move back to the "up-front front." On November 2, 1943, Col. Arnote received orders for Division Artillery to cross the Volturno River and move to the high ground north of Venafro, Italy. The Thunderbirds would soon be back on the line.

Clark's Fifth Army had maintained its division abreast formation as the line swept northward. As the allies moved northward, the 45th would maintain its position with the United States 3rd and 34th Divisions as they marched aside each other and into the teeth of the German defense. Venafro was 15 miles northwest of the Corps reserve rest area, nudged up against the Bernnard Line approximately 9 miles south of the deepest and most fortified German positions in the Gustav Line. The little town of Venafro was set amongst rugged rocky mountains and hills with little or no road network. In many instances the terrain was so severe that pack mules were the only efficient means to move supplies forward. With the allies slowed, the Germans had time again to fix and conceal their positions in the high ground of the mountains. The tactical advantage was certainly with the Germans as they strung together an elaborate maize of pill boxes, mortar, and artillery positions. In the hills around Venafro in November, the guns of German artillery, 88s and 105s, as well as their heavy mortars, already were registered on the key road intersections and buildings within the town itself. As the division moved forward, the Germans had the Thunderbirds in their sites. They patiently sat and waited with their fingers on the trigger.

On November 3 the Infantry Regiments were advancing on the town of Venafro under constant shelling and the following day the 179th Infantry Regiment was on the outskirts of Venafro. On November 3, 1943, Jack moved to a house in the small village of Malrati where the Division Artillery set up its command post. From here, Jack worked to assist the field battalions in locating and firing on the German artillery position in order to relieve the constant pressure on the advancing infantry units. It became another artillery duel with the Infantry units crawling for very inch. By the end of the day on the 4th , Venafro was certain to fall and McClain, along with Jack, went in with the Infantry units to identify a suitable location for a command post.

Although November 6, the division had total control of the town of Venafro there was in no way a sense of security. High in the hills and mountains around Venafro, the German artillery remained able to rain their steel and lead down into the town. It was left to the infantry and forward observers to spot the Germans out so that Division Artillery could place its counter-battery fire on the 88s and 240s. By this time, the men had grown awkwardly accustomed to the distinctive sound of the German artillery shells whistling through the mountain air. By now, the sound alone told them whether or not the round would be near, or far, whether to yell out "in-coming," or whether or not to keep on doing your business.

The 45th, with the fall of Venafro, had penetrated the second of the German lines of defense. Venafro was inside the Bernard Line and now the Gustov line was the only string of defense left for the Germans in Italy. Jack knew that with the 45th now at the door of the German's last line of defense, the Thunderbirds would most likely be there for awhile and better thought to be inside than out with the cold rapidly approaching. On November 6, the Division Artillery CP was moved into a multi-level abandoned fascist palace near the center of town. Jack was grateful for the chance to be shielded from the weather. Moving, Jack spotted a corner of a second floor room that most assuredly would be the most comfortable. With his backpack and bed roll thrown down, he had staked his claim, free of contest from Balkum and the others. Next, the men hurriedly moved about to set up camp so that the S-3 section could get down to business with the sound of German artillery heard in the distance. Then, as if the Nazis knew when Jack had thrown his bedroll in the corner, it started. At approximately 10:30 a.m. on the morning of November 6, it became evident that the Germans had "the Palace" zeroed in. Under direct fire, the entire command post was under seige and hysteria set in as shell after shell was lobbed from the hills and into the CP. Jack high tailed it down stairs seeking refuge in the corner of the first floor as men screamed at the top of their lungs "in-coming." Smoke and fire filled the room. It was impossible to see. Only after the third and fourth rounds could you hear the cries of anguish and death as men fell wounded and dead while survivors shouted "medic." It was a horrible scene. The men trapped in the CP were powerless. The decision to move about, or

The old church buildings of Venafro, Italy provided refuge to the Thunderbirds who were constantly shelled from the surrounding mountains.

The smaller homes in the town of Venafro allowed a brief escape from the horrible cold and winter of 1944.

not, literally became a life choice as the shells screamed inward, walls fell, and the palace crumbled. The ground itself seemed to shake uncontrollably as the shells exploded. There was little you could do but "take it," and pray that an 88 shell did not have your name on it. For an hour and a half, the Nazis sent their reign of terror down on the Division Artillery CP. By noon, 20 rounds of the German's biggest guns, the 105mm, had found their mark.

Mercifully, the shelling stopped shortly after noon. As the smoke and ash cleared, the sound of in-coming rounds ended, replaced by cries for "help," "I'm hit," and "medic." The CP had nearly become a morgue. The accuracy of the German guns had reeked unbelievable destruction in the town. Jack was incredulous at the fact that he was not dead or wounded. But as he searched through the rubble, brick, blood, and moans of men wounded and dying, it was not so for Harry Balkum, his closest friend. On the floor, blood spewing in all directions, Balkum was down, seriously wounded but thankfully not dead. The medics quickly got Balkum out and as Jack watched Harry's body loaded onto the cot he wondered if he would ever see his old pal again. The sadness was overwhelming as Harry was carried away. Jack's good friend Master Sergeant Basil Thompson of Oklahoma City made the final sacrifice in that hour and a half as did five others of Jack's comrades, Captain Ray Washam, Sgt. Paul Waddle, Capt. Fred M. Felker, Private Lamuel Williams, and Private Paul V. Meyers. Sergeants Rumple, Zymsho, Pixler, and Shell were wounded, but alive.

The resilient 45th did not waste time striking back. On November 7, 1943, all three Infantry Regiments pounded their way north of Venafro. On the 8th, the Germans attempted a counterattack and Division Artillery made the Nazis pay. November 9 found the 180th Infantry Units in Monte Croce and Monte Corno, towns north of Venafro routing the Germans out of their high altitude fighting places. On November 12, the Division Artillery struck their hardest blow back at Germans hiding in the hills around Venafro; 2,475 rounds were unleashed on "Hill 640" to support the advance of the 157th Infantry Regiment. As the torrential rains of Italy fell across the entirety of the allied advance, with cold setting in, the war became one of attack and counterattack with neither side gaining or losing substantial ground.

In the face of stiffening opposition, increasing casualties, and incredibly bad weather, General Mark Clark called a halt to the operation so that the Allied Forces could rest, resupply, and secure reinforcements. From a practical standpoint the sweep up Italy was stopped on November 15. The war had become a stalemate that would spark the Anzio invasion.

For Jack Neville, the worst day of his life turned into his worst month. With battle lines now frozen and static, the war effort became one of artillery fire coupled with mostly combat patrols. It seemed that the German positions high in the hills were locked into the location of the Division Artillery CP, as well as the CPs of the Infantry Regiments. Not only because of their elevated positions, the German's incredible accuracy also was thought in part due to spies hiding within the City of Venafro. Accordingly, all "suspicious persons" were rounded up and detained. The American Civil Liberties Union would have thrown a fit as detainees were not afforded benefit of counsel or due process. They were lucky they were not shot. Despite these efforts, the incessant German shelling continued. On November 10, 1943, the CP was again hit, this time at night. Luckily the only casualty of this attack was Col. Arnote's clothes as they were completely torn up. After determining that no one was hurt, Arnote located his fatigues holding them up to the lightbulb hanging from the ceiling. They looked like swiss cheese. The sight of Arnote's rags provided the only moment of levity that could come from such a shelling. Jack, of course, could not help himself. Despite their rank differential, the Master Sergeant observed that the Colonel would most likely have to fight the rest of the war naked. Even Arnote could not help but laugh. Thunderbird luck held on again when "in-coming" was shouted on November 14. Remarkably, the German rounds turned out to be duds. To Jack and the rest of the CP the sight of the giant 105 shells buried in the ground and into the walls was truly a wonder of the world. The shelling continued on November 16, with a half-track loaded with ammunition exploding just outside. Again, no one was wounded or hurt. By mid-November the S-3 section had relocated its position across an alley way from the palace. The alley way separating the S-3 room from the palace was quickly and appropriately named "Shrapnel Alley."

The G.I.s had renamed Venafro "Purple Heart Alley" and "Deadman's Corner." On November 21, at 10:00 p.m. the roof of the CP was torn off by 105 rounds, this time with Jack's good friend, Bill Collins, seriously wounded. Before the end of November, the Division Artillery CP remained in German sites and shelled on five more occasions with deadly results as three men were killed and several wounded. Jack escaped each time without so much as a scratch, but many of his comrades did not. Sadly, medics and stretcher bearers became frequent visitors at the Division Artillery CP.

Thanksgiving in 1943 was a series of 88 and 105 shells lobbed into the center of town by the Nazis to disrupt the division's holiday. Not even the arrival of the head man himself, General Mark Clark, at the Division Artillery CP did much for Jack's spirits on this otherwise dreary day. Clark had not exactly won himself great acclaim in the lower enlisted mens' ranks and the whispers amongst the men renamed Clark, General Mark "Mark Time" Clark. As many of the men viewed things, all the division did in Venafro was "Mark Time," sit there and get clobbered by German artillery. The news in Venafro only went from bad to worse in those cold, gray November days in 1943. General Troy Middleton had become a beloved, respected commander leading the division since October of 1942. He, like Ray McClain, was a leader at the front, always visible to the men in combat and the epitome of the Infantry motto "Follow

Me." He finally gave out in Venafro, Italy. Impaired by the cold and mountainous terrain, Middleton's knees became so arthritic that he could barely walk, and he was ruled medically unfit for combat command. To Jack Neville's chagrin, he said good-bye to another friend on November 22 when Middleton quietly handed over the reins of the Thunderbirds to General William Eagles. Little did Jack know that Ray McClain would be the next to go.

The November of 1943 "inventory" was not at all a bright spot in Jack's life. Static lines of defense subjected him to constant shelling by German artillery. Maybe his last vision of Harry Balkum was that of his best friend being carried out on a stretcher, covered in blood. Bill Collins, wounded. Basil Thompson, killed. The list of horror just went on, punctuated by the departure of Middleton. The sad exclamation point however had to be Thanksgiving day in Venafro, Italy, amid the rubble and ruin of the city. In his first ever Thanksgiving away from home at the age of 23, there was no such thing as the "good ole'" turkey dinner with mashed potatoes, carrots, peas, and that pumpkin pie with real whipped cream. His day had to be the sadness of good friends gone and lost, of ducking German artillery, and hoping he had not lost the key to open a can of C-Rations.

REFLECTIONS THANKSGIVING, 1968

After four great years of Florida weather and good times for the brothers, Jack was moving on up the ladder of Madison Square Garden. In 1962, Jack was given the ultimatum he knew was coming. If upward mobility with the company was to continue, a move to New York City was necessary. We all kept quiet as we knew there would be no family vote Jack's decision was quick and final. There would be no New York City. He promptly resigned and by December of 1962, we were on our way to Tulsa, Oklahoma and a new company in the pipeline construction business, Crose United. Opportunity spurred opportunity and Jack got his shot at owning a piece of a company he could call his won, Curran and Co.

In the summer of 1968, Jack and Leota picked up roots in Tulsa and moved to Littleton, Colorado, a suburb outside Denver. Jack viewed the move as a great adventure and at the age of 48 he was in full pursuit of the American dream. Colorado and the western plains were on the eve of a pipeline construction boom as the United States population base grew west. Curran and Co. was right in the middle of it. Jack would parlay his experience in the pipeline construction arena with Crose-United of Tulsa, to become vice president and chief financial officer of Mike Curran's aggressive venture into pipeline construction. While Jack was ever the explorer, Mom was more cautious and suspicious. Her concerns would prove well taken. By 1972, they would be back in Tulsa.

The house in Littleton was fabulous. About 3 miles west of I-25, almost up against the eastern slope of the Colorado Rockies. The scenery was spectacular. The house was perched atop a small hill with a tremendous view in all directions. The City of Denver dominated the skyline to the north. On the best days, you could look out a large window in the front living room and see Pikes Peak. Mom loved it and Dad worked.

By 1968, brother Richard was in his second year at Purdue University, West Lafayette, Indiana. Richard had gained great credibility with everyone as the years had gone by. At Christmas he generally was the only one in the family who could read and understand the directions for erector sets and other such contraptions still necessary to placate the enthusiasms of eleven-year-old Bob. Through high school and the first years of college, Richard had become by far the most sophisticated and smartest of the three brothers. We always were proud to announce that Richard went to Purdue on a Naval ROTC scholarship. While Richard also was considered the most stable and sane of all the Nevilles–Dad's brothers and sisters included–he disliked Purdue and yearned for the chance to return home to Oklahoma. Having summoned the courage to announce his intention to transfer to the University of Oklahoma, Richard raised the issue with the master of the household. Richard's plea was met with summary disposition by the old master sergeant. Not only "no," but "hell no, you'll walk out of there with a God-damn fine education that you can be proud of. You're staying." There was no appeal, no further discussion, the decision was final. Richard graduated from Purdue University, went on to get his masters, and served on the USS Enterprise for five years. Now, he is in banking in Seattle, Washington.

With Richard coming home on Thanksgiving from Purdue, and Drew driving his yellow Mustang from Norman, this particular Thanksgiving was a special homecoming. Neither of us knowing anyone in Colorado, all of our college buds at home in Oklahoma, it was a forced togetherness. As the weekend wore on, no one seemed to mind.

Thanksgiving morning was always near hysteria. By 10:00 a.m. you could smell the turkey. Leota, supposedly in charge of all kitchen activity, was continually harassed by Jack through the morning hours, his claim always being that the turkey was not cooking fast enough and not basted properly. One of Mom's "looks" was generally sufficient to force his retreat from the kitchen, albeit for only a short time. Jack's strategic withdrawal was most often made to the large jug of wine in the dining room always available on holidays. It was okay to drink before noon on Thanksgiving.

Close to noon, the complaints of "when do we eat, I'm hungry" and "isn't the turkey ready yet" became numerous. These complaints surfaced before noon not only because we were starving, but, the traditional Detroit v. Green Bay game, followed by Dallas v. Washington, was close to kick-off. It was the routine to "stuff" before game time.

The real signal that your starvation was soon to be relieved came when Mom instructed Jack to get the giblet gravy ready, and for Bob, Richard, and Drew to deliver the mashed potatoes, stuffing, green beans, and salad to the table. We were close to the big time.

We were never an overly religious group. Jack and Leota always required Sunday church service and in the younger years Sunday School and 11:00 a.m. Church was part of the required agenda. Dinner prayers were rare, but always preceded Thanksgiving and Christmas dinners. As noon brought the turkey to the table for the traditional Jack-carving, we all took our seats–Jack at the head of the table, Mom at the other, the three of us in a scramble to get the chair closest to the turkey platter. We all knew that the Thanksgiving prayer would come before anyone could get their hands on the turkey. And, while we were anxious and enthusiastic at the thought of the feast, the three brothers always harbored anxiety, sometimes fear, that you would be commanded by Jack to deliver the Thanksgiving prayer. This command always was given by Jack after we all sat down, none of us knowing who would be selected. As a result of Jack's secrecy, the three of us labored over the thought of what to say.

On this Thanksgiving, after we all settled in our chairs, starving, Jack made the announcement. "Richard, would you please lead us in prayer?"

Then the most startling event occurred in the history of Neville Thanksgivings. After napkins were folded, heads bowed, and hands clapped, the immortal words of Richard were forever burned into the annals of Neville lore, "Dear God, rub-a-dub-dub-thanks for the grubb - yea God!"

It truly was a historical moment. The Jack eruption was beyond description and the shellacking of Richard's lifetime was administered in non-Thanksgiving tones. It was ten minutes before the firestorm subsided and we all were ordered to return to the table where it would be done right this time.

Only this time, as we took our seats, Bob was administered to say grace. At 11 years old, the white fear of the occasion had not yet drained from Bob's face. In an incredible display of eloquence Bob delivered the Thanksgiving Day prayer. Bob spoke and spoke and then some. Bob thanked God for Mom, Dad, Richard, Drew, "Tex" the dog, his school, the President, the mountains, his bike, and on and on. It was a fifteen-minute sermon by my count, but it got the job done. Actually, he was afraid to stop.

During dinner, things returned to a degree of normalcy but with Richard having little else to say. Afterward, we all grabbed our pumpkin pie with whipped cream and found a place in front of the television to watch the second half of the Detroit versus Green Bay football game followed by Dallas versus Washington.

Jack promptly went to sleep in the same chair that he always went to sleep in after Thanksgiving dinners. It was 10 degrees and snowing outside.

CHAPTER XVII
CHRISTMAS IN VENAFRO

In Whitlock's *The Rock of Anzio*, life in Venafro is described as "unrelenting misery." It continued through December of 1943. The ground had become so hard that the men could not dig foxholes to escape the shrapnel and were forced to take refuge amongst the ruins and rubble that once was a beautiful City. The shelling continued. By Christmas, the 45th was supplied by pack mules and, according to the ranking company medic for I Company, 157th Infantry, "the whole division froze its feet." Division Artillery would throw the giant shells into the mountains and hillsides, and the Germans would throw them right back into town. It became the artillery version of "Annie Over" as shells were traded back and forth with deadly results.

Through the first two weeks of December, the Allies attempted to break the German lines of defense by aerial attack and bombing. Division Artillery "marked" the towns of Concasale and Viticuso for the bombers and ground attempts were made to push the Germans back. It was to no avail. The lines on the situation map had become literally frozen by the weather and fatigue of two armies who had slugged it out day and night. With Christmas of 1943 quickly approaching, Jack and the Thunderbirds hoped for something good. Christmas just had to be better than Thanksgiving.

If there was anything good of static, fixed lines of defense, it at least provided Jack the opportunity to write home. Between the shelling and shooting, Jack's major method of communication home was through "V-Mail." V-Mail was a small, 3-inch-by-3-inch postcard that usually contained a Bill Mauldin cartoon of Joe and Willie. There was just enough room for a short hand-written message and Jack fired as many V-Mails home as he could under the circumstances. To read them, you would not have known he was in the misery of war far away from home. His messages always were simple and upbeat, intended to let Leota know that things were just fine, even though it was horrible.

Christmas of 1943 was Jack's first away from home and his first away from Leota since 1937. On their first wedding anniversary, he was busy dodging enemy shrapnel. In Venafro, there was no Brown's Department Store or Streets.

In fact in Venafro there was no Christmas sale. Nothing was being sold in Venafro on this Christmas because there were no shops or stores left in Venafro. The only present Jack could muster for Leota this Christmas was one V-Mail. Always early with everything, Jack carefully crafted a message of Christmas cheer with a "love you Jack." He mailed the V-Mail Christmas card on November 11, 1943 to ensure a safe reliable arrival for Christmas. Interestingly, Jack's final note was "Just barely time to write." "Barely" time to write was a masterful understatement. On November 10, the CP was directly shelled, and the 11th was spent preparing to give it back to the Nazis. On November 12, the Division Artillery unloaded 2,475 rounds on Hill 460. It was a victory to get off anything in the mail, but somehow he found a way.

If you were fortunate enough to get a Christmas package in Venafro it was opened immediately. Peer group pressure allowed no solitude in opening presents and packages were too cumbersome to carry around while dodging shrapnel. After a horrible breakfast of powdered eggs it was Christmas fun to goad your buddies into opening their presents in front of all–even if you were standing in Venafro's muck. Christmas cheer from home brought an interesting array of items. Col. Arnote received a polka-dotted tie, Captain Large got house slippers, and several others received, of all things, Spam. For Jack, he received the best of all, Christmas cards with pictures and letters from every member of the family right down to his new young nephews and nieces. Jack could not help but laugh. After knowing Leota's parents for six years and having not seen them for an entire year, they signed their Christmas card "Mr. and Mrs. Stauffer." One thing was for certain, Mr. Stauffer would never change, not even if his son-in-law was fighting a war. Leota's card was a pretty "cheesy" pin-up like full body picture taken laying on a sofa. It brought on whistles and shouts from the S-3 room. Scribbled on the bottom:

> Here's to the day we can say Merry X-mas in person. I love you forever and always your own Leota

No matter what you did to make it feel like the Christmas holidays, the front was still the front and the 45th's Division Artillery delivered their own presents to the Germans. On Christmas day, 1943, 2,055 rounds were hurled at German troops attempting to take tactical advantage of this day of supposed peace. On December 30, in the snow, rain, and ice, artillery plastered 5,274 rounds on the enemy attempting to reinforce their positions for a feared New Year's eve attack. Jack's S-3 section welcomed in the New Year with support for the 180th attack on Mount Molino. As reported in The History of the 45th Division Artillery, "at midnight the Division Artillery shelled all known German positions, . . . thus 1944 really came in with a bang." On New Year's Day, 1944, Jack Neville was still in Venafro. Would they ever get to leave?

On January 2, 1943, Walter Arnote summoned the S-3 staff together for a planning session. He advised Jack and the staff that something was up, but he did not know exactly what. Arnote told the small group that the 179th Infantry Regiment was infiltrating off the front lines, and that Division Artillery was ordered to make ready for their own move rearward. Arnote's news was a belated Christmas present to say the least. The thought of leaving Venafro's hell-hole energized all. Arnote's instructions were given more substance when on January 3, 1943, the 179th began its pullback, and it became official on January 4, when the division received orders to begin infiltrating back to rest areas near Telese; the 3rd Algerian Infantry Division was to take over for the 45th Infantry Division. It should be noted that the French Expeditionary Force 3rd Algerian ran into substantial enemy resistence in taking the 45th's section of responsibility. The 1st and 2nd Battalions of the 180th, on January 10, manned their trucks and raced back up to the front to assist the French in beating back the Germans and establishing the French position. It was not until the 15th that the two battalions rejoined the regiment. For this extraordinary display of gallantry, General Charles DeGaulle awarded the 45th the Croix de Guerre Citation.

Jack's artillery was the last to receive its order of movement, but it came on January 5, 1944. The little-asked question was "why was the division, after being locked in head-to-head battle with the Nazis being moved to the rear areas?" No one seemed to know or care; they were leaving Venafro and that was all that seemed to matter. The scuttlebutt had it that Division Artillery would be moved to an area just north of Naples. On Jack's birthday, January 7, 1944, his hopes of celebrating his 24th in Naples with vast quantities of wine and song were dashed. The instructions came down. Naples was off-limits and the nearby rest areas around Naples were closed because of the prevalence of typhus and exceptionally high rates of venereal disease resulting from "horizontal fatigue."

On January 9, 1944, the 45th Infantry Division was officially relieved of its responsibilities in Venafro, Italy, and Jack and the Division Artillery were moved to the south and to the Grand Hotel near Telese after having been on the front since November 6, 1942. As Whitlock reported in *The Rock of Anzio*, since Salerno, the division had been in actual combat 110 out of 121 days. The death toll and casualty list provided the evidence of the cost of war: 651 killed in action; 2,550 wounded; 256 missing; 61 captured; and 9,492 sick or hospitalized. Adding up the numbers, almost the entire division was a casualty in one form or another, and it was incredible that Jack Neville was not wounded, injured, or killed.

As the Division Artillery settled into Telese for a much needed and welcome relief from battle, the inevitable question arose "what was next?" In early January no one seemed to know, but it would not take long to find out.

The Thunderbirds of the 45th Infantry Division would skirt around the Gustav Line to fight on the west coast of Italy south of Rome. Anzio would be one of the bloodiest battles of World War II, and as he did in the Sele Corridor, Jack would once again have to dig a foxhole and fight for his life.

CHAPTER XVIII
HOMEFRONT CHRISTMAS, 1943

In November and December of 1943, on the homefront in Oklahoma City, the 45th Infantry Division nearly dropped off the radar screen. While reports of the war in Italy appeared every day in *The Daily Oklahoman* and the evening's addition of the Oklahoma City Times, the location and movement of the division continued to be shrouded in the vague generalities of press releases issued by the Allied Supreme Headquarters in Algiers, North Africa. Most often, the radio and paper's daily war reports referenced only the "Fifth Army" or "General Mark Clark's Fifth Army" with the location or movement of specific units never revealed. The homefront, and Leota, knew the division was somewhere in Italy, but that was about it. As Jack prepared to move into Venafro on November 6, *The Daily Oklahoman* reported "Isneria Taken, Nazis Fleeing for New Line." Then, on November 6, the paper reported "Allies Overrun Entire German Front in Italy" as "the Americans" were fighting north of Venafro. Of course, at Venafro, the 45th had not exactly "run over" anyone, they were lucky to have survived the daily German shelling of the town. These reports never referenced the Thunderbirds and rather optimistically suggested that the Allies would capture Rome by Christmas. Not reported to the folks at home in early November was that the 45th was locked in a huge stalemate struggle with the Germans along the so-called Winter Line, and never was there a report that Jack's unit and the Division Artillery CP had experienced the death and destruction of German artillery. So general was the war news, it almost was no news.

Many of the articles clipped from the paper and pasted in Leota's scrapbooks were stories written by Ernie Pyle, the great World War II war correspondent. While Pyle's articles rarely identified the division unit he was with, he often would identify the company, or artillery battery he was following. Pyle wrote of life at the front, what the men ate, where and how they slept, how they were feeling, and what they were wearing. In the true sense he wrote of the "upfront front" to the home folks. Pyle provided rather graphic descriptions of the daily struggle of war. Appearing in the paper almost every day, Pyle's articles gave Leota the clearest picture of what the war was like. There are enough Bill

Mauldin cartoons in Leota's scrapbook to fill a small room. All Oklahomans knew Mauldin was with the 45th, so his often sarcastic and hilarious portrayal of two G.I.s Willie and Joe provided a pictorial link from the Thunderbirds to Leota and the Oklahomans. So irreverent and sometimes disrespectful were Mauldin's cartoons that General George S. Patton attempted to have Mauldin booted out of the European Theatre, or at least censored. Eisenhower over-ruled Patton and Mauldin sent the unshaven, filthy faces of Willie and Joe cartoons back to Oklahoma City on almost a daily basis. Judging from Leota's scrapbook, it is evident that Willie and Joe at least somewhat relieved the daily anxiety of never really knowing where Jack was or what he was doing. In early November of 1943, Hollywood brought much needed relief from the daily routine of monitoring the war to Oklahoma City. Opening at the Criterion downtown was "In Old Oklahoma" staring John Wayne, Martha Scott and Gabby Hayes. "Phantom of the Opera" made its Oklahoma debut at the Mid-west Theater. You could escape the constant thought of war for a couple of hours if you could afford the 25¢ admission.

By mid-November the reality of the death and damage of war was finding its way into the Oklahoma press. Many wounded from the invasion of Sicily and the early fighting at the Salerno beachhead were evacuated back to the United States and the Army's medical facility in Temple, Texas. The news correspondents naturally descended on the Oklahoma heroes to get their eyewitness accounts of the fighting. On November 18, 1943 under the headline "51 Days On The Line at Salerno," the first graphic accounts of the Salerno struggle were reported. Lt. Col. Jess Larson's interview told of the desperate straits of the 179th Infantry Regiment and their last- minute rescue by McClain's artillery and the battle of the Sele Corridor was revealed for the first time by the soldiers who actually fought. These reports provided little solace to Leota and the Neville family. Grateful that Larson had survived, his account provided information that Jack was in harm's way each and every day. On November 20, 1943, the grim reality of war came to the Stauffer home from Maxine Balkum, when she sent a Western Union telegram to Leota. The message was simple and to the point: Have just received word Harry seriously wounded in Italy, November 6.

Shock and dismay riddled Leota. Immediately she hooked up with the operator for Jackson, Tennessee and the Balkum home. Both hysterical and overjoyed that Harry was still alive, Maxine knew none of the details with the word "serious" never defined or described. All Maxine knew was that Harry had been evacuated to the rear area hospital complex where he was at least momentarily safe. Leota's world was now in a tailspin. Jack and Harry were together and they were nearly inseparable. Wherever Harry was, so to was Jack. If Harry had been hit, had Jack been hit? Or worse, had he been killed and that telegram not yet delivered? Worry and fear jumped to yet a higher level. Leota and Jack had become close friends with not only the Balkums, but also Basil and Eileen

Thompson. Eileen, Maxine, and Leota all followed their husbands to Crewe, Virginia for that last good-bye in May of 1943, only a few months ago. Together they caught the train westward, and home. The fickleness of war-time combat struck a hard blow at Leota, as Basil Thompson's death was reported to have occurred on the same day Harry Balkum was wounded. By mid to late November of 1943, Leota now knew that of those around and in daily proximity to Jack, his two close friends, one had been killed and the other wounded. But, there was no word about Jack. Leota reached for the positive. If the threesome had been together, and Jack killed, word would have reached her near the time Basil's death was reported, and surely by the time that Maxine had learned that Harry had been wounded. Leota's supposition was that on November 6, 1943 at some unknown place in Italy, Jack was the lucky one. As November crept to a merciful end, each passing day provided small relief from the little known events of November 6. After Maxine's telegram and the report of Basil's death, Leota rushed for the postman coming down the street each day. It was the irony of all ironies, no news was in fact good news. As the cold of December arrived, Leota finally concluded that Jack had survived.

With the first war-time Thanksgiving and Christmas near, along with a first wedding anniversary, November was not too early to start planning on what could be sent to Jack at the front for Christmas. It would take several family meetings to make the decision of just the right present for the war-time front. The subject was a hot topic in both the Neville and Stauffer households. Surely they had some of the comforts of home in the hills of Italy–a toaster, a waffle iron, a radio. Certainly all of these would be welcome gifts. Sylvester objected because the quartermaster corps, whom he greatly distrusted from his own World War I days, would steal and sell any appliance on the soldiers' black market. Most of the family quickly dismissed this reason as being paranoid. Leota quickly seized on the deficiency of the present. How was he going to carry it, and perhaps more importantly, where was he going to plug it in? Italy did not have electrical sockets, at least according to Jim Neville. A toaster was not practical. Of course, sister Helen would think of clothes in war-time, however the small group rather summarily rejected this idea. After all, the United States Army provided Jack's wardrobe from head to toe. Helen's only retort was that Brown's had a Christmas sale on slippers for $1.99 a pair. What could you get for the man who had everything? Leota was left with the task of taking charge. While everyone had a great time debating the "up-front" present, the results of such chatter yielded little results, and time was wasting. A decision had to be made.

What Jack Neville needed the most at the front in Italy were memories of home. Memories of family and those who loved him were the presents that meant the most in this time of struggle and sacrifice. Seizing on this thought Leota organized a picture-thon. This proved to be a rather monumental effort. Talking Rosa, Roselle, Helen, Jim, Creighton, Nat, Billy Lou, Sylvester, Lottie, and Eleanor into posing individually was a task akin to herding cats, now made more difficult by the arrival of new nieces and nephews. By December of 1943, brother Jim and Mary had brought along Gib and Pat, and Roselle and Pete had wasted little time in turning out Jim Pete MacKellar. Even in war, the family was growing. But Leota, as she always did, somehow got it all together. Seizing a picture of every member of the family, Leota took pain-staking effort to trim from the pictures full-body shot of each Neville and Stauffer family member. Thereafter, she bought a multi-paged red, five-by-eight booklet, and carefully pasted pictures of each person to a single page so that every family member would have their own page to write Jack a bit of Christmas from home. It took some time to get it done, but at one of those Sunday pot-roast dinners at Rosa's, the family again convened and made to write Jack a word of Christmas. Of course, every brother grumbled at the thought of having to say a word to their "little brother," but the truth was that it brought a bit of Christmas cheer to the Nevilles in war-torn December of 1943.

The family Christmas card to Jack in December of 1943, was not without some controversy. Posing in a rather suggestive reclining position, nearly horizontal, hair down and shoulder length, with her skirt pulled slight above the knee, legs exposed, Leota's picture had a near pin-up quality to it. Sylvester Stauffer voiced strong opposition to both the pose and the picture. He did not quite label it as pornographic, but he came close. Both Leota and Eleanor were too much for him, but once Helen, Roselle, and Billy Lou got into the battle, he was rather quickly overcome. Sylvester Stauffer however did not go down without a fight. While retreating, he let it be known that the younger generation's value system was in a state of decay, and he did not see how America's future could survive in a time of such moral decline. Conspicuously absent from his speech, however, was the fact that the entire younger generation was spread out across the world fighting a fierce battle for America's future.

As Leota hoped, the pictures of family and home were a welcome sight to Jack. The booklet of brothers, sisters, mom, and wife Leota were special. This Christmas card, put together in November of 1943, was found in Leota's scrapbook in March of 2000, shortly after her death. Jack obviously made considerable effort to keep and protect the card and its pictures. Some 60 years later the red of the card is now faded to a near pink, and the handwriting wishing Jack a Merry Christmas nearly invisible from time gone by. But the significant family statement is that Jack clearly felt compelled to keep the card among his personal possessions for more than a year and a half. The card itself evidences that he received it in December of 1943. He and the division were still fighting in the mountains of Venafro, shelled almost daily. He had yet to make the amphibious landings and fight at Anzio. Southern France was months away, and the one-year fight through southern Europe, Germany, and into Dachau were all in destiny's way. The entirety of Jack's handwritten journal, regrettably did not survive the war, but somehow, incredibly, that Christmas card of 1943, made it through. Leota wanted to create the memories, give him a bit of home and family, and she did. The nights in Venafro were cold and miserable, Anzio would be full of death, but Jack, with those pictures, now had a way to reach back to family in Oklahoma. In the bombed-out buildings of Venafro and the foxholes of Anzio there were few opportunities for solitude and reflection. But when the shelling and rifle fire stopped, when those preciously few quiet moments came, Jack had his pictures to remind him of good times, good things, and what it was all about.

December 25, 1943, was the first Christmas the Thunderbirds were away from home. A by-product of the World War was that it drove people and family together. Every Thunderbird family bonded over this difficult Holiday season, worried about the future, and everyday fearful that sons and daughters would never return home. For most, Christmas took on a real meaning, more than just the present, or what was under the tree. Christmas day for the Neville and Stauffer families was bittersweet. All gathered at the table at Rosa's for the traditional turkey dinner. There were two empty chairs–those of Jack and Gene Neville.

Through mid-December and Christmas, the exact location and operations of the 45th Infantry Division remained invisible. The press continued to report progress by the Allies on the Italian front creating a sense of false optimism for an early end to the Italian Campaign. On December 8, 1943, newspaper headlines read "5th Army Past Worst Barrier' Rome is Ahead" with the article reporting that the way was open for an all-out armoured assault on Rome. Again on December 20, 1943, the Allied Supreme Headquarters press release resulted in *The Daily Oklahoman* headline "Yanks Take San Pietro." The first hint of any stalemate on the Italian front came on December 16, where in a back-page article it was reported that ground fighting had been brought to a halt because of the miserable weather. Of course never reported was the fact that General Mark Clark had ordered all offensive operations to cease as early as November 15, 1943, because the men of the 5th Army, including the 45th Infantry Division, were physically exhausted, low on ammunition and supplies, and in need of reinforcements. In today's world of instant news and live television reports from the war fronts, perhaps a case of intentional dissemination of misinformation could be made. The facts were what the Army created, by omission if not by out right misstatements, a program of deception intended to disguise the location and strength of Allied Forces. During World War II such efforts by the Allied Supreme Headquarters were necessary for the protection and security of Allied lives. If the Nazis knew that the 45th was nearly out of food and ammo while stuck in the Venafro mud, it would only be an invitation for a full assault. The war-time press releases were written not only for Leota and people at home, but also for the Germans. They could read our newspapers just like we could read theirs.

As Leota reached for the paper after December 25, 1943, Jack became lost in the other news of the day. On Christmas Day the United States announced that General Dwight Eisenhower would lead the now certain invasion against the Axis somewhere along the northern European coast. On the homefront, a war of sorts broke out amongst the railroad workers who threatened a nationwide strike if they did not get their way. President Roosevelt saw it as a crisis that threatened the war effort. In a dramatic stroke, Roosevelt seized control of the railroads with United States Army Troops so that the flow of material and supplies would not be interrupted. The families and loved ones of those fighting overseas were furious at the railroad workers' selfishness in times of war, and Roosevelt's action may have been the only time Sylvester Stauffer applauded the action of the President in his entire life.

As plans were made to surreptitiously withdraw the Thunderbirds off the Venafro line, the attention of the Oklahoma press turned toward the University of Oklahoma when on December 29, 1943, George Lynn Cross was named its president. Cross would become an educational icon in the State of Oklahoma, leading the university to national prominence through the difficult war years. And to top off the year, Hollywood continued its string of patriotic war movies. Cary Grant and "Destination Tokyo" came to the big screen in Oklahoma City. The people of Oklahoma City were trying to cope with the absence of their boys from home, they were trying to move on. However, not even Cary Grant and submarines did much for Leota. Jack was on the other side of the world.

When the books closed on 1943, there were more debits than credits. Gene Neville's death was confirmed in January and after six months of marriage, living out of suitcases in rented apartments far from home, Jack and Leota had to say good-bye to each other in May for an unknown and uncertain future. For Leota it became a gut wrenching game of wait and worry. For Jack, Basil Thompson had been killed and his close friend Harry Balkum seriously wounded. At the young age of 23 Jack had witnessed death many times over and had seen and participated in the total destruction that only war can bring. The huge credit on the other side of the ledger, Jack Neville was still alive.

As Oklahoma City turned from 1943 to 1944, the whereabouts of Jack and the division remained clouded in ambiguity until January 23, 1944, when Leota woke up to the headline "Allies Smashing Inland For Highway To Rome." Correspondent Don Whitehead reported that American and British troops had landed practically without opposition on beaches south of Rome in a "daring successful seaborne blow." While the division was not specifically mentioned, it was a significant hint that Whitehead was the major contributor to the article. In the preceding months, he had reported many stories that tied him directly with the Thunderbirds, and the logical conclusion was that if Whitehead was reporting the war events, he was with the 45th Infantry Division. Leota and the Nevilles broke out the Atlas and the map of Italy. It did not take much study to identify the location of "the beaches south of Rome."

Leota was right, Jack and the 45th were in Anzio.

CHAPTER XIX
BLOODY ANZIO

War historians write that Anzio was one of the greatest battles in the history of modern warfare. It certainly was one of the bloodiest. Without question, it was the greatest defensive struggle of World War II, some say as much a test of sheer will as armor and artillery. The courage and daring of America's finest at Anzio never has been surpassed. With six German Infantry Division barreling down the Via Anziate Road, the 45th Infantry Division, from cooks, bottle washers to infantrymen, and artillerymen, with their backs literally to the Tyrrehenia Sea, fought off Hitler's last major attack in Italy. In essence, the Italian campaign ended near the beachhead at Anzio with the critical stage of the battle occurring during only a few hours of one day–February 18, 1943. Incredibly, the biggest part of the struggle was waged within a postage-stamp-sized area, only a few square miles. Located approximately 40 miles south of Rome on the west coast of Italy, Anzio would become the "Coloseum" of modern warfare with the world's gladiators fighting it out at close quarters. For Jack Neville, he and the others of the 45th Division Artillery headquarters would dig in near the Via Anziate road at a place called the Overpass as part of the last line of Allied defenses.

General Dwight Eisenhower was one of the best "planners" the Allies had to offer. His qualities of diplomacy and planning were probably the two factors that most contributed to the decision to tap him for command of the Normandy invasion. Even before the invasion at Salerno, Eisenhower was concerned about the ability of the Allies to move up the boot of Italy. As he saw it, weather and terrain could become as much the enemy as the Germans. Events proved him correct. With this in mind, he started serious consideration of an amphibious-end run around the central German defenses in Italy. While Jack and the 45th Infantry Division were treated to a 10-day respite from the front line, Eisenhower discussed the feasibility of an amphibious sweep at a planning command conference in Carthage, Greece. Anxious to continue further pressure against the Germans in the south, Eisenhower's thoughts were enthusiastically embraced by Winston Churchill, and accordingly the planning process was stepped up a notch.

The first considered landing site for the end run was the city of Gaeta just north of Naples. This plan was rather quickly scrapped because of the perceived strength of the German coastal defenses. Next, a landing north of Anzio was put on the table but rather quickly negated, because the northern site put the invasion fleet outside the umbrella of fighter protection. Almost by process of elimination the costal resort town of Anzio, Italy, was chosen as the landing site. The operation was approved and code-named "Shingle" on November 8, 1943, only two days after Jack and the division had established residence in Venafro. The "go-date" was set for January 15, 1944.

After November 18, however, a planning calamity of sorts broke out amongst the commanders, as well as the Allied leaders, while Jack and the division sat in the mud south of the Gustov Line. Forever the stepchild of "Operation Overlord," the key to the success of the Anzio invasion was the availability of shipping, in particular LSTs and LCIs. By January 15, all available shipping was to be committed to Operation Overlord in the north. Accordingly, on December 18, 1943, General Mark Clark vetoed Operation Shingle because his forces would be plagued by a lack of sufficient shipping and landing craft necessary to sustain an attack. Mark Clark's veto of Shingle infuriated Churchill, especially since Clark's Fifth Army and Montgomery's 8th had become stalemated in central Italy by the German's Winter Line of defense. Churchill was nicknamed "Bulldog" for good reason. Unwilling to accept Clark's veto, Churchill took his case directly to Roosevelt on Christmas Day, 1943. Unable to withstand Churchill's unrelenting pressure, Roosevelt reluctantly yielded and allowed the southern Allied Forces to retain 56 LSTs for Shingle. It now seemed that the daring end run was now back on, but not without more debate and dissension led by Clark. Not only was the lack of shipping a concern to Clark, but he "strongly protested the inadequacies of supplies" necessary to sustain a ground force north of the Gustov Line. Clark's concerns were rather summarily dismissed. At a detailed planning conference on January 7, 1944 in Marrakech, Churchill single handedly took over the planning for Operation Shingle. The debate over the effects of the plan continued to rage even amongst the British ranks. The Naval commanders expressed concern that they would have difficulty maintaining two divisions on the Anzio beach; sustaining three would be precarious; and, without question, it was impossible to maintain four divisions once on shore. Even the head of British Intelligence operations argued that the Anzio invading force could probably sustain a deep thrust inland, but that German strength would preclude a decisive punch without at least a break through at Cassino, or somewhere along the Winter Line. If the Gustov Line could not be penetrated and German forces diverted to the south, the fear was that the Anzio landing force would face annihilation. General John P. Lucas, the American who would command the Anzio ground forces, was openly disturbed over the small size of the landing force. Clark was so pessimistic of Shingle's outcome that he recorded in his diary that he felt as if he were being asked to perform the impossible. Intelligence reports had it that the Allies would face at least 14,000 German troops at Anzio. At the last minute, anxiety over the lack of shipping was momentarily relieved with the approval of some 25 additional LSTs, and, with this, on January 8, 1943, Eisenhower gave the green light for Shingle to go forward. Even with the dissension amongst the planners and commanders of both the British and American forces, all agreed that the attack could not be self sustaining or successful unless there was a break through at the Gustov Line in the south. The Allies would roll the dice and take their chances.

The fundamental plan for Shingle called for a one-two punch at the Germans. First, the United States Fifth Army and the British 8th would punch through the Gustov Line to the south of Rome, diverting German forces from Anzio and Rome to the south. Secondly the United States 3rd Infantry Division, the British 1st Infantry Division, two British commando battalions, and three battalions of American Rangers would hit the shores of Anzio and move quickly inland. The 45th Infantry Division was given the clean-up hitters' role and would come in after the initial landings. The Allies would only have three weeks to plan a major amphibious landing.

Weary and exhausted, elements of the 45th were withdrawn from the Venafro line as early as January 4, 1944. On the day after Eisenhower gave the final stamp of approval on Shingle, Jack and the Division Artillery were withdrawn to rest, resupply, and refit in Telese, unaware of the raging debate over the Anzio plan. The Allied commander was basically against the mission, only Churchill seemed to be a true believer, at least on the surface. Shingle was undertaken with a shortage of supplies, shipping, and manpower amid rather emotional debate with a short period of time to plan details, yet a president yielded to the persistent pleas of a British Prime Minister. Of course caught in the middle and at the low end of the totem pole were the pawns of this world chess game, people like Jack and the Thunderbirds who faced the risk of the ultimate sacrifice. The chances of Dad dying at the junction of the Sele-Calore River and in Venafro were considerably high, and now substantially made higher by a gamble principally decided upon by Winston Churchill, and acquiesced in by Franklin Roosevelt. In January of 1944, the free world was at great risk, it was a desperate time that required desperate measures and Churchill was not afraid to pull the trigger. Jack had seen the horror of war, the death of it all, since July 9, when the division landed in Sicily. He wanted it over, he wanted it ended, he wanted to go home; and even though he was a pawn in the game, he too would have rolled the dice across the table in hopes it all could be done with.

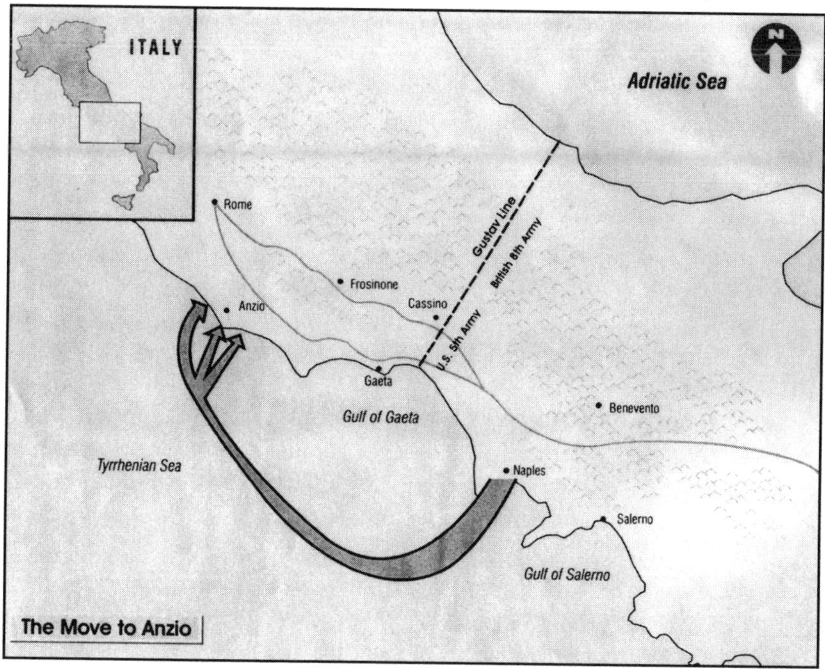

The "first punch" of "Operation Shingle" called for elements of the 5th Army to attack through the Gustav line toward Cassino in mid-January of 1944, with the 45th and other elements of the 5th Army to make an "end-run" from the Naples area behind enemy lines to Anzio.

REFLECTIONS DISTRICT COURT OF TULSA COUNTY, STATE OF OKLAHOMA, 1981

Almost as soon as Jack and Leota arrived in Denver, the great Colorado pipeline adventure with Mike Curran came to an end. Mixed in acrimony over broken promises and Curran misdirection, Jack decided that separation was the only course. Jack was finished with Curran and Company, but the two parted in somewhat of an amicable fashion. It did not take long for Jack to get back on track.

Barney Barnes was an old Tulsa friend and business associate when Jack was with C.R.C. Crose United and United Supply. Barnes had left the Williams Company seeking his own ownership possibilities and backed with long-time Tulsa money. Jack too still was looking for an opportunity to have his own stake, vowing never again to have a boss. While Barnes had the bucks and little desire to operate a business on a day-to-day basis, Jack had the "sweat-equity" and the motivation to move a company forward, still in search of the American dream. They were a perfect combination.

Leland Equipment Company was an established Tulsa business that specialized in the manufacturing of custom-built trailers for off-road hauling. The company had been moderately successful with its operations mostly confined to the State of Oklahoma. Leland management had grown weary and was looking for a way to retire. They put the company up for sale, and it became the perfect target for takeover by Barnes and Jack. The deal was done quickly. Barnes initially fronted 95% of the money, Jack 5%, and Leland Equipment Company became theirs. Barnes would passively participate, Jack would operate the company as its president and chief executive officer. By the end of 1969, Jack and Leota were back in Tulsa at 2931 East 57th Street, just north of Southern Hills Country Club.

Jack's vision for the company was quickly formed. Parlaying his Colorado contacts, Jack extended the arms of Leland into Alaska and Canada. The construction of Al-Can Pipeline was about to begin and there was plenty of opportunity. For the next year plus, Jack spent most of his time away from home, either in Alaska or Canada. The contracts flowed and Leland's business expanded rapidly. Jack's enthusiasm and energy literally drove the company to success in Alaska and Canada all the way from Tulsa. Sales soared, profits soared, and so did Jack. It did not take long for Leland to become a serious business force not only in Tulsa, but across the State of Oklahoma. Leland was Jack's baby and he coddled it like it was his own child. His equity interest in the company climbed to ten percent.

Pressed into the labor force was the youngest son, Bob. At 18, Jack decided it was time for Bob earn his spurs. But Jack's plan was not Leota's. With ten new 18-wheelers and trailers in need of delivery from Tulsa to Juneau, Alaska, high school graduate Bob Neville enlisted in the Leland work force to drive one of those monsters all the way to Alaska. The woman who followed the boss to Camp Pine in 1942 was not happy. Words flowed but both Jack and Bob forced her submission. With nine other off-duty Oklahoma highway patrolmen, Bob Neville alone in the cab steered the huge 18-wheeler all the way. Jack kept up on the convoy on almost an hourly basis. Leland Equipment was his baby, but so was Bob. Jack pushed Leland outside the continental America. Recognizing a shortage and need for front-end loader tractors and other similar machinery, he turned his efforts toward the relatively new Komatsu Tractor Company, headquartered in Toyko, Japan. After almost a year of having the Japanese running through the Neville household, Jack secured the first Japanese distributorship for the Komatsu line in Oklahoma. It was a huge coup for Leland Equipment. By 1979, company sales had grown from $3.8 million to $17.5 million.

By 1976 Leland's success had become its own worst enemy. With the value of the company now at its highest peak, Jack's partner, Barney Barnes, decided it was time to cash in. In 1976, Barnes sold his controlling interest in Leland to a powerful Tulsa-based construction company. Things quickly changed. The mega-corporation conglomerate became omnipresent with their battery of accountants, consultants, and second guessers. Jack's minority interest was treated as a minority and a hailstorm of controversies erupted between the new faction and Jack.

Jack refused to back down, demanding that the future course of the company be guided by his own hand, rather than by a group of accountants who had never seen a truck or trailer, much less toiled in the world of pipelines. Relationships continued to boil until the fall of 1979, when it all exploded.

In a firestorm of heated words, Jack's thought-to-be long time friend, Bob Groth, an Arthur Andersen consultant to the company, delivered the ugly news. Jack was fired. In the mix of an explosive exchange in Jack's office that day, Groth was barraged with a word storm of reaction. Throwing down a shot of scotch at 8:30 a.m., Jack told Groth that he had spent a decade building Leland's success to what it was. Hurling the jigger across the room and into the open fireplace, Jack decreed that he would not give it up and there would be a fight. Jack dug in, and prepared for his own counterattack in the District Court of Tulsa County, State of Oklahoma.

In early 1980, Jack fired the first shot. He filed suit in the District Court of Tulsa County alleging that his employment contract with Leland was breached by Groth's termination of his employment on the morning of August 15, 1979. In 1969, Jack had entered into a written employment contract with Leland Equipment, Company, that could not be terminated "for cause." No "cause" having been given or even alleged, Jack claimed Leland owed him the value of his stock and the remainder of his salary and benefits. In those days, it was a hefty sum, more than $300,000.

Jack's move was met with Leland's own form of attack. Hiring a battery of Tulsa's finest attorneys, Leland defended with a scorched-earth litigation strategy. They would spend Jack Neville into the ground and force a settlement less than the contract value, or so they thought. Hurling a vicious barrage of personal attacks, his old friend alleged Jack was lucifer personified– womanizer, a gambler, and a drinker that was destroying the fabric of good business ethics and Leland. Therefore, they argued, Jack was terminated for cause. It was ugly.

Jack never flinched amidst the ugliness. He stood his ground, refusing to discuss settlement. He quickly conceded that his conduct was not that of an angel, always perfect; however, the pipeline and truck industry was not exactly angelic. Jack stared every allegation down, determined to fight it out. The case proved to be a fight to the death.

The case went to jury trial in the spring of 1981. It was a bloody affair. Throughout it all, Leota stood her ground. She had followed and supported him through Camp Pine, Fort Devens, Camp Pickett, and 511 combat days between January of 1943 to May of 1945, and she was not about to stay at home and miss this one. Every day, she attended the trial from start to finish sitting on the first pew in full view of the jury. Rarely evidencing any reaction to the testimony, the jury kept a constant eye on Leota throughout the entire proceeding.

Leland's case for "cause" blew up in their face. Witness after witness melted on cross-examination as Jack said they would. The success of the company was undisputed and it became obvious who was responsible for it. Even the pencil pushing accountants could not deny the numbers. Time and time again, witnesses described Jack as a tough task-master, but always fair to employees. Leland customers on cross-examination refused to implicate Jack in any malfeasance destructive to the existence or future of the company. Leland's case quickly was reduced to pettiness and jealousy of a few idealists.

The "coup de gras" came during Jack's own testimony. He came off as he truly was. Direct, unpretentious, tough, and compassionate, the jury loved him. The war years were passed over rather quickly but the jury saw a man who had been through hard times, who had raised a family, had a solid marriage, had built a business with his own hands, and was determined to get what was rightfully earned despite powerful opposition. The 12 people admired his guts and will to fight for what he thought was right. Pressing to find some way to get at Jack, Leland's lawyers asked him if in fact he had a shot of scotch at 8:30 a.m. during the acrimonious meeting with Groth, obviously in an effort to paint him as a morning alcoholic unable to direct the company. The response was devastating to Leland's case. "Your, God Damn right I did, Bob Groth destroyed the company I spent a decade building and I was damned upset." You could hear a pin drop as Leland's counsel slowly took his seat. No more questions. The outcome was inevitable. Jack would win and Leland would lose.

The jury took relatively little time to deliberate and make its decision. Sometime after the trial, the District court trial judge let it be known that the jury had only one question–"could they award Jack more than what he had asked for?" No was the answer, so the jury returned a verdict in Jack's favor awarding him every penny he had asked for in his suit. Because the case was one for personal service rendered, the Oklahoma law allowed for recovery of attorney fees and costs. This time the trial judge over-cooked the award. He gave Jack more than he was actually entitled.

Jack and Leland continued to battle. Leland offered a substantial settlement, but less than the jury's award, threatening to hang the case up in the Oklahoma Supreme Court. Defiant as ever, not willing to give an inch, Jack rejected all settlement efforts and ordered a halt to any further such discussion. The case wound its way through the Oklahoma Supreme Court. After a year, the matter was finally at an end. The Supreme Court affirmed the jury verdict, and reduced the award of attorney fees and costs to what it should have been. Jack had won, never willing to concede or compromise what he had earned with the sweat of his own hands. The case was over and Leland wrote Jack a check for more than $300,000.

Jack and Leota's reaction to the end was typical. It was over, move on. Tomorrow was for the future, not yesterdays. As Jack explained, "no one got shot or killed here," we'll move forward, start over, and make something happen with hard work and perseverance. He did just that in the oil and gas business, real estate, and a run for the Oklahoma State Senate at the age of 68.

Jack took Leland Equipment Co. international in the 1970s. Jack, at right, is shown here with one of Leland's trailers in Saudi Arabia.

CHAPTER XX
PRELUDE TO SHINGLE

On January 5, 1944, the headquarters of Division Artillery received its orders to report south to the Naples rest area by January 9, 1944. While the CP had been at Venafro since November 6, 1943, no one felt as if they were leaving home. Indeed, Division Artillery staff could not get out of town fast enough. Initial scuttlebutt had the Division Artillery headed for rest camps north of Naples. Excitement ran high at the thought of wine, women, and song in the city of Naples. As the Division Artillery motored to the south, however, the hopes and dreams of "party Naples" were dashed by General McClain. Hoping to celebrate his birthday in Naples, Division Headquarters shut down all the rest camps in the Naples area on January 7, 1944, Jack's birthday. He guessed they knew he was on the way. With the influx of refugees and the destruction of parts of the city, Naples was plagued by the prevalence of typhus, and with the soldiers being moved off the Venafro Line and into Naples for rest, very high rates of venereal disease were being reported. As Captain Art Large explained, the division had a war to fight and everyone would need their balls. Naples was off limits. With Naples essentially shut down, the command post of Division Artillery was moved to the Grand Hotel near Telese on January 9, 1944. It was not all that bad, but of course anything away from the misery and shelling of Venafro was good. Between cleaning weapons, refitting, and repairing equipment, calibrating the new 105mm Howitzer that had just arrived, and the new carbines, the USO made some good noise with shows provided by comedian Joe E. Brown and Humphrey Bogart. Even the Red Cross' Mobile Doughnut Unit brought great cheers from the troops, but not really because of the doughnuts. If you played your cards right you were usually lucky enough to get to visit with some pretty American Red Cross women. Of course, most of the guys went by the mobile unit in hopes of picking up much more than just a doughnut or two. Most were unsuccessful, but a few got lucky. After all, the most often used pick-up line, "I might never make it back," was fairly persuasive, and true. Besides that, the G.I.s refused to allow themselves to believe that the Red Cross women were there just to hand out doughnuts. Great imagina-

The much loved "Doughnut Dollies" of the American Red Cross.

tion fueled many a trip to the mobile doughnut units. There is no record of Jack attending the Mobile Doughnut Unit while at the Grand Hotel in Telese. Perhaps, however, the most welcome amenity of all was one of the simplest things in life–a hot shower. In January of 1944, Jack and the men practically emptied Telese of water washing the filth of the Italian mud off their bodies.

On January 14, 1944, in the late afternoon, Jack Neville lay fast asleep on the floor of his room at the Grand Hotel when suddenly there was a knock at the door, so loud that it sounded like the shellings at Venafro. Jack went straight up the wall as the door to the room blew open with great force and fury. There, to Jack's disbelief, standing in the doorway was Harry Balkum. It was sheer unconstrained joy as both 23-year-olds jumped up and down, hugged, and ran around the room as if they were little children. Harry had made it, and his return lifted Jack's spirits from the dead as both men shouted for joy amongst the most often used phrase "you son-of-a-bitch!" and "you made it!" Talking uncontrollably, interrupting each other after almost every word, the two headed out in search of Bill Collins. Balkum's arrival called for instant celebration, and for Jack Neville, it was life renewed with the return of his pal. Vast amounts of wine and beer were consumed by all with Balkum's return.

The revelry and excitement of Balkum's return, however, ended the next day. More than hung-over, Jack and Harry were summoned to the S-3 room in the Grand Hotel. There, Colonel Arnote handed Jack a stack of maps and aerial photos with instructions to get familiar with the area, the division was soon to move out. Crunched over the maps and now confined to quarters for reasons of secrecy and security, Jack, with magnifying glass in hand, set about to study the maps and photos. This, of course, was the next operation. After considerable time with the maps, Jack's conclusion was that the division was headed to a place just south of Rome and the twin cities of Anzio-Netunno.

Harry could only look at Jack, "never heard of it."

CHAPTER XXI
CALAMITY AT THE GUSTOV LINE

The critical first punch of the two-punch Shingle plan started on time east of the Gustov Line. At 6:30 a.m. on January 12, the French Expeditionary Force struck out at the Germans. The Germans were well entrenched and, again, stalemate occurred. On January 17, the British X Corps commenced its assault into the middle of the German defense. Initially making progress, the Nazis moved quickly to reinforce their positions throwing two divisions, the 29th and 90th Panzer Grenadiers, into the line. By January 20, the British were forced into withdrawal. Further west on the Gustov Line an unimaginable horror was about to unfold.

General Fred Walker's 36th "Texas" Division was to cross the Rapido River on January 20. High in the hills, the Germans were ready and waiting with heavy artillery and machine gun fire. The Rapido crossing by the 36th was doomed from the beginning, a victim of inexperience and bungled planning. At the point of crossing, there was very little cover, and the 36th's advance was exposed to the direct observation of the German Artillery, who, as always in Italy, had the high ground. The area selected by the planners for the crossing was only 50 feet wide and 12 feet deep in many places. Still, Clark ordered the attack and on the night of January 20, the 36th made its first attempt to cross the Rapido River. As Carlos D'Este wrote in Fatal Decision, "it was one of the bloodiest failures of the war." On January 21, the 36th made their last attempt to cross. Between January 20 and 21, the entire United States 36th Division was lost, slaughtered before they crossed the river. As Whitlock described, it was "unmitigated disaster," 1,700 men were dead, wounded, or missing, almost every man in the infantry regiments a victim of the murderous German fire. As concluded by D'Este, "The reality was that the allies hadn't a hope of breaking the Gustov Line in the foreseeable future." To say the least, the so-called "first punch" missed, and missed badly, a miserable failure. By January 21,1943, Operation Shingle was on the ropes and in serious jeopardy of failure before the 45th Infantry Division ever put a foot on Anzio soil.

With the failure of the Allied forces, General Clark and the commanders were faced with a critical decision. The lead elements of the Anzio invasion force were just out of Naples harbor and there was ample time to recall the armada. The 45th's Division Artillery was still in bivouac and their movement could easily be halted before it started. There was time to regroup and reconsider. Notwithstanding the first missed punch, Clark elected to go forward, his precise reason for the decision somewhat unclear in history. Clark later would be held to account before Congress for the Rapido calamity. In the little Jack ever said about World War II, his most often used phraseology about the General was that he was a "son-of-a-bitch" and a "chicken shit." Jack did not elaborate on the reason why and when these proclamations were made, but it was obvious by his tone and manner of delivery that he wanted no further discussion about Mark Clark. History does make clear the fact that the first phase of Operation Shingle was an absolute fiasco and failure.

As the clock ticked toward Operation Shingle's D-Day, macabre like events continued as the Anzio force prepared to shove off. The commanders decided that a rehearsal was necessary and so a "practice" landing was held to the south near the Salerno beaches. The British 1st Division's exercise went off without a hitch, but for the United States 3rd Division it was a dark comedy of errors. January 17 and 18 proved a disaster, as the 3rd Division unloaded at the wrong beach and a number of trucks, howitzers, and anti-tank guns were lost to the deep blue sea. Not a single battalion landed on time, and not a single combat unit hit the correct beach. The lost equipment and material would have to be made up from some source. There was not time to re-equip and supply from Sicily or Salerno. As a result, the 45th and the United States 36th,who was three days away from being clobbered at the Rapido, cannibalized their quartermasters and ordinance units to replace what the United States 3rd had lost during their practice session. Once again, as they had at Salerno, the 45th would go ashore with less than a full boat of supplies and equipment in an operation believed unable to sustain itself without a success in breaking the Gustov Line. While the United States 3rd floundered on the beach during practice and the 45th scrambled to resupply what the 3rd had lost, the German commander still calculated that the main thrust of the Allied attack to be along the Gustov Line, with an amphibious landing somewhere north only a remote possibility. Believing this to be the case, German General Albert Kesseling on January 18 sent two divisions south to Cassino to meet the expected attack. For the Anzio landing force it would be two less German Divisions to contend with, but for the Allies to the south, it was two more divisions the Fifth Army would have to encounter at the Gustov Line.

CHAPTER XXII
BATTLE LINES

The geography of Anzio would play an important role in this clash of titans. The twin cities of Anzio and Netunno sat together on the beach, and were easily accessible by ship. Several key roads, towns, and landmarks on and near the beach would make World War II history. Chief among them was the only north-south road that intersected Highway 7, the road to the coveted ancient city of Rome. The Via Anziate ran directly north out of Anzio. Its military significance was rather simple. It was the only paved road running to or off the beachhead. To the east and west of the Via Anziate road lay mostly farms and fields. Off-road terrain made tanks or motor movement extremely difficult. There were many deep gullies on either side of the Via Anziate and in the early part of the year the fields were mostly mud, making it nearly impossible for tanks and trucks to traverse the off-road areas. If tanks or trucks, or even infantry got off the Via Anziate, they easily became sitting targets for artillery, mortars, and rifle fire. Approximately three miles north of Anzio lay a stretch of wooded areas that ran east and west called the Padiglione Woods. North of the woods, the terrain was mostly a flat land except for a feature that would take its place in the history of the battle, the Overpass. Located at a point that Lateral Road, running east and west and intersected the Via Anziate approximately four and one-half miles up the Via Anziate north of Anzio, the Overpass, as the troops came to call it, was not exactly a southern Mediterranean architectural phenomena. The Overpass was an unfinished highway bridge and railroad tracks ran parallel to the road. High dirt embankments ran approximately 100 yards on each side of the uncompleted overpass. Like the Via Anziate, it too would come to have its own military significance. If tanks and troops were to get to the beachhead from the north, they would have to come down the Via Anziate and through the gap of the Overpass. Problematic to any approaching enemy, the gap was only 20 yards wide. It became known as the "Gate of Hell" for good reason. The farm fields north of the Overpass and east and west of the Via Anziate were known as "Campo di Carne," translated meaning "Field of Meat." These farm fields would live up to their namesake in mid-February of 1944.

Progressing approximately half a mile north of Lateral Road and the Overpass was the "Dead End Road" which ran only to the east of the Via Anziate and into an unused railroad bed labeled "The Bowling Alley." Another half mile north of the intersection of Dead End Road and the Via Anziate laid the next significant land feature, a rather complex set of caves and tunnels, appropriately named by the Allies, "The Caves." Some of the caves were as high as fifteen feet, and described by one who fought there as "a normal city block long." Legend and lore had it that The Caves, of which there were six, were built in during World War I to store gunpowder manufactured in Anzio. North of the The Caves was "The Embankment" which was a bridge to support an unfinished railroad track. To the immediate north of The Embankment, were the towns of Aprilia and Carroceto, approximately six miles from the Anzio beachhead and sitting aside the Via Anziate. From a distance, Aprilia had a factory-like appearance to those who would fight there and accordingly was tagged "The Factory." Roughly eight miles from the beachhead up the Via Anziate was the Campoleone Station, a key transit area and just north of Campoleone was the road to Rome. In what would become the eastern flank of the 45th's defensive perimeter around the Anzio beachhead was the town of Padiglione, located near the intersection of Lateral Road and The Bowling Alley at its farthest southeastern point.

In the Italian Campaign, it seemed as though the Germans always held the key high ground, and the Anzio battle was no exception. Approximately 14 miles due north of Anzio lay the Alban Hills. There, the Germans had unobstructed observation of the entire area, including the beachhead. From these hills, mounted on railroad cars and hidden in tunnels, the Germans could roll out their monstrous guns which the Thunderbirds called "Anzio Annie" and the "Anzio Express." These 280mm guns had the range and accuracy to lob their giant shells of 550 pounds of high explosives 14 miles, all the way to the beachhead in a chilling reign of artillery terror. Jack's Division Artillery headquarters would be in the sites of Anzio Annie.

On the very day of the Rapido fiasco, Task Force 81 slipped out of Naples harbor undetected by the Germans. In keeping with the plan, the British 1st and the United States 3rd Infantry Division set sail for Anzio with the 45th Infantry Division still in Telese. The trip around the Gustov Line and up the west coast of Italy was 100 miles and on January 22, 1944, 354 vessels with 40,000 British and American troops, and 5,200 vehicles were sitting in the darkness off the Anzio-Netunno beaches, the Germans still unaware of the armada's presence.

Within hours after the British 1st and United States 3rd departed Naples, the 45th Infantry Division and the Division Artillery were alerted on January 21, for movement "on order." First to leave would be the Infantry Regiments led by the 179th who would disembark on January 21. Last to leave following the Infantry Regiments would be Jack and Division Artillery. With the alert for movement on order, the hours for Jack at the Grand Hotel in Telese were numbered and the mood of the troops turned from smiles at the Red Cross Mobile Doughnut Unit, to the somber near frowns of knowing they were going back to the killing at yet another place never heard of. Maps, logistical, and artillery fire support plans were studied and studied again, as Jack paced about waiting for the order to move out. The duffle bag and war belt were kept nearby, ready to be picked up and strapped on in a second's notice. As Jack and Harry waited, not a single shred of information leaked to the anxious troops that the United States 36th nearly had been wiped out at the Rapido River. With trucks loaded, and men on the edge, the order to move to the ships would not come for three long days. In the meantime, no one was allowed out of the perimeter for security reasons.

One hundred miles to the north, on January 22, 1944 at 1:50 a.m. the attack on the Anzio beachhead started with British rocket launchers whistling off to hopefully destroy minefields thought to be on the beach. At 2:00 a.m., the LCIs lined up after circling for nearly two hours and beat a path through the slight chop of the sea for the beachhead. As the landing force hit the beach, there was a stunned silence. The landing took place without opposition. No machine gun fire, no minefields, barbed wire, no 88 shells whistling down the beach. It was a quiet walk onto the beach that morning. The Allies were grateful for it. The British and American units moved swiftly inland. The British 3rd sprinted northward two miles and set up a road block on the Via Anziate. This deployment resulted in the initial northern beachhead perimeter being established just south of the Overpass. The United States 3rd quickly shuttled three miles to the east with both artillery and armor setting up defensive positions near the Mussolini Canal. Both the British 1st and United States 3rd were mindful of the potential of the German counterattack. The Allies wasted no time, and General Lucas ordered the beach stuffed with men and supplies with all possible speed while the infantry regiments braced for an expected counterattack that surprisingly did not come. By midnight on January 22, 1944, 90% of the Allied strength was on the beach at Anzio. The Germans at least had been momentarily caught with their pants down. It would not last long as Lucas and General Clark elected to maintain the perimeter and sit on the beach to wait for the rest of the invading force, principally the 45th, to arrive.

Three hours after the substantial part of the invasion force had established a beachhead, German Field Marshall Albert Kesslring learned that the Allies had landed at Anzio. At 5:00 a.m., Kesselring ordered elements of two divisions to establish road blocks across all roads leading from Anzio-Netunno to the Alban Hills. Two other divisions located in northern Italy, including General Eberhard von MacKensen's 14th Army, were ordered to move out immediately. By January 23, 1944, the battle lines were becoming clearly defined, as Jack and

Rifles in hand, the Thunderbirds off-load their LST's to go ashore at Anzio. While the landing was unopposed, Anzio became the bloodiest engagement of the war for the 45th and the Germans.

Division Artillery waited at the Grand Hotel in Telese. It would take six days for the entirety of the 45th to arrive at the Anzio beach. In the meantime, Lucas was content to improve his defensive position and wait on the beach. While the Allies hesitated to move inland, valuable time was gifted to the Germans to marshal their own forces for the bloody battle to come.

On January 23, 1944, the first elements of the 45th, the 179th Infantry Regiment, boarded 18 LSTs and LCIs for the 100-mile shuttle to Anzio. Arriving on January 24, the regiment moved quickly to the north, unopposed, up the Via Anziate, and dug in near the Overpass. There they sat and waited, as the British 1st fanned out to the left providing the western flank protection of the defensive perimeter, with the United States 3rd along the eastern sector. The newly-arrived 179th held the center, a bit seasick after their ride.

The entire 29th Panzier Grenadier Division had made their new home only eight miles up the Via Anziate road at Aprilia. Now massed at The Factory on January 24, an entire German Division laid in wait. By the 24th, the Germans had fortified their position to the west of The Factory at the town

The 45th comes ashore at Anzio in January of 1944 for the most part unopposed.

of Cisterna. It was almost as if the two giant armies, separated by less than 10 miles, were just sitting and staring at each other, waiting to see who would throw the first rock.

As the Allies sat on the beach at Anzio while the Germans massed their forces, Jack and the Division Artillery were finally given the order to lock and load. On January 24, 1944, Division Artillery trucked from the Grand Hotel in Telese to a staging area in Pozzuoli, a small port just north of Naples. Again restricted to the area, they readied for disembarkation, sat, and waited. The Allies at Anzio also attempted to probe northward. The British sent a patrol up the Via Anziate and the United States 3rd made a run at Cisterna. Both efforts were rather quickly and forcefully beaten back by extremely strong German counterattacks. Lucas had uncovered a hornets nest of Germans, heavily defending a line running from The Factory eastward to Cisterna. Lucas hoped the arrival of the 45th would tip the scales and allow him to attack. The division, was still in Pozzuoli, could not get there for four more days. Lucas was unsure of what was in front of him, but one thing was for certain–the Tyrrehenia Sea was directly behind him.

As word of the landings drifted back from the Anzio beachhead, the emotions of the 45th were mixed. Great relief spread through the ranks that the landings had gone well, unopposed, and few casualties. On the other hand, the initial invading force was still on the beach, not moving inland but rather purposefully remaining on the beach. Why? In Sicily, and Salerno, the initial invading waves had moved swiftly off the beach toward their objectives with all speed. At Anzio, this was not the case. Jack Neville posed the question that echoed through the next four decades, "Why are we sitting on our asses?"

Jack was among the many Anzio veterans critical of the failure of the Allies to move off the Anzio beachhead. This stagnation, as he saw it, was one of the chief complaints voiced against General Mark Clark. Jack's conclusions never were burdened by any of the specifics of tactics, strategy, or politics that plagued Shingle. Jack always put it simply and directly, "We sat on that Goddamn beach and got the shit shelled out of us." That was how he expressed the entire Anzio experience, and beyond these rather descriptive words, he either evaded or refused further discussion. From Jack's foxhole, his observations and feelings were understandable and, in many ways, justifiable. Sixty years later however history allows a broader, more inclusive view of what happened in January and February of 1944 that caused Jack Neville to be on that beach at that moment in time.

The most common, often repeated, criticism of Operation Shingle is the failure of the British 1st and United States 3rd to move into Rome, only 40 miles away. The "highway to Rome was open," the argument goes, all they had to do was drive. With some hindsight, military history suggests that at the time of the landings, and within possibly the next two days, the road to Rome may have been sparsely defended by the Germans. Indeed, even with the failure of the Rapido crossing, and other failures to penetrate the Gustov Line east of the Rapido, Kesselring's initial reaction to the missed first punch was to send two entire divisions south out of Rome to beef up the German lines of defense.

Whether Lucas should have taken Rome after landing on January 21, 1944, has been the subject of considerable debate with history being rather unkind toward the general, as well as his commander and boss, General Clark. There is, however, credible evidence to support the view that Lucas' decision to exercise caution in the face of known facts was both reasonable and prudent. First, as all of the military commanders agreed, critical to the success of Shingle was the initial first punch–the penetration of the Gustov Line that would force the

Germans to move their troops south. The first punch was a miserable failure and both Lucas and Clark knew this. Certainly by the time he hit the Anzio beach, Lucas knew his two divisions could not be aided or rescued by a successful southern Allied Force. He had to feel as if he were alone. He was.

All planners and commanders agreed that while the initial wave of Anzio attackers could possibly move swiftly inland, they could not survive a prolonged ground assault without reinforcements and supplies that had to come in part from a successful penetration of the Germans' southern defense. As a result, Lucas, knowing of the Rapido failure while on the Anzio beach, did not have at hand his entire invading force. Only two of his divisions were on shore, with the 45th still waiting north of Naples. The pitiful shortage of shipping caused by Overlord priorities left Lucas shorthanded and under supplied at a critical point in time. Adding to Lucas' dilemma was a lack of confident, well-sourced intelligence about the location and size of the German defenders in the Anzio-Rome area. In other words, Lucas did not know what was out there in front of him.

With the 157th landed on the wrong beach at Salerno, the 179th had sped quickly inland only to be cut-off and surrounded by a superior German force. An entire regiment was almost lost at Salerno. Lucas most certainly did not want Salerno to repeat itself. With all of the above at play, it is difficult to condemn Lucas' decision making as arbitrary, capricious, or "ball-less" as some of the veterans, Jack included, more descriptively put it. Lucas was cautiously prudent and for good reason. While it can be said that Lucas' failure to move the invasion force off the beachhead resulted in Jack Neville's four-month visit to Anzio, the preponderance of the evidence does not suggest that Lucas, or Clark for that matter, were "at fault" for placing Jack's life in unnecessary jeopardy by making the decision in the dawn of the battle to maintain the perimeter.

Other issues arise from microscopic hindsight examination of the first three days of Shingle. As often said, the commanders proclaimed it critical that the "first punch" made at the Gustov Line succeed. As the invasion fleet was on the water, and as Jack and Division Artillery were still in Telese having not yet even moved to Pozzuoli, the initial failure at the Gustov Line was known, or certainly should have been known by Roosevelt, Churchill, and right on down to Eisenhower, Alexander, and Clark. Given the known failures, the Allied decision makers could have called the operation off until success at the Gustov Line was more assured. There existed persuasive evidence to suggest that the Anzio armada should simply have been recalled to sail another day. The world went to war beginning in September of 1939. For almost four and a half years the free world's existence had been at risk and finally, by the beginning of 1944, the Nazis war machine was starting to crack from its horrific losses at the hands of the Russians on the eastern front. The invasion of North Africa, Sicily, and southern Italy were pushing the Nazis backward as the Axis was being caught in a vice of British, Russians, and Americans. The Allies agreed that the quickest way to put a dagger through the Nazis was to land a monstrous invasion force somewhere in the north of Europe and strike directly at Berlin. Invasion in the north, the Allies became convinced, was the quickest route to victory. And so, long before Anzio and D-Day, June 6, 1944, the British and Americans became committed to a giant leap of men and material across the English Channel and into the heart of Germany. By January of 1944, the Germans came to expect a cross-channel attack, and at the same time they were having to deal with immense losses in the east, and sustained pressure in Italy. Keeping the pressure on in the south kept a substantial part of the Hitler Army from reinforcing the north. In essence, by January of 1944, Hitler was pinned down on two fronts and expecting invasion on a third. The "heat was on," as they say. This body of evidence suggests that Jack's foxhole was dug at Anzio because of the reluctance of the world leaders to give the Third Reich a place to breathe. The Nazis were down but not out, and despite the fallacy and deficiency of Shingle, the decision was made to not let the Maniac get up anywhere, keep pounding at him no matter what the risk, no matter what the price. The free world was hanging in the balance. With a gambler's roll of the dice, Shingle went forward and Adair, Oklahoma, would be represented on Anzio sand by Jack Neville.

The commitment to Overlord rendered Shingle a stepchild in the south. The practical reality of the build-up in England for the cross-channel invasion caused a shortage of shipping in the theatre, especially so for Shingle. Despite efforts to the contrary, the shipping shortage prevented all three divisions from landing at Anzio at the same time. In essence, the invading force was shuttled to a landing site over a week's period of time, thus preventing or restricting a decisive movement inland. A logical argument can be made that despite difficulties at the Gustov Line, had sufficient shipping been provided to land the entire Anzio force, Rome would have fallen within the week and Jack spared the awful ordeal of the Overpass. However, on this, the greatest world stage ever, how can one really fault the decision to prioritize Overlord, even though it sacrificed Shingle, placing life on the line at Anzio.

In late 1943 and early 1944, the American industrial machine was pedal to the medal. While the real Achilles Heal of Shingle was a shortage of LSTs and LCIs, it was not as if there was a surplus of landing craft anywhere to be found. Indeed, the military leaders believed there were not enough stockpiled, even for D-Day. Andrew Higgins in New Orleans, Louisiana, was throwing out as many landing craft as time, men, and material would allow. Twenty-four hour shifts were not uncommon as the ship-builders, tank-builders, and munition makers were stretched to the limit. With priority given to Overlord, the fact of life was that there was simply not enough boats to go around.

CHAPTER XXIII
"...COLONEL... WE'RE OUT OF AMMO"

After two days in the Pozzuoli staging area, the 45th Division Artillery finally got its marching orders. On January 26, 1944, Division Artillery and Jack loaded on to trucks at 4:00 p.m. once again for transport to the embarkation point just north of Naples. There they waited for yet another two days. It was not until six days after the lead elements of Shingle had hit the beach at Anzio that at 8:00 p.m. on January 28, Jack boarded the LST for Anzio. Along with Division Artillery, the 45th's 157th Infantry Regiment and the 158th Field Artillery Battalion also boarded ship for the ride northward. As late as January 28, the division's 180th Infantry Regiment was at Naples harbor waiting to load as there were not enough ships to take them up the coast. Although it was only a relatively short hop to Anzio, after a day at sea Jack gratefully walked off the LST at 6:40 p.m. on January 30, 1944. There was no time for rest or pause. Division Artillery HQ and the HQ Battery moved quickly north up the Via Anziate and set up the Division Artillery CP two miles inland just inside the Padiglione Woods and south of the Overpass. Last into the Anzio beachhead was the division's 180 Infantry Regiment who arrived at noon on January 30. By 8:00 p.m. the 180th had taken up residence, bivouacked slightly north of Netunno. Strung out over six days, it was not until the last day of January, 1944, that the entire 45th Infantry Division finally made its way onto the Anzio beachhead. Once on the beach, the Thunderbirds quickly realized they were not going anywhere. Frustrated and feeling like ducks on a pond, the 45th carried out their first order of business. They "dug in" and, once again, they waited.

Time had allowed General John Lucas to get the whole of his invading force onshore and deployed. However, the Allies' hesitation had worked to the advantage of the Germans. While Lucas now had at his disposal some 61,300 men, 237 tanks, and 500 artillery pieces, the Germans had surrounded the beachhead with 71,500 troops. The Allies were now outnumbered at Anzio, with the odds to only worsen.

With the Thunderbird's duffle bags barely off their shoulders, Lucas, again being pressured by Mark Clark and Churchill to break-out of the beachhead, marshaled an attack by the United States 3rd Division against Cisterno on the right flank. The attack on January 30, was led by Colonel William O. Darby and the "Darby's Rangers." Only 5 miles off the beachhead in the Padiglione Woods at the small town of Isola Bella, yet another bloody mess hit the Allies.

Lying in wait in the vicinity of the Pantano Ditch were the Germans with tanks and artillery. Darby's forces were quickly surrounded and virtually cut-off from escape. Nearly out of ammunition, First Sergeant Robert Ehalt, one of the original Rangers, radioed the last Ranger message back to Darby. "They're closing in on us, Colonel, we're out of ammo - but they won't get us cheap."

Darby's entire force was massacred. Of the 767 Rangers at Isola Bella, only six survived. While Darby was among the survivors, his beloved Rangers were annihilated. After two brutal days of combat, the United States 3rd Division called off the assault short of Cisterna. The break-out effort had failed. However, while the Allies blood flowed on the beachhead, the Anzio invaders were sucking the life out of the Germans in the north who were waiting for Overlord. Hitler transferred eight divisions to the south to deal with Shingle. It was eight less divisions for Overlord to deal with, and eight more for Shingle.

The Shingle scoreboard at February 1, 1944, read ugly. The effort at Gustov Line had failed miserably at the Rapido River. Two abbreviated efforts to get to Aprilia had failed, and a major effort toward Cisterna on the right flank had resulted in bloody disaster. As the reports got back to the Division Artillery CP in the Padiglione Woods, the Chairman of the S-3 section, Walter Arnote, called his men together to explain the situation. The briefing did not take long. "Gentlemen, our ass is surrounded." Harry Balkum looked at Jack, "Shit."

On February 1, 1944, General McClain summoned the entire headquarters staff together. The McClain style of leading from the front had put the Division Artillery CP virtually on the front lines and at substantial risk. The orders now came to move the Division Artillery CP off the perimeter front. Barely out of their duffle bags and suitcases, the command post was moved backward two miles and stakes were put down directly on the Anzio beach just off the Via Anziate. While no explanation was given for the order, it was clear that General Lucas did not want command posts on the front lines, especially with the Germans only a few miles away, and well within artillery range. By February 1, 1944, with the division now on shore, the infantry units took up their positions on the defensive perimeter. To the left of the 45th was the British 56th, and to its right, the United States 3rd Division. The small area being defended was only 15 miles long and seven miles deep with one paved road down the middle. The mission of the 45th Infantry Division and Jack's Division Artillery was clear. The Thunderbirds were surrounded and their orders straight forward–they were responsible for the beachhead defense.

An aerial photo of HQ Battery, Division Artillery at Anzio, Jack Neville's unit. taken by Lt. McKay in February of 1944.

News of the demise of the Rangers and the failure of the United States 3rd to punch through cast uncertainty over the operations and planning. Initially the news created a dark cloud of depression about the camp, but then the adrenalin of survival kicked in. High energy soon took over. They had fought their way out of a tough spot at Salerno and had survived a pounding at Venafro. They would do it again. In the Division Artillery CP, every inch of the Anzio perimeter was plotted and gridded. Division Artillery set up an elaborate system of radio and wire communication allowing forward observers to pinpoint artillery fire anywhere along the perimeter. The Artillery batteries in support of the infantry units calibrated their 105s and 155s to swing the entire area. Before long, Division Artillery, in coordination with ships off shore and the United States Army Air Force, constructed a precise and deadly plan of artillery fire capable of bringing a curtain of lead down on anyone in the area. Five hundred artillery pieces, off-shore cruisers, and batteries were registered and ready to go. Within seconds, the artillery could hail lead and steel down on virtually every inch of Anzio ground. In the meantime, every artillery shell possible was stuffed into the chain of supply. Nobody was going to run out of ammo in this fight. By February of 1944, the Artillery had developed a deadly firing technique called "TOTs," or "time-on-target" that massed an enormous amount of artillery fire power on a single target all at one time. Through rather complicated mathematical calculations, theoretically every artillery gun, on command, could fire their weapon at a given time, and with correct calculation of distance and velocity, every round fired would arrive at the designated target

A 105mm howitzer of the 158 Field Artillery at Anzio in February of 1944.

at the precise, same time. The destructive and deadly firepower of "TOTs" was incredibly devastating. The attitude of the Thunderbirds turned into one of dogged determination. If the Germans were going to take the beachhead, they would pay for it.

Only a short month before Jack had experienced the mountains of Venafro, he was ready to fight on the beaches of Anzio. At Anzio it was nearly impossible to live above the ground during the day. The Germans, high in the Alban Hills, could observe all activity on the beach, and at times determined by the Huns to be the most disruptive, would roll "Annie," or the "Express" out of their tunnels and throw a few of their 550 lb. shells down on the beach. The soldiers labeled one of the huge railroad guns the "Anzio Express" because standing on the beach you could hear the shells coming, as if it were "a runaway train roaring through the sky." One soldier observed that several boxcars could be put in the center of the explosion of one of Anzio Annie's shells. The Division Artillery CP lived in a constant state of anxiety quickly elevated by the sound of the Express roaring down from the Alban Hills.

Never out of artillery range, the men literally lived under ground in "dug outs." Digging as deep as they could without running into water, the Anzio G.I. slept and ate underground. Many of the dug outs took on rather sophisticated designs for the occasion. Utilizing boards or logs, some underground digs were roofed and walled. Others had doors and wood floors, but no awards were given by Architectural Digest at Anzio. It was still the filth of sand, dirt, and mud. The Division Artillery CP remained on the beach for three months. The big downside to any architectural excellence in dug-out design was the concussion that always came with Annie, or the Express. Concussion waves ripped through the air and ground caving in the walls and collapsing the roofs. And then, you had to dig out, and start all over. So intense was the shelling, that even tanks and jeeps were two-thirds buried in the Anzio sand for protection.

For Jack on the beachhead, he tried to keep out of sight during the day, and only move about under the cover of darkness. Once the night settled in, trucks ran off the beachhead carrying ammunition, food, water, and supplies to the infantry troops dug in along the perimeter. At Anzio, even the hospitals were on the beach. It seemed as though everything was on the beach at Anzio.

Oddly enough there were a few niceties at Anzio, three of which were steaks, hamburgers, and yes, whiskey. The area north of Anzio was largely farm land, most of which had been long abandoned when it became obvious that war would take them over, or destroy them. As a result there were considerable "unattended" cattle and sheep. The men described it as purely accidental that roaming bovine would accidentally step on a mine or trip a wire. Of course, there was only one thing that could be done with the fallen carcass. The men carved the meat up for steaks and hamburger cooked over an open fire. There is no historical record of how many of these animals actually fell from a shot with a .45 pistol or an M-1 rifle, and any inquiry into the demise of these animals always was met with denial. Despite the population of cows, goats, and sheep, the primary bill of fare was the "C" and "K" ration which would be heated up

On the Anzio beachhead, the Thunderbirds lived in dug-outs. "170 MM Lane" refers to "Anzio Annie," the German gun that shelled the beachhead constantly.

A mainstay on the Anzio beachhead was steak and hamburger as the soldiers of the 45th shot cows that wandered onto the battlefield.

Dug-outs built on the Anzio beachhead in the Spring of 1944.

A captured "Anzio Annie."

The German railroad car big gun nicknamed "Anzio Annie." Hidden in the Alban Hills above Anzio, the Germans rolled the big gun out to shell the beachhead occupied by the Thunderbirds.

with the old reliable Coleman stove. Oddly enough, the British soldiers were assigned rations of whiskey and liquor. While the 45th had beer available, they had none of the stronger stuff. The absence of whiskey only spurred American ingenuity, and a number of moonshine stills sprung up on the beach that seemed to have everything.

In between dodging the shells shot by Anzio Annie or the Express, the beachhead troops took their turn ducking the delivery of 1,000 lb. bombs dropped by "Popcorn Pete." Popcorn's payload usually arrived at night directly over the beach. Popcorn Pete's bomb usually exploded in mid-air, sending a stream of steel and shrapnel downward, and everywhere with a distinctive sound of popcorn being popped. Also available for your entertainment were the sounds of "Berlin Sally," the German version of Tokyo Rose, whose most often asked question was, "do you know what your sweethearts are up to." At the most, propaganda of Berlin Sally was an irritant and easy target for a barrage of four-letter words explaining in rather literative terms what "Sally" could do with herself. Make no mistake about it however, the Anzio beach was no beach party. Moonshine, whiskey, a charred steak, and Berlin Sally were only occasional diversions from the death and blood that would flow on the beach in the next four months.

The mainstay of the Thunderbird's amphibious assault was the "Higgins" boat built in New Orleans, Louisiana by the Higgins Company. Operations in Southern Europe were desperately short of these boats as the Normandy invasion was given priority.

By February 2, 1944, the deadly preliminaries of Anzio were over. Both armies were poised for the face-off. The Germans sent a large patrol into the western sector of the 45th area of defense. The sixty-man unit was able to penetrate the 157th's lines, but the Germans "were slaughtered at close range." The Germans also made a push toward Aprillia, but this time artillery, coupled with air bombardment, stopped the Germans in their tracks. Now the German generals, Von MacKensen and his boss Kesselring, had to stop, rethink, and regroup.

By the evening hours of February 3, the Germans had consolidated their troops. In a torrential downpour they threw two divisions at the British near Campoleone Station and north of Aprilia. New into the battle were the feared German "Tiger Tanks." With the Germans heavily reinforced, the British suddenly found themselves dealing with at least six tanks, perhaps as many as 17. It was too much for the British. For Jack, Division Artillery, and the Thunderbirds, the tensions now increased. The Germans had poked, prodded, and cracked the British north of Aprilia. The fight was creeping southward, and toward the 45th. On February 6, 1944, even in the rearward area only a few miles to the south, the order went out for Division Artillery to double the guard. The Germans would soon be coming. Captured German documents told the Allies that the Germans would hit the front again the next day at 4:00 a.m. The main enemy target was The Factory, Aprilia.

While the Allies prepared and waited, 4:00 a.m. passed without incident. It was not a sign of relief. Not a man left his post. While the British were positioned to carry the brunt of the fighting, the 45th worked to prepare themselves for a German break through along the entire line. For Balkum and Neville back on the beach, the constant worry was communication and supply. All the artillery firing plans depended heavily on maintaining the ability to talk with each other, and this was not a day to run out of shells. Check and recheck, the Thunderbirds waited. The Germans were seven hours late. At 9:00 p.m. on February 7, German tanks and infantry attacked on a eight-mile front slightly north of Aprilia. Now the 45th's 157th was being plastered with German artillery near Buon Riposo Ridge. The 157th and the artillery were ready. In a 24-hour engagement, the artillery fired more than 24,000 rounds, an incredible rate of fire over such a short period of time. Stung by the 45th's fierce resistence, Von MacKensen backed his troops off for the next two days. At Division Artillery CP, the celebration did not last long. It was obvious the Germans' would return. The men went back to work, restringing the "commo" wire to ensure communication, refiguring firing plans, and hustling more of those golden shells, food, and water up to the firing batteries. The Thunderbirds stayed at the ready praying that the beleaguered British could hold the line.

Knowing that the British north of Aprilia were badly bruised, the Germans focused their strength directly at the Aprilia defenders. Spanning the next two days, the Germans hurled three regimental-sized attacks at the British and Aprilia with the "London Irish" and the "Royal Berkshire" at the point of the German attack. It was too much for the valiant British fighters. By noon on February 9, the German 725th Infantry Regiment had taken the Factory. Word of the fall reached Jack and the Division Artillery quickly. If the Germans continued southward, the Thunderbirds were the last division standing in front of the Tyrrehenian Sea. The expected continued attack did not come. At the Factory, the Germans were exhausted. Low on ammunition and supplies, they were spent. The German forces to the west at Carroceto were still on the move against the depleted "Scots Guards." The Scots could not hold. On February 10, 1944, the Germans took Carroceto. Between February 4 and February 11, more than 2,563 Allied soldiers had been captured, 99% of which were British. In the CP bunker back at the beachhead Jack got out his red grease pencil to mark the new German position.

The Nazis were now solidly encamped at the Factory, seven miles from the beach.

Supplies stacked and hidden on the Anzio beachhead in January of 1944.

CHAPTER XXIV
"BILL, YOU GIVE 'EM THE WORKS"

With the British to the west pinned down and decimated, Lucas committed his last beachhead reserve, the 45th Infantry Division, to the battle. During a conference at Lucas' headquarters on February 10, the decision was made that the Thunderbirds would attack the Factory and Carroceto the next morning. As the meeting concluded General Lucas looked at the commander of the 45th, General William Eagles, and said "Bill, you give'em the works."

McClain now summoned his staff together and explained the situation. Division Artillery would provide heavy fire support for the 179th Infantry Regiment who would lead the assault. In preparation for the attack the division was reshuffled along the perimeter. The 157th moved into a position straddling the Via Anziate. The 180th was moved out to the far right, north of Padiglione, with the 179th now in the middle of its two brother regiments. In S-3 section back at Division Artillery CP, it would be an "all-nighter." While the boys of the 179th Infantry Regiment literally fixed bayonets, Division Artillery burned the midnight oil to provide for a vicious pre-dawn barrage to be thrown at the Germans. The pressure to get it right was turned up a notch when staff scuttlebutt leaked that General Lucas had asked Mark Clark for another division to reinforce Anzio. The Fifth Army Commander adamantly refused Lucas' request. Every fear of the deficiency of Shingle was now being realized, and with Clark's decision to not reinforce the beachhead, the position of the 45th became regrettably more precarious.

The Thunderbirds were the last division between the Germans and the sea. Each shell and bullet counted.

In the late hours of February 10 and early morning hours of the 11th, the seemingly endless stream of Anzio freakish events continued. The Germans had caught Darby's Rangers by surprise at Isola Bella, and now the Krauts had intercepted a critical radio message. They knew the 179th was coming at the Factory.

Just before dawn on February 11, Division Artillery delivered its pay load on the Germans at Aprilia, and at 6:30 a.m. the 179th moved out for the doomed assault on the Factory. The waiting German tanks and armor were too much

Between February 17 and 19, 1944, 155mm Artillery battery guns fired some 41,525 rounds into the on-coming Germans.

for the 179th. With bayonets fixed, the 1st Battalion fought their way to the southeast corner of the city before being forced to retreat. The casualty rate was abominable. Every officer in Company A and half of its men were killed. The next morning the 179th made another brave charge at the Factory. German tanks rather easily repulsed the effort. At daylight the battered battalion was forced to return to its original starting point and the effort to gain control of Aprilia was put on hold. Every inch of ground was now vital to the Thunderbirds' defensive perimeter. With the Germans entrenched in Aprillia, the front line troops of the 45th took up positions only 500 yards south of the Factory ruins. The beachhead defensive perimeter had shrunk once again. The noose around the 45th was starting to tighten.

CHAPTER XXV
"ARE THE 179TH WEARING OVERCOATS"?

For Jack, and every man in the division, it was now more than evident that the Germans were preparing a major attack down the Via Anziate aimed directly at the beach. Division Artillery huddled over their maps with ears fixed to the radios as reports flowed in of the giant German troop, tank, and armor build-up just north of Aprilia. On February 15 it was no secret to those on the beach that the Germans had massed nine divisions, 125,000 troops, for a frontal attack directly at the 45th Infantry Division. Division Artillery would mass every ounce of firepower up and along the Via Anziate.

For most of the day, Jack ducked and dodged the near constant shelling the Germans threw at the beach. The Express and Annie were unusually active, causing constant disruption on the beach. The Germans, however, were not doing it for practice, or pleasure; the barrages were the unmistakable precursor of terrible things to come. The clock was ticking for the big clash and everyone knew it would come. Expecting the fight to start soon, the 2nd Battalion of the 157th moved out of their foxholes and northward. Taking up a position west of the Via Anziate at the Caves, the infantry battalion locked, loaded, and waited. As the day crept by, the tension of the beachhead increased. Only a few miles separated the water from the giant German force that would barrel down at them within hours. It was as if everyone just wished it would hurry up and start, knowing the Germans were not going to go away. As if the desperation of the moment was not evident, at 10:30 p.m. on the 15th, the 45th Division Artillery headquarters received orders from Eagles to organize the beachhead defense. Most fearful of a massive tank attack, Division Artillery kept their guns fixed along the Via Anziate. Because of inclement weather, the Via Anziate was the only pathway that could support a tank. In anticipation of the worst, the Thunderbirds established lines of a last defense south of the Overpass consisting of four trench lines that if need be would be manned by every cook and bottle washer left if the Germans penetrated the "Gate of Hell." Once again, the Thunderbirds were taking up defensive positions to stay and fight as they did at Salerno. No one would evacuate the beach. The plans and operations called for the "last stand" to be at the Overpass.

Nearly forgotten by Jack was the failed "first punch" in the south. On February 15, the Allies made progress at the Gustov line. Two hundred and fifty-four bombers let loose, on a hill known as Monte Cassino built in 529 A.D. At long last the tough Gustov line had been cracked. For the 45th it was too little too late. The southern allied force would not reach Anzio in time. Late that day, the German line and time of attack was again reconfirmed. The British captured a German paratrooper who was rather quickly persuaded to spill his guts. Near Aprilia, six German divisions were fueled and ready for the morning attack.

No one slept the night of the 15th at the CP. Radio and telephone traffic flowed in from the field battalions and forward observers. German night patrols were picking at the front lines of the 157th. All Jack could do was sit and wait for the call of the grid coordinates in order to fix the precise location of the Nazi's advance.

As dawn crept up on February 15, Captain Felix Sparks, E Company Commander of the 157th clicked on his radio. Seeing movement just in front of his position he queried back to headquarters "Are the 179th wearing overcoats?"

The Division Artillery CP exploded in response shouting "Hell no, shoot 'em." And now the fight was on with the Artillery CP now fixed on an infantry attack just north of the Caves. At 6:30 a.m. an incredibly powerful German artillery barrage was laid down the Via Anziate that rocked the ground all the way back to Jack's position.

In the heaviest artillery barrage yet, the Germans massed the fire of 452 field guns, howitzers, and other weapons to provide a carpet of steel for a massive infantry attack that would soon come. In addition to the German artillery, what was left of the German air force found the unusually sunny skies of the 15th to their liking. With 270 planes, the Germans bombed and strafed the entire beachhead, no doubt their objective was to drive the 45th into the sea.

To the surprise of those at the CP, forty-five minutes was a relatively short period of time for a major tank-infantry attack. Either the Germans were incredibly confident, or they were low on ammunition to fuel a prolonged attack. Little did the Thunderbirds know that the Germans were suffering shortages of artillery ammunition and strict controls had been imposed on the German gunmen. The 45th Division Artillery, on the other hand, had piled tons of shells on the beach and with creative nighttime movement leading up to the 16th had supplied all of the gun pits of the 105s and 155s of the Division Artillery. The 45th could shoot until the barrels melted.

With the end of the German artillery barrage, the inevitable infantry attack would surely begin. For Jack, all ears were primed to radios and telephones waiting for reports of precise enemy positions. Reports of the enemy attack came quickly. The Germans were attacking down the Via Anziate literally in human waves. The 157th's regimental historian described it as "wave upon wave, a grey blue" as the advancing tide of tank support came down a road and open fields. The German assault waves had no cover as the forward observers called in the positions of the advancing Germans to Division Artillery. Described by Whitlock as a "turkey shoot," the Allies hammered the German attack with 432 big guns, batteries of 90mm anti-aircraft fire, and shells from two British Cruisers sitting off-shore. The Germans were annihilated as the ground literally exploded around them, but not before their line of advance had taken them 500 yards south of the Factory. The radios cracked back to the Division Artillery CP. The 179th and 180th were holding their positions on the right, and it was now evident that the main thrust of the German force was at the 157th. The guns were focused northward, directly up the Via Anziate.

The slaughter only momentarily stopped the German attack. Sensing weakness in Spark's E Company, the Germans again came hard at the 157th. At

On February 16, 1944, the Germans started their big push down the Via Anziate into the position held by the 157th Infantry Regiment of the 45th. At this time Jack's position was south of the Overpass in the Padiglione Woods.

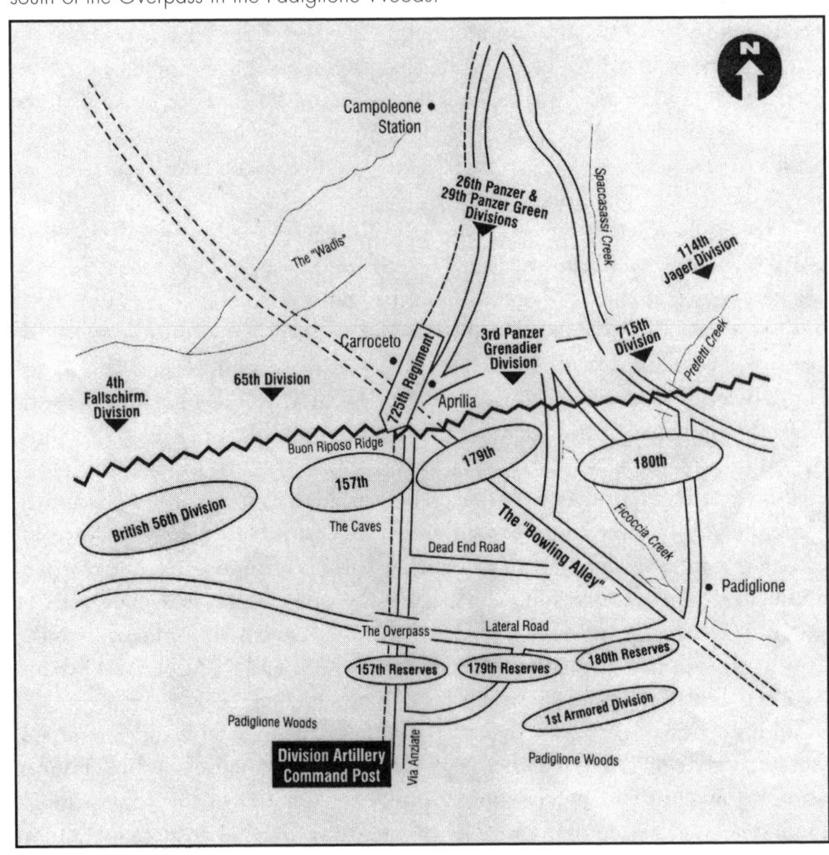

11:30 a.m., the 157th radioed the Division Artillery that they were being attacked in the vicinity of the Caves, and near the Underpass. In a moments notice, the Division Artillery CP massed the fire of 144 guns on the enemy near the 157th, with precisely placed TOTs. It was devastating, a German blood bath. The second effort to swamp the 157th was stopped and again the German losses were abominable. For the attacking 29th Panzer Grenadier Division, it had become "do or die."

The German effort again proved relentless. After pausing, the Nazis regrouped and another third attack was launched down the Via Anziate at the 157th. This time, it was too much. Sparks radioed back that fire support had to be put directly on his position. Jack and Balkum cringed at the brave call of the infantryman to call fire down on their own. Most likely, in an effort to stop the Germans, Division Artillery would end up killing their own. Jack did not have time to think about it, Division Artillery just did it. This time, however, it was not enough. Elements of the 2nd Battalion of the 157th were overrun by the 725th Regiment of the 29th Panzer Grenadier Division. the attack was once again halted.

Just as the 2nd Battalion of the 157th was being overrun, the 3rd Battalion of the 157th dug in near the Overpass and came under heavy German artillery fire causing more horrific casualties to the Thunderbirds. With the 2nd and 3rd Battalions of the 157th in disarray, the 179th to the right now became the object of serious concern. At 8:30 p.m. on the 16th, Division Artillery CP got the word that thirteen German Panzers were barreling down on the 3rd Battalion of the 179th. The Division Artillery could not get on the tanks fast enough and the two battalions of the 179th were virtually decimated. The 179th was forced to retire rearward. The beachhead perimeter defense continued to sag and shrink in the center. Further, to the right of the 179th, however, the 180th barely held their line. As Jack saw it from the CP, the 45th was bending, but not broken. When smoke on the battlefield cleared, the fury of the German assault became apparent. Prisoners and dead Germans from 16 different regiments were identified in the assault, seven divisions in all. Without question, artillery had saved the day. As Carlos De'Este wrote, artillery "again King of the battlefield." Despite such battlefield platitudes, Jack Neville found little "royalty" in the days effort as they had to fire on their own guys. As the day ended the burden of shooting at their own became heavy. At the close of business on February 16, as Jack penciled the maps, the Germans had made progress at staggering losses. While they had finally smashed through the 157th and 179th, they had advanced only just south of the Factory. While the attack had been stopped, there was no cause for celebration at Division Artillery CP. The Germans, only six miles from the beach, showed little sign of quitting.

The task of Division Artillery's communication with forward elements of the rest of the division had become more difficult. The system of wire communication once so elaborately planned by the S-3 section was in near shambles. Artillery fire had destroyed their own lines of communication. Now the principal method of communication and intelligence, apart from the radios, was messengers and prisoners.

Late on the 16th, at 11:15 p.m., the 171st Field Artillery Battalion took a young German prisoner. He was immediately hustled back to the Division Artillery CP for interrogation. Jack could not believe he was seeing the enemy, the prisoner could not have been more than 18 years old. His face was drawn and chiseled, eyes sunk far back into his head, caked in mud and filth from the battlefield, he had miraculously survived the day. While the young German had kept himself away from death, the fear of the battle and especially the effect of the artillery was told by looking at his hands. The young soldier had attacked the 157th's position over open ground and when the Division Artillery barrage fell he had no place to hide, except to try to dig. In a desperate attempt to avoid the deadly artillery shelling that massacred his comrades, the young soldier's fingers were literally worn down to the joints trying to dig into the fields to escape the lead that was thrown in all directions from the exploding shells. It was a horrible site to see even if he was the enemy, and Jack felt none the better for seeing it. Eyes dazed, his lower lip trembled in fear as his captors stared down on him, he quickly waived the constitutional rights that he did not have. The boy Nazi told Division Artillery that yet another attack would come, February 17 at 3:00 a.m. from the Factory, down the Via Anziate. Jack and the S-3 section went to work.

During the 16th, the rates of fire of Divisional Artillery evidence of the desperation of the hour. The 189th Field Artillery, led by Hal Muldrow of Norman, Oklahoma, averaged eight rounds of 155mm shells every 45 seconds, often barrel citing their rounds at the enemy. The training routine called for four rounds a minute. The division's four battalions unloaded an incredible total of 8,616 of 105mm and 155mm rounds at the enemy that day, an almost inhuman, exhaustive performance. They would have to do it again on the 17th.

CHAPTER XXVI
I'LL SEE YOU TOMORROW NIGHT

General Kesselring and Von MacKensen, despite advancing only 500 yards south of the Factory, sensed the 45th was on the ropes and ready to go down. Yet Kesselring was angered at Von MacKensen's inability to end it all on the 16th. Despite the aggressive mood of their Generals, the Germans' ground pounders were dispirited. In just two days of fighting, their ranks lost 2,569 men mostly to the savagery of the 45th's Artillery. Now, on the 17th, they would have to face yet another day attempting to advance over open territory that had become a killing field, no longer a farm field. The captured German soldier taken back to Division Artillery was right. The Germans would attack again, but earlier than expected. Von MacKensen would focus what was left of his two divisions against what was left of the 179th, and 157th, once more down the Via Anziate.

Again, there would be no sleep on the beach at Division Artillery. All ears stayed tuned to reports of movement. At 12:30 a.m. on the 17th the 179th was hit by German infantry. The frontal elements of the 157th were engaged by German troops before the midnight shift of the 16th, and by the next morning Felix Sparks' E Company, 157th, the Battalions were forced to retreat to the Caves. Elements of the 157th, including Sparks' company, were now surrounded. Incredibly, they still had a radio that could call on the Artillery. With radio in hand, every time the Germans approached or passed, Sparks radioed for fire to stop the Germans' advance.

Just before dawn the Germans pointed their 450 artillery pieces down the Via Anziate to lay down a barrage that would precede the next major tank-infantry attack. Once the barrage lifted, the Germans threw fourteen infantry battalions at the 45th positions in a human wave assault to split the 157th and 179th, and roll on to the beach. In support of the attack, there were 60 Tiger tanks rolling right at the 179th and 157th. To the right of the Via Anziate, it was almost too much for the 179th. Both the 2nd and 3rd Battalions of the 179th were forced to withdraw to the south in the wake of overwhelming enemy numbers. For the Artillery, the efforts became frantic–shoot and shoot as fast as you can.

By 9:00 a.m., the skies had lifted sufficiently for Allied air forces. Coordinated with ground artillery, British and American aircraft dropped 1,100 tons of explosives on the Germans tank-infantry attack in an attempt to stem the tide of the German advance. It slowed them up, but the Germans just kept coming and the bodies kept piling up on the Italian farm land.

The sheer weight of the German attack, despite heavy air and artillery bombardment, devastated the Thunderbirds. Most of two battalions of the 179th were either dead or wounded and the 157th was scattered. By noon, what was left of the division retreated south down the Via Anziate. At the intersection with Dead End Road, the Thunderbirds attempted to reorganize their line of defense. The Germans were now well south of the Factory, five miles from the beach, and only a few hundred yards north of the 45th's last line of defense at the Overpass.

Miraculously, the 157th and 179th somehow hung on through the afternoon. As dark started to fall, there was only one company of Thunderbirds left to defend the Gate of Hell. I Company of the 157th formed a semi-circular defensive line a few yards in front of the Overpass prepared to fight to the last man. Near dusk, the Germans sensed a moment of weakness. Two German Mark IVs rumbled down the Via Anziate supported by infantry. As the two tanks attempted to breach the Overpass, they were blown to bits and the machine guns of I Company annihilated the Germans who became entangled in concertina wire only feet in front of the companies defensive line. It was enough to halt the German onslaught. Not knowing of the condition of I Company, or of the small numbers of Thunderbirds in front of them, the remaining German tanks concealed themselves behind the remaining few farm houses near the Via Anziate and Dead End Road. There were momentary sighs of relief as what was left of the 157th and 179th stood yards from certain annihilation.

Five miles to the south, the S-3 section gathered their forces to assess the situation. The 2nd Battalion of the 157th was now surrounded, but still in radio contact with Division Artillery. The remaining elements of the 157th, specifically K and L Companies, were withdrawn and consolidated with I Company to defend the Overpass. What was left of the 179th was brought back to a position just yards north of the Lateral Road, to form a line with I, L, and M Companies of the 157th. Incredibly, the 180th remained in tact further to the east near Padiglione. All four of the Division Artillery's battalions remained in relatively good shape at the end of the day. Although substantially reduced in numbers, the Thunderbirds were well stocked with ammunition and supplies. While the infantry ranks had been decimated, Division Artillery still packed substantial fire power. There was plenty of fight left in the 45th, and no one was leaving the beachhead.

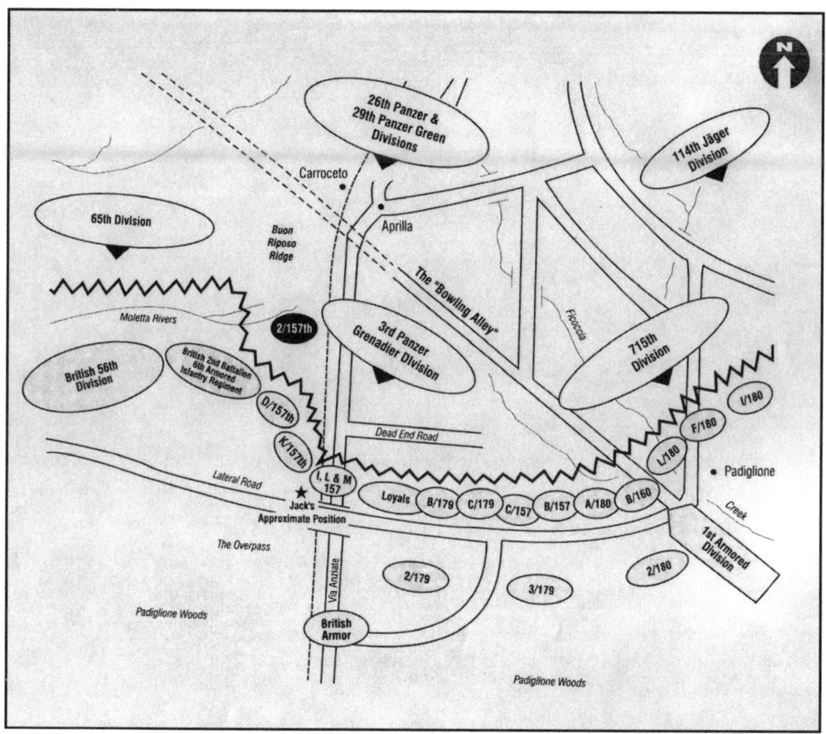

By February 18, 1944, the German's had pushed the 45th lines of defense to a position slightly north of Lateral Road and the Overpass. On this day, Jack's position was north of the Overpass and west of Via Anziate by only a few yards. From these positions, the Thunderbirds were able to beat back the German attack and save the beachhead.

CHAPTER XXVII
"868-293"

In filling in the missing war years of my parents one raises the question of whether there was a particular moment–a day, an hour–where fate and future actually hung in the balance. Certainly, at the Sele Corridor in September of 1943, death and fear permeated the junction of the Calore-Sele rivers as the division beat back the Germans. Jack had to feel angels on his shoulders when German artillery ravaged the CP on November 6, 1943. Many had seen the end because of well-concealed land mines on the narrow mountain roads leading to Venafro, and it had to be almost pure luck that one of "Annies" or the giant shells of "the Express" did not bring death or serious injury to Dad before February of 1943. War-time death seems random with little time or thought given to whether or not a bullet was actually traveling your way, and it is difficult to imagine, much less describe, a parent's fears and feelings standing in such harm's way some 60 years later. However, in following Jack and Leota through World War II, the day and time when a German bullet may have had Dad's name on it was in the early morning hours of February 18, 1944. Without any doubt, at this time, at this place, death was at Dad's door. The future did in fact hang in the balance on this rainy and cool Friday morning in Italy.

The epic struggle at Anzio on February 18 conjures up many visions of history. For the Germans, and Von MacKensen in particular, it was a sort of "Pickett's Charge," or a "Charge of the Light Brigade" without Errol Flynn or Ronald Reagan leading the way. For the 45th Infantry Division and Dad, February 18 took its place with "The Alamo," and "Custer's Last Stand," although without the total annihilation that Custer's 7th Calvary suffered. To borrow from the sport's world, it was a day when two world heavy weights staggered out of their corners, bloodied and bruised, for the last and final round in the southern European theatre. Carlos D'Este wrote in Fatal Decision that the single most important day of the battle of Anzio was February 18, 1944. While this conclusion is unquestionably correct, it is not a bridge too far to also suggest that the 18th was also the critical day in the history of World War II in the southern European theatre. All of southern Europe would be won or lost on this day. And for Dad, February 18 would be his closest call with death in combat.

By the 17th, the battle had dictated that the final fight would take place in an incredibly small area. Through the night of the 17th and early morning hours of the 18th, just north of Dead End Road, the Germans assembled the 715th Infantry Division, 5 battalions of the 114th Jager Division, and what was left of the 3rd Panzer Grenadier Division. The 45th's constant nemesis, the 29th Panzer Grenadier and the 26th Panzer also would be part of the show. This force was amassed slightly less than one mile from the Overpass. The main thrust of the German charge would again be aimed directly at the 157th dug in directly in front of the Overpass and the Gate of Hell, and the beat-up 179th Infantry Regiment sitting on the right flank of the 157th along Lateral Road. When the action got started, it would become a shoulder-to-shoulder battle in an area of approximately one square mile. However, for the Germans to reach the Thunderbirds, they would have to again travel an open, muddy field and charge down the Via Anziate without cover. To the S-3 section at Division Artillery CP back on the beach, the point of the German attack became obvious. Every available 105mm and 155mm was cited and leveled across the field known as Campo di Carne. When they came, the Germans would be caught in a murderous cross fire of heavy artillery.

In the early morning hours of February 17 and 18, while the Germans were regrouping near Dead End Road, the 3rd Battalion of the 157th, aided by the 2nd and 3rd Battalion of the 179th, slipped out of their trenches and foxholes and moved northward along the Via Anziate in an attempt to relieve the besieged 2nd Battalion of the 157th at the Caves and reclaim lost ground. The three battalion forces walked directly into Von MacKensen's tanks, artillery, and infantry before they could reach the Dead End Road. The effort to reach the beleaguered men at the Caves failed, the Thunderbird force was cut to ribbons and had to fight their way back to the south with fixed bayonets and hand-to-hand fighting. I Company of the 157th again fell back with L and M Companies to their foxholes just in front of the Overpass. Word of the failed attack by the 157th and 179th reached back to Arnote's S-3 group at Division Artillery. The German strength was formible, more than enough to push three battalions backward. There was no question that the dawn of the new day would bring a massive attack from Lateral Road directly at the Overpass. Division Artillery fixed their guns accordingly as convoys of trucks from the service companies hidden by the dark of night raced shell after shell to the forward firing battalions. As the Division Artillery History records "This was the big day."

General Kesselring and Von MacKensen were not without their own problems on the morning of the 18th. After three brutal days of combat, the German ranks had been ripped. Heavy casualties caused by the Allied pinpoint shooting had crushed the morale of the German soldiers. Too many had seen their friends and comrades literally disappear in the smoke and steel of the

45th's 105s and 155s. High casualties and low morale were now compounded by yet another serious problem–the Germans were running out of ammunition, especially the artillery. Kesselring was now faced with a similar dilemma as was Clark only weeks before. He could call off the attack, consolidate to the north, and fight another day or, he could take the gamble and throw the dice down the Via Anziate despite the problems that plagued his 14th Army. As the German intelligence saw the battlefield, the weakest link in the Allied chain was the 157th at the Overpass. Von MacKensen believed that if he could break the 157th at the Overpass, he could split the beachhead, race down the Via Anziate, and roll all the way to the sea. Von MacKensen decided to make the gambler's choice and crush the 45th at the Overpass.

The mood was somber and glum in the S-3 section of the Division Artillery CP in the early morning hours of the 18th. The infantry units, or what was left of them, were dug in. The artillery pieces were trained and ready, the basic firing and battle plan in place. On the beach all they could do was wait. McClain gathered his staff for the final situation briefing before sun-up. The beach would not be evacuated, the division would hold the line at the Gate of Hell. The Germans, massed along Dead End Road, would most likely preface their tank infantry attack with the usual artillery barrage. When it lifted, they would

The intersection of the east-west railroad and the Anzio-Albino Highway on the Anzio beachhead. Called the "Flyover," a British term for overpass, it was the scene of heavy fighting during the German push to drive the invaders into the sea. The flat landscape made any unobserved movement impossible, and as soon as a target appeared enemy artillery observers called down a rain of shells. Along the embankment are two American Sherman tanks and several other burned vehicles knocked out during the bitter battle. Jack's foxhole position is believed somewhere within this picture. (Courtesy of the 45th Infantry Division Museum).

charge. Staff and Jack would remain on the beach at Headquarters. However, if the 157th came under severe strain, the CP would be stripped down with all staff to take defensive lines north of the Overpass. The Germans were directly in front of the division's three infantry units, in some places separated by less than 1,000 yards. The forward field battery battalions would have to see them and shoot them. There would not be a lot of time for CP communication from the front. Jack and Harry kept their warbelts and rifles nearby. It looked like a Salerno rewrite. General McClain, never one to mince words, had made the situation crystal clear. With that, McClain wished his men God's best. Always an inspirational leader to those around him, the Oklahoma City banker announced that he would be spending the night at the front, with his artillery units. With that he disappeared into the dark Anzio night.

At 2:00 a.m. on February 18, 1944, the day that would either win or lose southern Europe began. From the Factory, the Germans threw a massive artillery barrage at the Overpass. Every piece they had was calibrated down the Via Anziate in a withering, earth shaking rumble of explosives. The best the Thunderbirds could do was hunker down and stay below ground. The artillery shells usually blew "up and out," not down. If you were below ground you had a chance. With bayonets fixed, rifles and machine guns locked and loaded, the 157th kept their faces in the mud of their foxholes and waited for the barrage to end. At the Division Artillery CP on the beach Jack stayed in the dug-out. The Germans had not fixed their sites on the beachhead CP, but the shaking ground and tremor told the story of what was happening only a short distance away. All night, and for one constant three-hour period, the Germans unloaded their arsenal on the 45th.

At 5:00 a.m., the barrage lifted and the Germans' version of Pickett's Charge began along the Dead End Road south. The Thunderbird infantry could now raise their heads above the rim of their foxholes, and through the mist of the early morning could see the gray overcoats of the Lehr Regiment slogging their way across the muddy fields of Campo di Carne. The men of the 157th and 179th rested their weapons just over the dirt rim of their foxholes, each man citing in a target, but waiting until the wave got into their effective range. However, as for the Division Artillery, they did not have to wait. The Lehr Regiment was in range, easy targets as the two-legged figures were unable to move with any real speed because of the mud. The radios cracked the news to the CP. The 189th, 171st, and 160th Field Artillery Battalions had them in their sites and it was now their turn to return fire at the on-rushing Germans. Firing as fast and furious as humanly possible, the artillery pumped shell after shell into the Germans. The Germans did not stand a chance; entire groups of men literally disappeared in the smoke of the artillery explosions. German bodies lay everywhere and screams of men dying and wounded pierced the morning air. Miraculously small groups of Germans survived the fanatical charge, and with little choice, they continued forward. For almost two hours the battle across the Field of Meat raged with 105 and 155 shells, mortars exploding everywhere, and the 157th and 179th barely holding on in hand-to-hand, foxhole-to-foxhole fighting. After what seemed an eternity, at approximately 7:30 a.m., a small counterattack pushed the Germans back. For the moment, the Thunderbirds held the line.

The momentary pause would give the Thunderbirds little time to assess their situation. Communication with the front and the 157th still was in tact and as the first wave of German assault slowed, the state of the perimeter defense at the Overpass was reported back to the Division Artillery CP. While the first assault had been momentarily beaten back, things were not good. The German attack had fractured the line of the 157th just in front of the Overpass and the 157th regimental CP had been forced to a position 800 yards southwest. The 157th's line in front of the Overpass had been breached, and now only thinly defended by three decimated companies of the 157th. The situation was perilous. Arnote gathered the S-3 staff together for the difficult news. The Germans had broken the 157th's position at grid coordinate 868-293. Everyone crowded the map tables to ascertain the precise location of the breach of one of the last lines of defense. Located on relatively flat terrain, 868-293 was just west of the Via Anziate, and only a few hundred yards north and just in front of the Overpass. The position was in the direct line of the German attack. Silence fell over the dug-out room. Arnote looked grimly at his troops. The CP would be stripped down. The orders now were that all available men of the Headquarters, HQ Battery, of Division Artillery Staff would grab their weapons, war belts, and as much ammunition as possible, prepare to move out, and assume positions to reinforce the 157th at 868-293. They all were now in the infantry, congratulations. No one saw much levity in Arnote's remarks, and certainly nobody viewed what had to be done as a promotion. For Jack Neville, just after 7:30 a.m., rifle, war belt, bandeleros, and pockets stuffed with shells, he, Balkum, and the others climbed aboard the 2_-ton six-wheeled trucks for the ride. As the truck rumbled northward on the Via Anziate on this gray, hazy morning, there was no chatter or banter on board. Each and every man, heads down staring at the floorboard of the truck, was asking himself in silence, "would I live or die on this day?" After 15 minutes, all faces turned toward the north. Only a few hundred yards in front of the convoy was the Overpass, still shrouded in the smoke and haze left by the first giant German wave of attack. There were no words as the men passed silently through the Gate of Hell, now virtually the last line of defense. The trucks lumbered to a slow creaky stop. None of the men wasted any time getting off; over the sides and out of the back they exited as quickly as possible. As a group they were targets for German artillery.

At this moment in time, the men were struck by the "eerie" silence on the battlefield. It was almost as if the Germans were waiting for the last of the

45th to take their place on the stage before the final curtain call. In silence, the new infantry moved out to the west, in a column of twos at route step. Moving quickly along, Jack had to keep his head down, in an effort to avoid the craters that had pocked the farm land. There was an occasional look backward at the Overpass. You could not help but wonder how in the world it was still standing. Almost every inch of the north side was plastered with the holes and scars of mortar and military fire. The Germans had thrown everything they had at the Overpass. After 30 minutes, the column halted approximately 300 yards west of the Via Anziate, less than a 100 yards north of the Overpass. Jack had arrived at 868-293. As the column came to a halt a slight breeze whipped up from the north, the smell of the battlefield drifted around the men. It was the smell of death, burning flesh, and for the first time, rather than looking backward at the Overpass, Jack looked forward, toward the north. The site was appalling. There were grey clad bodies everywhere as if a carpet had been laid with German overcoats. At some points Jack could not see the ground, the bodies were so many, laying shoulder to shoulder, faces twisted, unrecognizable as human. A few hundred yards in front of Jack were multiple strings of wire, the last physical barrier before reaching the foxholes of the 157th. German soldiers hung on the wire as if they were scarecrows, lifeless, helplessly entangled where machine guns and rifle fire raked the barbed wire. As Jack now stared northward, the air was occasionally pierced by the screams and moans for help of men beyond the wire. Help that would not come. German youth were dying only a few yards away. Jack unbuckled his war belt and retrieved his entrenching tool. At Anzio, you did not go anywhere without your shovel. It was time to dig in. On this morning, as the point of Jack's shovel hit the dirt and he gazed across the battlefield, it was nothing but a scene of death. It was rough stuff for a guy 24 years old from Adair, Oklahoma.

Digging a foxhole at Anzio was a difficult process. The dirt, mostly sand, was soft enough to dig a hole about as deep as you wanted. However, after about two or three feet, one usually hit water. On the 18th of February, a little water was not going to keep you from digging deep enough to get your head below ground. While the effort required a little ingenuity, one could usually work down until water was struck, bail it out with your helmet, and then resume the excavation once again. At the Overpass, on this day survival was the mother of invention. Jack got his hole deep enough to at least kneel down and peer over the sand rim resting his rifle on the ground. Standing or kneeling in a little water, even if it was ankle deep, would be the least of his problems. Everyone on this day stood their post for the fight about to come. Through common fear, everyone generated a strength and resolve to fight on, to hold the line.

Kneeling and crouching in that foxhole, Jack peered through the open cite of his rifle, sometimes fixing the weapon on the dead German bodies strung up in the wire only a few hundred yards away. With bayonets at the ready, loading his eight-round clip into the magazine, chambering the first round, Dad edged the safety to the off position, resting the rifle on the dirt in front of him. He was as ready as he could be. With a carefully placed shot he perhaps could bring the enemy down at 400 yards. At 200 to 250 yards he really would have to make it count. At 100 yards he better not miss. They waited for the Germans as heavy rain and overcast skies darkened the battlefield. Death was about to come.

Shortly before 9:30 a.m. the Germans prefaced the second wave of their attack with the predictable barrage of artillery, now inter-mixed with rockets, and Neberwerfers, known as "screaming meanies." For Jack, there was nothing he could do but keep his head below ground and listen to the screams of the German '8s whistling overhead and heading for the Overpass. Of course, he could pray that a round did not drop right into his lap. After what seemed an eternity, the shelling stopped and a quiet crept over the battlefield. Jack peaked over the edge of the foxhole. The Germans were coming.

At approximately 9:30 a.m., the Lehr Regiment and their friends were back on the Campo di Carne and the Via Anziate for another try. At 900 yards, the rumble and spewing of the German tanks could be heard, and then at 800 yards the faceless grey coats appeared on the horizon. Some were in a sprint, some at a brisk walk, others in a jog of sorts carefully stepping around their fallen comrades. It almost seemed a macabre like dance of sorts as the Germans moved across the landscape. They just kept coming over the open field in a bonzai-like suicide charge frantically yelling and screaming in an effort to find the courage to go on. Careful that only his eyes peaked out of the foxhole, Jack aimed his rifle down range selecting his targets who were still too far away. Never one of his virtues, he would have to be patient. Dug-in and concealed behind the embarkments forming the Overpass were the 45th Division Artillery. As the gray wave reached 700 yards, the ground erupted and shook as giant artillery shells raced out of the barrels of 105s and 155s screaming over Jack's head at the wall of attacking Germans. The results were appalling and devastating. There, yards in front of Jack, entire groups of men literally disappeared, evaporating in black and red smoke. Body parts sprayed in all directions, bodies fell everywhere as the Division Artillery delivered its deadly blow. As the Germans moved forward, for every one artillery round shot by the Germans, the Allies responded with twenty. It was impossible to believe that anything or anyone could survive this concentrated pounding. Somehow they did. The German survivors continued to rush forward. For those in the foxholes the German assault wave next came within machine gun, small mortar, and rifle-range, and at 300 yards the last barrier of defense had to open up. As the morning wore on, the German corpses were literally piling up in front of the Oklahoma foxholes. Lines continued to hold with everyone firing as fast as they could chamber a round. By mid-morning the sheer weight of the German numbers were starting to take their toll on

The famous German Mark IV tanks knocked out by Division Artillery at the Battle of Anzio.

the Thunderbird line to the east. While the 157th already was backed up to the Overpass, the 179th on the right flank had been forced 800 yards backward to a line along Lateral Road. The 179th was near total collapse. Then, as if God's hand and Thunderbird luck swept over the field of battle, the Germans inexplicably shifted the focus of their attack away from the beleaguered 179th giving the 1st Armored Division time to set-up and reinforce the battered regiment. Somehow, the 179th line held.

Although the Germans had been beaten back again, by mid-morning the entire beachhead perimeter had shrunk to within five miles of the sea. For the small group of Division Artillery transformed into infantrymen, only the water was at their back. With the momentary lull in the assault, Jack rested in his foxhole. As he laid in the mud of the hole, rifle across his chest not daring to get up, the clouds lifted and the sky started to clear. Slowly circling above was a Piper Cub, the last remaining forward observation plane in the division. In a bizarre way, the site and sound of the single-wing, single-engine piece of cardboard sputtering over the battlefield at 2,500 feet brought a grin and a giggle to Jack's face. Somehow Captain William McKay had found a way to get the old crate started and airborne. More incredibly, McKay had found the guts to fly it over Campo di Carne, refusing to leave his buddies behind. McKay could not shoot anybody, but maybe he could see the Germans, and radio their position to the Artillery.

The events which took place over the next few hours are the stuff of which legends and movies are made. General Von MacKensen, not knowing of the plight of the 179th, still believing that the 157th at the Overpass was the weakest link, was busy reorganizing his army of surviving infantry and tanks near Carroceto and the Factory for yet another charge at the Thunderbirds.

High in the air over the battlefield at 11:00 p.m. McKay got on his radio to

Arnote, one of the few remaining at the Division Artillery CP. McKay reported that 3,000 German troops, with tank support, were moving down the Via Anziate just south of the Factory and headed for the Overpass. McKay was confident the German force could be destroyed quickly. Arnote was stunned. A force this size would be the final straw, the shot that would do the Thunderbirds in once and for all. In disbelief, Arnote radioed back to McKay, "surely you mean 300." McKay's response was quick, " Hell no, not 300, 3,000." Arnote got the message this time and immediately got in radio contact with the forward firing batteries. In three minutes, near high noon, Walter Arnote had 17 Allied Artillery Battalions pouring fire directly into the advancing German force. For one hour, 224 guns pummeled the exposed Germans. The force that potentially could have destroyed the Overpass, pushing its defenders into the sea, was nearly annihilated.

What was left of the German force refused to retreat. Miraculously, Von MacKenson regrouped the survivors of one of the biggest barrages of the war, and at 2:00 p.m. he commenced yet another attack. Slogging across the already corpse-littered Italian farmland, and down the Via Anziate, came the last of Von MacKensen's force. Again, the scene of death and destruction was replayed. Division Artillery ripped holes in the German advance and Dad waited again for the German rain coats to get within rifle range. As pockets of Germans rose up to charge forward that afternoon, they were met with volley after volley, the artillery pieces leveled to near ground elevation. For Jack and his buddies, they just kept shooting, triggering round after round, watching the German faces fall into the mud only a short distance in front of them. It was horrific, but they held.

By late afternoon, the 157th continued to hold its own. However, the 179th was once again in desperate straits. At 5:48 p.m., Colonel Darby, now commanding the 179th, asked General Eagles for permission to withdraw and reorganize. Eagles refused. Everyone would stand their position. There would be no withdrawal, no retreat. In hand-to-hand fighting, Darby's regiment miraculously fought the Germans off.

As the day neared 7:00 p.m., the frequency of the German artillery lessened, and the seemingly endless stream of human tidal wave assaults came to a halt. The giant German attack could go no more, the Germans were now starting to retreat northward, back to the Dead End Road. Von MacKensen's forces were literally spent. His artillery ammunition supply dwindling, most of his infantry troops now either dead, wounded, or incapable of sustaining the fight; and his tank force now nothing but burning steel hulks along the Via Anziate, Von MacKensen had no choice but to fall back. At approximately 8:00 p.m., as dusk came, the bloodiest day ever in Europe thus far, mercifully came to an end. In the most literal sense, the 45th Infantry Division had destroyed the German force attacking the beach with an unbelievable 12,557 rounds of artillery fired in one day, approximately 9,200 of which ripped into German infantry and tanks. It was Hitler's last major attack in Italy during World War II.

For Jack at the Overpass, he did not dare get out of his hole in the ground. He was alive, and he would stay down. As darkness covered the Overpass, the supply trucks rushed forward with food, supplies, and ammunition. Jack could get out of his hole for a brief stretch. For the small convoy carrying the vitals of war to the front, the trucks were not free of cargo going back to the beach. The dead and wounded were evacuated back to the water's edge in the trucks that brought life-saving supplies. With their bellies full and bandoleros re-stocked, the Thunderbirds crawled back into their foxholes to wait and see if they would make it through the next day.

Another German Panzer tank victimized by the Thunderbirds at Anzio.

CHAPTER XXVIII

WHAT SAVED OUR BUTTS WAS THE ARTILLERY.

On February 19, 1944, any serious German threat to split the beachhead defense was over. The Germans were down, their numbers decimated, but they were not out. At 4:00 a.m. north of the Overpass, the Germans attacked the British Loyals. They were beaten back by the Artillery seven hours later. The 1st Armored Division mounted a counterattack supported by artillery and air cover. Allied bombers unloaded on the Factory and Carroceto where the Germans continued to hide and General Harmon's armored division rushed northward to reclaim the Dead End Road by noon. The Germans were falling apart, more than 700 prisoners were taken on this day. The remaining Germans did what they could to attack the Overpass. Their ranks cut to shreds, they were no match for the Artillery and Jack thankfully had far fewer targets to shoot at. At 5:00 p.m. the Germans made one last failed attempt to overrun the 179th. They were blown away by the Artillery. While there would be a series of attacks and counterattacks, most notably at the Caves, by the close of business on February 19 the beachhead crisis was beginning to end. The various recorded unit history yield no evidence as to when Jack would have once and for all left his position in front of the Overpass.

The cost of Italian farmland was high. In the four-day assault, the German casualties were 5,389 killed in action, wounded, or missing. The 179th lost more than half of its officers. The 45th Infantry Division suffered 400 killed in action, 2,000 wounded in action, 1,000 missing, and 2,500 non-battle casualties. February 19 the 2nd Battalion of the 157th still was surrounded at the Caves. The decisive blow during the four days was delivered by the Division Artillery. In three days, February 17 to the 19th, Jack's unit fired 41,525 rounds, while in 23 days of fighting in the Sicilian Campaign, 14,697 rounds were fired.

Without question, February brought victory for the Thunderbirds. The Germans, not entirely pushed off the face of the map, still huddled up at their favorite hiding place, the Factory. There were enough Germans remaining to keep Jack pinned on the beach. Outside the semi-circle forming the beachhead perimeter, 10 German Divisions were on their way.

REFLECTION THANKSGIVING, 1965, OKLAHOMA; THE IA DRANG VALLEY, SOUTH VIETNAM

With the spring of 1965 came America's first substantial troop build-up in South Vietnam. On March 8, 1965, the Second Marine Battalion moved into Da Nang, two more Marine Battalions arrived in early April, and by April 20, 1965, approximately 8,605 men of the 9th Marine Expeditionary Force had landed in Southeast Asia. In early May of 1965, United States Army ground troops set up camp and by the end of May, 46,500 young Americans were in a far away land marshaled between two Vietnams who had been at war for decades. Although President Lyndon B. Johnson had declared Vietnam a "combat zone", there was no Roosevelt-like speech and no Congressional Proclamation of war. At best, in the spring of 1965, America's Vietnam mission was vaguely and loosely defined. And, for the most part, America's youth was asleep during the storm warnings of death and civil disobedience this conflict would breed over the next few months and years.

In Tulsa, Oklahoma, in the spring of 1965, the Thomas Alva Edison Class of 1965, wrapped in their cocoon of safety and social security, looked forward to high school graduation. Oblivious to the Vietnam build-up, there were many events that occupied a higher place on the social and political agenda. College admission, and rejections, dominated the airways of the Edison hallways. There was a sprint to the mail box each afternoon to see what hand the colleges had dealt. At Edison High School, there were 33 National Merit Finalists, then a national record for one school. The paramount question of the spring was where you would go to college, not "if" you would go to college; and there was never a thought or word that anyone would be drafted, or voluntarily join any of the military services. Filling out those college application forms, and racing to the mailbox each afternoon was far more important to affluent southeast Tulsa, than the landing of the 9th Marine Expeditionary Force in Southeast Asia. Not a single "Eagle" from the Class of 1965 was drafted out of high school for military service. We all figured we had more important things to do, and the United States Army was considered a second-class occupation.

In the spring of 1965, Richard Slicker had pitched in 18 consecutive Edison baseball games, an Oklahoma high school state record. The locker room talk was whether he could throw his round-house curve ball in a 19th game and carry the "green and white" to the State Finals. He did it. As had become the usual spring event, Melanie Bates had taken her customary spring break to the Bahamas and returned to school sporting an incredible tan and driving a new baby blue Buick Riviera. Although there were many fantasies of getting Melanie up to "Golf Ball Hill" that spring for a midnight rendezvous, none of us ever had a chance with "Miss Edison." Prom night at Tulsa's downtown Mayo Hotel was not far away.

Jim Kothe, Kent Dunbar, David Dimit, Kermit Holderman, Bob Dillman, and myself spent many hours engaging in conspiratorial activity, the objective of course being to stay out all night and party at least until the crack of dawn. These well-made plans were rather quickly scratched by Mom and Dad who had participated in their own conspiracy with the other parents to snuff out such revelry. At 2:00 a.m. breakfast would be served at the Neville house and attendance was required. Our house looked like a grocery store of eggs, bacon, biscuits, and gravy as Dad took the orders and Mom served them up. Dad could not resist firing up the new Hasty-bake, and if you were lucky, a sliver of steak found its way mixed in with your eggs and bacon. With the Vietnam commitment slowly escalating, Bob Dillman was accepted at Stanford, Kothe and Dimit were off to Vanderbilt, Steve Kaplan to Harvard, and Alan Fedman to Brown. With the pomp and circumstance going on for graduation at the Tulsa Convention Center, United States Army combat troops in Vietnam were not on our radar screens. Totally unnoticed by the Eagle Class of 1965 were the first student protests against the war by the Students for a Democratic Society. On April 17, 1965, 15,000 protestors draped the steps of the nation's Capital shouting "Hell no, we won't go." As for Kothe, Dimit, and myself, our conscious and thoughts were fixed on the newest line of tuxedos offered at Big Al's Formal Wear, with prom night specials of $20.00.

For those of us in Tulsa over the summer of 1965, we continued our separation from political awareness and world events. French fries, cokes, and black bottom pie at Pennington's Drive-in on Peoria was the number-one activity after the evening movie at the downtown Orpheum Theater. Fraternity rush parties dotted the social calendar as "Rush Week" on the Oklahoma, Oklahoma State, and Tulsa University campuses were not far away. With gas less than 19¢ a gallon, transportation was only a function of how many times you could fill the 16-gallon tank of your three-speed Mustang to get to the next event. The summer of 1965 had become a vacation land of sorts as we all looked forward to college days and girls.

For Dad, however, those 6:00 p.m. evening dinners in the summer of 1965 began to take on a new tone as I made every effort to stuff it down and bolt from the house to pick up Dunbar and Kothe. For the last 15 minutes of the Huntley-Brinkley Report, Dad was fixed to the television set listening to the now daily reports of increasing hostilities and casualties in Vietnam. It was clear by the look on his face that he was troubled, but he remained silent. By July, American soldiers were losing their lives in the undeclared war with little national commitment or support. On July 1, 1965, the United States Marine Forces guarding the air base at Da Nang were attacked by the North

Vietnam Army and sustained horrendous casualties and by July 28, 1965, Johnson had sent 50,000 more troops to Vietnam, none of which came from the Class of 1965. The "Body Count" was becoming a fixed graphic on the NBC, ABC, and CBS evening news. But for me sitting at the dinner table in the summer of 1965 the primary concern was whether or not I could get some new Cole-Hahn penny loafers –after all Kothe had some.

By August of 1965, our summer of party began to wind down in preparation for the new life of college. Leaving home for the first time did not seem particularly disturbing as Mom packed a trunk and a couple of suitcases containing most of my worldly belongings. This process seemed only a Mom thing as Dad ducked in and out of the bedroom watching but saying nothing. August 15 was the magic date for all freshmen to move into the dorm rooms for the start of "Rush Week." For me, it was Setliff House, Cross Center in the far southeastern part of the University of Oklahoma campus, roommate unknown. In the week before, all of the old high school buddies moved from one parent's house to another gathering, as we saw it for the last time, pledging to keep in contact, and promising that at Thanksgiving we again would all rendezvous to see just how worldly we had become. On the morning of the 15th John Gibson and Mark Finnety picked me up for the 150-mile drive to Norman. John's four-door blue Chevy Impala was stuffed, and because Mark was the smallest he was required to squash himself into the back seat. Once loaded, Mom gave me a big hug and Dad the traditional "dad-man handshake" accompanied by a "good luck and giv'em hell." As for Bob and Richard, there was nothing but joy. The oldest was finally gone and there was finally the certainty of their own bedrooms, at least for a couple of months. Although school was only two hours away, as John maneuvered his way out of the driveway Mom's eyes watered up, Dad's face remained stern with that lower lip a slight quiver. I was the first to leave home, but not because a 1930's depression forced my departure, and at least none of us were leaving from Hampton Roads on the USS Leonard Wood.

As the Edison Class of 1965 departed the Tulsa sanctuaries of Pennington's, Southern Hills Country Club, and the Orpheum Theater for Rush Week at our respective colleges, the Vietnam situation grew worse. On August 9, 1965, another huge protest against America's involvement took place in Washington, D.C., and, for the first time, the war in Vietnam was brought into the living rooms on television. In retaliation for the attack on Da Nang the Marines hit the village of Cam Ne in force on August 3, 1965. On board one of the helicopters was CBS correspondent Morley Safer and a television camera crew. Forever imprinted on America's mind was the television image of a lone United States Marine using a cigarette lighter to ignite a fire that would burn down Vietnam grass huts in Cam Ne. Safer reported there were few enemy in the village after the Marine force took on small arms fire and casualties. Safer's report fueled the protestors and cast the American soldiers and their leaders as villains in a civil war between the two Vietnams. These staggering events went unnoticed at Cross Center as my new friends Jon Axton, Larry Beach, and I decided once and for all that we would pledge Beta Theta Pi, not Sig Alpha or Sigma Chi. In phone calls home, Dad and I never discussed the goings on in Vietnam or the war protestors on the left and right coast. The giant cocoon had spread to Norman.

As the summer of 1965 turned to fall, the Vietnam situation continued to heat up at home and abroad, but still, not at the Beta House in Norman. At 800 Chatauqua Avenue the two biggest concerns were finishing up our fraternity pledgeship and Oklahoma University football. In those days the upper classmen required Friday night study halls that were proctored by the grade-mongers of the Beta House. With study hall over at 10:30 p.m., we were required to report immediately for an all-night house cleaning that usually ended just in time for all of us to run back to Cross Center, shower, shave, dress in coat and tie, and be prepared to meet and greet the Beta alumni who started to arrive by 10:00 a.m. Of grave concern to all of us was the plight of Sooner football. College football icon Bud Wilkinson had retired as head coach to run for the United States Senate. Amazingly, he lost to liberal, anti-war Democrat Fred Harris. The Sooner faithful were now in the hands of long-time assistant Gomer Jones and the fate and future of the Sooners occupied most every conversation. The war was rarely, if ever, mentioned and the Huntley-Brinkley Report conflicted with intra-mural football practice. The Beta defense of the intra-mural football championship outweighed the significance of any national news.

As the phone lines burned up organizing the Thanksgiving rendezvous with the old gang the gravity of the Vietnam conflict and its anti-war sentiment became more heated and violent nationwide. By November of 1965, protests were popping up all across the United States and the burning of draft cards became a favorite form of civil disobedience. A gruesome expression of anti-war sentiment took place on November 2, 1965. Norman Morrison, a Quaker, set himself on fire after pouring gasoline all over his body just outside the Pentagon. It was the first public display of death against the war on United States soil. More would follow. As Mike Cawley and I prepared to watch Oklahoma State beat Oklahoma for the first time in 40 years, the troop build-up in South Vietnam gradually climbed and the United States was now aggressively seeking out the enemy with search-and-destroy missions. And, of course, the body count continued to rise. For the first time in the war, only a few days before Thanksgiving, United States Army troops engaged the North Vietnam Regulars on November 14, 1965 in what became known as the Battle of the Ia Drang Valley. Lt. Col. Harold Moore's 2nd Battalion, 7th Calvary found themselves surrounded and were almost totally annihilated.

What was left of Moore's battalion gallantly fought their way to safety and finally were rescued. The casualty rate was horrendous, with much of the fighting brutal hand-to-hand combat. At one point Moore was forced to call artillery fire and napalm down on his own position. With the United States dead and wounded at Ia Drang reaching into four figures, many Americans became even more suspicious of the Vietnam commitment. Any victory now appeared far away and possibly at too high a price.

Without a care my freshman year, high school classmate and new pledge brother Blaine Schwabe was my ticket home. Both of us from Tulsa, much was made of the fact that "it had been forever" since we had been home. It had been all of about three months. It served as sufficient enough excuse to skip Wednesday morning classes in time to get home in the early afternoon and plan nighttime shenanigans with Jim Kothe and David Dimit. They too had skipped their Vanderbilt Wednesday classes anxious to get home to compare the first half of the first semester of our first college year.

The timing worked out perfect. After being home thirty minutes, the phone rang twice within 30 seconds. Kothe and Dimit were on their way over. Dunbar called to say we would all meet at the Dillman's at 7:30 p.m. Let the good times roll, the old times were back. The door bell rang at 1:30 p.m. So familiar were Dimit and Kothe with the Neville household they knew all they had to do was knock or ring and come right on in. Of course we all acted as if we had not seen each other in decades and had lived worlds apart. But as soon as Kothe and Dimit walked in the front door a sort of culture shock quickly set in. Gone were wheat jeans, Polo shirts tucked in, and penny loafers. "In" came the grunge, Bib-like white shirts bloused out over scruffy blue jeans frayed at the bottom and 10,000-mile looking tennis shoes with no socks. They both looked as if they had just emerged from the homeless shelter, rather than a fine southern college. This was Vanderbilt I asked? Also gone were those close cropped haircuts, and the biggest shock of all–Kothe and Dimit had let their hair grow down to their shoulders. There was no question about it, Kothe and Dimit had gone "hippie" in the fall of 1965. There was even a brief discussion of earrings and jewelry. It was incredible. I roared with laughter as they both hurried through the front hallway and into the living room. It was a great reunion even though two of my best friends looked as if they were out-of-work vagrants. For the next two hours, we exchanged stories of our freshmen adventures as Mom ducked in and out with bowls of popcorn, cokes, and the always-present-during-holidays chocolate chip cookies, right out of the oven. Mom never said a word about their appearance, and only occasionally did they attempt to proffer an anticipatory defense of their grungeness, obviously attempts of friendly provocation. Mom never took the bait, and performed her usual masterful job of avoiding the engagement. To Mom, as she seemed to evidence, Kothe and Dimit looked the same in November as they did in August, and she was not about to allow either to believe she felt otherwise.

At the strike of 5:30 p.m. Dad rolled in from work through the side door of the house leading to the driveway. Kothe and Dimit were frequent visitors to our house, and Dad was anxious to see how they both had fared their first time away from home. Genuinely excited to see them both, the initial pleasantries that go with a two-and-a half-month absence were exchanged. This was done without a single remark directed at the length of their hair or their appearance. I knew however that it would not last long. Dad would not be able to resist such an inviting target. The first topic of course was school. "What classes are you taking? Got any grades yet? How often do you study?" Next up was the social scene. "Are you drinking any beer? Any girlfriends? Don't get married until you're out of school. Girls will screw up your grades if you don't watch out." The interrogation of sorts continued as

Thanksgiving, 1965, from left, Drew Neville, David Dimit, Kermit Holderman, and Richard Neville. Jack gave David $10 to get a haircut before he allowed Dimit into the house. David got the haircut.

Mom just watched shaking her head with an occasional "Jack" intended to let him know to slow down. Bob and Richard of course had long cleared out finding the "older" guys boring, but not first without nine-year-old Bob remarking that Dimit looked "weird." Now sensing that Dad had "warmed-up," I tried to steer the conversation toward more important topics. Our fraternity brother Ron Shotts had missed a 32-yard field goal in the last few seconds and for the first time in four decades O.U. had lost to O.S.U. Glances from Kothe and Dimit told of the response–who cares? They go to Vanderbilt. Try as I did to move the conversation away from what I knew was about to happen, the pathway was now wide open for Dad and the "barbs" that were surely to come as a result of their "hippie-dum."

"Does the University have a barber shop? Have you thought about curlers, jewelry, or dresses?" In a good natured but relentless fashion Jack threw spear after spear at Kothe and Dimit's new look with neither offering much of a defense.

Then, things started on a downhill slide. Now my two high school friends actually began to defend themselves. Their justification for shoulder length hair and over all ragged appearance was actually a purposefully designed political statement. Their appearance was a protest against the Vietnam War and the "establishment," whoever they were, that had unlawfully dragged the United States into this undeclared war. I sat in stunned silence now convinced beyond certainty that no one cared to discuss who the next O.U. quarterback would be. To my shock and surprise Dad was in much agreement with what both had to say about the war. He stopped short however in describing the war as "illegal." He thought it unfortunate that the boys fighting the war lacked solid America commitment. He questioned South Vietnam's ability to put a formable force in the field, or carry on after the conflict was over, if it was ever to be over in light of the continued troop build-up. The politics of Vietnam seemed disassembled and there was an undefined uncertainty about our true purpose in Vietnam. Surprisingly, between the old World War II veteran, now all of 45 years old, there was an amazing convergence of views. I remained silent, initially fearful when the war talk started that certainly Kothe and Dimit would be tossed out. Jack still could not resist forceful jabs at both. How in the world did dirty long "girl hair" serve to further political opposition to the war? To Dad, it was a disconnect.

Now feeling emboldened, Kothe began his explanation, and I now knew "it" was about to hit the fan. "It" was the familiar theme of baby-boomer 1960's civil disobedience. "Our voice, the voice of the people, is not being heard. Protest is the only form of revolt being heard. Protest is the only form of revolt that will bring real attention to this unjust war. Those who have to fight the war must stand up and be counted, refuse to go. Burn your draft card, carry placards, chant Hell no, we won't go. Send the signal, just tell them, we won't fight. If we have to, we'll go to Canada, we should all become conscientious objectors, that will show'em."

At this point in the conversation I decided it was useless to attempt to steer the dialogue toward Oklahoma's newest top football recruiting class. I did not know what to say or do. They both seemed from another planet and spoke a foreign language. I even wondered if I actually went to high school with these guys. This conversation was just going to have to play itself out. Uncharacteristically Jack remained silent as Kothe and Dimit railed the viles of Vietnam explaining the ways the citizenry should act to end the war. Then, Dimit took the conversation a bridge too far. He spoke of protest against the soldiers. Try to keep those going, from going, by throwing rocks, water balloons, flowers, anything to let them know that they should throw down their arms and take up with the people. Those going off to war, or coming home from it should be jeered, not cheered. That was the way to stop it; a revolt in the ranks, insurrection. With this, Mount Vesuvius erupted. Dad's face and ears turned red, nostrils flared. "How dare you candy-asses denigrate those who fight for their country? Boys are dying in that war. They should be honored." Fifteen hundred young men just lost their lives in the Ia Drang Valley and casualty rates were high after the attack on the Da Nang air base. Dad ran off a litany of facts and figures about the build-up in Vietnam and the war that was both impressive and staggering. Both Kothe and Dimit were speechless. "You boys want to protest, you want to oppose the war in Vietnam, you take it to Johnson or McNamara, but for the men who wear the uniform, and fight the fight, they deserve your respect and honor. You leave them alone. They were not the ones who made the Vietnam war happen, they regretfully have to fight it." With this, the Kothe and Dimit's Wednesday afternoon ended. Arguments over the politics of Vietnam were one thing, but disrespect for those compelled to fight a war, just or unjust, was out of bounds in Dad's book. With my two friends fairly "FRIED" from the heat of the conversation, Dad rose from his chair, reached in his wallet, and withdrew two ten-dollar bills. He handed each ten dollars with the comment "Get a God-damn haircut if you want to come back to this house."

As Kothe and Dimit left the house with me following closely behind prophetically apologizing, Dad retreated to the back yard to fire up the Hasty-Bake. He never said a word to me about the incident, never offering apology or explanation for the more-than-heated exchange with two long-time friends. As for me, I withdrew to my room believing that the best strategy was to stay out of the line of fire. Embarrassed that I knew so little about America's involvement in Vietnam, I felt ill-equipped to take Dad on, but in my gut I knew he was right. Those in uniform fighting for their country, most probably not wanting to be there anyway, were off limits to the civil disobedience of which my friends spoke.

Believing two friends had been forever lost, in the quiet recess of my room I searched for the reasons behind Dad's emotion and strong feelings for the men fighting in Vietnam. It seemed a contradiction of sorts yet he obviously meant every word he had said. He was opposed to the war, yet he obviously felt genuinely protective of those actually fighting it. In November of 1965, I could not reconcile this perceived inconsistency, yet 37 years later I can understand his emotion and feeling about the soldiers fighting the fight. In 1965, I had never heard of the Overpass, or the Sele-Corrider. Dad had fought the good fight. He had been there, and in a sense, he was with those young men who fought in Vietnam; and for Dad, they too were heroes, and should be honored as such.

Two hours after Kothe and Dimit left the house, the front door bell rang. Mom was gone and I knew Dad would not answer the door. A man in his mood tending to his smoked turkey was not to be disturbed in any event. I shuffled to the door to see who it was. Opening the door, I could not believe my eyes. Kothe and Dimit were standing there, both clean shaven and with hair cropped closely behind their ears. Gone were both long hair and jewelry. Kothe even wore his Southern Hills golf shirt. Without me saying a word, almost in unison, they chanted, "Is your Dad here?"

They had finally both returned to Tulsa.

CHAPTER XXIX
ANZIO IN OKLAHOMA

By February of 1944, the war correspondents were becoming more skilled at their trade. Now often traveling with combat units, they were allowed to release their reports to the homefront within a day or two of the action. Still screened and censored by the Allied Supreme Command and the Supreme Headquarters Allied Expeditionary Force, the reports were more timely, but still in most cases purposefully vague. In Oklahoma City, Leota still rushed for the paper to at least get a glimpse of the action in Europe. In the first few weeks of the Anzio battle, the news releases by the Associated Press never specifically mentioned the 45th Infantry Division and only referred to the "Allies" or the 5th Army and Mark Clark. At times, the news from the front made it seem as if Mark Clark was fighting the entire Nazi nation single-handedly. Although the daily news reports never mentioned the "Thunderbirds," Leota and all of Oklahoma City knew their boys were at Anzio. On February 2, 1944, *The Daily Oklahoman* reported the 5th Army attacks at Campoleone without mention of the division or the fact that the famed Darby's Rangers had been wiped out at Isola Bella. Over the course of the next few days the citizens were told that the German thrust at Carroceto had been stymied even though Hitler's own elite SS troops had been thrown into the battle. As the war continued, more and more of the wounded and crippled were being sent home. And, while the 5th Army Headquarters always attempted to tell the story with the most optimism, the men who had fought the war were telling it like it was. As the wounded and dead returned home, it became widely known, but officially unconfirmed, that the Thunderbirds were at Anzio in the thick of an awful struggle with the Germans who were not close to quitting.

There were times when Mom wished she had not read the paper as the reported events only continued to dominate every moment and thought. While General McClain had achieved legitimate hero status, anxiety levels spiked upward with a quote from a returning veteran of Anzio.

"Whenever a fellow would see McClain, he would say 'let's get the hell out of here, we're near the front'."

While quotes such as these were headline grabbers, they only fueled concerns and worries. Wherever McClain was, Leota believed Jack was not far away. And, if these stories were accurate, he was in the line of Anzio fire.

Leota did everything she could to find a distraction. Her work helped. On February 2, 1944, McDonnell Douglas started a seven-day-a-week work schedule. Now there would be a sort of reprieve from those sometimes long Sundays where there was too much time to think. In addition to the daily trek to Midwest City and the McDonnell plant, the events of the day in Oklahoma City often provided a much needed comic relief of sorts. While most of the young men were off fighting the Nazis, Oklahoma's aggressive crime fighting District Attorney George Miskovsky was burdened with the task of destroying some 20,000 pints of whiskey recently confiscated in county-wide raids. Mom suggested the booty should be sent to the 45th in support of the war efforts. Sylvester Stauffer did not believe the suggestion very funny. With most of the "boggie-woogiers" in the European Theater of operations, the social talking heads of the day were on a crusade to save the young. The new theory of the day held that "jive boogie woogie" provoked juvenile delinquency and accordingly this type of music should be closely monitored, even censored. Never mind that most of the "juveniles" across the nation were being called for military service, a sure-fire way to bring a halt to delinquency. Hollywood continued to bring the war to the big screen. There was only so much of this Leota could take, but the Fighting Seabees, opening at the Midwest starring John Wayne provided an evening's entertainment, along with Air Force at the Uptown and Iron Major at the State. Before the end of the war, Leota laughed, John Wayne would fight in every branch of service and in every theater of operations across the globe. In any event if you bought a war bond, you got an extra seat at the movies, and by February 3, 1944, the Sooner nation had over subscribed its 4th Victory Loan Drive. Leota did her part.

Leota and Oklahoma City did not escape the horror of the furious German counterattack that took place February 16th through the 19th. In unusual, almost "real time" reports, the Associated Press brought a new level of agony and worry to the families with sons and husbands in Italy. In one of the first indications of serious difficulty on the beachhead, only one day after the massive German counterattack of February 18, 1944, *The Daily Oklahoman* headline boldly stated that "Anzio Defenses Sag, But Absorb all Nazi Blows." While Oklahoma City was told that the division had held the defensive line, it was clear that it was not without the cost of lives. It only meant that Leota had to wait to see if "the telegram" would arrive in the next few days. The gravity of the Anzio battle was over, when the paper reported that in one of the most crucial battles of the war, the Allies had fallen back but that German dead "carpeted" the battlefield; and on February 21, 1944, the Associated Press reported that "German dead were strewn across the meadows of Anzio." There was neither mention of the Allied dead or wounded, nor of the great struggle of the Thunderbirds at the Overpass. On one hand, it was exhilarating to learn that the Nazi tide had been stemmed; but on the other hand, no one, including Leota believed that victory was achieved without death. The misery of victory was that of waiting to see if your loved one had paid the ultimate price. There was little good about any of this. But fortunately for Leota, "the telegram," did not come and as each day passed without the postman coming, she found the optimism to go forward with the next day.

It was not until March 11, 1944, that the Army first let it be known that the 45th Infantry Division had saved the beachhead and Operation Shingle from oblivion. Oklahoma City's pride swelled with the report that the 45th Division Artillery unit had destroyed 30 Nazi tanks at the beachhead. The entire division received a unit citation for gallantry. Almost a month after the great German counterattack was beaten back, Leota was finally able to breathe a guarded sigh of relief. The postman did not ring. Jack had apparently made it through; and the wait and worry only began anew.

CHAPTER XXX
OVER AT ANZIO

While a great victory had been won at the beach, the men of the 157th, 2nd Battalion were still stranded and surrounded by Germans at the Caves, less than one mile from the Overpass. On February 18 and 19, as the rest of the division was fighting to the south, the beleaguard 2nd Battalion literally taking cover and hiding deep in the Caves, fought off three different German attacks. By February 20, the Division Artillery staff and Head Quarters Battery had reassembled at the beachhead command post. All eyes and ears were focused on the 2nd Battalion with hopes that they could somehow be rescued. On February 21, the British made a valiant run to save the Americans. Their efforts, although gallant and brave, failed. The British sustained horrendous casualties in their attempt to rescue the Americans. Most of the 7th Queens were annihilated. The next day, the Germans made their own full-scale attack to wipe out the surrounded battalion held up and hiding at the Caves. Incredibly, the 2nd Battalion was still in radio contact with Division Artillery and the other artillery units. As the German attack pressed forward, the call Jack and the others loathed to receive came through. So desperate were the men of the 2nd, that they called artillery fire down on their own position. For the fourth time in the war for Jack, plans and operations were made to fire on their own Thunderbirds. The German's attack was beaten back. After the Artillery fire lifted, the 2nd Battalion made the decision that they would attempt to break out. It was the only real choice they had. Back at Division Artillery Headquarters, Jack waited and listened. Leaving their dead and wounded behind, what was left of the battalion began a fighting withdrawal, infiltrating southward at 2:00 a.m., the morning of February 23. What was left of the 2nd Battalion walked out that night, hooked up with the British, and made their way back to the rest of the Thunderbirds. There were not many left. Captain Felix Sparks was the only survivor of E Company, all others perished. As for the entire Battalion of some 700-plus men, only 142 survived. By sunset on February 23, 1944, the battle for the Caves was over. And by the 24th, the Germans were well entrenched where the Thunderbirds once had been.

Bloodied and battered, German Commander Von MacKensen finally decided that he could not break the 45th Infantry Division and so he shifted what troops and guns he had left toward the eastern perimeter of the Allies beachhead lines, and the United States 3rd Division. While this provided some momentary relief to the Thunderbird Infantry Regiments, there was no relief for Jack and Division Artillery. On February 28, 1944, the Germans made a weak attempt to overrun Carano. On the 29th, Division Artillery poured down 66,000 rounds on the Germans. Once again ripping holes in the advancing German infantry ranks, the attack was repulsed. The Nazis made two more attacks without success as the German assembly areas had been detected and targeted. The Artillery rained lead and steel into the assembly areas before the German attacks started. The Americans continued to hold the line. A stalemate of sorts developed and on the scale of the battle field, the Anzio front was "relatively" quiet through March.

Throughout March of 1944, Dad spent most of his time in his bunker, taking on an almost mole-like existence. The threat of direct frontal assault by waves of German infantry had subsided, but it was still too dangerous to move about the beach in daylight hours. The Germans continued their daily random shelling and no one strayed far from their foxholes. Living on Anzio slipped backward in time to the activities and recreation enjoyed before February 7. Baseball was the favorite, but by the afternoon innings, the Anzio Express usually found a way to break it up. On March 1, 1944, the Division Artillery CP was moved to a location just outside the sister city of Netunno, on what was called the "Anzio Penhead." Dad believed the move was made to make the CP less inviting, a less visible target. It did not work. While the Germans were apparently incapable of mounting a ground attack,

Somehow the Thunderbirds found a way to have some fun at Anzio with a "mule rodeo" easily observed by the Germans in the nearby hills.

what was left of the German Air Force bombed the area almost every other day throughout the entire month of March. After the Luftwaffe made their run, which usually was brief, Anzio Annie and the Express were rolled out just to spice things up. Jack spent March running from one bunker to the next, as did everyone else on the beachhead. Aerial attacks were the event of the day.

As the March stalemate wore on, supplies and materials continued to pour onto the beach. It became evident that plans would be made for a break-out from the Anzio beachhead. The only question was when it would take place. While Jack's CP remained on the Penhead, yet another sign of break-out evidenced itself. During the weeks of relative inactivity for the Thunderbirds, the 45th was refitted, resupplied, and repositioned. By the end of March, the division was deployed on a new three-mile line that ran northeastward toward Carano. For the most part, the division was facing northwesterly toward Rome.

With the stockpiling of the beachhead and the new deployment of the division, scuttle-butt was rampant that break-out was soon to come. Anxiety levels were elevated when on March 17, 1944, Jack and the S-3 section spent the entire day pouring over maps and plans for "Operation Centipede." Hopes to move forward were dashed when the operation could not get enough air cover. Centipede was scrubbed.

In early April, General Mark Clark was summoned off the Anzio beach to Washington D.C. to meet with General George Marshall. Plans for the invasion of Normandy, Operation Overlord, were being finalized with the cross-channel invasion anticipated to be sometime in late May or early June. It was therefore critical that German assets be put to the test in the southern European Theatre in order to drain German infantry and tanks away from the Normandy beachhead. At the very least, it was necessary to paralyze German forces in the south to keep them from reinforcing their German brothers in the north and it was critical to launch the attack in the south in order to maximize success at Normandy. Clark was told that on or about May 11th, the 8th Army would mass its forces and once again attack the Gustov Line. This time however, to ensure success, the Allies would not spread their force and attack across a broad front, but rather tank armor and infantry would be concentrated at the mouth of the Liri Valley, and ram though the Gustov Line to capture Highway 6, the road to Rome. The attack on the Gustov Line was code-named "Diadem." Clark's 5th Army role was to breakout northeasterly from the Anzio beach and move to cut Highway 6 at Valmonte to link up with the advancing southern allied force. Code-named "Buffalo," Clark was to attack with his forces once the Diadem battering ram had cracked the Gustov Line.

The signs were unmistakable that the Thunderbirds were finally near pushing their way out of Anzio. By early April, the Division Artillery had perfected their deadly "time-on target" firing missions. With careful planning, Division Artillery could place 1,000 rounds on a single target at one time. It was an incredibly devastating, deadly, and effective artillery tactic that allowed Division Artillery to pick-off selected German targets. After the S-3 section devised the "Casale Program," for counter-battery fire, Division Artillery engaged in an incredible 85 TOT missions between April 4 and April 16, designed to knock out key German gun implacements and troop assembly areas. It was as if the Division Artillery was going to blast the Thunderbirds off the Anzio beach. Of course, Jack was not aware of Mark Clark's trip back to Washington, D.C., but by mid-April Colonel Arnote, Captain Large, and General McClain were summoned south for planning conferences in Sorrento. Their departure told the troops that things were getting ready to happen.

While McClain's departure to Allied command for meetings and conferences usually signaled that a major offensive was about to begin, this was not the case. Jack never had much good to say about Mark Clark, but he held Arnote and Large in high regard. As for Ray McClain, both Jack and Leota absolutely revered the man in charge of Division Artillery. McClain had that "intangible," he was a great leader of men who made efforts to earn the respect of his men. McClain was visible to his troops, as often said he was "out front," sometimes far ahead of even the infantry. While he was aggressive, his reaction in the battlefield was measured often in terms of saving lives, not risking lives. McClain, at Salerno nearly single-handedly rescued elements of the 179th and to his tremendous credit, on the evening of the greatest German counterattack in World War II, McClain told Jack and his staff that he would sleep with his men at the front. It was obvious to all that he could have gone to the rear. He did not. For Dad, Ray McClain was a role model he needed at the young age of twenty-four. Clearly, McClain, in the awful time of war, had become both father and friend to Jack despite his high rank and station in life.

While the shelling at Anzio was near constant, time was found for religious services and prayer.

CHAPTER XXXI
ANZIO BREAK-OUT

On April 23, 1944, McClain returned from Sorrento and on the next day gathered his staff. In an emotional farewell departure, McClain explained that he was being transferred to England to assume command of the 30th Division Artillery. On April 24, 1944, McClain received the Silver Star for his rescue of the 179th in Sicily, and with that he was gone.

McClain's departure from the Thunderbirds was an emotional blow to the troops. For the next few days Jack worried how they would fare without the leader who had been with them since September of 1940. Events gave Jack little time for thoughts or sorrow. Any doubt of the Anzio break-out was removed on April 30, 1944, when the Commander of the Thunderbirds, General Eagles, arrived at the Division Artillery CP. The main topic of discussion was the break-out attack. One plan, "Operation Turtle," called for Division Artillery to support an attack up the Anzio-Albano road, moving to the northwest and toward Rome. The second plan of attack, code-named "Buffalo," had the line of attack moving toward Valmonte, cutting Highway 6, trapping and killing a retreating German 10th Army pushed northward by operation "Diadem." The third alternative, "Grasshopper," called for an advance to the southeast. It could not take long for the operation to become bogged down with high level jealousies and egos. Irrespective of the plans decided upon, Mark Clark was obsessed with the capture of Rome first, no matter what.

While McClain was sorely missed, it did not take long for Col. J.D. Meyer to take command of Division Artillery. On May 9, 1944, Meyer confidently took control. Thunderbird artillery would not miss a lick.

The following day it was evident that the higher-ups favored Buffalo and steps were taken accordingly. For the first time since the Anzio landing, the Headquarters Battery of Division Artillery moved off the beachhead and north of Lateral Road.

On May 11, 1944, Operation Diadem to the south commenced on schedule. At 11:00 p.m., the Allies massed 1,660 artillery pieces at the point of attack and the great assault against the Gustov Line began. The first punch had

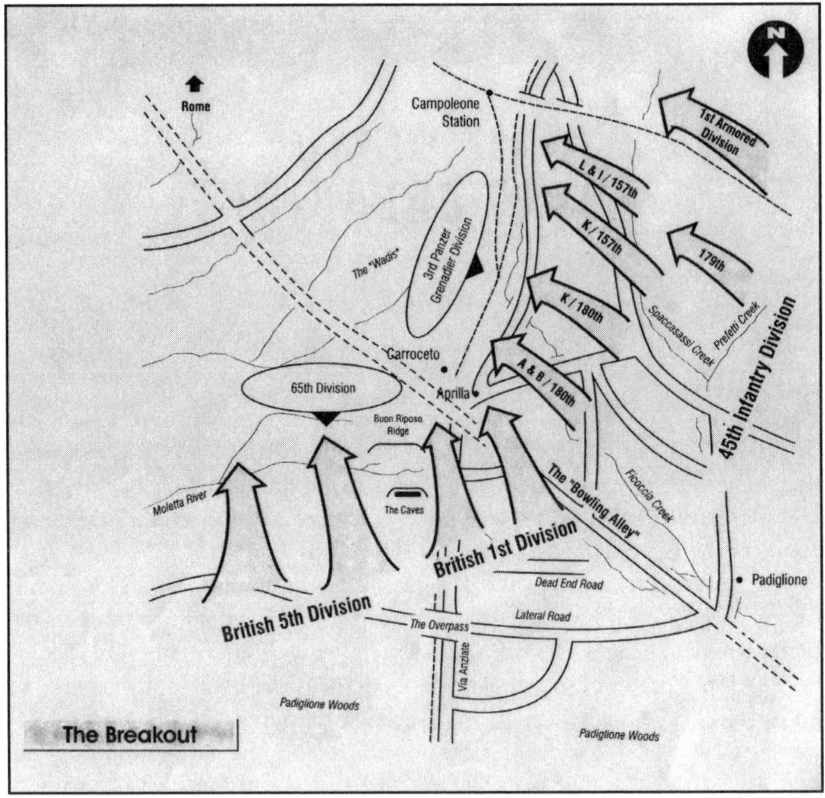

By mid-May of 1944, the Thunderbirds had shifted eastward of the Via Anziate in preparation for the "break-out" from the beachhead.

been thrown, and the green light was given to the troops in Anzio to attack. The break-out at Anzio would commence May 23, 1944.

As Jack studied the maps, the division was to move northwesterly toward the German's favorite hiding place, the Factory. In implementing Buffalo, the Division Artillery utilized its own form of deception on the Huns. On May 11, the S-3s implemented "Fire Plan Buffalo." This plan called for artillery fire in rather exposed situations designed to induce the Germans to return fire, which they usually could not resist. The return fire gave away the German artillery positions, and thereafter the rest of Division Artillery could focus its deadly TOT mission on the German location. Fire Plan Buffalo proved critical in eliminating, or at least reducing, the deadly effect that German Artillery could otherwise have on advancing Allied tanks and infantry troops. It worked. Although it had become evident to Jack and the S-3 staff, it was not until May 16 that the S-3 staff were given specific orders to start plans for the Buffalo plan of attack. Tensions ran high. For the first time since January 29, the division and the Allies would mass for an attack against the Germans. The "bunker-down"

The bridge over the Mussolini Canal, just off the Anzio Beachhead, was utilized by the troops to cross the canal in May of 1944.

strategy was over. To support the attack, and get closer to the front, for the first time in three months and 21 days, the Division Artillery command post was moved off the beach to a series of gullies east of the Via Anziate and slightly behind the infantry regiments planned line of attack. It did not take long for Jack to clean out his beach bunker, and there was by no means any sense of leaving home. It was now "get back" time and, as Flint Whitlock, so eloquently wrote, it was time to leave this "savage wilderness." After being cooped up and shot at, Jack and the rest of the Thunderbirds were ready.

On May 17, Clark and Alexander clashed once again over Buffalo as Diadem in the south was showing signs of success. Alexander demanded that Valmonte be seized and Highway 6 blocked in order to capture the German 10th Army. Clark, on the other hand, was obsessed with the capture of Rome, arguing that the 10th German Army could easily escape by way of any number of secondary road networks. Clark secretly worried that objective Valmonte was purposefully designed to bog VI Corps down so that the British could get to Rome first. As Clark confided to his inner circle, "The capture of Rome is the only important objective." However, as Buffalo was about to begin, Clark had little choice but to follow orders and move to take Valmonte. Clark's ego would swiftly change the plan.

On May 20, 1944, Colonel Meyer and Arnote called together the entire staff to discuss and coordinate the break-out attack. The anxiety level rose as Jack carefully noted the plan of infantry attack that would be protected by heavy artillery support. If the division was to move off the beach, the artillery fire would have to be on the money. The Thunderbirds' mission called for the division to drive between Aprilia and Carano to provide left flank protection for the 1st Armored Division who would move northeasterly and capture Cisterna. Jack and the S-3 staff hovered over the maps as Arnote briefed the logistical details of ammunition and supply to the firing batteries. It was a grim planning session. Buffalo called for the Thunderbirds infantry regiments to advance across open fields just as the Germans had attempted in mid-February. The Germans had been murdered by vicious artillery fire. If those April TOT missions had been successful, perhaps the infantry would not have to suffer similar carnage as the Germans. Every round counted with coordinates plotted and replotted. For the 45th, the break-out at Anzio began in the early morning hours of May 23, 1944. On the evening of May 22, "all troops were in position, waiting for the time for jump-off." As the evening calmed before the storm, Col. Meyer once again called the staff together to read a message from General Truscott.

> ". . . You are free men, against whom no slaves of a tyrant nation can ever stand. Our comrades in the south are fighting their way toward us. The eyes of the world will be upon us. Be alert, be vicious, destroy the hated enemy. Victory will be ours."

For Jack, all he could do was stare at the sky and pray that the division would not be annihilated. There was no sleep in the foxholes this night.

May 23 began early. Up long before the attack was to start, Jack stuffed himself with an awful combination of both C and K rations. This unique delicacy would probably be the only bit of chow he would have the rest of the day. As the S-3 staff gathered hours before the attack, the unanswerable questions resurfaced time and again. How many German tanks were out there? During the months of March and April had the Germans brought up artillery sufficient to turn back the attack as the Allies had in February? Where exactly were the Germans along the route of attack? You could not look at your watch enough in anticipation of H-hour. Jack stepped outside the S-3 tent for one last smoke. Radio and telephone traffic were relatively quiet now. All was in place for yet another great battle that could mean the difference in the southern European Theatre. It was a cool and cloudy Tuesday morning, as if there was ever a good day for men to die. At 6:00 a.m. on May 23, the Anzio break-out started. The Division Artillery laid down a 30-minute hail of steel in preparation for the Infantry attack, and at 6:30 a.m. the men of the 157th, 180th, and 179th Infantry Regiments went over the top in their own form of a "Pickett's Charge" across relatively open fields. As the attack was under way, the German's responded initially by bringing up strong tank support. Now having TOTs perfected to a near science, the Division Artillery blew apart some 24 German tanks with well-planned and executed fire. To the great relief and surprise of all was that the German artillery was relatively absent, certainly not sufficient to stop the hard-charging Thunderbirds sprinting across the open field. The German 3rd Panzer Grenadier Division was in retreat and by sundown the Thunderbirds had taken the railroad bed north of Aprilia, their first objective. By day's end, Division Artillery had fired some 13,000 rounds. The day was marked with numerous acts of courage and bravery as the Thunderbirds took the fight to the Germans. On this day Sgt. Van T. Barefoot of the 157th, a Choctaw Indian, earned the Medal of Honor near Carano when he almost single-handedly took out three German machine guns. There was no question, the division was there for the fight.

By the second day, the Germans had regrouped somewhat to form a counterattack. On the division's west flank, the Germans hit the 180th with a tank attack and on the eastern division flank at Spaccasassi Creek, the Germans attempted the same tactic. The Division Artillery again hammered the German Panzers. The division had moved successfully on all objectives between Aprilia and Carano.

May 25 only added to the list of bizarre events that seemed to characterize and haunt the Anzio campaign. In the south, the Allies were finally achieving hard-earned success at the Gustov Line. The German 10th Army was retreating from the Liri Valley was in danger of being caught in the deadly vice of Allied forces moving from the south and Clark's forces moving from the north. However, Clark's ego and absolute obsession for Rome got the better of him. That morning at 8:30 a.m., Clark conferred with Truscott over the possibility of diverting the 45th, 34th, and 36th Divisions toward Rome rather than continue the line of attack toward Valmonte. For the first time the Allies were in a position to crush the Germans at Valmonte, and with indications of Diadem's success, Clark's paranoia that the British would be first into Rome only grew. Some accounts hold that Truscott reminded Clark that the mission was to the northeast toward Valmonte, not toward Rome. Clark made his often repeated argument that the German 10th could easily escape on secondary roads at Valmonte, and that the real prize was Rome. Throughout the morning and early afternoon, the Allied success in the south and near Anzio became undeniable. German resistance was showing signs of collapse as the United States 3rd Division took Cisterna.

In yet another bizarre twist of Anzio history, Brigadier General Donald Braun, Clark's G-3, summoned Truscott for a mid-afternoon meeting. The orders were that the 45th, 34th, and 36th Divisions were to reverse their course and move toward Rome, and the United States 3rd Division and the 1st Special Forces would proceed to Valmonte. Clark had ordered his forces split. As D'Estes wrote, "Clark suddenly dismembered operation Buffalo." The order, of course, was passed down to Truscott's Division Commanders, one of whom of course was General Eagles of the 45th. At the Division Artillery CP, the confusion caused by the change in orders was sorted through rather quickly. Instead of turning to the right, the division would turn to the left. Jack Neville really did not care. The Thunderbirds wanted to break-out, get away from the beach, and just about any direction except backwards was embraced with enthusiasm.

The Thunderbirds fought hard and fast, and by late afternoon the division had the German 3rd Panzer Division against the walls of Aprilia. The Germans had reeked havoc and death on Anzio, most often assembling and hiding in the nearly-destroyed town of Aprilia. Now they had the Krauts cornered. At 2:40 p.m. on the 45th, Division Artillery laid an incredible series of TOT fire on Aprilia and as Division Artillery history recites "the Germans evacuated their favorite nest." As the German 3rd Panzer Division fled, the artillery did not let up.

"We fired TOTs on the departing guests to speed them on their way."

By nightfall, one of the most significant landmarks on the Anzio landscape, the Factory, was finally in Allied hands as the Germans quickly retreated.

The move toward Rome started in the late morning of May 25, with H-Hour at 11:15 a.m. The Rome offensive from the southwest would be spearheaded by the 45th. For Jack, the Division Artillery CP remained slightly south of Padglione to plan and coordinate fire support for the advancing infantry regiments as they attacked toward Campoleone. For the Division Artrillery, H-hour, started at 11:00 a.m. as more than 300 pieces of artillery blasted the Italian countryside clearing a path for the infantry with precisely placed TOTs. The attack moved forward with relatively light resistence and by 3:00 p.m., the air observers flying their Piper Cubs over the battlefield reported to the Division Artillery CP that German tanks and troops were moving quickly to the north. So focused and well planned was the Division Artillery this day that they were able to place more than 1,000 rounds on a single target at almost the same time. The 45th found more success. Again utilizing carefully planned TOTs, Division Artillery took out machine gun nests and mine fields clearing the way for the 180th, 157th, and 179th. Effective German Artillery fire was noticeably absent. The German shelling was becoming lighter and less frequent, but of very heavy caliber. The S-2 section concluded that this was a sure sign of retreat as the enemy was getting rid of their heavy ammunition. They could not carry it and get away fast enough. By May 28, German resistance at Anzio was in shambles as 5,156 prisoners were taken.

After May 28, the race for Rome was on as the Anzio break-out and destined for success. Whitlock described it in *The Rock of Anzio* as the Italian Grand Prix. As the 45th infantry climbed aboard anything that would move, Jack and the S-3 section hovered over the maps of the road networks and key targets surrounding Rome. On May 31, General Meyer stamped his approval on "Fire Plan Rome" as the artillery hurled 11,170 rounds at the Germans in a single day in preparation for the liberation of Rome. With the Germans now in full retreat, Jack and the S-3 Section packed up the CP for the last time on Anzio soil. Loaded onto trucks, the Division Artillery CP raced up the Via Anziate to establish the Division CP near the railroad tracks near Aprilia. As they zoomed through the "Gate of Hell" for the last time, all heads turned in unison to look backward, and then at each other. Balkum and Neville could not help but look at each other, shaking their heads with a slight grin. How in the hell did they survive?

With Division Artillery now positioned to support the final assault on Rome, the last German counterattack in Italy came. On June 1, 1944, the Germans attempted to halt the Thunderbirds' rush for Rome. The artillery was ready. On this day, the Division Artillery shot 15,956 rounds, and once again the Germans were slaughtered by a curtain of steel and lead. After the counterattack, the only substantial German resistence was now holed up on a hill south of Rome. The last of the Germans were barricaded behind concrete emplacement as the 179th attempted to fight up a steep slope to force them out. At dawn, the morning of June 3, as the Division Artillery unleashed another wicked barrage in what came to be called the Battle of K-9 Hill, the 179th fought their way up the slope behind 16,241 rounds fired in support of the attack. Strong tank support finished off the Germans, and for all practical purposes the Battle of Anzio, and Rome, was over.

With the Germans fleeing, Jack anxiously awaited for the next order to move the CP on to Rome. Then came an unexpected halt in the action. The Germans had once again sustained heavy casualties and there was no question that they soon would abandon the Eternal City. Over the radio to Division Artillery CP came the voice of the German commander asking for a cease fire, a two-hour truce to evacuate their dead and wounded. In the heat of the Battle of Salerno, such requests by both sides had been honored, but at Anzio-Rome,

A partially-destroyed German 88 destroyed during the move on Rome, in June of 1944. The German 88 was one of the most feared German weapons of World War II.

the four months of hell and death were too much, the price too heavy. The operations report for June 3, 1944 recited in The History of Division Artillery treated the event with brevity.

> ". . . the Germans requested a two hour truce to evacuate their dead, but it was refused to them . . . enemy losses were heavy."

With the Thunderbird refusal to grant the enemy any quarter, the Germans were now in a full sprint to get out of town.

Back at the Division Artillery CP, the S-3 section hung on every word of the radio transmission reporting the movements of the infantry units toward Rome. At 9:00 a.m. on June 3, the 180th was moving rapidly just south of the Tiber River. The next day the 180th secured a bridge over the Tiber River, only five miles southwest of Rome. With the bridge secured, the word came to Jack to prepare to move out. The Division Artillery CP was headed to Rome. The emotions and anxiety were high as Jack and the men of the S-3 section climbed aboard their trucks for the ride to Rome. As the convoy finally made Highway 6, there were cheers and tears as many had made the final sacrifice and were left behind at the Anzio beachhead.

By late afternoon on June 4, Rome fell to the Allies with the 45th Infantry Division just outside the southern city limits, as General Clark, amidst great pomp and circumstance, drove his jeep through the City of Rome in triumph. On June 5, 1944, the Battle for Italy was over for the Thunderbirds and the Allied Forces.

In the evening hours of June 5, as the sun was about to set over one of the greatest cities of the world, the Division Artillery and Jack's unit crossed the Tiber River. At 8:00 p.m. on January 5, Jack Neville from Adair, Oklahoma, was in Rome, Italy, and more importantly, still alive.

With the entire division now encamped in fields west of Rome, the service companies were quick to rush in hot food. Relatively new to the war scene were shower trucks. Jack could not stand under the shower of water long enough and was grateful for every drop. For the first time since January 29, Jack could rest free of the worry of being bombed, strafed, shelled by "Anzio Annie," or shot at. The horror of Anzio was over, and at least for now the killing stopped. Clean shaven, and with a new uniform, socks, and boots, it was a June holiday.

On June 6, 1944, Jack made his way through S-3 tent. With the fear of being killed at least momentarily over, thoughts shifted toward home. He now had been away from home and Leota an entire year. It was not getting easier with the constant question always resurfacing and repeating itself, "will I ever get home again?" With the S-3 section's radios tuned to the British Broadcasting Company's frequency, the despair of thinking about Leota, and Oklahoma, was broken.

Over the radio came the news that relieved the entire free world.

The Allies had landed in Normandy, D-Day June 6, 1944.

Casualty rates and statistics in war-time were difficult to keep and often conflicting and confusing. There is one common certainty, however, that runs through the cold numbers–the casualties at Anzio were horrific. The combined Allied and German losses for the four-month battle totaled 94,000, almost seven divisions. At the Anzio beachhead, the Allies suffered 7,000 killed in action and 36,000 wounded in action, missing in action, or otherwise injured. In the short period of time between the breakout and the fall of Rome, the 45th Infantry Division lost 442 men killed in action, 3,200 wounded, missing, or lost. The great Italian campaign was essentially over when Anzio was won and Rome fell. From Salerno to Rome, 20,000 Allies were killed in action of which 12,000 were American. During the Italian Campaign alone, the Thunderbirds' casualties totaled 33,905.

To further put the horror of Anzio and the entire march through Italy in perspective, the casualty count in Sicily was 3,914. The division suffered ten times that in Italy. Fifty-four percent of the 45th Infantry Division's war-time casualties were in Italy. A morbid statistical twist of the numbers also suggests that every man in the division, while fighting in Italy, was a casualty approximately two-and-a-half times.

Without question, Winston Churchill was one of the world's greatest leaders. His personal courage and spirit literally saved a nation that was on the brink of Nazi occupation. Curchill was rarely short of words and depsite his role in Operation Shingle, his candor should be noted: "Anzio was my worst moment of the war. I had the most to do with it."

Battery A, 1st gun section, 189th Field Artillery Battalion on June 4, 1944 between Anzio and Rome two days before the liberation of Rome. It was artillery units such as this that saved the day at Anzio annihilating German infantry and tanks attacking down the Via Anziate.

REFLECTION ANZIO'S IMPACT ON THE NEVILLES

On more than one occasion, Dad emphasized to the brothers to not sit back and wait for any inheritance to line our pockets, that we all better get out there and learn how to make a living for ourselves. We always giggled at these types of statements, but events proved him serious. Dad and Mom traveled the world in the 1970s and 1980s–China, Russia, Hong Kong, Turkey, and Japan, just to name a few. In addition to those mentioned, in the late1970s, they both traveled to Naples and Rome with two other couples. There were never any extended discussions about this expedition, or the real reason for going. Mom always simply put one of the reasons as "Your Dad was in the war there." Dad never offered an explanation for the trip, other than it would be a great adventure. I always suspected a hidden agenda or secret purpose, but nonetheless summarily dismissed the thought of extensive probing. Upon their return, their stories were of the beauty of Rome and Naples, of the great food and restaurants, and, of course for Mom, the shopping. Most of the "booty" they bought was shipped back, not carried back; and while they both regaled us with stories of their trip, never was a word spoken about the war, or of the Anzio battle.

The city of Aprilla, not affectionately known by the Thunderbirds as the Factory, was completely destroyed in the fighting during the four months of the battle. The city was rebuilt entirely, except for the tower that gave the city its namesake. The Overpass survived for 32 years after the war and was destroyed in 1976 to make room for a new bridge. Where Dad made the last stand at Anzio, with the passage of decades, there is little left to remind visitors that anyone ever fought a great battle there. Even the infamous Via Anziate is simply relabeled Highway 207. Anzio-Netunno, as the twin cities did decades ago, still serve as a favorite summer retreat for the Romans; and remnants of the Caves are still visible, if one takes the time to look. Isola Bella, where Darby's Rangers saw the end, was renamed "Via Ranger," to honor those who fell. However, the most poignant reminder at Anzio of the grievous loss of lives during the awful struggle is found at Netunno, where the American cemetery is located.

There seems little question that Dad's closest war-time friend was Harry Balkum. To this day, Harry Balkum's name is still listed in the Jackson, Tennessee, phone book. A young athlete of considerable legend in Jackson, Harry left high school and joined the United States Army. He and his wife Maxine met up with Dad and Mom at approximately the time the division moved to Camp Pine. The foursome was nearly inseparable, as Mom chronicled in her scrapbook. At sometime, Harry again was seriously wounded at

Anzio. A head wound plagued his health the rest of his life. The facts surrounding Harry's wound are unknown. For his action at Anzio, he received the Purple Heart, but his physical condition would not allow him to return to the front. Harry Balkum returned to Jackson, Tennessee, in July of 1944. Maxine Balkum died of cancer in 1975. Thereafter, Harry married his old high school sweetheart, Claudia.

Like Dad, Harry never seriously discussed Anzio, or the war for that matter, even to the extent of refusing to discuss how he was wounded. In fleeting comments about the war, he made light of the food, joked of the lack of toilet paper, and of not being able to take a shower. Like Dad, there was never mention of battle and efforts to probe were pushed aside. Claudia and Harry enjoyed vacationing in Virginia. Several occasions were spent in Norfolk, near Hampton Roads, the 45th's point of de-embarkation. Claudia was surprised and even laughed when she learned that Harry had set sail for Europe from Hampton Roads. He never spoke of leaving. Like so many others, gregarious, fun-loving guy Harry Balkum, the star quarterback on the Jackson High School football team, Mom's jitterbug partner at Camp Pine, preferred to let the war remain in the recesses of his mind, his thoughts and feelings forever lost in the decades of history. Harry Balkum died in Jackson, Tennessee, in 1990.

In all of the hours and days we spent as kids with Mom and Dad traveling across the country in a car, through all of the baseball games, football games, trips to Adair, morning breakfasts, evening suppers, sunrise breakfasts, trips to the zoo, graduations, marriages, my own service in the United States Army, the words "the Overpass" were never spoken.

CHAPTER XXXII
NEWS OF ANZIO

As 1944 moved into the first weeks of June in Oklahoma City, for Leota it was the same old guessing game about where Jack and the 45th were. The March press releases only confirmed what everyone knew, but as the Allies broke out of the Anzio beachhead, there was still no mention of the division's location. Of course, not surprisingly absent from any news report was Clark's decision to move the 45th west toward Rome. The lack of information was commonly frustrating, now even to the point that respected New York columnist William Safire complained that he learned more from London media than our own government. But for Leota, her major concern was not the morning headlines, but what the postman would bring today. After now being separated from Jack for slightly more than one year, she still froze at the sight of a green Army Hudson sedan cruising down Classen looking for a street address. In those days Leota was always in a hurry to get to work at the Douglas Aircraft Plant. United States Army sedans and mail did not come to the Douglas Plant. It was often a relief just to be at work and away from home where all you did was worry.

As *The Daily Oklahoman* and *The Oklahoma City Times* reported, "Allies Hammer Outer Defensive Line at Rome" and "Americans Surround Velletri." It was clear to the home folks that the Thunderbirds were off the beach and headed somewhere else. With Tommy Dorsey and his Orchestra performing at the Municipal Auditorium and the Blossom Heath, to the applause of some 5,000 fans, the United States 1st Armored Division rolled into Velletri and Valmontone. In reporting the generic "American" move off the beachhead and toward Rome, the words "45th Infantry Division" never were printed.

Early June 1, Leota and Oklahoma City received a double dose of major war-time news. Allied bombers saturated the Normandy coastline of northern France, near Calais, a sign certain that the cross-channel invasion was eminent. So excited were the Citizens that the paper began a contest of who could correctly pick the invasion date. Guesses flooded in. Only three days later, the news that the Neville-Stauffer clans waited for the most came as the paper reported "Rome Defense Crumbles, Nazis Retreat; Allies Say Liberation of City Imminent." June 5, 1944, brought the big news that finally told the whereabouts of the 45th. "Anzio Fighters Liberate Rome" was the headline Leota woke up to and while the article only related "a force from the old Anzio beachhead mopped up Rome," without mention of the division, it was close enough. There seemed little doubt that the Sooners had taken the Eternal City. The very next day the homefront was treated to the news that had been talked about for more than a year. The greatest seaborne assault in the history of modern warfare had crossed the English Channel in awful weather to attack Hitler's supposedly impregnable fortress. The Oklahoma City papers reported the German broadcasts because General Eisenhower initially refused to confirm the invasion. The headlines screamed across Oklahoma "Germans Say Allied Paratroopers and German Forces Land on French Coast." As the Allied Supreme Headquarters felt confident to confirm that the Allies were on the ground in Normandy, the later editions told Oklahoma City "100 Mile Coast Invaded." For a few precious hours, Oklahoma City let themselves celebrate as Leota, her pals, and most of Oklahoma City stuffed themselves into the Cow Shed for six hours of entertainment by Bat and the Rhythm Cats at a cost of 75 cents. For those with less energy or ambition, the Paseo Plunge in the Paseo District provided a great place to let it all go in a night-time swim. Through the rest of June and into July, Leota followed the reports of the Allies' move inland and sweep across northern Europe, always searching for word of the 45th. The division once again had become invisible, and even the 5th Army's move to new positions north of Rome took a back seat to the news reports of the advances by the Allies into and across the Cherbourg Peninsula. The 5th Army had become fourth-page news as it took Civita, 38 miles northwest of Rome.

For the first time Leota and her buddies believed the war might end. The Germans, in the space of only three days, had been run out of Rome and kicked off the Normandy Coast. It was now safe to say that the Nazis were being pushed back to Germany. The optimism of war's end, however, did not seem to slow up Oklahoma City. By March of 1944, the Douglas Aircraft Plant had produced 1,000 C-47s.

As Leota and the rest of the wives of war rushed to the west side of the plant, Douglas completed its 2,000th C-47 on July 1, 1944, to the cheers and pride of its mostly female work force. As the good news in the European Theatre rolled off the presses, the Oklahoma Railroad Company and the Pacific Northwest Railroad continued to advertise "War Workers Wanted." As the war in Europe continued, so did the war on the homefront. With battlefield victories, a new wave of patriotism swept across the plains. On July 4, 1944, more than 3,000 people toured the Naval Air Station in Norman, Oklahoma, and the Oklahoma Tire and Supply Company ran the first advertisement to buy war bonds, kicking off Oklahoma's fifth War Loan drive. Even across the Atlantic on Independence Day, the American flag that flew over the Capitol on December 7, 1942, was raised in Rome's Piazza Venizie to the thunderous cheers of the American soldiers and the Italians as well.

With no news of the 45th, the attention of many was on the local political scene. Embattled, often controversial Oklahoma County District Attorney George Miskovsky was locked in a heated battle with Warren Edwards. The Miskovsky campaign was a war itself, but Edwards prevailed. On the national political front, Franklin Delano Roosevelt was nominated again on the very first ballot at the Democratic National Convention in Chicago, with Harry Truman nominated for vice president. Little did Truman know that in less than a year, with Roosevelt's death, he would assume the presidency as the war in Europe came to a close.

Despite the wave of new optimism that spread across the Heartland with continued reports of Allied victories there remained grim reminders of the death and destruction of war. With the loss of the battleship Oklahoma at Pearl Harbor, the Sooner nation fixed their ears to the radio as Congressional hearings commenced on the December 7, 1942, surprise attack on Pearl Harbor. By July of 1944, the newspapers carried daily body counts. By July 2, Oklahomans had suffered more than 2,000 dead, wounded, or missing. Despite the euphoria of recently won victories and record numbers of planes manufactured, Sergeant Wayne Clark, recently returned from the front with the 45th Infantry Division, put matters in real perspective for Leota when he told Oklahoma City "Everyone's scared . . . sometimes we were scared we were going to die, and other times we were scared we wouldn't."

Of course, Jack did not know it then, but his war would last less than another year. However, as the dog days of summer baked Oklahoma City, the Thunderbirds, unknown to Leota, were on their way back to Naples to get ready for the division's fourth major amphibious landing. The battle of southern France was about to begin.

CHAPTER XXXIII
SOUTHERN FRANCE

The center stage of the war was now northern France as the Allies hammered away at the German Army in Normandy; but for Jack, life in bivouac west of Rome was not half bad. The freight train sounds of "Anzio Annie" and the "Express" forever had been silenced. Free of being shot at and shelled, it was the first time in the war that he and his pals in the Division Artillery could relax. For ten days, Jack and the others could actually shave, sleep, rest, take a hot shower, get a hot meal, put on a fresh uniform, and write letters home. Added to these fine amenities were a few site-seeing trips to Rome. Passes were freely issued and the boys were trucked into Rome to see the Eternal City. For Jack, it was his first time to see the Coliseum, the Vatican, and the wonders of the old world. He gladly would have traded it all to be home.

The Roman holiday ended on June 17, 1944, as the entire division struck their tents and moved into assembly areas. After four days Jack and the Division Artillery climbed aboard trucks for the ride back to the Salerno beachhead. By June 21, the Division Artillery CP staked their tents in San Martino, Italy. Two days later, the rest of the Thunderbirds were encamped at various locations around Battipaglia, Italy, some 25 miles north of where the 45th had landed on the Salerno beaches. There the training started all over again as the 45th practiced and practiced amphibious beachhead assaults. By now, the veteran Thunderbirds knew these sessions were not just for the sake of practice. The amphibious training was a strong signal that the Thunderbirds were being readied for yet another seaborne assault somewhere in southern Europe. In looking at the maps, the scuttle-butt again ran rampant. Would the division sweep around the 5th Army advancing north of Rome, similar to Shingle? Would they be put ashore in southern France? The new replacements viewed the debate with enthusiasm; the veterans, like Jack, met the prospect of yet another seaborne invasion with a deep sigh of anxiety. Would it be another Anzio? On June 30, 1944, Arnote called his S-3 staff together. Arnote was leaving for a division planning session in Naples, that's all he knew. Arnote's brief departure provided the sure sign of things to come. Amphibious practice landings coupled with division level planning sessions told only one story, another major operation was in the works.

Planning for Operation "Anvil," later renamed Operation "Dragoon" actually began before the 45th sailed for Anzio. As early as October of 1943, the Allies were considering three courses of action in southern Europe. The Russians saw two of the strategies as follows. First, the Allies could take up defensive positions north of Rome or, second, attack and push the Germans through Italy and into Germany. The Russian proposal, of course, benefitted the Russians because its armies were pushing the Germans westward. As they saw it, the shortest Allied link-up came with a push through Italy, not France. The British and the Americans on the other hand liked the idea of an attack in southern France, synchronized with Overlord. This strategy benefitted the British and Americans as Anvil could provide the necessary diversion to Overlord and provide another needed line of supply. As was usually the case, the British and the Americans won the debate and the southern France assault operation was approved at the Cairo conference in December of 1943.

Only one week before the 45th Division Artillery combat-loaded for Anzio, and amidst the debate over Shingle, the strategy of Anvil also fell into disagreement. Eisenhower believed that the invasion of southern France was vital to Overlord, and that both operations should be planned to take place at the same time. The British, as well as Ike's own staff, argued that it was impossible and dangerous to now withdraw troops and supplies from Italy to coincide with D-Day. This time, the British and Ike's own staff won the battle, ultimately convincing the Supreme Commander at a conference in England on January 21, that the southern France operation should be postponed until July largely due to a lack of landing craft. It can be argued in hindsight that this decision substantially contributed to the Anzio success story. If there had been a shortage of men and material at Anzio, because of Anvil the case could be made that the 45th would have been pushed into the Tyrrhenian Sea. There was disagreement over the military value of the southern France invasion. Churchill saw no value to it, Eisenhower's staff believed it vital to the logistical support of Overlord because of the port in Marseille, and Roosevelt believed that if Anvil was canceled it could offend the Russians. Nonetheless, the decision was made. Operation Anvil was now on.

Southern France was defended by the German 19th Army, Army Group 6, consisting of eight divisions. This time the advantage of manpower and geography belonged to the Allies. With the success at Normandy, the Germans were pulling troops out of the south. To ask the German 19th to defend a stretch of coast between Nice and Marseille was too much. In southern France, the Germans were spread too thin and were unable to aggressively deny the beaches to the Allies.

On the Allied side of the table was the newly constituted 7th Army under the command of General Alexander Patch. The Seventh would consist of the 1st Special Service Force, The Devil's Brigade, the United States 3rd, the 36th, and the fighting 45th.

With the "okay" given to Operation Dragoon, things began to happen with the Thunderbirds. While the infantry regiments continued their training on the beaches of Salerno, the Division Artillery, with the exception of Jack's Headquarters

S-3 unit was moved to an area near Battapaglia on July 1, 1944. After two weeks the Division Artillery CP was reshuffled to the familiar area of Pozzuoli, Italy on July 17, 1944. Once there, it was all business. Training and physical conditioning were cranked up a notch and the S-3 section went into hibernation to plan their part of the invasion of southern France. This time Jack was not confined to a small room on a ship, perhaps worse. Along with Arnote and Large, Jack and the others were consigned to a blockhouse just north of Naples where the S-3 section labored over the details of Dragoon. There, for the first time, Jack officially learned that the 45th would go ashore in southern France.

The basic plan of attack called for the 7th Army to land approximately 50 miles east of Marseille. Prior to the landing, the 1st Special Service Forces would take two key islands south and west of Tropez. The United States 3rd Infantry Division would hit the beach near St. Tropez. On the far right flank would be the 36th Infantry Division going ashore near Cannes. The 45th Infantry Division would take the center point of the attack between the 3rd and 36th, with the Thunderbird 157th and 180th going in first followed by the 179th. General Meyer, and the Division Artillery, learned habits from McClain. Jack would go in behind the 157th Infantry Regiment. Once ashore, the 45th would move with all dispatch off the beach and toward Grenoble, France. D-Day would be August 15, 1944. The more broad objective was to push the Germans out of southern France and link-up with Patton's 3rd Army who was rushing eastward across northern Europe. The more immediate and tactical mission of the 45th was to capture the coastal towns of St. Maxime and Villepey.

Transport ships are loaded for the invasion of Southern France in August, 1944. Jack left Italy for the last time on August 9, 1944 aboard LST 321 and landed on the French Riviera near St. Maxime, France on August 15, 1944.

DAD'S HONORS

Dad never spoke of the war heroes. In the 45th Eight there were plenty. Eight Thunderbirds were awarded the Congressional Medal of Honor, four of which were won for gallantry and courage in action in the Italian Campaign. Neither Mom nor Dad ever spoke of the medals Dad received for action in Italy. It was not until after Mom's death, while combing through her scrapbooks that we discovered that Dad was awarded the Bronze Star. On July 25, 1944, in the "staging area," most likely near Pozzuoli, before sailing for southern France, Dad was decorated with the Bronze Star by Major General Eagles, commanding General of the 45th. The citation reads in part as follows:

> *"Jack L. Neville 2830236 FA Master Sergeant . . . for meritorious service in combat July 10, 1943 to April 28, 1944, in Sicily and Italy. Master Sergeant Neville's unusual initiative and organizational ability have been instrumental in his combat section maintaining its high efficiency throughout the Sicilian and Italian Campaign. His remarkable abilities and untiring efforts are worthy of praise. Entered military service from Oklahoma City."*

Considerable and unsuccessful efforts were made to research and identify what specific acts Dad performed to earn this decoration. What occurred seems forever lost to the ages. However the citation spans the period of time from the division's landing in Sicily to a point in time approximately three weeks from the Anzio breakout. This period obviously included the battle at the Sele-Calore River near Salerno and the German counterattack at Anzio. Whoever wrote the words of the citation captured Dad perfectly. "Unusual initiative" and "untiring efforts" described much of Dad's persona. When the Monroe Elementary School Redbirds needed a baseball field, he built it. When fledgling Leland Equipment Co. struggled, he went to Japan and Alaska to open new markets. Who knows how many times we were were hauled out of bed at the crack of dawn to go to Adair and fish the Spavinaw. Mike Gonzalez, curator of the 45th Infantry Division Museum finally concluded that Dad's award itself was unusual–"it must have been a hell of a plan carried out in extraordinary fashion." The other interesting bit of family lore taken from the citation is found in Dad's handwritten note to Mom at the top of the citation.

> *Beetle, this medal was presented to me on or about July 26, in the staging area before sailing for S. France by the C.G. of the division.*
>
> *Love*
> *Jack*

None of us ever conceived that Dad had a nickname for Mom, much less if he did that it would be "Beetle." How or why he came up with this name is beyond the brothers. We never heard Dad refer to Mom as Beetle. From reading early telegrams from Camp Barkeley and the few notes in the scrapbook written by Dad, it was a nickname of some duration, and quite clearly an expression of affection.

As for the medal itself, it has never been found. Dad's note inferentially suggests the possibility that he sent the medal home through the mail to Mom. On the other hand, Dad could have kept the medal with him throughout the last remaining months of the war, only to lose it in the confusion and hysteria of moving through France and Europe. The possibilities of the medal's ultimate demise are endless speculation, yet its absence tells another story about Mom and Dad. Dad obviously was proud of the Bronze Star. He clearly wanted Mom to share the moment, knowing it would make her feel better in her time of loneliness while he was away. Mom went to extraordinary lengths to preserve the meaningful and, to her, really important memorabilia from the war pictures of family, of Camp Pine, Camp Barkeley, Harry and Maxine, Christmas cards, and on and on. It was not so much that the Bronze Star was unimportant or insignificant, but in the end neither of their thoughts were of war-time decoration. Dad's Bronze Star was never the subject of conversation, and neither was Mom's nickname, "Beetle."

At the close of July, 1944, the Thunderbird's Italian Campaign was coming to an official end as they readied for the invasion of Southern France. It was only fitting that those who distinguished themselves in this great campaign be recognized. On the eve of Operation Dragoon, the real heroes, the ones who paid the ultimate price for freedom were not forgotten. On July 30, 1944, General Meyer gathered his Division Artillery together for an emotional and inspirational tribute to those who lost their lives or were forever missing in action in Italy. Grateful they were finally leaving Italy, the Thunderbirds prayed for better days ahead. Strengthened by thoughts of home, and of those who would not go home, the 45th was ready to reek havoc on the Germans on the French Riviera.

Like checkers on a board, the division moved from place to place, queing up on the Italian west coast for departure from Italy. On August 1, 1944, Division Artillery moved to an area 30 miles north of Naples with the rest of the division returning to the embarkation area near the town of Pozzuoli. By August 6, Jack and the Division Artillery CP had moved into the "Texas Area" near Pouzoulli where now, all together, the Thunderbirds waited for the orders to combat load for France.

The Thunderbirds did not have to wait long to board ship. The next day, the Infantry Regiments loaded onto transports and assault craft. The division, once again at full strength, would sail to France in 22 LSTs, 34 LCTs, four APs, two AKs, and nine Liberty Ships. The U.S.S. Biscayne would serve as the division's flagship. For Jack, the Division Artillery CP did not step off Italian soil for two more days. At 8:00 p.m., on August 9, Jack left Italy for the last time in the war. Division Artillery CP boarded LST 321 at Pouzoulli. Other elements of the artillery boarded LST 322 and the British transport ship, Ascania. At long last, the Italian Campaign was over for Jack as LST 321 pushed off the dock.

Once at sea, the division command confirmed the obvious. The public address system on LST 321 announced that the Thunderbirds had received orders for another seaborne invasion in southern France. The division was headed for its rendezvous point to meet the rest of the invasion armada off the coast of Torre Ammunizicta, Italy. Once there, the 45th dropped anchor to wait on the rest of the invading force, the United States 3rd Infantry Division , and the 36th Infantry Division. By August 12, the entire Dragoon force had gathered and at 4:00 p.m. the course was set for the French Riviera.

As the division chugged its way toward the coast of St. Maxime, the usual pre-invasion preparatory bombardment commenced with great fury, essentially signaling to the Germans the location of the attack. In the early morning hours of August 14 and 15, a staggering aerial bombardment blanketed the coast from St. Tropez to Cannes designed to knock out the deadly German artillery positions. In the early morning hours the 45th's task force crept close to the beach as the sun cracked the horizon. As they would later say, it was a beautiful day for an invasion. The weather was perfect, cloudy and cool. As the sun rose Jack grabbed his binoculars and, with the rest of the S-3 section, rushed to the 321's port side railing. As the sky broke behind them, it was an awesome sight. From 7:00 a.m. to 7:30 a.m. on August 15, heavy bombers unleashed their loads on the beaches assigned to the 157th, 180th, and 179th. Then, as the Army Air Corps was passing over the beaches, the Navy destroyers ran in close to shore to lose a forty-minute bombardment on the shoreline and hills just beyond the landing area. Jack fixed his glasses on the hills above St. Maxime to find the location of any German return fire. Not altogether surprising at this stage in the proceeding, none came. As Jack continued to scan the beaches hoping to locate any enemy return fire positions, the invasion went off like clockwork. By 7:49 a.m., the infantry regiments were fully loaded and racing toward the beach. At 8:00 a.m., the 157th hit the beach and rapidly advanced for St. Maxime. The 180th, on the right flank of the 157th, headed for St. Aygulf with the 179th right behind them. As had become the custom with McClain, Jack went ashore with General Meyer and others of the Division Artillery Headquarters staff to stake out the Division Artillery CP and await the arrival of the rest of the Division Artillery. To great relief and surprise,

In August of 1944, the Thunderbirds hit the beaches near St. Maxime in Southern France. After the Battle of Memiux, Jack, second from right, Frosty Munson, far right, and Harry Balkum, far left, celebrated at the division's enlisted men's club.

the Thunderbirds encountered little to no resistance. By 3:00 p.m., the entire Division Artillery was on the French Riviera at St. Maxime, France. By the end of the day on the 15th, the Thunderbirds had secured their initial objectives with Jack located at the Division Artillery CP, just northeast of St. Maxime, ironically in a German hospital. The History of the 45th Division Artillery recorded the relative ease of the southern France invasion.

> " . . . the landing came off without a hitch."
> " . . . the movement was inland, swift, and orderly."

If the run for Rome after the break-out was a war-form of the Italian Grand Prix, the advance off the French coastline was equal to the Daytona 500. In the next seventeen days, the command post for the 45th Infantry Division would be moved eleven times as the Seventh Army raced northward to link up with Patton's Third Army. By mid-August, the German troops in France were not concentrated in any substantial line of defense, but rather widely dispersed. Incredibly helpful to the Allies were the French Resistance, and the Force Francaises de l'Interievr, FFIs, who located the German pockets of resistence for the Allies. For Jack, compared to Italy, the move north was more of a truck ride than a fight like the division had experienced the past year. In fact, through August of 1944, the Artillery's shelling of the Germans was comparatively light with only 6,648 rounds fired that month–hardly one day's worth at Anzio.

The "Thunderbirds" move north out of St. Maxime, France on August 16, 1944.

Only three days after landing, the Division Artillery CP moved twice to Salernes and Taverns for the division's attack on Barjols, approximately 40 miles north of St. Maxime. The next day, Barjols fell. Two days later the CP was moved again to Le Puy to support the attack against elements of the 11th Panzer Division. Just east of Grenoble, 1,000 Germans were taken prisoner. In two days Jack rumbled through Cadenet, Lauris, and Lairmarin. On August 23, Grenoble, France, many times the host city to world class skiing events and Olympic Winter Games, fell to the 36th Infantry Division pushing inward from the 45th's right flank.

The move northward gathered more momentum as reports of the Allies' advance on Paris flowed in. French partisans in Paris openly were shooting at the Germans in the streets. Hitler ordered the city burned and destroyed, but his own troops refused to obey. On August 25, 1944, the German garrison surrendered and the Allies triumphantly paraded through the Arc de Triumphe with Paris now a free city.

As the 179th moved in to Grenoble to replace elements of the 36th Infantry Division, Jack's Division Artillery sprinted a war-time incredible seventy-five miles in one day, one of its longest moves in combat. By now, Division Artillery and the Thunderbirds were moving so far, so fast, that they were out running their supply lines.

Only eight days after Dragoon's landing, it was becoming obvious that the Germans were running for the "Vaterland." The 45th however was in hot pursuit, knowing that the sooner they caught the Germans, the sooner they had the next big fight, the sooner they could go home. The division rolled through town after town to the cheers, flowers, and kisses of the now-liberated French people. Many of the newly-freed villages and towns, not much larger than Adair, Oklahoma, only provoked memories of the Eby General Store and the farmers and ranchers who came to Neville & Co. hoping Bart Neville would extend just one more month of credit for flour, food, and clothes. The small-town French had not suffered through a depression era 1930s, but they had nonetheless been smothered by German soldiers who stole and confiscated their goods and products to support their occupation. Bart Neville, Rosa, and Jack's eight brothers and sisters would not have taken kindly to hostile troop occupation by German forces in Adair. As Jack motored through southern France, certainly every opportunity was taken for French wine and other liberation-amenities, but for the most part, the game plan was refuel, and move out.

This map reflects the advance of the 7th Army through Southern France with the 45th in the center moving from St. Maxime to Grenoble.

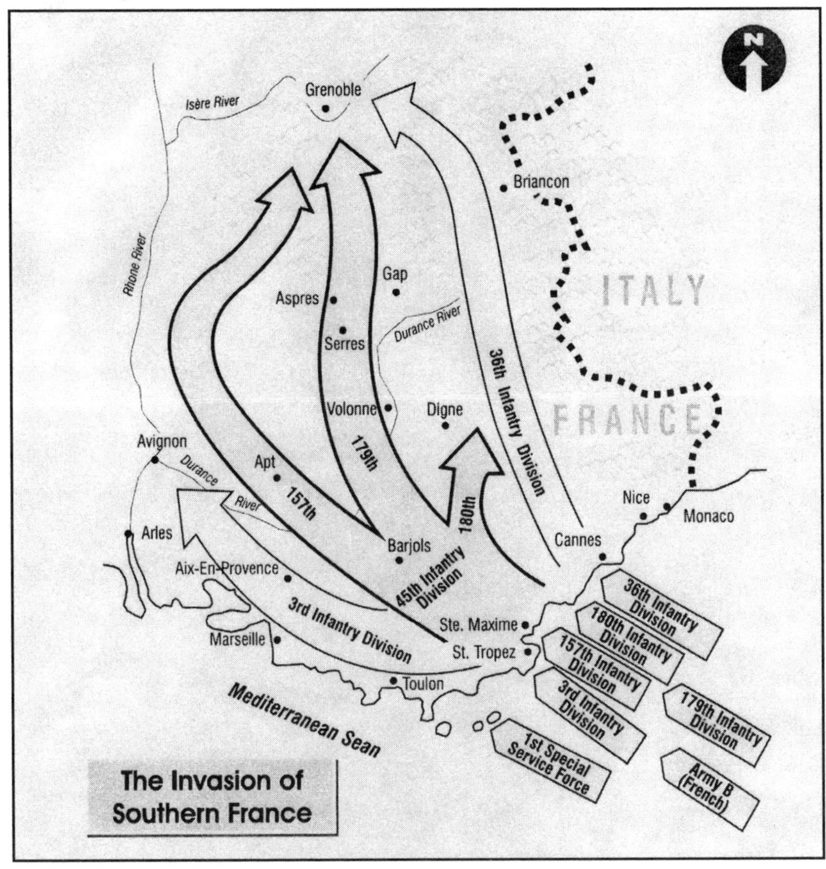

On down the road, Division Artillery continued northward through Gap, Crest, and Briancon. At the town of Chambre, the 179th took another 1,000 prisoners and continued the march. As Oklahoma City University started fall classes, the Thunderbirds rolled into Lyon, France, and Memiux on September 1. Elements of the 11th Panzer Division attempted to slow the advance at Memiux. It did not take long. The so-called "Battle of Memiux" was over September 2, 1944, and the Thunderbirds set their sights on Bourg, France, 20 miles to the north. By September 4, the Germans were routed out of Bourg and with 4,781 enemy captured, representing eight German Divisions and 12 Luftewaffe units, the German occupation of Southern France continued to disintegrate. The movement was so swift that the Thunderbirds were far ahead of the operation's schedule. Once the division had reached Bourg, the Thunderbirds had steam-rolled the Germans for 318 miles since landing August 15.

This map reflects the division's movement through Southern France.

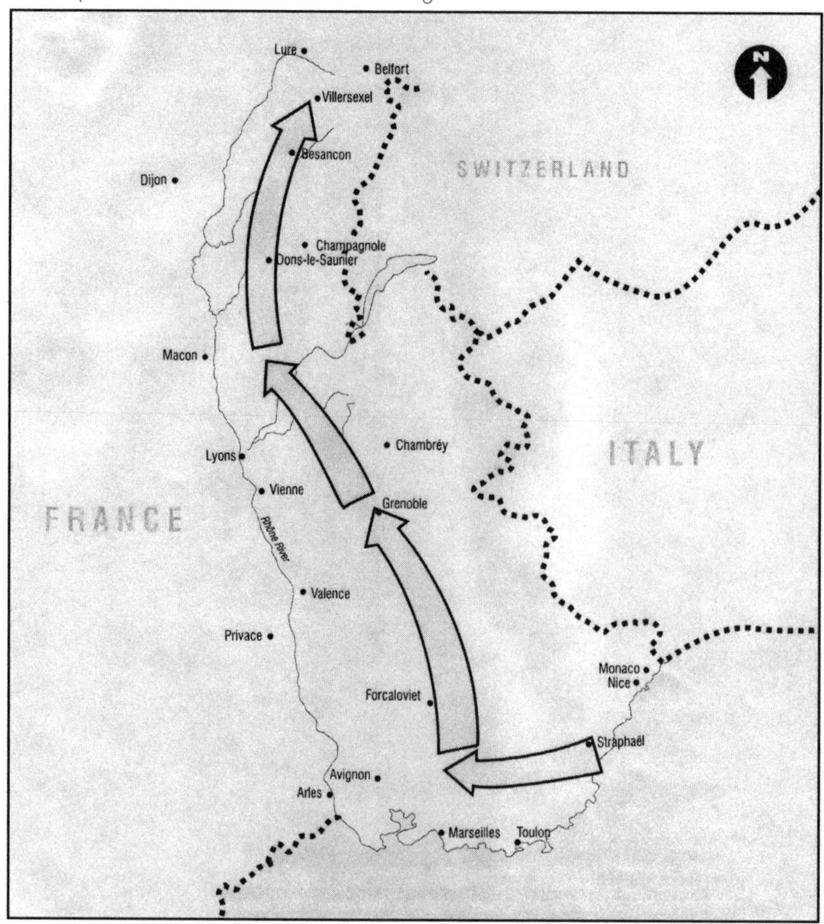

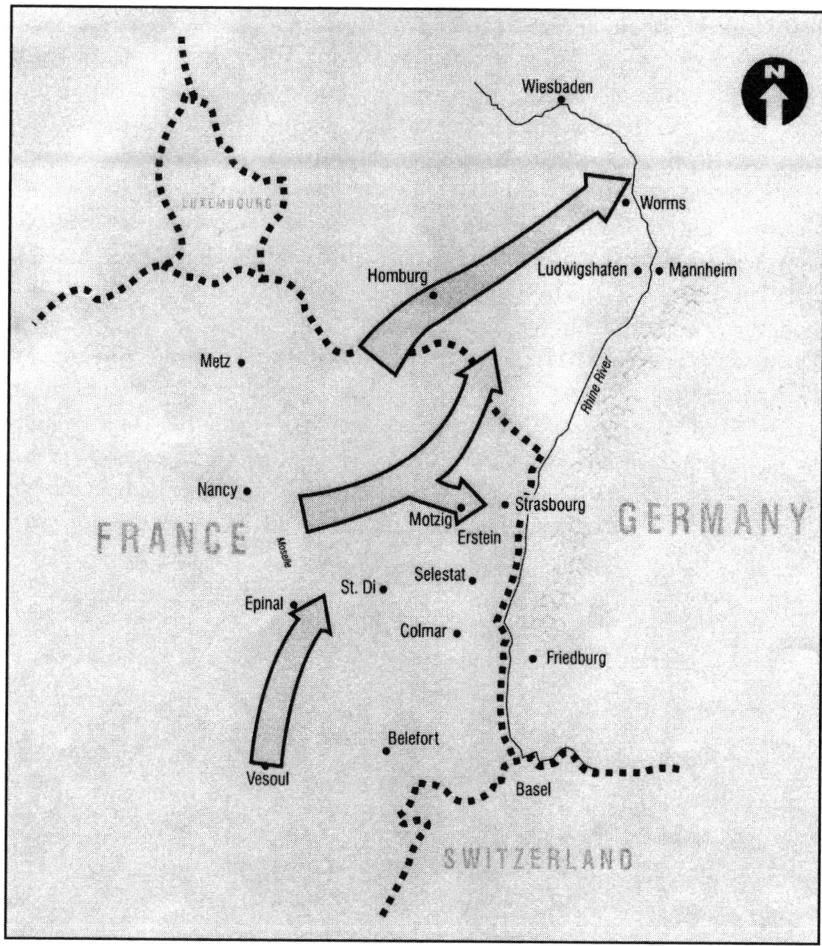

After crossing the Moselle River near Epinal the division split forces advancing on Bitche and Strasbourg, as well as Homburg and Worms to the north, crushing the infamous Maginot Line and Seigfried Line along the way.

With the Germans retreating north, the next attack came at Baumes-les Dames. Surrounding the town, the Division Artillery shot the Germans out of town and by September 9, Baumes was in the hands of the 45th. Two days later, the Thunderbirds ran into a "hornet's nest" of Germans at the town of Abbenans. Division Artillery again surrounded the town and blasted the Germans away.

On September 12, one of the principal objectives of Dragoon was accomplished. Elements of Patch's 7th Army linked up with Patton's Third Army at Chatellon-sur-Seine, near Dijon and 18,000 Germans were taken prisoner. The significance of this event goes largely unnoticed in the histories of the war in the European Theatre of operations. For the first time in the war the Allies had formed a single line of force that ran from the Normandy Coast south to the French Riviera. The Allies now had a line of supply and material that could flow from both the northern ports of Europe, like Antwerp, as well as the southern ports in the French Riviera. Joined from south to north, the tidal wave of Allied power was poised to surge eastward toward Germany.

Jack and the Division Artillery continued to roll on Chateau de Bournel across the Dowds River and toward Geney. Once again, the speed of the Division Artillery's movement had out distanced their supply lines. The chase for the Germans slowed up to wait for the service companies to hurry ammunition, fuel, and supplies to the front.

On September 16, 1944, the Thunderbirds were realigned for a turn and attack northeasterly. The 45th was now to advance and take the town of Epinal, a city of 27,000 people along the Moselle River and close to the Vosges Mountains. In support of the attack on Epinal, Jack and the Division Artillery CP moved to an area near Bain Les Bains and established their CP on September 20. The division started its assault on Epinal the next day. The 180th moved

On September 22, 1944, a 45th M-4 Sherman tank crossed the Moselle River near Arches, France.

directly at Epinal, while the 157th on the left struck at Igney and the 179th on the 180th's right flank hit Arches. The attack was enough to force the Germans across the Mosselle River at Epinal. As the Germans retreated they blew every bridge possible to slow the advance of the 45th. Division Artillery struggled for a fix on the German columns retreating. Once again, Captain William McKay threw caution to the wind in getting his Piper Cub observation plane airborne above the battlefield. With fire all around the plywood plane, McKay radioed to the Division Artillery CP the German position. McKay's radio transmissions allowed Division Artillery to blast the retreating Germans column to pieces. As Jack listened to the excited reports coming in from McKay, evidencing the destruction of Germans running out of Epinal, his plane was hit by German fire. The S-3 staff looked at each other in disbelief as the radio told of McKay's plane spiraling downward. In one last effort to save himself, McKay jumped to his death from the plane. For Jack and S-3 it was a staggering loss. The man who had tempted the odds at Anzio by getting his small plane airborne, the man who spotted Von MacKensen's 3,000-man force at the Factory staying over the battlefield to radio the enemy's position, and the man whose courage under fire may well have saved the day in Italy was dead. On September 24, Epinal fell to the 45th and on the 25th, Division Artillery moved across the Mosselle River free from German fire.

The Germans were now running so fast that they were leaving their belongings behind. With the fall of Epinal, the 45th captured 15 German loco-

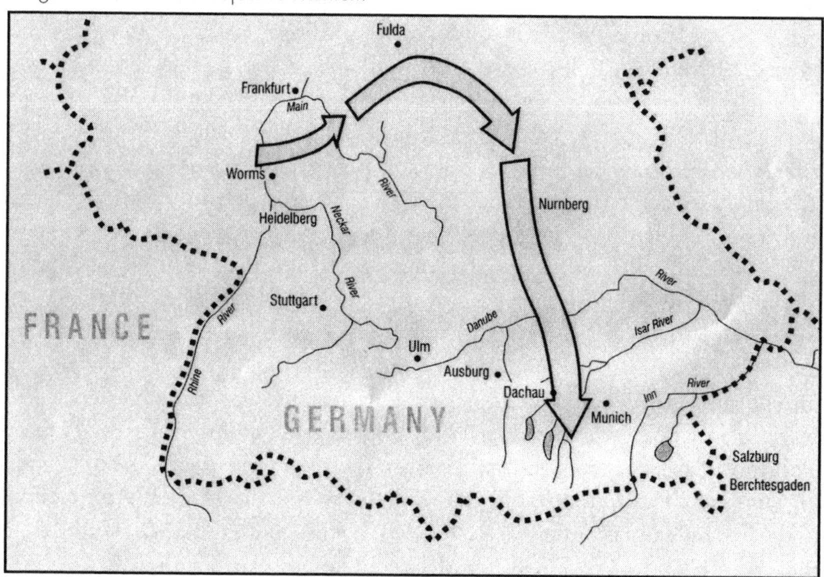

From Worms, the Thunderbirds moved eastward with very bitter fighting in Aschaffenburg and Bamberg before they were ordered by General Patch to pivot southward to Nuremberg with the ultimate objective Munich.

motives, 11 coal cars, and substantial stashes of ammunition. These seizures were both timely and important to the division. The Thunderbirds were still moving at such a fast clip that the Army supply points were well behind the advance. By September 23, the division's service company trucks were traveling distances between 105 to 465 miles for supplies. Necessity became the mother of invention as the Thunderbirds appropriated and put to their own use the German supplies and ammunition.

As Jack and Division Artillery pushed into the foothills of the Vosges Mountains, the first signs of another European winter set in. The speed of advance was being held up by heavy rain and the inevitable mud that plagued the road network. Additionally, while the Germans were retreating at a high rate of speed, they were fighting an aggressive withdrawal. The roads and fields east of Epinal were heavily mined and the tall pine trees were strategically felled by explosives in order to delay pursuit of the fleeing Germans. On September 27, Division Artillery found themselves trapped in a minefield just short of the village of Deyvillers. Jack was lucky again. At 9:00 a.m., a Division Artillery truck struck a mine and was demolished. No one was killed, but five were seriously injured. By the evening, Division Artillery CP pitched their tents in Deyvillers and readied themselves to support the infantry attack against the towns of Grandvillers and Rambervillers. Again, the Thunderbirds made short work of it. On September 30, the 179th and 180th occupied Grandvillers. On the same day, Division Artillery laid a fifteen-minute barrage on Rambervillers. Rambervillers fell on October 1 as the 157th surrounded the town and routed the Germans from the village's streets and buildings. For Jack, it was time to pack up and move again.

By early October the Nazis were retreating to fixed fortifications along the Meurthe River, four miles east of the Montagne River. For the Thunderbirds, their advance was slowed by stiff resistence along the Montagne River and through the Vosages Mountain foothills. Additionally, the division was extended far beyond its points of supply and it was necessary to pause and allow the supply trucks to catch up with the vitals of the battlefield. Becoming more and more problematic was the weather. Heavy rain, cold, and mud bogged down the entire division. Along the Montagne River, the Germans were fighting for every town and village. To slow the Thunderbird juggernaut, the Nazis were now forcing the citizens of these small French towns to evacuate into the hills of the Vosages Mountains, turning their life-long villages and homes into nothing more than armed barricades, eventually destroyed. In essence, the Nazis were causing the destruction of decades and centuries of rural France. This forced evacuation of the French from their homes proved to be the Nazi's undoing. While the country French were forced to seek refuge and protection in the foothills and mountains, the farmers, bakers, and shop owners infiltrated their way back to the Thunderbird lines. Having lived in these areas most of their lives, the Frenchmen knew every trail, building, haystack, nook, and cranny of the countryside. Having been kicked out of their homes and businesses, they knew the location and strength of the German troop positions. Having made their way back to the American lines they were only too happy to disclose this vital information to the Thunderbirds. For Jack and the S-3 staff in Division Artillery the French citizens had become the forward observers for the artillery. One of the better episodes of French resolve is chronicled in *The Fighting Forty-Fifth*. It was not often that Division Artillery could play a tactical role in the liberation of American prisoners of war, but in October of 1944, they did. In mid-October, displaced French citizens told Division Artillery of American and French prisoners of war being held in the city jail of St. Die. Officers of the Division Artillery, agents of the Office of Strategic Services. forerunner to the CIA, and the FFI collaborated and devised a daring escape plan. Division Artillery fired a concentration of 155 shells near the jail. The explosions scattered the German guards momentarily as OSS agents and French citizens rushed in, overpowered the remaining guards, and freed more than 40 prisoners while the 45th's Artillery continued to provide diversionary fire. The success of the rescue provided a tremendous boost in morale within the Division Artillery.

Jack must have marveled at the French people so eager to tell of the enemy's size, strength, and location in their hometown, all the time knowing that the places they had lived and worked forever would most likely be destroyed in the fight. As he studied their faces, they were really no different than the town's people of Vinita, Wewoka, Elk City, Clinton, Pink, or Adair. They had built a life scratching out a living in the small rural countryside, fundamentally content with life, only to see their freedom and way of life stolen by the Nazis and the war. So eager were the French farmers and citizens of rural France to see the Nazi menace forever eradicated, that they were willing to sacrifice the buildings, schools, shops, churches, and businesses of their towns and villages so that the evil of it all would be run back to Germany. The French could rebuild their streets, shops, and homes, but they wanted their way of life forever liberated and restored. The Thunderbirds had a kinship of sorts for the farmers and villagers of southern France that added to the resolve to fight on.

For the first two weeks of October, the Thunderbirds pressed their attack against the Germans along the Montague River. On October 15, 1944, the Division Artillery moved into St. Die, or what was left of it. For the first time, Jack saw the evidence of what the Nazis could do to the non-combatants of countries they had occupied. In reprisal for the jail break that rescued both Americans and French from the city jail, the German 716th burned and destroyed the entire town.

In preparation for the attack across the Montague, Division Artillery calibrated their sites on Bru and Jeanmenil. The Germans were heavily packed

In November of 1944, the Thunderbirds hit the famous Maginot Line in Southern France. The fighting was fierce, but the Germans were pushed back. Two Thunderbirds stand in the ruins of the Maginot Line near Wissemburg. By mid-December of 1944, the battle for Southern France was over.

into both towns until the Artillery carefully massed the deadly TOTs on both towns. The Germans were no longer massing their forces along strategic natural barriers such as rivers and hills, rather they continued to defend from the towns and cities they occupied. The 45th and Division Artillery were killing Germans, but in the process decimating French villages that dotted the countryside. On October 23, the division crossed the Montagne, the town of Montagne fell, and by October 30 Bru, Jeanmenil, and St. Benoit were in the hands of the Thunderbirds. By October 30, Jack was encamped at the Division Artillery CP at Autry. In less than two weeks, three French towns had been reduced to ashes to get at the retreating Germans. The German 21st Panzer Division and the 716th Infantry Division dug in to wait on the next Thunderbird assault. The Thunderbirds did not waste much time with the 21st and 716th. By November 3, the division had crossed the Meurthe River, with the 45th's left flank anchored at Baccarat. There, the Division Artillery CP staked their tents.

By November 8, and Thanksgiving only a few days away, the Thunderbirds had been in Europe 542 days, 352 of which had been spent at the front. After 86 days of continuous action, having captured 11,000 German prisoners, the division was replaced in the line by the newly-arrived 100th Infantry Division and moved back to rest areas near Bains-les Bains. However, rest and relaxation was not in the cards. Division Artillery remained in the line to support the 100th Infantry Division. Rather than pack his bags for the truck ride to the west, Jack stuffed his duffle bag as the Division Artillery CP was moved to Luneville to support the continued attack toward Strasborg. With the 100th successfully moving through Phalsbourg and Savern northwest of Strasbourg, Jack finally got his first break since the St. Maxime landing. At 6:00 p.m., November 16, the Division Artillery was relieved from combat duty to rest, refit, and resupply for a few days in Lunneville. He would need it. As German soil drew nearer by the day, the assault on the Maginot Line was about to begin.

During the 1930s, the vaunted Maginot Line was built by the French after World War I at a cost of $200 Million, then an unheard of amount of a country's resources. Named after the French Minister of Defense Andre Maginot, it consisted of tank traps, pill boxes, barbed wire, and gun emplacements, some of which were encased in 10 feet of concrete. In all, it was an 87- mile stretch of forts designed specifically to keep the Germans out. It did not work. French warfare was a remnant of World War I. By World War II, stagnant lines of defense were outdated. "Case Yellow" was the German plan for the defeat of France. Simply put, the Germans Blitzkerig would fly over and go around the Maginot Line with their tanks, airplanes, and 117 Divisions. In 1940, German Army Group C under General Wilhelm Ritter Von Leeb struck at the Maginot Line. Thought to be impregnable, Army Group C made short work of it and early in World War II, the Maginot Line fell into German hands. Directly across and east of the Maginot Line, at some points as close as 10 miles, was the German counterpart to the Maginot Line, the Siegfried Line. In 1939, the Siegfried Line had become a substantial defensive obstacle that guarded entry into Germany. There were thousands of concrete bunkers, some as wide as 21 feet and as high as 18 feet with multiple levels. The bunkers were constructed to ensure that each had inter-locking fields of fire with the others. In front of the bunkers were pill boxes and mine fields with heavy barbed-wire barriers. There were miles of anti-tank ditches. The Siegfried Line had an imposing aura to it, but it suffered from the same deficiencies as the Maginot Line; it could be outflanked, and the bunker system picked off one at a time. Additionally, the now awesome firepower of the United States Artillery could be brought to bare on the bunkers, forcing the Germans to remain underground as infantry units worked their way forward in a frontal assault. It would be dirty business, but the Siegfried Line, formidable as it appeared, was not impregnable.

Jack's rest lasted only six days. The division was alerted for movement on November 22, 1944. On Thanksgiving Eve, Arnote summoned the S-3 staff together for the next plan and operation. The XV Corps was to attack the Maginot Line, with the 45th Infantry Division to assault the forts along the line at the town of Mutzig, in what the maps labeled as the Colmar Pocket. For Jack, his second Thanksgiving in Europe was spent in a truck chowing down on K-rations and C-rations as Division Artillery set up camp in a field between Blamond and Richeval to support the Infantry Regiments who moved to Romansville in preparation for the attack at Mutzig. In the attack on the Maginot Line, the Thunderbirds methodically went about their work. Division Artillery pounded the bunkers as elements of the Infantry Regiments scratched and crawled their way through the mine fields and under the barbed wire to drop their grenades into the portholes of the Maginot bunkers. Other Infantry units flanked the now German bunkers. Once making their way to the bunker itself, grenades were dropped down the ventilation shafts causing the Germans to promptly vacate. As the Germans ran from the bunkers, the 45th saw to it that this day was their last. One by one, like dominoes, the bunkers fell ripping giant holes in the Maginot Line. After three days of intense action, Mutzig fell on November 25, 1944. With the Mutzig objective achieved, the Division Artillery CP moved to Suherlenheim and then in a twelve-mile trip Jack trucked it to Bouxwiller. Slowly but surely, the Nazis were being pushed off the Maginot Line and out of France. However, despite withdrawal, the Germans were still fighting as pockets of determined resistence were developing along the Thunderbird line of march.

Setting aside possibilities of being ambushed along the roads leading to Venafro, Italy, shot at Salerno, being both shot at and shelled at Anzio, and as much time as Jack spent in a truck or jeep on the narrow roads of Italy and France, it was amazing that he was not hit by the shrapnel of an exploding mine triggered by the wheel of the truck. A German mine did not know the difference between a General and a sergeant. Pure luck meant the difference in touching off a mine, or avoiding its explosion of steel that could rip off a leg, arm, or worse, kill you. On November 30, General William Eagles' luck ran out. Now with the Division Artillery CP at Bouxwiller, to support the division's move eastward toward Engwiller, the Germans somehow found the resources to mass a 20-tank and infantry counterattack in an attempt to break the eastward drive of the Thunderbirds. As the fight started, Division Artillery was able to put their hands on a German Artillery forward observer who got himself so far forward that he was captured. The prisoner did not have to talk. After being searched inside and out, the German had tucked away in his pants map overays of the German positions. Quickly, the Division Artillery put together a cocktail of deadly TOTs on the German position. The German attack never started. Eagles, like Middleton and McClain, did not spend a lot of time in the rear areas. He was found as often at the front as he was in the back. In the melee of the thirtieth, Eagles' jeep hit a land mine, knocking him out of the jeep, and, sadly for his followers, out of the war. Like checkers moving forward, with the German counterattack stopped, Jack's CP moved into a field in the vicinity of Printzheim to wait for the next move. As Dad climbed aboard the two-and-a-half ton truck, he could only ask himself how it could happen to General Eagles, and not happen to Sergeant Neville. For Jack, it was the fortune of war, he had thankfully dodged another one.

With German resistance fading, Division Artillery laid a heavy artillery path in front of the infantry regiments. Engwiller, Kindeviller, and Bitschoffen all fell in succession as the Thunderbird morale soared. As Jack's S-3 section broke out the maps at the end of the month to plot the next session, excitement ran through everyone.

"The division was now precariously close to German soil."

At the end of November by Jack's map, the Vaterland was only 40 miles down the road. Things were moving very fast. By December 3, the division took Zinswiller and Meitesheim. On the more eastern flank, Mertzwiller fell on December 5 and by December 9 the Thunderbirds were 20 miles further east at Niederbrom.

By December 12, the Thunderbirds were on the outskirts of Lembach in the heart of the Maginot Line, a key city controlling a vital pass into Germany. Col. Dwight Funk, commanding the 158th Field Artillery, radioed Col. Walter O'Brien of the 157th Infantry, " . . . Say the word and we can toss a concentration into Germany."

O'Brien responded, "fire away."

Thus the first shots of the 45th were fired into Germany. The assault on Germany was only beginning. On December 13, the forward observers of Division Artillery had the artillery of the German 245th Infantry Division located and bracketed. By now General Meyer's S-3 section had TOTs down to an art form and with the German position pin-pointed, it was no contest. The 45th Division Artillery wiped out the German artillery support on December 13, 1944.

Only one day later, the Thunderbirds had control of Lembach, and the battle for southern France was essentially over. Now, the guys from Oklahoma were ready to jump into Germany. Morale sky rocketed at the thought that the end was in site. For Jack, the Division Artillery CP remained in Niederbrom approximately 20 miles to the west and south of Lembach, to await the inevitable beginning of the end. Jack Neville was about to invade Germany.

REFLECTION THANKSGIVING DAY WAR TREASURERS

There is not much written of "looting" by the American troops and the 45th Infantry Division in particular, but it nonetheless certainly happened. This type of "souvenir" hunting took on many forms but the uniqueness and ingenuity of Dad's efforts should be recorded. We brothers never heard the mention of Rene Jules Lalique. He was a Frenchman born in 1860 in the village of Ay in the Champagne region of France. Lalique came from a family of jewelers and goldsmiths. In the 1900s Lalique developed very special skills with glasswork and crystal. His artistry with crystal in particular became world recognized, and to this day Lalique crystal is considered a coveted prize. Prominently displayed in a dark oak hutch in the dining room of the 57th street house in Tulsa were four prominent and beautiful pieces of Lalique crystal of considerable size, and twelve wine glasses of unusual design. We brothers were aware of their presence, but I suppose because we were "guys" our curiosity never prompted inquiry of their significance nor their history. They did not, however, go unnoticed by Bob's wife, Judy, at one of the Tulsa Thanksgiving dinners. Mom always made sure that the Lalique wine glasses were put to good use on special occasions, especially Thanksgiving and Christmas. Given the rather raucous nature of the festivities, their use on the 4th of July was absolutely forbidden. As we sat at the Thanksgiving table waiting for the pumpkin pie to come out of the oven, Judy twirled her wine glass of Kendall Jackson Chardonnay, with the question to Mom, "where did you get these beautiful wine glasses?" Both Mom and Dad broke out with grins and laughter at the question, with Mom rather quickly responding "Jack stole them." With this, the caper was uncovered and what would have been an otherwise dull conversation about wine glasses turned into a spirited cross-examination of Dad's extra-curricular war-time activities. Richard, Bob, and I barraged Dad with question after question, accusations of being a "looter," "thief," and "robber-baron." Dad's weak attempt to defend himself was to no avail as Mom roared with laughter to the point of near tears. Dad's only pitiful defense was that he did not steal anything, but rather the Lalique crystal was "liberated from Nazi occupation." I reminded Dad that his defense was weaker than my own when caught stealing bubble gum from the Katz Drug Store at the age of seven. We were having so much fun poking fun at Dad, that the details of this alleged theft were never developed in any coherent fashion. Other than France being identified as the country, the actual crime scene was never revealed by Dad as he mightily professed a lack of recollection. Dad's memory lapse brought on another round of laughter as the thought of a branded thief not being able to recall the crime venue lacked any credibility. Nonetheless, he stuck to his guns.

After the first round of pumpkin pie with whip cream on top, Dad finally conceded that he and his pals nearly emptied the store front of a small glassware shop in one of the small towns that the division rolled through in southern France. Initially, Dad attempted to mitigate the circumstance, professing that he initially recognized the value of Lalique crystal and therefore was determined to capture it for "your mother." This brought a roar from Mom that forced Dad into further retreat. He had no idea that the crystal had value or history, all he knew was that it was beautiful enough to "finger" for Mom. We then reminded him that "Mom made me do it" was not much of a defense and that this tactic never worked for any of us. But, for Dad, it was enough for the Thanksgiving Day trial. Richard, being the most logical thinker of the group, then thought of the next logical question, "how did you get four pieces of large Lalique crystal and eight wine glasses from southern France back to Oklahoma during a world war?" After all, you could not just stick them on the back of the truck or jeep and expect them to survive. Now it was Mom's time to squirm a bit. By the fall of 1944, Jimmie Smith, Mom's brother-in-law, had joined the ranks of the 45th and was assigned as a truck driver with one of the service companies. Jimmie's route ran from the various points of supply directly to the division front lines, allowing Dad and Jimmie to occasionally hook up. They did so in a conspiratorial effort to get their wartime booty home. During the war it was the custom and practice of the truckers to name their trucks. Only creativity limited name selection which was usually stenciled on the side of the door in white paint, or as still goes on today, name plates were attached to the front or back of the truck. For Jimmie Smith, his vehicle was christened "Sick, Lame and Lazy." And, as Dad could not resist pointing out, over the vocal objection of Mom, the name of the truck perfectly described Jimmie's most dominant and admirable traits. In any event the twosome took great care to tightly pack the Lalique pieces in boxes stuffed with padding and put them in the front seat of Sick, Lame and Lazy. For Dad, he would not see the souvenirs until he returned home, and for Jimmie Smith, he worked his ill-named truck all the way back to the port of Marseille where he bribed a buddy of his to stowe them on board a ship headed for Hampton Roads, with instructions to mail the packages to Oklahoma City. Somehow, miraculously, the Lalique crystal and wine glasses survived the journey from southern France to Oklahoma City, arriving sometime in early 1945. To this day, they remain in the family, and 62 years later prominently displayed and still only used on special occasions. With the end of the very few wartime stories ever told, Richard could not help himself observing that no less than 5 or 6 felonies involving the misuse of government property had been committed in the episode. Now the lawyer in the group had to come to the aide of the accused. With the passages of decades, certainly the statute of limitation had passed. Dad was safe from prosecution. With this, we all adjourned to the living room. Detroit and Green Bay were about to kick-off.

The crystal tells yet another story. On Shawnee Street, I recall visiting the homes of friends whose fathers had fought in the great war. Often prominently displayed were rather exciting memorabilia that captured the eyes of a ten year old–guns, knives, swords, German helmets evidence of conflict and conquest. But for Dad, the only evidence of liberation that returned from Europe were the Lalique crystal and a small Nazi flag which was not discovered until March of 2000. As Dad sped through the southern France countryside, seizure of the trappings of death and destruction were not on his agenda. Rather than stop to claim an instrument of war and killing somewhere along the way, he paused long enough to retrieve something that would make Mom smile. With rather extraordinary effort and incredible luck, that crystal made it all the way from southern France to Oklahoma, safe and unbroken. And, so did Dad. Mom and Dad could both look at the beautiful pieces and remember a time gone by.

Looking back after all these years to that Thanksgiving, it was obvious that the Lalique crystal held a special place in the hearts of Mom and Dad. It was a fond memory of a tough and difficult time. Together with the seemingly out-of-place poster, "It's a Long Way to Tipperary," the George M. Cohen songs so loudly played on the 4th of July, and the Lalique crystal–all told a story about Mom and Dad's missing war years that they chose to remember in their own quiet way.

CHAPTER XXXIV
FALL, 1944, OKLAHOMA CITY

In August of 1944, the frustrating and agonizing wait in Oklahoma City went on. Although the press continued to report the increasing body count of Oklahoma casualties, the citizens were starting to see a slight glimpse of light at the end of the dark tunnel of war. In the dog-days of the Oklahoma summer, the allied forces in Europe were driving unopposed on Paris, France. United States tanks were moving swiftly for the City of Light. As WKY and KOMA Radio reported, Allied control of Paris, France and Florence, Italy were near collapse, the Nazis hung eight of their own general officers thought to be involved in the plot to kill Hitler. By mid-August, the Germans conceded Normandy as lost. For the first time in the war, Leota could see that the Germans were cracking under the weight of Allied power as the Army was being pushed back to the Vaterland. Despite the optimistic reports in the paper and over WKY Radio, the 45th Infantry Division once again had slipped into anonymity. While convinced the division was stashed in secrecy somewhere on the Italian mainland, the location of the division remained shrouded in secrecy and unreported by the print or broadcast media. A big lift to Leota came when Lt. Col. Hal Muldrow returned to Oklahoma City on a 30-day leave in early August, 1944. Muldrow's return was of special interest. Leota knew Muldrow commanded the 189th Field Artillery and accordingly had to be somewhat near Jack. At the least, Muldrow's words were the closest she could get to Jack. Muldrow had been there, he had been at awful Anzio and on August 8, 1944, he told the story to Oklahoma City. Hal Muldrow's report stirred every emotion from pride and exhilaration to concern and despair. Muldrow did not mince words as he explained to his home state that the artillery served the "Sunday punch" at Anzio. "It was all a matter of teamwork" he explained. On the other hand, Muldrow was candid about the plight of his men, and the artillery specifically, "the artillery suffered like the infantry." By August all of Oklahoma City knew of the carnage of the infantry ranks at Anzio. Leota knew by August that Jack had least survived the Anzio battle and by her best guesstimate was alive and well somewhere in southern Europe. Nonetheless, it was disconcerting to all Nevilles for Muldrow to equate the "suffering" of the artillery with that of the infantry. Muldrow's statement only served to reinforce belief and fears that no one was safe in this war, especially those within the fields of fire. Secondary to worrying whether Jack was dead or alive, were concerns of how he was doing. Could he sleep and eat with some relative degree of comfort? How does he keep his head up and not drown in the despair and depression that had to come with death all around? Muldrow provided the words the Oklahoma homefront needed to hear, "No one has to worry about the morale of the 45th"

And with that, Norman, Oklahoma's Hal Muldrow went back to war.

In the late summer, former Oklahoma boxer turned head football coach Dewey "Snorter" Luster took to the field with the University of Oklahoma Sooners, all fifty strong. It did not exactly catch the front page headline but the invasion of southern France did. In mid-August, Leota got the first hint of where the Thunderbirds were headed with *The Daily Oklahoman* reporting on August 13, 1944, "Invasion Looming in the Southern Zone." With Hal Muldrow home on leave it was unlikely that the division was part of the 5th Army's continued advance in Italy. With Muldrow's departure, the best bet was that Jack was in southern France with General Patch's 7th Army. Only two days after the LCIs hit the beach, the news reported the seizure of the French Riviera. Again, with sighs of some relief, Leota learned that Patch's command had taken 70 miles of beachhead with light casualties. Once again, the best source of information about the 45th came from those returning from the front. While the Allied Supreme Headquarters, for security reasons, still attempted to mask the movement and location of division level operations, those returning from Europe could not wait to tell their story. Only one day after the France invasion, Sergeant Cecil Creel, hospitalized in Chickasha, spilled the beans telling *The Daily Oklahoman* that the 45th was now with Patch's 7th Army. Sergeant Don Robinson confirmed the location of the Thunderbirds to all of Oklahoma City when he leaked it that the division was first to hit the beaches at St. Tropez, France. Those at home could not help but see the irony and comic of the Creel and Robinson reports–the generals would not reveal the whereabouts of the Thunderbirds, but the Sergeants and privates never hesitated to tell the homefront where the "boys" were once they got home. At least by late September of 1944, Leota could follow Jack's move through France knowing with some certainty that the Thunderbirds were with Patch's 7th Army.

As the Thunderbirds moved northward, reports continued to flow home that the division was encountering little resistence. Sergeant Robinson wrote home "It seemed like a furlough after Italy." While vague, "light resistence" did not provide much comfort to a skeptical wife at home waiting on her husband. "Light resistence" meant that the Germans still had rifles to shoot at the Thunderbirds. Leota did not see much "light" about a German that could shoot at Jack. The reports of "light casualties" did however provide a slight measure of comfort making it easier to go to work at the Douglas Plant.

A prideful diversion for Leota was found on October 4, when Geromino was officially christened as the Douglas Plant's 3,000th C-47.

For Leota, at the age of 24 and by necessity still living at home, life had to have had its moments. Sylvester Stauffer had a passion for politics and was vocal about the issues of the day. A day did not pass that Sylvester would not bang out a letter to his Congressman or Senator. In the fall of 1944, as the war in Europe heated up, so did the politics at home. In September of 1944, Sylvester, purportedly against any form of government control, saw it as a communist plot that the Oklahoma County District Attorney's office poured some 8,000 pints of whiskey into the sewers of Oklahoma City. High on Sylvester's list was Roosevelt's "OPA," the Office of Price Administration. As Sylvester saw it, the core of freedom itself was under assault when the OPA once again considered rationing coffee, and refused to increase the price of oil. Sylvester saw absolutely no humor in Leota's rather quiet observations that her father's politics, and conversation, were perhaps driven by the fact that he liked coffee, loved whiskey, and increasing the price of oil put money in Sylvester's pockets. Also un-American were the labor unions that remained active and hostile during the war. In early October, 50,000 workers went on strike in Detroit, Michigan. Strikes were not infrequent, and Sylvester cheered when a group of servicemen stormed a picket line aroused by a wartime work-stoppage at North American's Bomber Plant. Too proud to admit it, Sylvester Stauffer was incensed at the thought that war-time workers would stop working while he had a son-in-law still fighting in Europe.

Sylvester's rather libertarian view of politics was not without contradiction as Leota often pointed out. In mid-October the Social Hygiene Society proposed that all teenage girls in Washington, D.C. be returned home as they were "too immature to be running loose in Washington." Sylvester was in favor of this control proposal. But perhaps Sylvester's biggest shift away from his conservative political dogma came with the presidential election of 1944. Thomas E. Dewey, staunch conservative Republican Senator from New York decided to take on the powerful Roosevelt in one of the most vicious presidential elections in American history. In early October, Dewey accused the Roosevelt Administration of being backed by the Communists and that New Deal politics were creating a "corporate state." Dewey accorded Roosevelt with little respect for the war effort when he accused the President of failing to have an "intelligent" program for dealing with the invasion of Germany–Dewey proclaimed that the Americans were paying in blood for Roosevelt's idiocy. Dewey even made his way to the Municipal Auditorium in Oklahoma City to an audience of 3,500 and called for the restoration of integrity in the White House. He further accused Roosevelt of causing the death of many American soldiers by failing to prepare the country for war. The war between Gore and Bush, and Bush and Clinton in the 1990s, was tame in comparison to Dewey's attack on Roosevelt during 1944 war-time. Dewey's rhetoric proved a bridge too far for Sylvester Stauffer, and certainly for Leota. Both saw Dewey's rantings as nothing short of treason. The war could not be won with a divided house and both believed that if Hitler was to be defeated, a unified America was critical. Moreover, it could not help Jack, still fighting the war far away, for Dewey to label the Commander in Chief as unprepared, unintelligent, and perhaps worst of all, un-American. The boys in the field needed to know that their Commander in Chief was doing all that could be done and that he was behind them all the way. The cause was not helped by calling Roosevelt's Administration a bunch of Communists as it only played into Hitler's hand. Dewey, despite the Republican he was, had stepped across the line. In the only time Sylvester Stauffer would pull the lever for a Democrat, he voted for Roosevelt in the 1944 election. Of course, two days after the election, Mr. Stauffer was back on the Republican bandwagon assailing the OPA's refusal once again to increase the price of oil. For Leota, the decision to vote for Roosevelt was easy. She did not care about price controls or war-time production goals. She only cared about getting Jack back home alive. With the Allies near the German border, and with victory after victory piling up on the European battlefield, Leota thought Roosevelt was the man to get Jack home. On November 7, 1944, Franklin D. Roosevelt swamped Thomas E. Dewey and became the only three-term elected President in American history. Roosevelt carried the State of Oklahoma by a then incredible 75,000 votes.

In 1944, Leota saw the effects of men who fought in war. Jim Tunnel would never again be a watch-maker with one arm. Denny Morison would never play professional baseball with just one leg. Even survival had its costs that changed people's lives forever. More present as the war went on were those green Hudson sedans with United States Army stenciled in white on the side. If Leota saw one cruising down Classen she prayed it would not turn east on 42nd Street. Gene Neville's death was tough enough, she could not imagine if it were Jack. For many of the wives who waited and worried at home, family values were a product of the war. They loved and appreciated what they had and were determined and committed to keep it together if only they could get through the war.

The diversion to politics and the worry of war was entertainment, especially on the radio. By October of 1944, Leota's favorite was back on NBC Radio. Jack Benny was at it again, this time with Mary Livingston, Phil Harris, Rochester, and Abbott and Costello were on every Thursday night. Harry James and his Orchestra made a return trip to the Municipal Auditorium, and soldier-sailor-airman John Wayne once again transformed himself into a western hero in *Stage Coach* and Tall in the Saddle showing at the Uptown Theatre.

A World Series got to the Midwest and the St. Louis Cardinals won the Championship in the sixth game behind shortstop Marty Marion. Of lesser interest to Leota, Snorter Luster's Sooners were having a tough time losing not only to Texas, but to of all teams, the Norman Naval Air Station Zoomers, never mind that the Zoomers were loaded with former professionals who had been drafted and assigned to Norman. Perhaps the most unique oddity of the entire decade of the 1940s arrived on October 22, 1944. For the very first time, Oklahoma got a look at the electronic wizardry that would later come to dominate American life. In a tour through 19 cities sponsored by WKY, Oklahomans got their first look at television.

In the fall of 1944, the entire world was truly at war. Not only were substantial gains being made on the European battlefield, but the war in the Pacific Theatre was swinging in favor of the United States and its Allies. Despite the diversions of television, radio, entertainment, and sports, the war across the globe was in Leota's face every day. In October, General Douglas MacArthur's forces retook the Philippines, previously abandoned to the Japanese in the early stages of the war. The United States Navy trounced the Japanese Navy in the Battle of the Philippine Sea. While Jack, the United States Army, and the Allies were pushing into parts of Germany, B-24s were in the air bombing Tokyo. By the early fall of 1944, 5,000 tons of supplies per day were pouring into Naples and American's industrial might was turning out a rifle every 32 seconds and more than 11ships a day. In short, the good guys were starting to win and it was difficult to see how the forces of freedom could now be stopped.

Nonetheless, the determined Germans found the will to hold on. In October of 1944, the United States 1st Army gave the German forces occupying the 1,100-year-old city of Aachen the ultimate ultimatum–surrender or die. Hitler responded telling Aachen citizens and his troops to "stand and die." As the fanatical Nazis fought to the death, the ancient city, home of Charlamagne, was totally destroyed. Not known to Jack was the fact that the Thunderbirds would face their own Aachen, but on down the road in the southern German city of Aschaffenburg. After Aachen's annihilation, Leota woke up to news reports that Hitler had decreed that both young and old, women and children, would fight to the death as part of a newly-formed home guard to defend the Reich. By the fall of 1944, the Germans were killing their own heroes in blind allegiance to Hitler. German war hero Field Marshall Erwin Romel's death was reported as a result of wounds suffered when a United States fighter strafed his command car. In fact, Hitler's Gestapo and SS troops forced Romel's suicide believing he was part of the conspiracy to assassinate the Furher. Just before Thanksgiving, Dwight D. Eisenhower gave Leota a jolt of realism affirming America's worst fears by predicting that Germany would fight to the death.

For the 45th Infantry Division, with the battle for southern France over, the fight for Germany was about to begin. The road into Germany would be long and bloody. Ahead for the Thunderbirds was Aschaffenburg, Nuremberg, and the death camps of Dachau. It would be yet another Thanksgiving and Christmas without Jack.

While the four-month race through France was swift, it also was deadly. There were 20,181 Thunderbird casualties in France, 5,269 of whom were killed in action and another 1,449 missing in action.

REFLECTIONS KATZ DRUG STORE, OKLAHOMA CITY, SUMMER OF 1955

By the time my neighborhood pal, Richie Roth, and I reached the age of eight years old, our delinquency had graduated to a more sophisticated level. Rather than throwing rocks at cars, petty theft had now made its way onto our conspiratorial agenda. Located at the corner of 19th and Portland, the Katz Drug Store had an abundant supply of bubble gum and chocolate Hershey Kisses all wrapped and sitting out in large open bins. Katz usually had a special on Saturdays. For 1¢, you could get two. Richie and I reasoned however that it would be more fun and challenging to grab a handful for free, rather than fork over the 5¢ that the both of us could scrounge together for ten pieces. Stealing bubble gum and Hershey Kisses took a great deal of planning and stealth. First, our wardrobe for the occasion had to be just right. Your shorts had to have large pockets in which to stuff your loot; and you could not wear your shirt tucked into your shorts, it had to be bloused out and over your pockets to achieve maximum concealment. Only a stupid thief would try to walk out of the store with the goods actually in your hand. Tactics were of course an integral part of the plan. Late Saturday morning provided the most affordable opportunity. By then, the barrels and bins would be stocked full and the store clerks busy with Saturday morning traffic. A lookout was the key to the heist. Richie and I usually played three rounds of "paper-rock-scissors" to see who would play the role of sentinel. Whoever won could easily evade capture if there happened to be an arrest. After all, the lookout could easily claim "I did not know anything about it" and there would be no evidence to prove otherwise. On this particular Saturday morning, I lost. Richie would guard the action and I would make the grab.

It was pretty easy work this morning. With the coast clear Richie gave me the signal, and with a quick flash, one handful of kisses and another of bubble gum were stuffed into my right and then my left pockets. Perfect, the entire operation so far undetected. The process of escape had to be carried out with almost equal stealth and daring. To exit the store together was a mistake, it could raise too much attention. So Richie and I split forces, I went one way, he the other, we would rendezvous outside for the journey home. Richie's exit was rather easy with no risk. I, however needed some form of cover. Nearly attaching myself to the nearest female adult to give the appearance that I was really "with Mom," the departure from Katz came off quite easily. Once well away from the store and in safe harbor, we sprinted home in victory to inventory our booty. Richie and I had scored again and of course we proclaimed ourselves brilliant.

While fooling the Katz store clerk was one thing, fooling Jack Neville was another. My entire life I felt as if he had radar to detect misdeeds, and try as you might to lie out of it, once those steely blue eyes bore down on you with those nostrils flared, the jig was usually up, quickly followed by a confessional. When Richie and I arrived back at my house that morning, we encountered our first miscalculation of the soon to be ill-fated mission. For some unforeseen reason, as we entered the front door there to our horror was Dad sitting in the living room reading the The Daily Oklahoman. How could he have betrayed his usual practice of tending to the yard this Saturday morning. Absolute fear rushed through our bodies as we marched on through the living room. It was too late to turn back. As we moved past him, with my arms held rigidly down my sides in an effort to better conceal the loot bulging from my pockets, I could sense the radar beams bouncing off my body. He was attempting to detect if something was up. Somehow, we moved on by at a high rate of speed with a quick "Hi Dad" followed by the response "What are you two doing?" I gave him an equally quick reply, "nothing." Richie and I motored into my bedroom and shut the door mistakenly believing we were free. It took many years for me to understand that "nothing" in response to his question was taken by Dad as a certain sign of delinquency, especially if "nothing" was followed by the sound of the door being closed. To Dad the sound of the door closing was akin to an artillery shell going off.

Believing ourselves finally safe, Richie and I spread our loot over the bedspread in preparation for equitable distribution. Because I had taken the greatest risk this morning, the greater share would go to me. In this instance equitable distribution did not mean an equal split. Richie could not argue with this proposition. Rolling our hands over the candy as if it was long lost treasure, we were too busy to notice that the bedroom door had been swung open without even a courtesy knock. The question came again, this time a little louder "What are you guys doing?" Now fear rushed through our veins, pulse rates spiked high, and red flushed over faces. "Nothing" was again the response that jumped from my mouth knowing that neither of us could withstand lengthy inquiry. Dad's radar-like blue eyes continued to hone in on me, yet I still decided that my only chance would be to lie my way out of it. This tactic would prove fatal in short time. The next round came with "Where did you get the candy?" "From Katz" was the quick answer. The next round of question and answers would unravel the entire caper. As only Dad could do, he cut immediately to the chase "You stole it didn't you?" Before I could answer, my pal Richie put a knife right in my back with "Mr. Neville, I don't know anything about this, I was just in the yard." Richie's traitor-like reply did us both in as his attempted self defense wholly failed for want of any credibility. Still, with the traitor in my midst I felt a false comfort in numbers knowing that if I were to be shot on the spot. I would not go alone. On this day, however, Richie was spared summary execution and only suffered the embarrassment of being dismissed from the house. Now I would have to go it alone.

Death by hanging was sure to come next, but at the very least the mother of all butt-kickings was sure to follow. With Richie slithering out of the house like the snake he had become, I was braced for the volcano that I knew would erupt with the traitor's departure. Remarkably, the expected explosion did not come.

Rather the order came down that I was to retrieve from the kitchen a small grocery bag, into which the entire stash was to be transferred. Surely, I thought, I wished and hoped that this meant only that the goods would be thrown away and that the only punishment would be deprivation of the candied treasurers. But this fantasy remained only in my dreams as the next order came, "come on" and "bring the bag." Dad's new tactic, "calm in the midst of storm" was by now becoming a source of confusion and tension. Through the years I had achieved a sort of immunity from world decibel records being broken with even minor infractions, a sort of "tougher skin" if you will. But silence in the aftermath of felonious activity was not only new, but more than disconcerting. The fear factor and pulse rate quickened with each passing silent moment as I followed him out of the house with me carrying the bag of stolen goodies. Absent were the usual "God Damn Its" and "you don't have the sense God gave a goose."

With Jack proceeding down Shawnee Street at a rather brisk pace and me attempting to keep up a few steps directly behind, it became evident to my neighborhood buddies, all of whom including the rat Richie were now watching while riding their bicycles in circles in the middle of the street, that this was not exactly a father-son outing to the local drug store. It was more of a walk of shame down the sidewalk than a Saturday afternoon stroll to the store with Dad. With each step, the trek took on the trappings of the Bataan Death March, or of one of Jean La Fite's pirates being forced to walk the plank. Either way, it seemed as if punishment was certain and imminent.

As the journey continued I prayed for the "why" question, hoping I could defend myself in Richie's absence blaming the entire episode on him. I could at least attempt to mitigate my circumstances by admitting to aiding and abetting, but yet deny any conduct as principal, as if it would make any difference to Dad. It would not. Dad was never going to ask the "why" question and I knew it. In our house, there were no constitutional rights of due process or trial in matters such as this. Judgments were usually summary. You either did it or did not do it. If you were guilty, the step between crime and punishment was a short one. As we moved east along 19th, my fate became more evident, and with the turn to the south at 19th and Portland, it was only confirmed. Jack was marching me back to the scene of the crime with the bag of stolen goods in hand. Into the store we went. Dad wasted no time with quick inquiry of the first clerk sighted. "Your store manager please." By now, the entire episode had turned from ecstasy to pure agony as I attempted to muffle the groan that oozed out of my mouth. Much to my regret the boss of Katz too quickly appeared. A rather fat, short officious looking fellow, his face and manner did not seem to possess the slightest ounce of compassion. He looked like a hanging judge to me, a real Judge Roy Bean. A silence fell over our threesome before Jack issued the next order, "Well you've got something to say don't you?" That was it. Part of crime's punishment was a public confessional to the victim. The humiliation was overwhelming as I explained the planning and commission of the caper standing there in the aisle of the Katz Drug Store, making Richie the dominant player in the heist, especially since he was not there to defend himself. Finally concluding my plea of guilty, the bag full of stolen candy was tendered to the victim. With full restitution made but for the two pieces eaten, I knew that the pronouncement of sentence was near. Fully expecting to be hauled away handcuffed and in leg irons, I waited for the store manager to render his non-appealable judgment. There did not appear to be much deliberation to his decision now with sack in hand, Judge Bean explained that I should be arrested and prosecuted for such delinquency, and that if I aspired to a life of crime I was well on my way to it. With that tongue lashing, the store manager entered a suspended sentence of sorts. Without the company of one of my parents, I was banished from the store for six months; and if recidivism set in, arrest and prosecution would most assuredly follow. With that, I apologized with the most remorseful face of contrition a seven year old could muster given the fearful circumstances. By apologies end, my mouth was nothing but cotton, my skin a pale white, and, worst of all, my pants were wet. Frightened beyond words, I had peed in my shorts. Death by hanging would have been easier. The exit from Katz was only slightly less embarrassing, akin to leaving the courtroom with all of the spectators eyes on the now convicted. Would it ever end?

The journey home seemed longer than the walk to Katz. Not a word was said as Dad and I marched along in silence, with my chin on my chest only occasionally glancing up to see my way. The indignity of it all just would not go away. At least my pants dried out before we turned onto Shawnee Street to move through what seemed a gauntlet of my neighborhood buddies who remained at their posts anxiously awaiting news of the outcome. By now, of course, Richie was conspicuously absent from the scene. Dad's backward glance with those steel blue eyes left the unmistakable message that the march home would continue uninterrupted by any neighborhood kid press conference or debriefing. On through the front door and into the house we went. Once inside, the avalanche of "God Damn Its" and "you haven't got the sense God gave a goose" commenced in rapid fire succession. With the decibel level establishing a new Neville family record, it was made crystal clear that any further criminal activity would be met with summary execution. It was a no tolerance policy unless it was my desire to spend the summer in the Berry House Juvenile Detention Center newly constructed on Classen Boulevard. The message was loud and clear as fear once again weakened my already wilted body. With the admonishment finally over, I was banished to my room until called for dinner with instructions that the bedroom door would remain open. At least bread and water would not be the evening bill of fare.

I never stole anything ever again. To my knowledge Richie successfully escaped all accountability.

REFLECTIONS MONROE ELEMENTARY AND SKELLY STADIUM

Certainly, Jack and Leota's lives during the war years were marked with victories, defeats, and disappointments. The broader more philosophical question is whether these events played a role in shaping their post war views on the ways of life. However, we will really never know as such philosophical musings were not a topic at the dinner table. We never knew enough to ask and neither Mom nor Dad were about to talk about it. Now, however, a few observations are in order.

In the 1950s baseball was the king of kid's sports. After Dad almost single-handedly built the baseball field at Monroe Elementary, team practice started. All thought of ourselves fearless; however baseball at that age had its terrifying moments. For some reason, a baseball leaving a pitcher's hand and headed for home plate or worse yet, me, was traumatic. In those days, there was no such thing as a pitching machine, and the kid-game had no place for a parent who actually pitched in the game lobbing it over home plate, for the players on his own team to smash away, as is done in many leagues today. It was kid-on-kid in the 1950s. Dad had a rather unique idea of how to rid our team of the fear of being hit by a baseball. Standing on the mound in a rather imposing fashion during batting practice, Dad would occasionally and intentionally throw a ball straight at us. His theory was simple. If the ball hit you, it wasn't going to hurt that bad anyway, he used to say. So he would occasionally try to hit you with the ball so you would get over the fear of being hit. Of course, no nine-year-old player believed this actually would work. Second, if you swing the bat and hit the ball, the ball would not hit you. The wisdom of his methods escaped most of us and were routinely disregarded. If the ball was headed for my face, I was going to bail out of the batter's-box pronto. I didn't care what he said. Most of us were convinced that before any and every pitch was thrown, the ball was first going to hit us in the face. If the ball was not going to hit us in the face, the next feared area of impact was our balls. Teammate Doug Rich always reasoned that it far better to be smashed in the teeth rather than have your balls crushed by the speeding white sphere. Neither prospect was particularly appealing. When we stepped to the plate, hitting the ball became secondary to protecting our precious body parts.

Next to getting hit with the ball was the fear and humiliation that went with striking out. Of course, the fear of being hit by the ball was counter productive to both swinging the bat and actually hitting the ball. It was a true athletic feat to "bail out" of the box and at the same time hit the ball. The truth is that you prayed your "at bat" would end quickly, hopefully with a walk to first base. Billy Grimes of the Madison Magpies was the biggest nine year old in the post-war era. Parents were quick to claim that Billy really was not nine years old, my God he probably had to shave. The controversy was quickly put to rest when Mr. and Mrs. Grimes produced his birth certificate, which most of us thought was fake. With Grimes now proven to be nine, we were all faced with the unhealthy prospect of facing Billy's fastball. To us, the Grimes fastball coming at you looked like an aspirin accompanied by flame and smoke as it sped through the atmosphere. It was impossible to guess whether the speeding bullet would be thrown over your head, behind you, or at you. One thing was for certain, the Grimes fastball rarely made it over the plate and its unpredictability struck fear in your heart.

During practice, many of Dad's instructions, at least to me, were preceded by the three words "God Damn It" spoken within a split second and at a decibel level that could be heard for blocks. "God Damn It Stay In the Box," and "God Damn It Swing The Bat" were the two most often repeated instructions given during the course of Monday, Wednesday, and Friday practices. However when Mom showed up at practice, or during the course of the game when other parents and teams were around, the offending phrase precedent to the instruction was dropped. Finally the day arrived to battle Billy Grimes and the Magpies on our home turf. Batting third in the line-up, I would not have to wait long to meet the speed-baller from Madison Elementary School. In the bottom of the first inning, Grimes' first pitch to Ronnie Kise was three feet over his head and behind him. My eyes darted down the bench toward Dad waiting to see if he would explode in anger at Grimes' wildness. It did not happen as Dad in an encouraging, but loud tone yelled at Kise to "stay in the box." With eyes now big as saucers, Ronnie stepped back into the box for the next delivery. This time the aspirin came hard and low, right at Ronnie. Almost instantly, our first batter dropped to the ground. He was hit in the balls. Dad and the Magpie coach rushed to Ronnie's aide as we sat in stunned disbelief waiting to see if Ronnie was dead or alive. Finally Ronnie got up, dusted himself off, and gently holding his crotch walked down the first base line to the cheers of the crowd. Dad walked back over to the bench seemingly unphased by Kise's near-death experience. He clapped his hands in encouragement with "we've got a runner on, let's get him home." A sense of amazement swept the bench, Kise's balls had been crushed but he was standing on first base, still in the game. Next up for my Redbirds was Jim Stacy, our smallest player. Not a single batting helmet fit Jim's head and he constantly had to tip the bill of his hat upward so that he could see the pitcher. Jim was petrified and frozen at the plate. By now Grimes had collected himself and despite Dad's mega-voice instructions to "swing the bat," the Louisville Slugger stayed on Jim's shoulder for three straight strikes. Called out on strikes, the batting helmet falling off his head as his chin went to his chest, he broke down in tears as he walked back to the bench to "polite" parent applause. As Jim took his place on the bench, Dad marched down the row of now forlorn players patting Jim on the shoulder, "next time, you'll get 'em your next time up," followed by "next batter, let's go, runner on, let's get him home."

To my regret, I was the next batter up and my inventory of events said things had not gone exactly as hoped. Our first batter had been hit in the balls and our second batter was called out on strikes and broke down into tears. I was determined it would be neither for me. In an incredibly athletic feat on Grimes' first pitch, which was far outside to the right, I managed to both bail out of the batter's box and swing wildly at the ball. Of course, I missed by at least three or four feet. But I had accomplished my goal of not being hit, and not letting the bat stay on my shoulder. This exercise was repeated twice more as I went down swinging, my bat never coming within two feet of the ball.

Dad's only response as I briskly moved back to my place on the bench was "good effort, it was close, almost." In truth, it was none of the above, only an effort of survival.

As our first baseball game wore on, the Magpies crushed our team by double-digit runs. We never got a runner past first base after Ronnie was hit in the balls, and no one even hit a foul ball. Only mercy ended the game as Dad huddled his troops around him. He delivered the post-game speech in a decibel level that could be heard downtown. "Keep your chins up; it was a good effort, be proud of yourselves, we'll practice next week and get better, I promise. Let's go get some ice cream."

Despite a pathetic performance, there was never a negative word said. One hour after the game, as the team slurped down banana splits at the Dairy Queen on May Avenue and 48th Street, it was all behind us. Frowns turned to grins as we relived the Grimes fastball with laughter and fun, all bonded together. We were ready for the next game with a smile on our faces.

As I moved into high school, Dad's kid-coaching days came to an end, but his enthusiasm for the game, whatever the sport, never waivered. We played them all back in those days, no one played only one sport, and Moms and Dads never missed an event. With the Nevilles now living in Tulsa, as I left the house for those high school football games at Skelly Stadium, Dad never once lectured me or instructed me "to win" and I never recall him angry if we lost. His often repeated phrase, which I sometimes still hear today, was "give-em hell, play hard." There were many victories along the road, there also were many defeats and hard times. A dropped punt at the 10-yard line against Tulsa Central in 1964 cost us the football game; a missed free-throw against Conanstance Junior High cost us the county championship; a false start kept me out of the finals of the conference 100-yard dash; and a twisted cartilage in my right knee put me out for the football season my senior year. Never was a negative word ever said about defeat.

Jack Neville's energy and enthusiasm was limitless, usually only restrained by Mom. He worked hard and played hard. He was emotional, quick to anger, and no one ever had a problem hearing his words. He was plain spoken, and direct, with little ambiguity or vagueness about the message he intended to deliver. If you missed a curfew, got back to the Beta house on a week-day night over--served, did not show up on time, failed to shake hands with a grown-up, ran out of gas on highway 69, missed work because you wanted to sleep in, stole candy at the Katz Drug Store, lied to Mom, threw rocks at cars, or made up lame excuses for not doing something you were told to do you were in for the shellacking of a lifetime, a major ass-kicking that was unrelenting.

However, for missed fly balls and free throws, dropped punts, grounders that went between your legs, last second losses, and strike-outs, there never was an angry or demeaning word spoken. For Dad, fighting the good fight was the victory, and if you did that there was little else that really mattered to him.

Whether the war shaped Dad's attitude on such things I suppose is forever lost to the ages. However, one observation is for certain. In Reipertswiller, France, in 1945, and at Anzio in 1944, Dad saw a lot of young men die.

On the Monroe Elementary School baseball field in 1955 and at Skelly Stadium in 1964, no one was going to die.

CHAPTER XXXV
GERMANY

Jack benefitted greatly from the tremendous leadership of the Thunderbird Divisional Commanders. Key, Middleton, Eagles, and McClain were authentic World War II heroes who acted in the best interest of their men, and in so doing so saved lives. With Eagles' wounds incapacitating his command, on December 3, 1944, Major General Robert T. Frederick took over as the 45th Infantry Division's Commander. The morale of the troops sky-rocketed. A 1928 graduate of West Point, Frederick was the youngest divisional commander in the European Theatre, he was fearless. He had formed and trained the American-Canadian 1st Special Service Force which came to be known as The Devil's Brigade. Although Frederick was glamorized in Hollywood's version of "The Devil's Brigade" with William Holden in the lead role, Frederick was the real thing. He had been wounded in combat nine times. There was no doubt that he was a fighter. Frederick inspired trust and confidence in his men. For Jack, he saw Frederick as a leader who would "kick some German butt, and take names later." He was the perfect choice to take the Thunderbirds into Germany.

It was, however, a rather inauspicious start for Frederick's administrators. On November 30, 1944, during a practice amphibious landing in Southern France, the Thunderbirds' entire payroll was lost at sea. Nearly $2,000,000 went to the fishes in the surf of the French Riviera. On the eve of stepping foot on German soil, the men took the loss philosophically. It was not as if they were going to be able to do Christmas shopping in Germany anyway. For many, much of the payroll would only go toward the bad end of a game of craps or cards.

Despite being swept back toward Germany, there was plenty of steam left in the Nazi war machine. In the German planning stages since mid-September was a massive counterattack code named "Watch on The Rhine." On September 16, 1944, while Jack sped through France, Hitler brought his most senior officers together at Wolf's Lair in East Prussia. It was from here that Hitler gave the order for the most famous counterattack of World War II, which came to be known as "Battle of the Bulge." Approximately 200 hundred miles north of the 45th Infantry Division, the Germans, by December of 1944, had managed to hide 250,000 men and 1,100 tanks in the Ardennes Forrest, aided by the horrible winter weather of northern Europe. The objective of Hitler's last gasp was to create crisis in the Allied lines sufficient for the Germans to seize the port city of Antwerp. It was Hitler's demented belief that if the Allies key point of supply at Antwerp would be captured, the German Army could regain the initiative and perhaps turn the tide of the war.

At 1:50 p.m. on the day before the German counterattack, L Company of the 180th Infantry Regiment of the 45th Infantry crossed the German border from Lembach and headed for Bundenthal and Niederschlettenbach, Germany. For Jack, however, and the Division Artillery staff and headquarters, they remained on the border of France to support the advance on the two German cities.

As the 45th advanced eastward on Bundenthal, the German 5th and 6th Panzer Divisions hit the United States 28th in the Ardennes. Caught totally by surprise, General Sepp Dietrich's 6th Panzer Division raced westward toward Antwerp, capturing 8,000 American prisoners. The Battle of the Bulge was on with fury.

As the German counterattack moved westward to the north of the 45th, the Thunderbirds continued eastward in the south. The Division Artillery CP moved to Lembach on December 17. As the Battle of the Bulge raged on, the Thunderbirds, having blown a hole in the Siegfried Line, were encountering stiff resistance at Bundenthal, Germany. While G Company of the 157th had moved aggressively on its objectives, two of its platoons had been surrounded and trapped. With the advance eastward in a semi-stall, Division Artillery moved further east to support a rescue attempt of the encircled platoons of the 157th. For Jack Neville, he first crossed the German border near Lembach, France. On December 18, along with his unit, Jack entered the town of Niederschlettenbach, Germany, just across the Lauter River and east of Bundenthal. There was no time for celebration or pause. Although now in Germany for the first time, the division was encountering a tough enemy fighting for their homeland with spirits buoyed by events in the Ardennes.

By December 20, the Thunderbirds were now feeling the impact of the German offensive in the Ardennes. With the two platoons of the 157th still surrounded in Bundenthal, Eisenhower ordered all offensive action to cease until such time as the German counterattack in the north could be dealt with. In this regard, the United States 103rd, which provided right flank support for the 45th, was ordered to withdraw on December 21 and moved to aide the beleaguered American forces in the Bulge. On December 22, the 45th's lines were spread even thinner when Division Artillery and the Infantry Regiments were ordered to assume responsibility for the departed 103rd's sector. Although under orders to cease all offensive operations, and with lines spread thin, General Frederick refused to allow his surrounded troops to remain at death's door. The word came down to all staff levels that Frederick was going to get his boys out no matter what the orders were, or the situation was. The Division Artillery S-3 staff put together their part of the plan, and at dusk on December 23, the Artillery registered on every enemy location in Bundenthal. At 6:00 p.m., the artillery let loose 1,000 rounds of high explosives clearing a path for a daring rescue of the surrounded platoons trapped in two houses on the edge of Bundenthal. Perfectly timed, the shelling lasted 45 minutes, allowing the Thunderbird patrols to race in for the rescue. In dramatic fashion, wounded comrades were carried out under intense German machine gun fire. The Bundenthal rescue was a Christmas present for the entire division, and especially for those who got out safely.

While the weather turned pitifully bad, Christmas in Niederschlettenbach, Germany, was not bad by war-time standards. Indeed The History of Division Artillery records that " . . . it was a fine Christmas Day Dinner." The mail service was not half bad either as Jack enjoyed another round of Christmas Cards that Mom had gathered up from the entire Neville-Stauffer clan. Somehow, those 1944 Christmas cards made their way back to Mom's scrapbook. Despite the morale boost of hearing from loved ones and family at home, in the dark of night Jack could not help but ask whether or not he would have to spend yet another Christmas in some war-torn town fighting the Germans.

To the north, the Allied forces had finally taken control of the German Ardennes offensive. With Germans unable to take the key city of Bastogne, the Battle of the Bulge was nearing an end. By January 8, 1945, the German forces in the Bulge were withdrawn at the horrendous cost to the Germans of some 70,000 casualties, 50,000 prisoners, and 600 tanks.

While the last of the German counter-punches were ending in the north, things were only beginning for the 45th Infantry Division in the south. It did not take long for the Germans to discover that Eisenhower had moved forces out of the south to defend the Ardennes offensive in the north. The perceived point of greatest Allied weakness in the south was the western flank of the Thunderbirds.

By December of 1944, the Allies intelligence network had broken most of the German codes. The German intercepts were decrypted under the code-name "ULTRA" at Bletchly Park in England and thereafter disseminated to those units' effected. ULTRA had uncovered a large German build-up of forces in the Black Forest area near Bitche, on the western most flank of the Thunderbirds, and by Christmas Eve it was clear that the Germans were prepared to attack from the south. The word was sent to the 45th to get ready. On December 27, 1944, the Division Artillery staff gathered for an "all-hands" meeting. Colonel Arnote's normally infectious smile was gone and it was evident by Captain Large's manner that the situation was serious. Arnote briefed the staff that the Germans were apparently massing their forces approximately 40 to 50 miles west of the Division Artillery CP with the intent of attacking somewhere near Bitche, France. A quick look at the map told the story. Division Artillery and many elements of the infantry regiments were in the eastern one-third of the division's sector and forward of the units in the western sector. If the Germans could successfully seize key road networks and terrain, in the western sector, it was conceivable that they could work their way to the rear of the Thunderbird's positions. Accordingly, General Truscot had ordered that should the Germans attack in the 45th western sector, the Thunderbirds were to give up ground in the east and come to the aide of the units to the west. Arnote went on to conclude that staff was to immediately study positions and scenarios for a "retrograde movement" that followed the line of the former Maginot Line. The staff was incredulous. The division had just taken the Maginot Line and was slowly but surely wiping out what was left of the Siegfried Line. They were about to give up what they had taken, a bitter pill for any soldier to swallow. For Jack and his buddies, Billy Williams and Frosty Munson, Arnote's instruction to "plan a retrograde movement" simply meant one thing–the division was retreating back to France.

The ULTRA intercepts would prove correct. Somehow, someway, despite the enormous expenditure of men and material by the Germans in the Ardennes, they had managed to collect seven divisions for an attack in the Black Forest Region near Bitche. This time the Germans would throw their elite SS troops at the Thunderbirds, the 12th Mountain Regiment. The German units were battle hardened, skilled, and very well equipped for winter fighting.

For the Thunderbirds on the western flank of the division's section, 1945 started out with a bang. One hour before midnight, December 31, 1945, the Germans attacked with five divisions and two Panzer Divisions held in reserve. The desperate Germans struggle to survive was on in the south. On January 2, 1945, Jack and the Division Artillery pulled out and headed back to meet the German thrust from the West. The History of Division Artillery tells the story–"January 2 – Retrograde Movement."

It was an unhappy group of Thunderbirds that left Niederschlettenbach, Germany that day. They had paid dearly for the real estate they were leaving and it was unthinkable that they might have to buy it back again somewhere down the line. Jack thought he was riding backwards through Hell, and he was. The entire division was. As the Thunderbirds climbed aboard their truck headed back toward Lembach, France, faces were grim and sullen, and so too were those of the people the Thunderbirds were leaving behind. Dad and the others had formed an attachment to these townspeople. Along the border towns it was not uncommon for the citizens to bring the soldiers baked pies, pastries, and other amenities that evidenced their own thrill of freedom from oppression. It was their way of expressing gratitude to the soldiers from small town America. The Thunderbirds reciprocated in their own way, often giving up a canteen, their mittens, or their chocolate as an expression of thanks. The small German and French villages along the way were not unlike Vinita, Wewoka, Norman, or Adair, and it was heartbreaking to think about what might happen when the last Thunderbird truck pulled out, and if the war was lost, the first German truck pulled in. As Division Artillery retreated, the scene was the same in each town. The free-French flags were taken down and white flags raised in hopes what was left of a house or barn would be spared from destruction should the Germans return. Only the old men and children remained in the villages, wearing tattered ragged clothes and shivering in the winter cold waving good-bye. Some huddled by roadside fires started with wood that once was their tables or their beds in hopes they could eat at least one last hot supper and avoid the bite of freezing temperatures. When the division arrived, they were greeted with wine, song, flowers, and cheers. Now going out, the Thunderbirds saw only sadness and tears. As Jack motored by, it was easy to see the dark clouds of despair rolling in behind the people they were leaving. It was a tough scene to watch.

By January 2, the Division Artillery CP had "retrograded" to a building outside Reichenhoffen. With the expected point of German attack later confirmed to be at Bitche, the CP was moved to Schillersdorf on January 3, 1945 to meet the attack. There was no celebration on New Year's Day as the artillery spent its efforts getting ready to shoot at the Germans. The Artillery got their chance when the 12th SS hit the 45th hard at Wingen-sur-Moder, pushing the division line backward. By day's end, the Thunderbirds were facing fanatical German effort on its left flank. It took only one day for the 180th to get their act together. As the 12th SS moved in for what they thought was the kill, the 180th cut the German troops off. Surrounded and out of contact with their own, the SS sustained 1,000 casualties and 270 taken prisoner on January 5. The German assault was stopped.

The German SS was not about to give up. Hitler had commanded his elite to "stand and die" and on January 11, 1945, it became evident that they intended to do just what the Fuhrer ordered. Once again the Germans came through Bitche aimed at the 180th and this time the Thunderbirds were forced to retreat some 600 yards. In this attack, the 180th again inflicted very heavy casualties on the SS and the Germans were forced to halt their advance and regroup. General Frederick, sensing the opportunity and need to stem another German thrust that was certain to come, rushed in the Thunderbird 157th for a counterattack north and east of Reipertswiller. In the Division Artillery S-3, all hands were on deck to provide the critical supporting fire for the 157th counterattack.

Thus began perhaps the most dismal chapter in the history of this fabled division. On January 14, the 157th attacked the 256th and 257th Volksgrenadier Divisions in the snow-packed, forested bitter cold mountains north of Reipertswiller with Division Artillery providing coordinated artillery support. The fighting was extremely heavy. In the early afternoon of the 14th, the 157th came under vicious German 88 fire and the regiment was forced to dig in. Even Col. Felix Sparks reported that "It was the worst beating we ever took from terrific concentrated artillery barrage, including Anzio." At 9:00 a.m. on January 15, Division Artillery gave it back to the Germans with a heavy artillery barrage of their own. The 157th broke out and moved forward rapidly taking their objectives, two hills, Hill 420 and Hill 400, by noon. The problem now created by their success was the fact that their rapid aggressive advance of some 1,500 yards had created a salient and by the late afternoon the regiment was being hit by the Germans not only from the front, but from the left and right flank. By 5:00 p.m. the Germans correctly sensed that they had the opportunity to completely surround the entire regiment. "They came hard and in force." It was brutal as the 157th sustained very heavy casualties and "enemy dead were piled up like cordwood in front of our position." Dark finally fell and the now nearly-surrounded regiment dug their foxholes in the snow to await the morning light.

Early on the morning of January 16, the SS started to tighten the noose around the neck of the 157th. At Division Artillery, the S-3 staff had all ears on the radio listening and waiting for the word to give the 157th the fire support they might need. The sounds over the radio were ugly. At 1:00 p.m. the German SS delivered a "staggering blow" to the 3rd Battalion's K Company, overruning the Thunderbirds left flank. The radio transmissions at Division Artillery were becoming more sporadic and desperate. Division Artillery sprang into action as 3,294 rounds were fired on the 16th in hopes of staving off the German effort to encircle the regiment. It was not enough. All Jack could do now was listen as the expected terrible news came at 4:00 p.m. Two companies, I and K, were completely surrounded by the Germans. The noose would only tighten as the Thunderbirds dug in for another night, low on ammunition, supplies, and medical equipment.

On January 17, the surrounded companies attempted to break the German vice by an attack northward. Their efforts failed. Heroic and hectic efforts to resupply the stranded Thunderbirds went on most of the day. All failed, and as yet another night fell, the 157th dug in. For Jack, the S-3 staff and Division Artillery it was an all-night affair, but by morning they had a bold plan. The 157th had requested that Division Artillery plan for a "running barrage" at the rate of one round per gun, per minute to be lifted on the call of other infantry units assigned to attack the encirclement. After considerable debate, it was decided that the artillery would shoot everything they had left in an effort to break the German vice, hopefully allowing infantry units to rush in and rescue the surrounded companies. It was a desperate measure for a desperate hour, but the Thunderbirds were not going to let their own die on those hills without trying to get them out. The Oklahomans were not about to surrender to the German SS. The Thunderbirds would fight it out, do or die.

As the morning of the 18th came, Division Artillery let loose with all they had. In a blistering shooting spree, Division Artillery laid down a 45 minute rolling barrage of 1,427 rounds. At 5:30 a.m., the S-3 section received word to lift the barrage and elements of the 179th sprinted forward to rescue their besieged comrades. Extremely heavy German fire forced the 179th rescuers to dig in and by 9:10 a.m. the entire effort ground to a halt under withering German fire. Artillery frantically attempted to contact the stranded companies in the melee. The Germans had enveloped and infiltrated G Company's positions, and the fighting was turning hand-to-hand and bare knuckles. Suddenly, all radios and telephones of G Company went silent. While other German SS kept the men of the 179th pinned down, elements of the 12th SS overran all positions of G Company, but the Thunderbirds were not about to give up. At 3:00 p.m., the 179th put together yet another attack to rescue their brethren. It too failed. The German fire support was just too strong. In a furious effort to blast the 157th out of its trap, and to support the determined efforts to rescue the 157th, Division Artillery fired an incredible 5,018 rounds. It was not enough, and by days end it looked as if three entire companies had been annihilated, with the remaining companies trapped inside a deadly ring of German artillery and infantry. For Jack and his S-3 friends, the failure to blow the Germans out of their position was becoming more frustrating and depressing. The snow and overcast conditions made aerial and forward artillery liaison observations impossible. While the two remaining companies were maintaining radio contact, all wire lines to the companies had been torn to shreds by German amd American artillery fire.

January 19 proved no more successful. The 179th made another futile effort to get to the stranded survivors. Once again, the German artillery, machine guns, and mortar fire, aided by inclement weather, forced the 179th to fall back and by the end of the day on the 19th, the chances of rescue were openly discussed as remote at best. The Thunderbirds refused to quit. On January 20, at 12:45 p.m. efforts were made to resupply the trapped men by air. The air effort never got off the ground, again defeated by the snow and clouds.

Arnote and Large called the staff together. It was a grim group of sergeants that Arnote explained that efforts to reach the stranded 157th were being called off. Still in radio contact with the survivors, the message had been given that if they were to get out they would have to fight their way out by attacking to the southwest. Told to keep alert, Large told Jack and the staff to plan for supporting fire should the remainder of the 157th decide to make a break for it. As Jack and Frosty Munson listened on the radio, the Germans sent a

Colonel into the encircled and cut off Thunderbirds with a white flag. The 12th SS demanded that the Americans surrender or die. The besieged Thunderbird response was quick and defiant. After tying white flags to the muzzles of their guns, the weapons were turned upside down and thrust into the snow. The signal to the German Colonel was made unmistakenly clear. Freezing, out of ammunition, food, and no way out, the remaining brave men of the 157th told the Germans there would be no surrender; if you want us, come and get us. With the German Colonel's departure, one of the last radio transmissions from the besieged soldiers was made to Division Artillery at 3:30 p.m. "We're coming out. Give us everything you've got."

With that, the Artillery unloaded all they had left. Within the hour the awful news came that this effort also failed, there would be no escape. K Company reported for the last time that they could not break out, and that of the entire five companies, there were only 125 men left. Gloom, despair, and devastation took over the Division Artillery Headquarters as the last order was given to those still standing–break up and infiltrate back to the 45th's line as best as they could. There was no response, as all radio communication went out. By nightfall, the German SS had closed the trap, all five companies had been annihilated.

Of the five companies trapped by the Germans between January 15 and January 20, only two men, privates Walter Bruce and Benjamin Melton, made their way back to safety. It was a catastrophic loss for the entire division. Seven company commanders and 30 platoon leaders were killed or captured and when the division was finally relieved from the front it took 1,000 men to bring the division back up to battle strength. Despite heroic and valiant efforts to save the five companies, it was the single worst defeat the Thunderbirds would suffer in their 511 days of combat. As for Jack's unit, they blasted 20,261 rounds in a furious and failed effort to save their fellows. It was the most rounds fired at enemy troops during the entire war, and despite their frantic, courageous efforts, failure plagued the day.

While the 157th battled valiantly for their survival, the 179th and 180th fought hard to hold the line, emboldened by the last stand of the five lost companies. The 45th Infantry Division's stubborn resistance brought the German counterattack from Bitche to a grinding halt. Worn out and exhausted, the division was replaced in the line in late January by the 42nd Division. For Jack, the Division Artillery CP was moved to La Petite Pierre, France on January 20.

With German counter-offensive stopped, the German lines eroded into pockets of organized resistence. One by one, the 45th moved to eliminate each area with Division Artillery providing the necessary support. By early February of 1945, the Germans were once again on the retreat, headed back toward Germany and the Siegfried Line.

CHAPTER XXXVI
MARCH ACROSS THE RHEIN

With the 42nd Infantry Division relieving a mauled and battered group of Oklahomans, the Thunderbirds moved into reserve areas in the vicinity of Epinal, Baccarat, and Luneville, France to refit, resupply, and reorganize. It was a welcome and much-needed rest. Division Artillery CP remained at La Petite Pierre and were glad they did so. On February 10, 1945, General J.D. Meyer saw to it that every enlisted man in Division Artillery was issued more than their fair share of gin. It was not exactly a country club martini party, but in the bitter cold weather of France, it provided a great form of anti-freeze even if the medicine was sipped out of a cold canteen cup.

By February 11, the Division G-2 had declared that the Thunderbirds were not in a hostile area and could stack arms. General Frederick nonetheless made good use of the time and during this brief pause. The Thunderbirds, including Division Artillery, spent their time preparing to enter Germany for the second, and hopefully, last time. In short, the entire division was sent to school. Although Jack was grateful for the lull in the fighting, he knew it would not last long. Nobody was packing their bags to go home, and indeed the so-called instructors were teaching the men quite to the contrary. Soon, they were told, they would be entering Germany in the last march to end the days of Hitler's Third Reich. Frederick briefed the men to expect a fanatical enemy. Intelligence was reporting that even the civilians in the towns they were about to attack would -be armed. Hitler's "stand and die" orders had in some cities created a home militia that would defend the Vaterland with women and children being forced to bare arms. Failure to observe uniformed troops and tanks did not necessarily mean that towns and villages would not be hostile. "Be alert and be ready" were the instructions. Striking a new fear into the men was G-2's revelation of concern that the Germans would fight their last days using chemical warfare. They had done it in World War I, and it was not expected they would do anything less in the second World War. As a result, in addition to practicing and rehearsing river crossings and the use of new fuses for the artillery pieces, Jack spent considerable time schooling for chemical warfare. Gas chamber exercises became the frequent afternoon activity, quickly followed by a trip to the rear area beer tent at the new Division Artillery CP at Rozelieores, France.

In early March of 1945, rest, rehearsal, and practice time was over. The beginning of the end of the war was about to start. General Patch's 7th Army was ordered to make a major thrust into Germany near Saarbrucker and to prepare accordingly. With the Division Artillery CP now at Sarreinsming, France, the Thunderbirds were ordered to hit the Seigfried Line east of the Blies River. The division would thereafter proceed with the greatest speed toward Homburg, Germany. H-hour for the attack was 1:00 a.m. on March 15, 1945, with the division moved by truck into the front lines near Sarreguemes with the old familiar United States 3rd Division on the right and the XXI's Corp's 53rd Division on its left. The night before, the 45th Infantry Division CP slipped into a prisoner-of-war camp at Steinbach, France to wait.

The second thrust into Germany began precisely on time, supported by the close air support of both British and American fighter bombers. To aide the aerial armada, the Division Artillery marked for bombing every town in the path of the Thunderbirds–Gershiem, Walsheim, Whitterheim, Briefurt, and Babeshiem. As the infantry troops prepared to board their boats to cross the Blies River, the S-3 staff plotted a deadly series of time-on-target rounds on Rehinehm, Niedergailbach, and Bliss Brucken. On March 15 the Infantry stormed across the Blies River with Division Artillery blasting away. By March 17, the 157th, annihilated at Reipertswiller and now restaffed, had reached the bunkers pill boxes and fixed fortifications of the Seigfried Line. The Division Artillery CP was moved up to Gersheim and once again the systematic destruction of Germany's last real line of defense began. With Division Artillery firing away at German concrete, keeping the Germans pinned down and unable to return fire, the 157th crawled out of their holes and attacked the world's greatest defensive fortification with flame throwers, bazookas, and grenades. With great courage and speed, the Thunderbirds eliminated bunker after bunker. German positions fell like dominos. The 45th was ruthless in their attack, marked by incredible acts of courage and bravery. Most notably, Lt. Jack Treadwell nearly single-handedly eliminated six German pill boxes and captured 18 German prisoners. For his actions, Treadwell was awarded the Medal of Honor. The entire division was on a rampage determined to pay the Germans back for Riepertswiller, get the war over, and get home. On the day of the 17th, the division captured almost 100 prisoners, scores of weapons and equipment, and inflicted unaccountable casualties on the Germans who refused to give up. With the Siegfried Line cracking, the Division Artillery CP was moved eastward to Bliesmenger, a 12-mile hop, for what was hoped to be the death blow to the Seigfried Line and the Germans fighting therein. In unrelenting, merciless fashion, all three Infantry Regiments, behind a shield of artillery fire, pounded the so-called impregnable fortress the entire day of March

18. Eighty-six pill boxes were reduced to rubble, 268 prisoners captured, and five key towns were taken in what was the last day of the Seigfried Line. By the 19th, the 7th Army and the 45th were pouring into Germany as the entire 17th SS Panzer Grenadier Division withdrew to the east side of the Rhein. The Thunderbirds now owned the Seigfried Line, and would never give it back.

On March 20, 1945, Jack and the S-3 staff received the news they were hoping for. At 8:50 a.m., division headquarters notified all units that the Germans were in a full retreat eastward. The Thunderbirds were not going to let the Germans up as orders were given that all regiments were to be in hot pursuit. To support the chase of the fleeing Germans, the Division Artillery CP again was moved eastward to Mimbach as the division now closed on Homburg. In the way of the Thunderbird land rush, the 45th lanced their way through the towns of Lautzkirchen, Nieder-wurzbach, Bierbach, Altstadt, and Ingweiller with the capture of some 2,055 prisoners in a day's time. Homburg fell to the Thunderbirds and the Division Artillery CP and Division CP moved into the bombed-out remains of the Homburg Hotel to plot the continued thrust eastward toward the Rhein. The taking of Homburg was a milestone for the division as it was the first German city of any significant size captured by the Thunderbirds. Even Division Artillery took pause for brief celebration as The History of Division Artillery noted, "Very Good Looting."

The Homburg holiday lasted less than 24 hours as on the very next day Jack and his pals got the order to "saddle-up" and continue the chase as the Germans were attempting to hot-foot-it across the Rhein. Ironically, Hitler made the chase easier and faster. In the 1930s, the Nazis built their own form of an interstate highway that they, of course, tagged as a "super-highway." There was no such thing in Oklahoma City, much less Adair, Oklahoma, and Jack was amazed at the monstrosity of these four-lane autobahns on which the Division Artillery trucks could race at nearly full speed over concrete rather than the rugged dirt roads of which they had become accustomed. The Nazi super-highways were originally built to stimulate economic development by linking northern Germany to southern Germany, and not altogether secondarily, to facilitate German troop movement. Interestingly, in the 1950s, Dwight D. Eisenhower would initiate a similar idea with a program designed to construct what came to be known as the interstate highway system. However, during the war, the 45th Infantry Division was using the German form of interstates to chase the Nazis east toward the Rhein River. On March 22, 1945, the Division Artillery made a then-incredible leap forward some 45 miles down the super-highway to set up the CP in the town of Eisenberg.

The showdown on the river's edge of the Rhein was about to begin with the 157th arriving on the west bank and the Germans bunkered down on the east. Jack could not help but note the date, March 23. On Leota's 26th birthday he was about to cross the Rhein River and fight the Germans. It would have been more fun to celebrate with her jitter-bugging at the Blossom Heath in Oklahoma City. With the 157th at the Rhein, the Division Artillery CP was moved 15 miles closer to the town of Gundersheim.

In anticipation of crossing the Rhein, the division spent most of the 23rd, 24th, and 25th in preparation. Intelligence suggested that the Germans might have the remnants of 21 divisions on the east side of the Rhein. To counter this expected strength, Corps command attached 15 additional artillery battalions to the 45th and on March 25, the Division Artillery CP was inched up another six miles to the town of Mulheim. It took the better part of two days to construct the pontoon ferries and other river craft necessary to make the crossing, but by March 26 the Thunderbirds were ready.

The fight on the Rhein River was unexpectedly brief, but nonetheless difficult. At 2:30 a.m. on March 26, 1945 the boats carrying the Infantry Regiments started their swim across the Rhein in a heavy fog between Worms and Hamm. The Germans opened up with their 88s and the initial resistance was strong. Although more than half of the assault boats carrying the 180th were lost, most of the regiments reached the east bank. Division Artillery from the west bank pounded back at the Germans and by 7:30 a.m. the Germans were broken in the 180th's sector. The 179th quickly crossed the river and swiftly cleared their area of Germans. By the end of the day, the battle on the Rhein River was essentially over with the capture of some 1,047 prisoners, sixteen 88s, and hordes of ammunition. It was a complete route. With the east bank now in the safe hands of all three infantry regiments, Jack moved across Germany's Rhein to the small town of Seeheim on March 27.

For the German soldiers, defeat now was only a question of time as what was left of its forces in the south fled 25 miles to the east and the next natural barrier, the river Main and the twin cities of Aschaffenburg and Schweinheim. In the north, the United States 1st, 9th, and 3rd Armies also were racing eastward gobbling up huge pieces of German territory with every thrust. With every day, Jack knew the end was near. It just could not be soon enough.

In combat since July of 1943, Jack thought he had seen all the horror and ugliness that war had to offer, that was until the division got to Aschaffenburg.

Aschaffenburg was a city of approximately 40,000 people located on the east bank of the Main River, 20 miles south of Frankfurt and 93 miles north of Munich. The city's principal war-time purpose was that of a convalescent center for the German wounded. As the Thunderbirds rapidly moved eastward, headquarters increased their warnings of organized fanatical civilian resistance telling the soldiers to beware as they moved through the small German towns and villages. For the most part, German and Nazi flags were being taken down by the civilians and replaced by the white flags of surrender. Civilians were generally docile and the closest Jack saw to resistance were the frowns and grimaces that came from only a few of the older town's people. It was not until the division reached the town of Sulzbach that the Thunderbirds first encountered armed civilians willing to fight; however, their efforts were scattered, disorganized, and dealt with rather summarily. This would not be the case in Aschaffenburg.

The Nazis handed the defense of Aschaffenburg over to a Nazi party extremist, a lunatic by the name of Major Von Lambert. With Division Artillery CP being established at Seeheim and ready for the assault on Aschaffenburg, Von Lambert ordered all civilians unwilling to fight for the Fuhrer to get out of town. Those left would stand and die for the "Vaterland." Along with the remnants of the German 36th Infantry Division, and approximately 50 of Himmler's most fanatical SS troops, the old men, women, boys, and girls barricaded themselves in the city to meet the Thunderbird advance. On March 28, 1945, the Battle of Aschaffenburg began.

As elements of the 157thcrossed a railroad bridge over the Main into Aschaffenburg, the three Infantry Regiments simultaneously negotiated the river by boat and pontoon. As elements of the infantry regiments entered Schweinheim and the outer limits of Aschaffenburg, they were met by the defense of young 15 and 16-year-old boys thoroughly indoctrinated into the Hitler youth believing it was better to die than surrender to the Americans. The young warriors were successful in extracting heavy casualties, and in self defense, the Thunderbirds were forced to shoot many of the teenagers in their foxholes as they refused to surrender. Over the next two days, 15-year-old girls were felled while firing a bazooka at a platoon of the 157th; children lobbed grenades off rooftops into clusters of Thunderbirds; and women and old men transformed themselves into snipers to stall the inevitable. By the end of the day on the 28th it was evident that the fight for Aschaffenburg would be an absolute nightmare for the infantry working their way through the streets. For Jack at the Division Artillery CP, as the radio reports flooded in, he and the rest of the S-3 staff were astonished at the Aschaffenburg resistence. As the division met with more and more casualties, it became obvious that General Frederick was not going to allow continued attrition of his infantry troops by shots being fired from those hiding in buildings or perched on rooftops. Arnote called his staff together with the order given to commence planning and operation to shell the city. If need be, Division Artillery would level all of Aschaffenburg if its street fighters refused to surrender.

In a last ditch effort to prevent the planned destruction of the city, the division made surgical efforts to bring the war in Aschaffenburg to an end. Discovering that the tallest church steeple in town was being used as an observation platform and communications center by the SS, the long triangular steeple was blasted to rubble with twenty-five rounds of high explosive. The awesome display of firepower that wiped out the steeple did not faze Von Lambert's SS troops or the citizenry. They continued fighting as the Thunderbirds continued to work their way through building after building. Intelligence sources located

Major Von Lambert's headquarters in the middle of town in an old castle-like structure that also served as Gestapo headquarters. Hoping to cut the head off the snake and destroy the command function of the street resistance, General Frederick called in sorties of P-51s. At 6:40 p.m. on March 30, the S-3 section tuned in their radios to the air attack that dropped rockets and napalm on the Gestapo hoping that the Allied air power would save the Artillery from razing the city. The air armada eliminated the Gestapo headquarters, but somehow Von Lambert survived and maintained control of his fanatical band. Street by street, the infantry regiments worked their way through Aschaffenburg until Von Lambert and his rebels were essentially surrounded and cut off from escape.

For 21 months of combat, Jack and the division had clawed and scratched their way through Europe fighting uniformed German soldiers and their tanks and artillery. Never had Division Artillery purposefully pointed their big guns at the civilian citizenry of any Sicilian, French, Italian, or even German town. Even in France, the Wermacht had forced the French and German citizens to evacuate their towns before a big fight. The SS and Wermacht were forcing them to stay and fight. Despite the war, the small-town soldiers of the 45th were more accustomed to delivering chocolates and K-rations to the homeless of conquered towns and villages. Now the S-3 staff had been asked to put together plans and operations that would not only destroy a town, but most probably its inhabitants that included women and children.

In Germany, the Allies were closing fast on all fronts in March of 1945. The Russians were racing westward, the British and Americans were surging eastward, and the city of Berlin was within the gun sights of all. Hitler, among others, was nonetheless exhorting the German people to pick up arms and continue the fight because in the end they too would die, and it was better to be dead than Russian Red or American Blue. Certainly the concern facing the 45th in the final days of the war had to be that the bypassing of Aschaffenburg would only send the signal that armed civilian resistance could save the German cities from being conquered, therefore preserving in a small way, the Nazi's Reich that Hitler proclaimed would last 1,000 years. If Aschaffenburg was not taken, how many other Aschaffenburg's would be down the road. The zero-tolerance signal had to be sent and thus the orders to eliminate Aschaffenburg, had to be given. From a more militaristic point of view, Aschaffenburg was a town of some size. In addition to its fighting citizens, the SS troops, and remnants of the German 36th Infantry Division were still capable of a fight. Aschaffenburg was too large a pocket of resistance to leave to the division's rear. Aschaffenburg had to fall irrespective of loss.

In the end, Von Lambert would erase any dilemma of Aschaffenburg's fate. On March 30, 1945, Division Artillery and airplanes dropped leaflets into the center of the city pleading for Von Lambert and the civilians to quit. Efforts to persuade a surrender were not altogether unsuccessful. A young German lieutenant attempted to convince Von Lambert that it was all over and that they should give it up. Von Lambert had the young soldier hung from a steel support above a wine shop with a sign stapled to his body "Cowards and traitors, hang.... Today there hangs a coward in officers garb because he betrayed the Fuhrer. . . ." As the hours clicked by, many of the civilians became dispirited in the face of the overwhelming power looking at them down the barrels of the 155s. They pleaded for Von Lambert to surrender the city and for their efforts they were shot. The surviving civilians were ordered to erect barriers, dig foxholes, and prepare to die. To ensure that the women, children, and old men of Aschaffenburg stayed in their positions, Himmler's SS troops were there to stand guard. Anyone who abandoned their post was executed. The crazed Von Lambert sent the word out–there would be no surrender.

The course now clear, the division and its Artillery began its systematic and violent destruction of the city. With its 105s, 155s, and even the giant 240 cannons, the immense firepower of the artillery leveled Aschaffenburg in methodical, brutal fashion. According to The Fighting 45th, "Artillery fell like machine gun fire." Building by building, house by house, shop by shop, and street by street, the city was reduced to dust and bricks as the Thunderbirds worked their way toward the middle of town and Von Lambert's headquarters over the next five days. By April 2, what was left of Von Lambert's troops were encircled in the middle of town in the remnants of the German Gestapo headquarters. Now facing certain death, Von Lambert failed to demonstrate the courage that he himself had demanded from so many of Aschaffenburg who had died spanning the last several days. At 7:00 a.m. on April 3, Von Lambert dispatched a captured American soldier as an emissary to the Division Headquarters. Two hours later, the monocled martinet of Aschaffenburg did what he had proclaimed would never be done–he surrendered the city to the 157th. As word swept through the city, the survivors clustered around Von Lambert's headquarters with even the German soldiers joining in the chant "schweinhund," or pig-dog, as 100 German officers and Von Lambert marched out of the ruins of the castle, all carrying white flags of surrender. More than 3,000 prisoners were taken and by 1:00 p.m. the city was declared secure. It was finally over.

In the six day siege of Aschaffenburg, the estimated German losses were put at 4,682. According to The History of the 45th Division Artillery, the city was totally destroyed.

Jack had witnessed the fanatical, diabolical nature of Nazism first hand. Their leaders had so little regard for human life that they had sacrificed the old men and women of the town, and perhaps even worse, the young. Would this have happened in America? In Adair? Surely a democracy and freedom would never allow it. There was no real battle in Aschaffenburg as the Thunderbirds had experienced in the last year, only the destruction of buildings, streets, shops, houses, and the death of German citizens. Now angry at the thought that Hitlerism may make them do it all over again in the next town down the road, Jack packed his duffle bag, threw it on the back of the truck, and climbed aboard to wait for the orders to move out. Looking at his pal Frosty Munson, shaking his head in disgust and thinking of how lucky in a bizarre way Harry Balkum was to be home, the big diesel truck engine turned over and they rode out of town on April 4, 1945. Looking back at Aschaffenburg through the dust kicked up by the wheels of the trucks, the constant recurring thought surfaced again and again, "my God will I ever get to go home? Please don't let us have to do this again."

Not far down the road was Nuremberg, then Dachau, and Munich. For Jack, Aschaffenburg added a new dimension to the horror of the war that sadly, in only a few short days, would be eclipsed many times over at the Dachau Death Camp.

With the fall of Ashaffenburg and the capture of some 33,180 Germans in the month of March, it was a clear road ahead for the Thunderbirds, at least for the next few days. Largely unopposed, the Thunderbirds moved swiftly and deeper into Germany. Jack and the Division Artillery sped eastward through Pfaffenhasen, Jossa, Speicherz, and Gesfeld between April 4 and April 7. For the most part, the resistance encountered along the way was scattered and disorganized.

Once through Gesfeld, the XV Corps delivered a surprising directive to the Thunderbirds. Rather than continue its eastward movement, the Thunderbirds were ordered to pivot their line of march to the right and proceed with the greatest speed southward. In a day's time, Jack motored 47 miles to Konigshofen and then further south to Ebern. As the division kept on the heels of the fleeing Germans, General Dwight D. Eisenhower broadcast another stern and chilling warning to not only his troops, but the American people. In addition to the expectation of Nazi civilian zealots taking on armed troops, as occurred in Aschaffenburg, the Berlin radio broadcasts were now proclaiming the existence of a so-called werewolf terrorist organization who would initiate a sort of guerilla warfare in cities attacked by the Allies. In a last ditch defense effort, the "werewolf terrorists," were instructed to assassinate any mayor or leader who attempted to surrender their village or town to the Allied advance. Fearful that they were now facing a series of Aschaffenburgs, the S-3 section broke out the maps to see what lay ahead of them. There would be no open farmland territory to the division's front. Now in the direct line of the Thunderbird's march were three key German cities–Bamberg, Nuremberg and Munich–all sizeable population centers. The thought of fighting three Aschaffenburgs was agonizing. While Jack was relatively safe from fire in an artillery siege of a town, the thought of planning and executing the total destruction of three more cities was sickening, even if it was necessary.

On the road to the south was the small town of Birnfeld. Expecting the worst, it did not happen. Without much of a fight, the 179th captured the last of the German 256th Infantry Division. Approximately 100 German soldiers were left of a division that once numbered 10,000. The Wermacht was in shambles and so was all of Germany. After Birnfeld, without pause, Colonel Arnote called the S-3 staff together for the next order of movement. Corps Headquarters now directed that the Thunderbirds proceed to the city of Bamberg, and attack with due speed. Intelligence reports suggested that the German 36th Infantry Division was held up within the city and that they were expected to put up stiff resistance. The German 36th was to be eliminated, and if that meant wiping out Bamberg, so be it.

Bamberg, Germany, had a pre-war population of approximately 65,000 which had been swollen by refugees and wounded soldiers. The town was garrisoned by some 2,000 German troops who initially sent the word out that they would die rather than surrender. Concerned that Bamberg would likely be another Aschaffenburg, Jack and the Division Artillery established the CP at Castle Seehof and leveled the big artillery pieces at the city to support the infantry's attack. On April 12, 1945, the Battle of Bamberg began with all three infantry regiments encircling the city. The infantry regiments quickly cut off all escape routes from Bamberg. Working their way toward the inner part of the city, the infantry reported their movement back to Division Artillery. Fingers on the trigger, the 105s and 155s waited for the first instance of substantial resistance. There would be no hesitation for snipers hiding in windows and on roof tops waiting to kill or wound a Thunderbird. The Artillery was not going to let Bamberg turn into a street fight like Aschaffenburg. Instead, they would level the city to save the lives of their brothers. As the infantry moved toward the middle of town, vast supplies of ammunition and bombs were discovered. Bamberg was too-well armed to bypass and the discovery of such a large stock of supplies validated the need to route out Bamberg's defenders. Facing mostly small arms fire, the infantry closed the ring on the German garrison with the civilians and refugees quickly fleeing for cover. Bamberg would be no Aschaffenburg. By noon on April 13, 1945, the Germans were surrounded in the center of town and by 5:00 p.m. it was over with the surrender of 2,000 Wermacht soldiers. It was with a great sigh of relief that the S-3 staff listened to the German surrender in Bamberg. At least on this day, Jack was spared the awful task of having to plan to shell civilians and destroy a city.

In the rubble of Bamberg and as the 45th mounted their trucks for the next move to the south, the Division Headquarters announced that President Franklin Delano Roosevelt had succumbed to a cerebral hemorrhage in Warm Springs, Georgia, at 3:35 p.m. the previous day. The United States had a new leader as Harry Truman from Missouri was sworn into office. Speaking directly to the Armed Forces and the American people, Truman vowed that the Roosevelt policies would continue and that the Germans would be crushed.

With Bamberg over, it only took one day for the 45th to receive orders for its next objective. It was a stunner. On April 14, 1945, the boys from the small towns of Oklahoma were ordered to continue southward and take the city of Nuremberg, Germany–the shrine of Hitler's Nazism. Bamberg had fallen with comparative ease and relatively few Thunderbird casualties. However, no doubt lingered in the minds of the Thunderbirds about Nuremberg. Germany's third- largest city would be defended to the death by not only its soldiers, but its fanatical Nazi citizens. As they sped along the autobahn, it was with grit teeth and grim faces that the 45th braced for a fierce fight feared to be bloodier than Aschaffenburg.

Nuremberg was a city of immense symbolic significance to the Nazis. With

With a population of 400,000, Nuremburg was the birthplace of the Nazi party. In mid-April of 1945, its leaders refused to surrender and most of the city was reduced to rubble by Division Artillery.

a pre-war population of approximately 400,000, the city was considered the birthplace of Hitler's Nazi party. Huge rallies were regularly held in the city's stadium marked by grand pageantry that honored the party and the Fuhrer. Once a year, the city hosted the Nuremberg Party Festival that lasted an entire week honoring Hitler Youth Day, Party Leader Day, Brown Shirt Day, and Army Day. During this week the Germans reveled in torch light parades and grandiose rituals climaxed by the inspirational speeches of their evil leader Adolf Hitler and others.

Often referred to as the cradle of Nazism, Nuremberg also was the birthplace of the most notorious and sadistic body of state-sponsored legislation that mandated the mistreatment of the Jewish race and those deemed inferior human beings in the judgment of the Nazi Party. Passed in 1935, the Nuremberg Laws set forth a statutory persecution of the Jewish race which included expulsion from all public authority depravation of citizenship made it a criminal act for a German to marry a Jewish citizen, deprived Jews the ownership of retail stores, and, in humiliating fashion, forced the Jewish people to register their property with the State. Also included within their lunacy were provisions for state-supported destruction of Jewish Synagogues and worshiping places. So proud of Nuremberg were the Nazi militarists that they made the city the campus of the German War College. At its zenith, Nuremberg stood as a symbol for everything evil and inhuman propagated by Adolf Hitler and his party of thugs bent on world conquest.

If Nuremberg was the birthplace of Nazi ideology, it also was its death place. Shortly after the war many Nazi leaders, including Herman Goring and Rudolph Hess, were rounded up and imprisoned in Nuremberg. Between November of 1945 and October of 1946 the surviving leaders of Hitler's party were put on trial before an International Tribunal in Nuremberg Palace of Justice in what history labeled as the Nuremberg Trials. It was an ugly unceremonious end for those responsible for killing millions of Jews and others in the death camps of Europe. Of the eleven convicted, ten were hung in the prison gymnasium. Only Goring managed to cheat the hangman's noose, somehow finding a cyanide capsule and committing suicide. With the exception of Adolph Hitler, who himself committed suicide in April of 1945, every major Nazi leader responsible for the birth of the most sadistic and oppressive political party the world has ever seen, was put to death in the very cradle of Nazism.

As the 45th moved toward Nuremberg in April of 1945, Mayor Gauliter Karl Holz busily printed and passed out leaflets admonishing the civilians that any German surrendering to the Allies would be shot. Also barricading themselves within the walls of the old city was the 17th SS Division.

With the German Artillery nearly non-existent, the Germans would use their 88s as the main line of defense along with their newest concoction of horror, the "Schnell" mine which could blow a soldier "higher than his head."

It would be a hostile greeting for the Thunderbirds.

On April 15, 1945, the Division Artillery motor columns made their way south toward Nuremberg, carefully maintaining 20-yard intervals in the event of ambush or attack. While moving down Germany's autobahn had the advantage of speed, the long truck columns were vulnerable from the flanks, especially in wooded areas that crept close to the highways. While riding in the trucks was certainly better than walking, there was a constant air of tension and fear that anything could happen at any time. All weapons remained at the ready, rounds chambered, locked, and loaded. While the truck drivers tried to keep their eyes fixed straight ahead, Jack and Frosty Munson kept a steady watch on the woods to both sides of the convoy. Grateful for the speed of movement, there was the ever present worry that an ambush could trap the division in the "no-man's" land of the highway without support or cover.

If Division Artillery had any hesitation or moral dilemma of having to reduce another German city or town to nothing, it was erased on April 15 on the road to Nuremberg. What was left of the German Luftwaffe constantly harassed the columns with thirteen air sorties. Initially fearing a ground attack from the flanks, the division was hit with a series of desperate air attacks from the German Messerschmidts. Jack spent most of the day scrambling out of the back of his truck and diving into the road-side ditches to escape the machine gun fire. The German air attacks never lasted long and rarely did any damage as the American P-51s quickly arrived on the scene to chase the Nazi pilots away. Nonetheless, Jack knew well the damage a 50-caliber shell could cause to an arm or a leg, or worse to your life. Before reaching the outskirts of the great city, the Germans made it clear that they would not go down without a fight. With emotions now near anger, the Thunderbirds were there to accommodate the SS. If they wanted a scrap, they would soon get it.

By the end of the day on the 15th and into the early morning hours of the 16th, the Thunderbirds positioned themselves for the attack on Nuremberg. For Jack, the Division Artillery CP was initially set up at Ebermannsaat and later moved to the village of Lauf when the S-3 began their operations and planning for Artillery support to begin at daylight. As darkness fell on the 15th, Jack could not help but chuckle at the latest intelligence reports coming into the S-3 tent. The Thunderbirds biggest nemesis at Anzio, tank Commander General Von MacKensen, had been captured by Patton's United States 3rd Army while moving toward Frankfurt.

At 9:00 a.m. on April 16 the 157th Infantry Regiment attacked coming in from the south and east of the city. Initial objectives were taken and while the infantry encountered intense 88 fire, the artillery smashed the German guns to scrap. By the end of the day, the giant artillery pieces and the 45th had the birthplace of Nazism nearly surrounded. Although he knew the response in advance, General Frederick would give the Germans one last chance to come out with their hands up. The outcome predetermined Gauliter Holz refused; instead they would fight to the death. Unlike Aschaffenburg, there was no thoughtful hesitation over preservation of this German city. The Thunderbirds knew to end it, they would have to kill the city. No better were the emotions of Jack's unit captured than in The History of Division Artillery:

> An ultimatum was sent to the town notifying the officials that the town would be destroyed if not surrendered. We were to have the pleasure of destroying it.

On April 17, the entire city was encircled and the assault toward Nuremberg began. With all three infantry regiments attacking abreast of one another, the 45th Infantry Division moved into the city. For Jack, the S-3 section planned heavy and intense fire on the city in support of the infantry advance. Unlike Aschaffenburg, the orders to the S-3 from General Frederick and Meyer were simple–no restriction on target. With no Nuremberg building, tower, or structure sacred or safe, Division Artillery laid 12 batteries of fire at the city's defenders as the 157th, 179th, and 180th moved in for the end. The powerful combination of artillery, infantry, and air support stifled any serious effort to stop the attackers. On April 17 alone, 4,869 prisoners were taken and the 157th infantry regiment stumbled into a prisoner-of-war camp just as they entered the city proper. Thirteen thousand Allied prisoners, mostly non-United States soldiers, were liberated from Nazi imprisonment. More than 45 powerful German 88s were eliminated along the way. By the 18th, the last of the German fighters were being pushed into the inner parts of the city. The German lines were totally broken and the defense of Nuremberg was reduced to pockets of resistance formed by small bands of German survivors. The fighting, like Aschaffenburg and Bamberg, became house to house and street to street.

Some of the most difficult fighting in Nuremburg took place at the Nazi Party Parade Ground.

On the 18th, Jack's unit moved into the outskirts of Nuremberg to be closer to the action. This time, without hesitation, if the enemy was even thought to be held up in a store front, office, or house, the big artillery guns would barrel cite their cannon at the objective and obliterate the target allowing the infantry to safely advance. Houses, churches, and shops were no longer taken, they were destroyed. By the end of the day, those Germans still resisting were forced into the inner sanctum of the city. The noose was tightening.

On the morning of April 19, the final assault on Nuremberg's inner city began. It lasted all day and into the next as German soldiers and citizens fought furiously. On April 20, 1945, at 6:15 p.m., the last 200 German soldiers who were willing to fight were cornered in a tunnel and refused to give up. The 45th accommodated their desire to die for their Fuhrer.

The next day, Jack stood in Adolf Hitler Plaza for XV Corp's flag raising ceremony. The American flag now flew over Nuremberg, the battle over.

One of Nuremberg's most notorious Nazi citizens was Julius Streicher. The owner of numerous newspapers, Streicher was a vocal advocate of the persecution of Jews and he organized and conducted many campaigns to ban Jews from education and public entertainment. He favored state expropriation of Jewish property and was a true believer that the Jewish race should be destroyed. Of the 10,000 prisoners taken at Nuremberg, Streicher was nowhere to be found. His professed loyalty to the Fuhrer was not enough that he would stay and fight with his comrades and instead he escaped the city. In July of 1945, an American patrol near Berchtesgaden captured Streicher on a farm while he was painting, pretending to be a farmer. He was tried, convicted, and hung in Nuremberg following the Nuremberg trials.

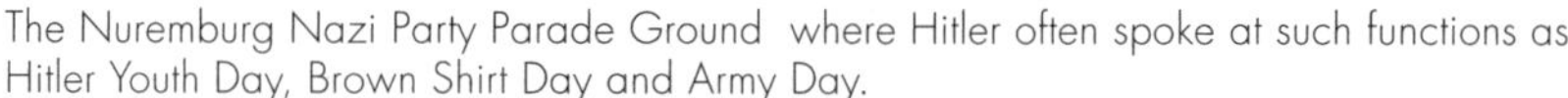
The Nuremburg Nazi Party Parade Ground where Hitler often spoke at such functions as Hitler Youth Day, Brown Shirt Day and Army Day.

With the fall of Nuremburg in April of 1945, the 45th marked the occasion with a parade in Adolph Hitler Plaza. The city would later be the venue of the Nuremburg trials of numerous Nazi war criminals, including Herman Goring.

With only a few hours rest after the fall of Nuremberg, the Thunderbirds were given their next objective, and told once again to move out with all possible speed. While Jack did not know it at the time, the city of Munich would be the last and final target of World War II for the 45th Infantry Division. For Jack, the end of the war was only a few days away. On April 21, the Division Artillery CP moved to Buttleborn. As Russian tanks moved into the city of Berlin from the east and the Allied Armies poised on the outskirts of western Berlin, Jack moved into the town of Roth, just outside of Nuremberg. After encountering a strong delaying action by the remnants of the 79th Volksgrenadier Division, the Thunderbirds moved across the Altmuhl River on April 23. The next day they were given orders to turn their line of march southeastward, across the Danube River, and continue on to Munich. So swift was the movement, no one in the S-3 section dared to unpack. With the Division Artillery CP moving into Monheim, the Thunderbirds prepared to cross the rapid currents of the Danube River. The Germans would not let it happen easily. On April 26, the German 79th blew the last bridge crossing the Danube leaving the Thunderbirds momentarily stranded on the north bank of the river. Dug in on the south bank of the Danube with their 20mm guns, the Germans prepared to stop the 45th's crossing of the historical river. To counter the last of the German Artillery, the 45th's Division Artillery rolled into position on the Danube's north bank and methodically picked off the 20mms as they attempted to obstruct the crossing. With the Germans now in total disarray and completely disorganized, the Thunderbirds prepared to cross the river. Jack Neville crossed the Danube River with the Division Artillery on April 27, 1945 to set up camp in the small town of Burgheim. The next day, the Division Artillery CP was moved to Schrobenhausen in position to attack Munich. As the S-3 section unfolded their tents for the night, the radios whistled with incredible news from the north. The previous day, the Russians and Americans had linked up at the Elbe River. Berlin now was surrounded and the Third Reich was in the last inning. Surely it would end soon. Knowing that in the morning the final days of the war would start, Jack, Munson, and Arnote lit their kerosene lanterns and hovered over the maps studying the route to the south. They were 40 miles from Munich. The town almost directly in the line of march was Dachau, 10 miles north of Munich on the Amper River. Arnote reviewed the S-2 reports advising his staff that Dachau had no military significance. Therefore it was not

The 45th's march through Germany was fast and furious with capture and imprisonment of thousands of German soldiers. Prisoners were housed outside of Furstenfeldbruck, Germany in May of 1945.

a target. No plans and operations would be necessary for Dachau as the division would bypass the town. Get ready for a fight at Munich was the standing order.

Spearheading the assault on Munich was the 3rd Battalion of the 157th Infantry Regiment along with attached units of the 171st Tank Battalion, two batteries of artillery, the 120th Engineers, and 50 tanks. With a formidable array of firepower, the task force would be led by Lt. Col. Felix Sparks, commander of the 157th, and survivor of Anzio and Reipertswiller. As events would unfold, Jack Neville would not be far behind.

On April 28, the lead elements of Lt. Col. Sparks' task force were less than 30 miles from Munich. At 7:30 a.m., Sparks received Frederick's order to move on Munich with all possible speed. Only a few hours later, Sparks received a change in his orders with instructions now to detour to the town of Dachau and liberate what was believed to be a prisoner-of-war camp to the northeast. According to Sparks' personal diary, the order "pissed off" the battle hardened leader of the 157th. Sparks did not see any military objective to Dachau and such a detour would only delay and reduce the firepower necessary for the assault on Munich, thought to be a key aircraft maintenance center that would be heavily defended. Sparks did as he was ordered. With two of the companies of 3rd Battalion in the assault mode, Sparks elected to send one company on toward Munich with I Company detailed to locate the camp and take it. As Sparks relayed his plan back to headquarters, he received orders that quickly

In April of 1945, the 45th began its assault on Munich traveling down the German autobahn that ran north of the city.

chilled his anger and peaked his anxiety about his newest assignment. Not only was Sparks to seize the camp, he was ordered to completely seal the Dachau Camp off with his forces and allow no one to enter or leave. Lt. Col. Felix Sparks had never heard of Dachau. What in the hell was at Dachau?

The small town of Dachau had a population of approximately 15,000. Prior to the war the town was principally known as an art community because of its unique light conditions which made the area conducive to painting on canvas. After World War I, as Germany attempted to climb back into the arena of world military power, an ammunition factory was constructed a short distance to the northeast where many of the Dachau citizens were employed. The factory's main product was gun powder. By 1933, Hitler's Nazi party had essentially seized control of Germany and the Nazi's tentacles of political oppression and tyranny reached everywhere. Hitler's principal method of dealing with his political opponents was to simply have them arrested and jailed. All free speech and political thought were quickly corralled and suppressed. One of Hitler's primary henchmen in these early days was Heinrich Himmler who rose in the Nazi party to lead Hitler's personal army, the SS. In the early 1930s Himmler was Munich's chief of police and it was in this position that he rounded up every "undesirable," "inferior," and political opponent that stood in the Nazi's way. It did not take long for the jails in Munich to overflow in the wake of Himmler's term as police chief. His solution to the jail's over-population and to further enhance the wave of Nazi suppression, was to seize the ammunition factory northeast of Dachau and turn it into a prison. Of course, Hitler did not label the converted factory as such, but rather the Reich's propagandists called it a "special camp" for the protection of communist detainees. In essence, Hitler's political opponents were gathered up and "protected" by being imprisoned at the Dachau Camp, or so the world was told. By April of 1933, a small group of the SS took over the operation of the camp, and by April of 1945, approximately 240 of the most sadistic of the SS watched over the camp's population. The Dachau Camp was not originally built as a "death" camp. In its beginning, the camp was intended to be a work camp, or slave camp to house political opponents or anyone else the Nazis did not like. However, as the years went by Dachau became much more. As Hitler's evil empire grew into the late 1930s and 1940s, Dachau evolved into one of the Reich's most sadistic and gruesome places the world has ever come to know. Dachau came to be known as the Nazi experimental medical station where the camp's population was the object of uncountable inhuman and grotesque medical experiments. Prisoners were regularly the object of biochemical experiments which included the purposeful injection of typhus, as well as other death-causing viruses and diseases, into their bodies. Other brutal and sadistic exercises included the infamous cold experiments–a process where poisoners were subjected to freezing water and cold in order to determine what temperature vital parts of the mind and body froze and became inoperable. Only the most sadistic and evil understood the reason for such torture, but it was all in the regular course of business at Dachau.

The Dachau Camp was of considerable size. Approximately 1,000 yards in width and 1,200 yards in depth, it was nearly self-sustaining. The western two-thirds of the camp consisted of an infirmary, a coal yard, a power plant, and railroad tracks dissecting the camp from the southwest to the northeast. The eastern third of the camp consisted of SS officer housing units and the prisoner compound and barracks. While not technically an extermination death camp, Dachau was equipped with a coal-fired crematorium to dispose of those who had died from starvation, over work, the cold, grotesque medical experiments, or those simply executed at the whim of their captors. Felix Sparks and those in the 45th had no clue of the horror just in front of them.

At approximately noon on April 28, 1945, Dr. Franz Blaha stood behind the main gate of the Dachau Camp gazing down the road that led to the freedom he was convinced he would never see. Blaha was a Czechoslovakian doctor imprisoned at Dachau for the last three years. He was 72- years old, and somehow had managed to stay alive only because the Nazis saw him as a useful tool for their sadistic ways. At gun point, Blaha had been forced to perform grotesque executions followed by thousands of autopsies of those murdered. He had survived Dachau, but at the near loss of his sanity. At times he tried to regain his loss of humanity by staring down the long lonely road, silently hoping and praying that freedom would come. By the 29th, most of Dachau Camp's executive officers had fled the camp leaving behind only a few of the most fanatical SS to stand guard over the prison population. At 72, there was little he could do but stay and wait for someone to come. On this day, as he stood alone looking down the road, two bright headlights appeared on the road in the distance. Dimmed by age, his old eyes worked hard to see who or what it was, anxious and scared that it was the Nazis returning to the camp to continue their madness. As Blaha squinted and strained to see ahead, the two headlights turned slightly to the right. Blaha could see that the lights were those of a single jeep pulling to a halt on the side of the road. His hands gripped the iron gate, and as he continued his stare down the road he could see a large outline of a single soldier stepping out of the jeep and staring down the road directly back at him. The man down the road stood motionless for what seemed like forever. Blaha, still fearful, dared not move as he thought the figure's eyes were fixed on him, watching and listening in silence but for the sputtering idle of the jeep's engine. Then, the figure got back into the vehicle. With the engine revving up, Blaha could hear the Jeep's gears being shifted as it turned around to speed away and back down the road. As the wheels of the vehicle turned to the left, Blaha was sure his eyes had betrayed him. On the right rear panel of the jeep he was certain that he had seen a white star. My God, the Americans were here. With all the excitement his old bones could muster, Blaha started his shuffle back to the barracks to tell the rest. Maybe his prayers had been answered and the nightmare over. Blaha did not know it then, but the solitary figure climbing from the jeep with binoculars fixed on the main gate was that of Lt. Col. Felix Sparks, with the 45th Infantry Division Thunderbirds not far behind.

The lead elements of Sparks' advance units reached the small town of Dachau rather quickly, only to find no German soldiers in the town and no prisoner camp as had been reported. After breaking out the maps and questioning a few of the town's people, Sparks redirected his forces back to the northeast of town in hopes of locating the camp. Speeding down the road hoping to lead to his objective, Sparks ordered his driver to bring his jeep to a halt. The war had taught Sparks to be cautious in these circumstances and he was uncertain about what lay ahead. Climbing from the jeep, Sparks fixed his field glasses down the road. As he moved the glasses back and forth and up and down trying to get a clear view he spotted a large sign hanging over what appeared to be a gate. Focusing the binoculars, the sign read "Arbeit Mach Free," translated "work will make you free." As Sparks continued to survey the gate, barely visible was the outline of one individual, clad in what appeared to be a blue stripped uniform with both hands above his head holding on to the rungs of the iron gate. Sparks momentarily continued his watch on the lonely figure, then climbed back into the jeep telling the driver that they were at the right place, they had located the camp.

Sparks' only intelligence reports suggested that the camp could be heavily defended by the SS, possibly even with tanks and mortar support. After reconnoitering what he believed to be the main gate of the camp and the surrounding area, he was convinced that if the camp was in fact defended, the firepower of the Nazis would most likely be focused on this entrance. Accordingly, Sparks sent reconnaissance east and west in search of an alternative approach. Shortly thereafter, Sparks decided that the most advantageous route of march was along the railroad tracks that entered the camp from the southwest. It was from this point that Sparks, and the Thunderbirds of I Company, 3rd Battalion 157th Infantry entered the Dachau Camp for the first time.

As they moved into the camp along the tracks, things were eerily quiet. Ever fearful of ambush and booby traps, the Thunderbirds moved cautiously forward down the tracks and into the western third of the camp. Now visible to the advance party of I Company were a number of railroad cars. Cautious that the enemy could be concealing themselves in the box cars, the Thunderbirds crept forward weapons at the ready. As the boys stepped closer and closer to the cars, many of the soldiers were quickly overcome with the horrible aroma of the rotting flesh of human remains to the point that many were physically stricken, vomiting and regurgitating. The horror and evil of Nazi Germany unfolded before the young soldier's eyes. Along the railroad tracks were 39 railroad cars. Literally stuffed and stacked into every box car and gondola type of car were the bodies of men, women, and children. All of the dead were in various stages of decomposition and the sight of it all, the order of such death was shocking, overwhelming. If any man questioned the reasons they fought, the Dachau Camp spoke the answer. The boxcars, which came to be know as the "Death Train," contained the bodies of 2,310 men, women, and children. Moving on past the Death Train, the Thunderbirds continued northeasterly through the camp. Many were so emotionally distraught that they cried, others were enraged. As the Thunderbirds moved from building to building, the SS would occasionally make their presence known by either attempting to surrender or ambush the on-rushing Thunderbirds. Sparks' men were in no mood for mercy. Any German uniform that attempted to raise his weapon was instantly shot, no quarter given. Roughly halfway into the camp, Sparks' party turned eastward. After moving approximately 700 yards east of the railroad tracks, the Thunderbirds ran directly into the crematorium. The sight and smell of the ovens was as ugly as the Death Train. Bodies were still in the ovens in various stages of post mortem, arms and legs twisted and turned in grotesque angles. The room next to the crematorium contained bodies stacked like cordwood waiting to be reduced to ashes.

The Thunderbirds continued east running directly into the prisoner compound only 60 yards east of the crematorium. As they approached the barbed wire and wooden fences that bordered the prisoner barracks, the air was remarkably still. Then, almost suddenly, the slave-prisoner population understood for certain what was happening, their freedom at long last had arrived.

According to Leota's scrapbook, this picture of snow covered bodies in a boxcar of the "Death Train" was taken by Jack. It snowed at Dachau on May 1, 1945 suggesting Jack was in the Dachau Death Camp at or about the time of its liberation by the 45th.

Their terrible ordeal was now over. Bluestriped uniforms streamed out of the barracks running toward their liberators, shouting and screaming for joy, deliriously happy, relieved that the Americans had come. The Dachau Camp had originally been constructed to house 5,000 with each barrack intended to shelter 208 prisoners. At the time the camp was liberated, almost 1,600 men women and children, many already dead or near death were found stuffed into each barrack. Incredibly, as many as 300,000 people entered the camp gate through the course of Nazi occupation. On April 29, 32,000 prisoners were liberated from the horror of the Dachau Concentration Camp. Despite the calamity and hysteria of events surrounding the liberation, it took Sparks' group only one hour to get the Dachau Camp under control. The next day, the 7th Army Headquarters took over administration of the camp as the 116th and 127th Evacuation Units moved in.

The liberation of Dachau was not without controversy or questionable incident. According to rumors, many of the Thunderbirds, sickened and angry to the point of emotional breakdown at what they had seen, shot and killed many of the SS who surrendered or attempted to surrender. After some fifty or so of the SS were rounded up along a wall near the camp's coal yard, a sudden burst of machine gun fire erupted killing seventeen. Controversy immediately arose as to whether or not the Germans were attempting to escape. According to an eye witness, investigations revealed they were either attempting to escape or attack. Although history has resolved the issue in favor of the 45th, the 42nd Infantry Division later claimed they were actually the

Two of the dead SS soldiers at Dachau, most likely shot by the 45th. According to Leota's scrapbook, these pictures were taken by Jack as he moved through Dachau sometime between April 29 and May 1, 1945.

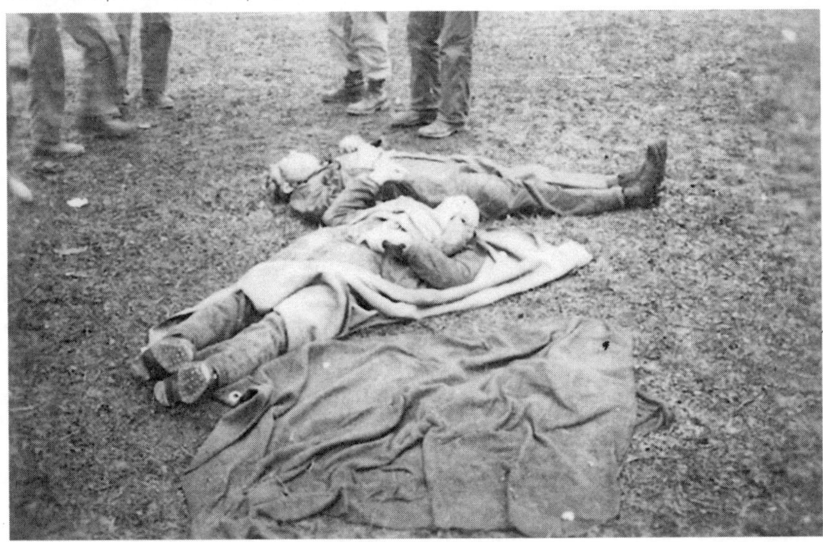

first into the Dachau Camp. Events proved the 42nd was about an hour and a half behind the Thunderbirds, but they did in fact reach the southwest corner of the camp at the railroad tracks. Two generals of the 42nd attempted to enter the main area of the camp only to be refused by Lt. Col. Sparks. Sparks had his orders to seal off the camp, let no one in or out, and this included the two generals of the 42nd. Sparks later was threatened with court martial and nearly arrested for following General Frederick's orders to let no one into or out of the camp. General George S. Patton, in front of Sparks' very eyes, ripped up his court martial papers dismissing the allegation of Sparks' refusal to obey the command of superiors as ridiculous under the circumstances.

After the war, and the Nuremberg Trials, the Allies refused to release to the next of kin the bodies of those hung in the prison gymnasium after trial for fear that their graves would become monuments or shrines to perpetrate Nazism and its beliefs. Although there is no real evidence, respected historians suggest that the bodies of Goring, Streicher, and the others were actually cremated in the ovens at Dachau. In any event, Dachau did in fact serve as the venue for the war crimes tribunal for the prosecution of those responsible for the murder of American prisoners at Malmedy during the Battle of the Bulge.

The Thunderbirds inspect the Death Train shortly after entering the Dachau Camp.

On April 28, 1945, I Company of the 157th entered the Dachau Death Camp. To their horror, they discovered 39 boxcars containing the bodies of 2,310 men, women and children.

The Thunderbirds called the boxcars discovered at Dachau the "Death Train."

Jack places a wreath at the wall of the Dachau's Nazi death camp known for its gruesome medical experiments on its inmates.

REFLECTIONS DAD AND DACHAU

So, where was Dad during the liberation of the Dachau Death Camp? Dad's silence on these matters and the passing of decades leaves us only to reason from the facts we do know. The record strongly suggests that Dad was not that far behind Sparks' task force, if indeed he was not part of it. Although the various histories do not specifically reference the participation of the Headquarters Staff, Headquarters Company of Division Artillery, it is unmistakable that Dad was witness to the atrocities at Dachau. Found in Mom's scrapbooks were several pictures of the Dachau Camp taken by Dad after its liberation. Prominent among the pictures are three of the Death Trains which clearly depict bodies stacked into the box and gondola rail-

Pictured is Dachau's main camp building. In April of 1945, the 45th Infantry Division was the first allied unit into the camp that imprisoned over 10,000.

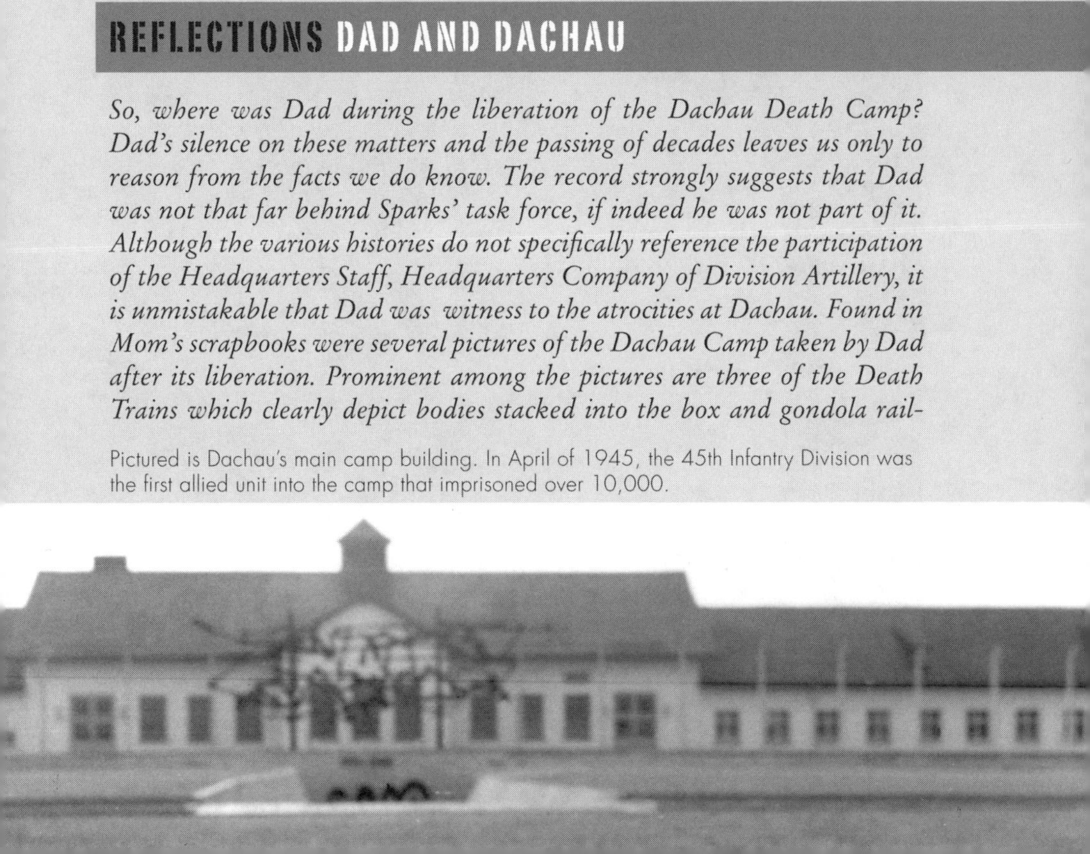

road cars that ran into the southwestern corner of the camp. We know that Sparks had orders to seal off the camp and let no one enter or leave on April 29, 1945. It is therefore fair to conclude that Dad was in the camp on April 29, the day of its liberation. If in fact, Sparks was successful in executing his orders, as he apparently was, and assuming no one could leave the camp, it follows that Dad was present at or about the time Sparks' men secured the camp. According to Whitlock's The Rock of Anzio, *it snowed in Dachau on May 1. While two of Dad's pictures are of numerous snow-covered bodies most likely in a boxcar, the pictures of the Death Train reflect the absence of any snow on the ground or in the boxcars, therefore suggesting that Dad was on the scene. Additional evidence, perhaps far more circumstantial, is the entry in The History of Division Artillery for the date April 29 to the effect that the 157th captured Dachau. "The place was filled with bodies of prisoners," further suggesting the presence of Division Artillery personnel*

May of 1971, Richard Neville is commissioned a 2nd Lt. in the United States Navy after graduating from Purdue University, with Jack and Leota at his side.

in the Dachau Camp at or about the time of its liberation. One certainty of Dachau does exist. Dad never spoke of it in any meaningful way other than to parenthetically reference that he "was there." Interestingly, his pictures of Dachau made their way home from Germany where Mom conscientiously made them part of her scrapbooks. Mom wanted somebody to at least see part of the story someday, even if there was no one to speak of it.

May of 1971, Drew Neville is commissioned as a 2nd Lt., U.S. Army, Signal Corp., and reported for active duty at Ft. Gordon, Georgia in September, 1972.

REFLECTIONS THE RUN FOR THE STATE SENATE, 1988

Politics in the Neville household were a hot topic. The issues of the day often dominated dinner time discussions with Dad poking and prodding everyone except Mom, always with the objective of creating as much turmoil as possible. Although Dad was an announced conservative Republican, it was often difficult to determine where he really stood on any particular issue. If you took one side of an issue, he would take the other. And, over the evening hours, the more J&Bs and water he washed down, the more cantankerous he would become. He loved the debate and argument. There were of course many occasions when the heat of the conversation got too high. In these times, Mom always played the role of moderator. Interrupting with a few "now Jacks" and a few shakes of her head, usually served the purpose. At the least, the decibel level lowered if only for a short time. In all of these conversations, rarely was a resolution or conclusion reached, but there was always conversation. On John Kennedy, Dad described him as the son of a rich, whiskey-running gangster. However if you attacked Kennedy as a liberal, Jack's response was that Kennedy kept America out of a nuclear holocaust during the Cuban missile crisis, he at least fought in World War II, and he pioneered space exploration as a national goal. On Lyndon Johnson, he was a crook who stuffed the ballot boxes in Texas to win the election in the Senate. But, if you attacked Johnson on the Viet Nam War policies, he defended Johnson staking out the position that the President had no support and was in an impossible position. His own President Richard Nixon was a crook, but he at least got us out of the Viet Nam War. Ronald Reagan was a "good-talk'n" movie cowboy, an over achiever who somehow found the way to deal with the Russians by spending the communists into their own form of national bankruptcy with the "Star Wars" initiative. On the sometimes more sensitive social issues of the day, Dad would often announce that a woman's place was at home with the kids, "God damn it, somebody needs to be home when they come home from school." On the other hand, if Mom wanted to work at the Gilcrease Museum, it was "okay." Women ought to be able to play golf any time they wanted to at Cedar Ridge Country Club, but they better not slow anyone up. On issues of abortion, school busing, and integration his views were always rather straight forward. If she does not want the baby, she should not have it, but if she has it she better damn well take care of it, not the government. In our under-10 basketball league in Oklahoma City, Dad entered our all-white Gilt Edge Cowboys team into a league with several all-black teams over the protests of several parents. Dad's response, "So God Damn what, we're play'n." If you had a thin skin at the Neville dinner table you needed to think twice about sitting down. Dad was a voracious reader who kept in step with the issues of the day, social as well as political, and often the evening supper was a test intended to provoke both thought and conversation. In all of these contentious, cantankerous dinner table conversations, World War II was never a topic of debate or extended discussion.

On July 4, 1988, the customary 4th of July festivities got underway with a bomb-shell announcement. Gathering the family around, Dad announced that a seat in the State Senate for the Southern District of Tulsa was open. Dad declared his candidacy for the Republican nomination to the State Senate with the primary to be held in August. Dad was 68 years old. His announcement was not met with great enthusiasm or support. Uncle Baird, could not help himself with the quip "what in the hell for?" Dad's answer, "because I want to." Pete MacKellar seized on the pecuniary, "I guess we've got to give you some money." Dad's answer "no, there won't be any campaign solicitations." "This is crazy" became the theme that ran through the pool-side beer and barbeque. There was no "stump speech," no cry for political contribution or even support, just "I'm runnin" and that pretty much ended the only "public announcement" of Jack's candidacy for the State Senate.

In the summer of 1988, the Republicans were running on a tidal wave of national support. Two-time elected President Ronald Reagan was stepping aside for George H. Bush from Texas, and it looked as if the Democrats would counter with relatively little known Michael Dukakis of Massachusetts. It certainly looked like a Republican slaughter. At home, Henry Bellmon was in the governor's chair for the second time. Senate District 35, where Mom and Dad lived, was stretched geographically into south Tulsa, but was dominated mostly by affluent Republicans. There would be no serious Democratic challenge and whoever won the Republican primary would most likely take a seat in the State Senate. Many of the local political issues revolved around the state's usual financial crisis. Bellmon was talking of a special session in the state legislature for improvements in the state's prison system, yet a measure calling for a $10 million cut in the state's welfare budget was on his desk. The Department of Human Services was in need of a $23 million bailout, and the Senate was deciding whether senior citizens should be given an additional $1,000 tax exemption. State Questions 617 and 618 were on the ballot, both measures intended to stimulate economic development in the state. For the race in Tulsa Senate District 35 there was plenty of political fat to chew on. On the national scene, abortion, human rights, economic opportunities for minorities, the defense budget, and equal opportunity for women all dotted the political landscape. Interestingly, George Bush's selection for vice president, Dan Quayle, found himself im-

mediately mired in controversy over his military service. The Democrats, and even some Republicans, went on the attack alleging that Quayle had purposefully avoided service in Viet Nam by joining the Indiana National Guard.

The 1988 Republican primary for Senate District 35 was one of the most unique races of all times. The Republican incumbent was Warren Green, a political veteran who had held the seat since 1964. Green was the odds-makers favorite, the only candidate who had a political organization in the district. The other challenger was a young attorney, Don Rubottom, 34 years old, the only candidate with a written plan and legislative agenda. And then there was Jack Neville, never a politician and retired at 68. It was going to be interesting.

After Dad's July 4 announcement, conversation turned toward Dad's political strategy for the upcoming race. What about Oklahoma's economic development? What about the state questions? Prison reform? The Department of Human Services bail-out? Abortion? Equal rights? What about Dan Quayle joining the National Guard and not going to Viet Nam? Each and every question was posed as a potential issue to "run on" with a constant plea that if he was going to be in the race, certainly he had to address some issues in order to get his message out. Each issue-related proposal and strategy was artfully and skillfully dodged, until finally, probably out of frustration from being badgered by those of the family who fancied themselves political geniuses, he announced his political issues agenda and strategy was that he did not have one. Republican candidate for the State Senate Jack Neville announced to the family gurus that he had no platform, no agenda. "I'm just runnin'," he said.

And so he did, in one of the most never-been-written about and bizarre races in state political history. Mom and Dad financed the campaign mostly out of their own pockets, but most of the family could not resist making at least some contribution. He never solicited campaign contributions from the public, he never bought television or radio spots, he never ran political announcements in the paper, and he never handed out leaflets. The closest he came to "organizing" a campaign was a trip he and Mom took to a local sign store to order 12" x 12" placards with a red background "Neville for Senate" stenciled boldly in white. His only campaign "staff" was Mom and together they stapled the placards to wooden stakes they purchased at a local hardware store. Dad did rent a "campaign headquarters" of sorts in a small strip shopping mall at 61st and Riverside Drive. Headquarters was about 900 square feet and consisted of one phone, one desk, and three chairs. At headquarters, several activities took place. Mom and Dad drank coffee, read the newspaper, called their pals telling them only that Dad "was runnin'," and putting their signs together. There was one "Neville for Sen-

ate" sign taped to the front door of headquarters. And, without question, all "campaign activities" ended at noon.

Dad's campaign style was just as unique as his political platform, and it was both fun and frustrating to follow him Saturday mornings on the campaign trail. He must have visited every coffee shop, Denny's, and waffle shop in south Tulsa, Bixby, Jenks, and Coweta. It never took much for him to "work the room" as he was totally at ease shaking hands with everyone approachable with his only salutation being "Hello, I'm Jack Neville runnin' for Senate." Dad never mentioned his opponents, never mentioned an issue, and never gave a speech. He never even mentioned that he was a Republican, he challenged no one to debate, and never was there a word said that he fought with the 45th Infantry Division in World War II.

In the purest sense, Dad was "just runnin'." Tuesday, August 23, 1988, was the big day of the primary. By late afternoon Mom and Dad had "headquarters" organized and ready for their own brand of a watch party on election night. It was not exactly "election central," but it was for the Neville family. Stocked with beer, scotch, gin, huge plates of hamburgers, hotdogs, and ribs, Mom and Dad waited at election headquarters for their supporters and political well wishers to drop by. By seven o'clock when the polls closed, the tiny 900-square-foot office was packed with people, and like the 4th of July, it was all family. The Sullivans and MacKellars traveled all the way from Oklahoma City, and the Nevilles from Okmulgee, Ponca City, and Muskogee. The place was alive with nieces, nephews, children, grandchildren, and the scene was turning into an unexpected exciting event, as we all stood together waiting on the election results. By election night Dad's political staff had brought two improvements to headquarters. One was a television and the other a huge rectangular piece of cardboard. In Mom's printing were all precincts of District 35 listed down the left column, and the three candidates for Senate District 35 stenciled across the top. Dad's staff intended to keep its own election night count. Who needed Tom Brokaw. After seven o'clock, the election results started to pour in and with each interruption in local programing a "hush" came over the Neville watch party. With each announcement, Mom posted the numbers in the appropriate columns to the now rather loud "oooh's and awww's" of the crowd. Throughout the evening, there was an "ebb and flow" to the results with Dad, at times, miraculously in the lead. The atmosphere became electric as the entire family exchanged their "I can't believe its" as the hour closed in on 9:00 p.m.

By 10:00 p.m. the anticipation was over and the results were in. Despite the Republican rush, Oklahoma voters turned out from office 12 incumbents across the state, one of whom was twenty-four-year veteran Warren Green. But Don Rubottom was too much for Dad. The final vote tally was

Rubottom 2,972, Neville 1,587, and Green 1,128. Despite the second place finish there was only jubilation at Headquarters with a claim of victory over incumbent Green. Second place did not bother Dad, and his enthusiasm over the race was infectious. There was not a sad eye in the place as the Neville clan partied on in celebration long after the results were confirmed with a call to the State Election Board.

And now, looking back to that one moment the night of August 23, 1988, there seems suspended in time a "oneness" of the Neville brothers and sisters, nieces, nephews, and grandchildren, that was never to be again. The Nevilles were aging, moving into the twilight of their years. That election night was the last time they all were together in one room, and in the coming years, the race of time would prove inevitable for the Nevilles of Adair. That's what the campaign of 1988 was all about.

CHAPTER XXXVII
FINALLY OVER

With the liberation of Dachau came the final collapse of Nazi and fascist power in Europe. As the Russians and Americans scrambled through the bombed-out ruins of Berlin, Hitler married his mistress of ten years, Eva Braun, and committed suicide in his bunker. Benito Mussolini also was captured attempting to escape from Italy. He was hung by his heels in a public square.

The only fighting for the 45th now remained to the south. The race was on for Germany's third-largest city, Munich. Five United States Divisions, including the 45th, barreled down the autobahn to the south. With Dachau still fresh on their minds, the Thunderbirds were ready for the final fight, trigger fingers itchy to wipe out the remainder of those who created the Dachau Camp. Jack's Division Artillery CP moved to the small town of Mittenhiem for plans and operations that would crush whoever or whatever was left in Munich. The city of Munich had a population of 828,325 and was considered a major aircraft industry center. By April 29, the city and its war-making assets had been bombed to near oblivion, but intelligence reports indicated there still existed a strong SS and fanatical Nazi presence. After Dachau, Division Artillery was of no mind to give any quarter to any German with a weapon. The actual attack on Munich by the 45th started on the very day that Dachau was liberated with the 180th and parts of the 179th bypassing Dachau and moving on to Munich. Jack and the S-3 section listened on their radios in anticipation of any engagement of the enemy by the 180th or the 179th. Expecting a wicked fight, it did not come, and Munich fell quickly in rather anti-climactic fashion. On April 30, the 180th fought off the last German resistance in the northern edge of the city and raced straight for the center of town unopposed. The great city of Munich fell in one day's time and at 6:00 p.m., April 30, 1945, the city was cleared and secured. Remarkably, the civilian population was relatively orderly, and the division was left to "ride herd" on some 125,000 surrendering German soldiers.

We always believed Jack was part law enforcement officer because of his experiences after the fall of Munich. With orders to take over the policing of the city, the Division Artillery CP was moved to a map reproduction center

By the end of May, 1945, the Thunderbirds were garrisoned in Munich and often policed the city, including Adolph Hitler's apartment on the second floor.

on the outskirts of Munich. For the next two days, Jack and the men of the S-3 section garrisoned their area of the city without incident, and at the same time fretted over the next assignment, the next objective. In the month of April, 1945, Jack had been accustomed to quick and rapid movement. In April alone the Division Artillery CP had moved 19 times and with some fighting still going on to the north around Berlin, the men were fearful there would be a next move, another battle, more shooting, and killing. On May 3, 1945, Col. Arnote called his S-3 staff and Jack together for yet another too familiar

The 45th Infantry Division at attention in Munich on Memorial Day, 1945.

meeting. All were convinced Arnote would instruct the men to make ready for Berlin, they would move out in the morning. Instead, the staff with glazed eyes and solemn faces stared at Arnote as he delivered the news Jack had convinced himself would never come. Arnote quietly announced that Division Artillery was ordered to stand down, they would not be committed to battle again in the European Theatre of operations. For Jack Neville, the shooting and killing ended forever on the northwestern outskirts of Munich, Germany.

To the north, with Berlin now in the hands of the British, Russians, and Americans. Hamburg Nazi radios announced Hitler's death and that he would be succeeded by Admiral Karl Doenitz. Loyal to the end, the Nazis announced that Hitler had fought to the end. Of course, the report was a lie, Hitler died at his own hand. Doenitz did not waste much time suing for peace. On May 7, 1945 the Germans ran up their last white flag and surrendered unconditionally. The great war in Europe was over, the Nazis finally crushed. For Jack, it was the first time since he boarded the U.S.S. Leonard Wood at Hampton Roads, Virginia in June of 1943 that, after 511 combat days in Europe, there was the feeling that he would finally get to go home, alive.

In 1973, Jack and Leota traveled to Southern Europe where Jack returned to the German death camp at Dachau liberated by the Thunderbirds in 1945 only a few weeks before the end of World War II.

CHAPTER XXXVIII
SPRING OF 1945 - OKLAHOMA

Although the Allies were piling up victory after victory in the European Theatre, the anxiety and frustration of the war wait reached its zenith for Leota in the spring of 1945 as she watched for the war to end. The two principal sources of information still remained *The Daily Oklahoman* and the radio. Surely, with the continued route of the German forces, the home folk would be told of the precise whereabouts of their loved ones fighting the war on the European continent. Quite the reverse was the case. Instead of less secrecy, the Supreme Allied Headquarters made it clear that there would be more secrecy over division level troop movements. By late March and early April, the Allies front line extended all the way from northern Europe, Denmark, and Holland, to the southern most regions of Germany where Leota was fighting. United States commanders feared that lifting the veil of secrecy and revealing the exact location of division level units would allow the German Army to pinpoint the spearheads of Allied advance in the final days of the war. Some of the most spectacular gains made by the advancing allies were camouflaged or not reported. The best Leota could do on most days was to continue to follow the reports of movement of the 7th Army as she had done in the months previous as all Oklahomans knew the Thunderbirds were in General Patch's 7th. By the spring of 1945, talk became more serious that the war could end soon. To Leota, it did not seem to matter much that the Oklahoma A&M Aggies won the national basketball championship beating NYU 49-45 in New York's Madison Square Garden. The 45th's battle at Aschaffenburg was reported in considerable factual detail, even outlining Major Von Lambert's use of civilians to defend the city to the death. Two weeks later, the Thunderbirds' victory at Nuremberg was reported, and moving into late April of 1945, Leota and the home front could see through the earlier promised veil of secrecy. By April 17, Leota knew the division had turned to the south and was headed for Munich at the same time Berlin was in an Allied vice that was tightening every day. All of Oklahoma City knew that the war in Europe would end soon. There was an excitement in the air at the thought of the boys coming home by, at least, the end of May.

In late March and early April of 1945, the talk in Oklahoma City turned to the victory in Europe. While most saw the expected "V-E Day" with joy and excitement, others were far more pragmatic, even to the extent of casting a cloud of depression over the anticipated victory over the Germans. The 45th Infantry Division had been remarkably successful in Europe, their battle record impecable, and the United States would certainly still be engaged with the Japanese in the Pacific Theatre once the Germans were beaten. Now the rumors swelled that with the defeat of the Nazis, the Oklahoma boys of the 45th would be sent to the Pacific isles to fight the Japs. Leota could not bring herself to deal with this issue. Jack was still in Europe, he was still fighting. Please God keep him alive in the final days. The thought of going to the Pacific would be dealt with later. Could he just get home?

Nonetheless, Oklahoma City and Oklahomans started to now more seriously consider the effect of the war's end on the homefront. By the spring of 1945, soldiers already were streaming back home. By April 15, approximately 1,700,000 servicemen already had returned to civilian life. The workplace and workforce was looking to make a major shift. Much of the labor force was comprised of women, like Leota, who were forced into the labor market because of economic necessity due to the absence of the men who had gone to fight the war. Now those same men were returning. Some forecasted the biggest post-war problem for the United States to be jobs, with estimates that 60,000,000 jobs would be needed nationwide when it was all over. Already, the Better Business Bureau in Oklahoma City was establishing advisory services for returning servicemen hoping to go to work or go into business.

On a lighter note, and already on the post-war agenda, was the proposal of the Oklahoma Malt Brewery Associations that all taverns in Oklahoma City be closed for 24 hours after "V-E Day" was declared. The citizens looked forward to ignoring the proposal on "V-E Day." While the economic impact of war's end was the high point of many a conversation, the grim and ugly reality of the post war lingered in the thoughts of many. At the Muskogee Veterans Hospital, 3,347 patients were admitted in one year and the War Department was recommending that 100,000 graves for Oklahomans be established. Oklahoma had lost many of its finest. Gene Neville was one of them.

Since the end of World War II, the "Baby-Boomer" generation certainly has experienced their share of uncertainty and fear that comes with catastrophic national and world-shattering events that impact the way one lives and thinks. They had lived the Cuban Missile Crises, the Kennedy Assassination, the Viet Nam War, Watergate, endless turmoil, war and death in the Middle East, the Gulf War, Iraq, the Murrah building bombing, Bosnia-Serb genocide and murder, and the horrific events of 9-11, Bin Laden, and now homeland safety. Many of Jack and Leota's generation lived to see and experience all of these events, and let us not forget – a world that was on the edge of destruction in 1945. While certainly not diminishing the horrible significance of the events referenced above, it is difficult to conceive and articulate the fear, anxiety, and uncertainty that must have run through Leota's mind with what occurred in only the last two weeks of April, 1945. While Jack was trying to stay alive fighting his way out of Nuremberg toward Munich, not knowing what lie ahead at Dachau, Leota and the world woke up to the news that Hitler's goal not only included global conquest, but the extermination, the genocide, of an entire race to include men, women, and children. With the Allies only 57 miles from Berlin, Dr. Bela Tabian, a survivor of the Auschwitz Death Camp, disclosed to the press that the Germans had murdered five million Jews over the course of the war. The gas chambers and ovens of Auschwitz were on the world stage. As the Allies closed on Berlin, the horror of the Nazi Regime was further exposed on April 21, 1945, when reports surfaced of the murder and mass cremation of the Jews at the Bergen-Belsen Death Camp. On April 22, a Congressional delegation saw first hand the horror of the Nazi's plan of "Final Solution" carried out at the Buchenwauld Prison Camp, and the 45th's liberation of those starving and near death at Dachau. In essence, the world became witness to Hitler's plan of world-wide murder, and for Leota Neville, 26 years old, living with her parents and waiting for Jack, it was inconceivable that such depravity could truly exist in the world. As if the exposure of the Third Reich's scheme of death was not earth shattering enough, during the final two weeks of April Leota saw the death of Franklin D. Roosevelt, followed by the suicide of Adolf Hitler, and the end of Mussolini in a public square. In 17 days, three of the world's most prominent players left the stage of world turmoil in death. The last two weeks of April, 1945, brought forth a collision of near insane events that would shape the world forever. For Jack, his mind was fixed on avoiding the machine gun fire of strafing Messerschmidts, most likely unaware of what was unfolding in other parts of Europe and the world. But for Leota at home, her world, and perhaps her future, seemed to be in a state of calamity and uncertainty. The world events was a list of horrors. Jack was still gone, still exposed to death, and now the fear that with the Pacific war still raging that Jack could be forced to fight even more.

Thankfully, May of 1945 brought much needed relief to those waiting in Oklahoma City. On May 1, *The Daily Oklahoman* reported that the expected battle in Munich never came about as the city was won in a day's time. On May 3, 1945, the Nazis finally surrendered Berlin, and now even Truman was calling for a "quiet V-E Day." Finally came the word that every American had been waiting for since December 7, 1945, the war in Europe had finally come to an end.

On May 8, 1945 at 8:00 a.m. Oklahoma war-time, Germany surrendered unconditionally. Truman would address the nation that evening. In Leota's quiet way, she always was very keen on politics and at times she often seemed quite savvy in her observations. Germany and many parts of Europe were now occupied by three of the four world powers–Russia, Britain, and the United

Headquarters, Division Artillery, Jack's unit, is pictured as a unit for the last time at the end of May, 1945.

States. The geographical boundaries of the post-war era were a hot topic that became hotter after Germany's surrender. Leota kept her eye on job and economic security necessary for she and Jack to resume their lives. But in early May of 1945, world politics and economics were relatively low on Leota's list. She had not seen Jack since May 28, 1943, when she left him at Camp Pickett, Virginia taking the train back to Oklahoma City. What would it be like to see him after all this time? Had the war changed him? Would they still be in love? Would he want to have children? Will they go to Spring Lake, jitter-bug at the Blossom Heath, hold hands, share a kiss, be together? There was now a mystery about their togetherness that would only be answered when he got home. All other things were second place. With it over, when would he be home?

In celebration of Memorial Day 1945, the Thunderbirds formed for the last time and paraded in Konigplatz in Munich.

CHAPTER XXXIX
GOING HOME

Even with the shooting and killing at an end, and the war over, it was not easy for Jack to get home. No one just went down to the shore and got on the boat. The War Department had devised a complicated system to rotate the United States forces back to the States. The system basically involved a calculation of "points." Going home required an accumulation of 85 points that was based on such factors as months of service, days in combat, overseas duty, and decorations. Many an hour was spent in the 45th's Adjutant General's office calculating points in hopes for the earliest departure. Jack's point total in May of 1945 was relatively high given his record of service, although the precise number is apparently not a matter of record. In May, the United States Armed Forces expected that 2,887,000 troops would rotate home over the next nine months, with 45,000 expected home in May. Jack's number was not enough to get him home earlier than June with only 23 Oklahomans back by May 14. More than 400,000 United States servicemen would remain in Europe for the near future. Jack, and most of the Thunderbirds at least for the time being, were among those, waiting with each passing day of service for their points total to reach the magic 85.

With victory in hand, the mission of the Thunderbirds became one of occupation, and for Jack and the Division Artillery this meant mostly being a policeman. Division Artillery was assigned to Landkriese Friedburg and Furstenfeldbruck, two Munich suburbs to the northwest of the city under Area Command Munchen. There, they maintained road blocks and assisted in general police duty, including the over site of some 125,000 German soldiers housed in a prisoner-of-war camp near Furstenfeldbruck. The civilian population was for the most part cooperative and peaceful, and the occupation was largely without incident. Oddly, one of the biggest problems policing the city came with the growing number of bicycles that seemed to miraculously appear. No one had cars, and a bicycle was the only German mode of transportation. They were everywhere, but all thought that the bikes were better than guns. What was left of the German air force surrendered near Munich shortly after the occupation of the city. At Reim airport, 115 German fighters surrendered with an acrobatic aerial show as their pilots landed their aircraft for the last time. Jack was not that impressed with the German pilots display of skill. Only a few days before he had been jumping out of a truck to avoid being killed by strafing Messerschmidts. And then on May 10, 1945, the Allies chief protagonist at the Anzio beachhead, General Albert Kesselring was captured.

The Germans were effecting peaceful surrender in Munich and other parts of Germany. The occupation of the city was not free of some good times while waiting for the Adjucant General's office to calculate going-home points. Munich had more than its share of beer halls, and without question Jack did his best to visit all of them. The Munich Beer Hall, also known as the Hofbrauhaus, was one of the favorites and most famous, even to the extent that Felix Sparks took it over as the 157th's CP. The USO did its usual great job of creating some diversion from the anxiety and wait for orders to go home. Frequenting Area Command Munchen were the musical combos of the Georgians, The Gotham Four, and the Poison White Swingsters. While all curfew limits had been lifted, there was a staggering shortage of women and for Jack, Frosty Munson was the worst jitter-bug partner he ever had.

Most of the 45th Infantry Division did not begin their march home until September of 1945. By then, the port city of La Harve, France, had been cleared of the ship wreckage blocking the port caused by the sabotage of the Germans in the late stages of the war. The bigger part of the division was moved by motor transport to Camp St. Louis, just outside of Le Harve, where they waited to board the "Liberty Ships" for the near two-week ride home. From Le Harve, France, most of the Thunderbirds steamed into east coast ports with the 179th and 180th landing in New York and the 157th at Boston. From the east coast, much of the division traveled by train to Ft. Bowie, Texas, where they were ultimately "separated from service" and discharged into civilian life.

Fortunately for Jack, and many of the Division Artillery, they would not have to wait three months until the fall of 1945 to go home. By May of 1945, many of Jack's unit were considered the "old men" of the division, having trained and fought continuously together since September of 1940. As a result, many reached the necessary 85 point level by the end of May. For Jack, May 14, 1945, had to be an emotional day. On this day, Lt. Col. Walter Arnote made his way through the ranks of his staff to bid them all a farewell. Having been Jack's boss, and leader of the S-3 section since March of 1942, the good Colonel was on his way back to Walters, Oklahoma. By the end of May, the unit that had seen four major amphibious landings and fought eight campaigns began to disperse to England, the Riviera, Paris, and Lyon. They were finally going home.

On Memorial Day, May 30, 1945, the ranks of the 45th Infantry Division Thunderbirds of World War II formed for the last time in the streets of Munich, Germany, in the Konigsplatz. Jack stood at attention with his brothers as General Robert T. Frederick paused to pay honor and remember those no longer there, but forever Thunderbirds "... wherever we go, we shall not forget our debt to our fallen comrades." For Jack, there had to be a lot to remember, never to be forgotten. For the 45th, the casualty count at the end of the war was a staggering 62,563 men killed, injured, or missing in action. Mathematically, every man in the division was a casualty four times. As a testament to their sacrifice, the Thunderbirds had the highest casualty rate among the 18 national guard units that fought in World War II, and only three regular Army divisions sustained higher losses. As Jack stood in the sunshine of the Konigsplatz remembering his fallen friends and his own brother Gene, he had to wonder how he made it out alive, and how lucky he was to be going home.

Within the first few days of June, 1945, Jack received his orders to board the troop trucks headed for Marseille, France. Just outside Marseille, he bivouced at Camp Lucky Strike to await orders to board one of several liberty ships that would sail him home. Around June 3, 1945, Jack boarded the liberty ship USS Phillips De Bene, at the port of Marseille. By June 16, the De Bene steamed into the New York Harbor and, for the first time since June of 1943, Jack put his foot down on American soil. But once in the United States, it was still difficult for Jack to extract himself from the beaucratic arms of the armed forces. The United States Army had their way and you had to do it their way. While Leota knew that Jack was on his way home, and most likely knew the point of de-embarkation, the families were told not to go to the port cities, that contact with the returning soldiers would not be possible. It was almost as if Jack was going to be put in a decompression chamber of sorts, or that the Army was attempting to deprogram him from war's way. However, if one looks at the numbers alone, the Army way was somewhat understandable. Almost 3,000,000 men would be home within nine months. Forty-five thousand had returned in May alone. On June 20, 1945, only four days after Jack's arrival, the Queen Mary chugged its way into New York Harbor with 14,526 men aboard. New York was big, but not big enough to accommodate the thousands that anxiously awaited the return of their loved ones. While cumbersome, the Army's plan called for the men to be shipped to 18 different locations spread across the United States where they would be discharged from so-called "separation centers." For Jack Neville, this meant Fort Smith, Arkansas. Climbing on board his last troop train and finally headed westward for home, he arrived at the Ft. Chaffee Separation Center, Fort Smith, Arkansas on or about June 20, 1945. In his hand was one duffle bag.

While the Army was successful in keeping Leota out of New York, there was no way to keep her and the other wives and loved ones out of Fort Smith. She headed to Fort Smith by train. Incredibly, even at Ft. Chaffee the Army continued to press its regimin on the soon-to-be separated troops. Now only hours from civilian life, the citizen soldiers were nonetheless restricted to the PX and required to attend counseling services that carefully and in detailed fashion explained the GI Bill of Rights and other veterans programs that would be available once they hit the streets. Kept to themselves forever were their thoughts and emotions of being reunited after more than two years of painful separation. Tucked away in Leota's scrapbook is a 24-hour pass issued to Jack on June 24, 1945, requiring that he not fraternize, consume any alcoholic beverage, and that he obey all laws, state and federal, while off the post. It is rightly concluded that after kissing good-bye at Camp Pickett on May 28, 1943, they were back in each others arms June 24, 1945. The edges of the 24-hour pass today are brown, and obviously fragile; but somehow, like Leota and Jack, they survived to provide a piece to the puzzle of missing war years.

On June 25, 1945, Master Sargent Jack L. Neville was honorably discharged and officially separated from the United States Army after four years, eight months, and nine days of service. After fighting a World War, his grubstake for the future was $200 mustering out pay, and one duffle bag.

REFLECTIONS HOME SWEET HOME

For Mom and Dad, the thrill of finally being home had to be exhilarating, exciting beyond words. Dad reveled in the joy of being back in "the City," and a return to normalcy, future of civilian life, and family. The simple luxury of reading the paper with a cup of coffee in the morning, rather than Stars and Stripes or the 45th Infantry Division News, while being shot at was quickly restored. The Dodgers were leading in the National League, Detroit in the American, and there still was no chance that Mom would go to the wrestling or boxing matches at the Stockyards Coliseum. Dad quickly found that there were still plenty of places to have a rollicking good time. The Rhythm Kings were opening at the Elwood Nite Club, the Hollywood Caravan was going on at the Municipal Auditorium, and Springlake Park, now with a monstrous roller coaster, had become the scene of big time show-biz attractions with dancing at the Pavilion. Dad finally got to jitter-bug the night away with Mom, a better partner than Frosty Munson or Billy Williams in the USO tents of Munich. To both Mom and Dad's delight, it was getting a bit easier to get around the capital city. "Motorized buses" were starting to replace the trolleys, and now there were 30 places Mom and Dad could go to see the movies. There was no way that Dad's "mustering-out pay" was not going to be spent having some fun and making up for lost time.

While it was thrilling to finally be home, the road out of Fort Smith was not easy. Half of the world was still at war as United States air and ground forces closed in on Japan. Americans were still dying in the fight. Gas and tire rationing continued in Oklahoma City and the most patriotic of citizens continued to observe "meatless" and "sweetless" days. While the Douglas plant near Tinker was scaling down from its peak of some 24,000 people employed in 1942, in late June of 1945, the plant cranked out its 5,000th C-47. Approximately six weeks after Dad returned home, the atomic age came alive when the little man from Missouri gave the green light to drop the atomic bomb on Japan, August 6, 1945. Three days later another was dropped on Japan, killing 25,000. The Japanese, now facing total annihilation of their island state, were finally pushed into surrender. In large bold headlines on August 15, 1945, The Daily Oklahoman read "President Announces Peace." The Japanese accepted surrender at 6:00 p.m. Oklahoma time. For the first time since the Japanese invaded Manchuria in1938 and the German's Poland in 1939, the world at war was over for Mom and Dad. There was peace.

The biggest threat to Mom and Dad's relationship had to be the war, but now with it finally really over, they could get on with putting their lives back together. There were problems ahead, but they paled in significance to the war-time separation and sacrifice they both had endured. The United States Army was expected to discharge some 5,000,000,000 men and with the industrial cutbacks sure to take place with peace, unemployment was expected to skyrocket. Jobs would be difficult. The war had created a huge public debt that was expected to be reduced by an increase in taxes. With the shooting war over, Mom and Dad faced another battle–higher taxes and reduced job opportunity. These problems were easier to deal with than the worry, fear, and wait of the war. It is unlikely that they saw the potential of a difficult job market and higher taxes as much of an impediment to rebuilding their lives.

Mom had a lot of Scottish blood that flowed through her veins, and living with her parents she remarkably was able to save a little money. This, in addition to a portion of Dad's Army pay sent home, allowed them to rent a small duplex on Northwest 30th Street. Dad had the vision to know that education was the key to the future. It was a theme he preached his entire life. With the aide of the G.I. Bill of Rights, and with Mom still working, Dad enrolled at the University of Oklahoma in the fall of 1945 and received his degree in the spring of 1947.

Well, as they say, the rest is history. Through good times and bad, for better or worse, for the next 51 years they went on. Together they built a business, raised and educated three children, and left a legacy of common decency, love of family, and love of life.

There are many life lessons to be learned from Jack and Leota's war years. In many ways, a world at war stole their best years. No one puts this more eloquently than Tom Brokaw in The Greatest Generation:

> *"At a time in their lives when their days and nights should have been filled with innocent adventure, love and the lessons of the work-a-day world, they were fighting in the most primitive conditions possible across the bloody landscape. . . ."*

When times are good and the way of life paved with success, it is easy to mark the way. But the real measure of man is how he stands when times are difficult and the path clouded by fear, doubt, and uncertainty. Mom and Dad stood tall in the wake of the worst calamity the world has ever seen. As Brokaw went on to write

> "They answered the call to save the world . . . they won the war . . . they saved the world."

Mom always seemed unflappable in the face of life's difficulties as we brothers grew up. Dad never encountered a problem he could not solve. They both had a natural constitution that enabled them to deal with life's issues no matter how large they loomed. Their ability to persevere was certainly shaped by the fact that they had seen and experienced far worse along the path of life. Dad loved life because at such a young age he had seen so much death, and to survive he had to deal with it and the hardship that went with trying to stay alive. Mom loved the togetherness of family and her children in part because she had to endure the awfulness of separation and loneliness that came with the war. They emerged from the war as two stars of their generation that now provide a light in the darkness, their lives a source of strength when times are hard, a beacon that guides our way in the future. Dad never thought or spoke of himself as a war hero, or even as one whose service to country was extraordinary. He was neither statesman, nor general of armies. He was a guy from Adair, Oklahoma, a citizen soldier who did his job and asked for no fanfare or adulation in return. Brokaw and noted historian Steve Ambrose both call it the "Greatest Generation" mankind has ever witnessed. Let this history record that Mom and Dad were part of it. All of us are the children of this generation, and let us always remember and never forget what they did here.

INDEX

A

B

T

U

BIBLIOGRAPHY

BOOKS

The Rock of Anzio, by Flint Whitlock
The Fighting Forty Fifth, by Leo Bishop, Frank Glasgow, George Fisher
D-Day by Steven Ambrose
The Victors, Steven Ambrose
Hard Times in Oklahoma, The Depression Years, by Kermette D. Hendrickson
The Story of Oklahoma, by W. David Baird, Danny Goble
Historical Highlights of Mayes County, by the Mayes County Historical Society
The Oxford History of the American People, by Samuel Elliott Morison
The Heart of the Promised Land, Oklahoma County, an Illustrated History, by Bob Blackburn
Oklahoma City, Centennial Portrait, by Odie Faulk
At Dawn We Slept, by Gordon Prange
Yanks in the RAF
James Fighting Aircraft from World War II
The Hinge of Fate, by Winston Churchill
American Heritage New History of World War II by American Heritage Association
The World's Great Artillery, by Hans Holerstat
The Second World War, by John Keegan
Closing the Ring, by Winston Churchill
Citizen Soldier, by General Ray McClain
Fatal Decision, by Charles D'Este
Anzio: Epic of Bravery, Fred Sheeham, Oklahoma University Press, 1964
We Were Soldiers When We Were Young, by Harold Moore
World War II, The American Heritage Picture History of World War II, by C. L. Sulbzerber
A Time for Trumpets, the Untold Story of the Battle of the Bulge, by Charles MacDonald
The Mammoth Books of Battles, by John Lewis
The Anatomy of the Nurnberg Trials, by Telford Taylor
The Nurnberg Trials, by Anna Tusa
Thunderbird, by Guy Nelson
The Heart of the Promised Land, by Bob Blackburn

MAGAZINES

Time-Life Series

INTERVIEWS

Mike Gonzalez, Curator, 45th Infantry Division Museum, Oklahoma City, Oklahoma
Geneva Eby
Roselle MacKellar
Jim Neville, Fort Drum Historical Museum
Charles Willits, 45th Division Ordinance, 45th Infantry Division Museum
Claudia Balkum

NEWSPAPERS

The Daily Oklahoman, 1939-1946
The Oklahoma City Times, 1939-1946
The Watertown Daily Times
45th Infantry Division News

MUSEUMS

The 45th Inventory Division Museum Archives

MOVIES/VIDEOS

Patton
Video interview of Felix L. Sparks, 45th Infantry Division Museum.

LETTERS

October 3, 1942, F. W. Trout letter to Mrs. E. B. Neville
October 5, 1942, F. W. Trout letter to Mrs. E. B. Neville
October 31, 1942, F. W. Trout letter to Mrs. E. B. Neville
October 7, 1942, R. F. Rowse, BBC to Mrs. E. B. Neville
January 18, 1943, Secretary of War to Mrs. E. B. Neville
January 19, 1943, Helen Neville to Mrs. Jack Neville

ARTICLES/PUBLICATIONS

July 15, 1943, Table of Organization and Equipment No. 5-10,
"Division Artillery Motorized Infantry and Motorized Division."
The 189th Field Artillery, Monograph No. 10, July 1988, by Brigadier General Otwa Autrey.
From Buck Private to Three Star General, by Glen Ray McClain, 45th Infantry Division Museum.
A Time to Honor, By Col. John Embry, 160th Field Artillery, 45th Infantry Division Museum.
It Was Worth It, by Harry Dobbyn, 45th Infantry Division Museum Archives.
Dachau at Its Liberation, Felix L. Sparks, 45th Infantry Division Museum Archives.
45th Occupational History of Germany, 45th Infantry Division Museum Archives.

MISCELLANEOUS

Jack Neville handwritten journal
Leota Neville two scrapbooks
The United States Census Bureau Reports, 1930, 1940
The 45th Division Artillery, Sheaf Field Press
Gene Neville Flight Log
45th Division Artillery Operations Report
Diary of the Sicilian Campaign, Brigadier General Ray S. McClain
Historical Summary of the 45th Infantry Division
Rene Lalique Biography 1860-1880, www.lalique.com